Reihe: Planung, Organisation und Unternehmungsführung · Band 129
Herausgegeben von Prof. Dr. Dr. h. c. Norbert Szyperski, Köln, Prof. Dr. Winfried
Matthes †, Wuppertal, Prof. Dr. Udo Winand, Kassel, Prof. (em.) Dr. Joachim
Griese, Bern, Prof. Dr. Harald F. O. von Kortzfleisch, Koblenz, Prof. Dr. Ludwig
Theuvsen, Göttingen, und Prof. Dr. Andreas Al-Laham, Mannheim

Dr. Swantje Hartmann

External Embeddedness of Subsidiaries

Influences on Product Innovation in MNCs

With a Foreword by Prof. Dr. Stefan Schmid,
ESCP Europe, Berlin

Bibliografische Information der Deutschen Nationalbibliothek

Die Deutsche Nationalbibliothek verzeichnet diese Publikation in der Deutschen Nationalbibliografie; detaillierte bibliografische Daten sind im Internet über <http://dnb.d-nb.de> abrufbar.

Dissertation, ESCP Europe, Berlin, 2010

ISBN 978-3-8441-0037-2
1. Auflage Mai 2011

© JOSEF EUL VERLAG GmbH, Lohmar – Köln, 2011
Alle Rechte vorbehalten

JOSEF EUL VERLAG GmbH
Brandsberg 6
53797 Lohmar
Tel.: 0 22 05 / 90 10 6-6
Fax: 0 22 05 / 90 10 6-88
E-Mail: info@eul-verlag.de
http://www.eul-verlag.de

Bei der Herstellung unserer Bücher möchten wir die Umwelt schonen. Dieses Buch ist daher auf säurefreiem, 100% chlorfrei gebleichtem, alterungsbeständigem Papier nach DIN 6738 gedruckt.

Foreword

In the International Business (IB) and International Management (IM) field we commonly assume that Multinational Corporations (MNCs) can be considered as intra-organizational networks. Perlmutter's Geocentric Firm, Bartlett and Ghoshal's Transnational Corporation, or Hedlund's Heterarchy are examples of intra-organizational network approaches. Furthermore, headquarters and subsidiaries, which constitute the intra-organizational network, are embedded in so-called inter-organizational relationships. As a consequence, they are commonly shaped by the interaction with their environment, and not only by the interaction with other organizational units from their intra-organizational network.

While traditional IB and IM literature has emphasized that competitive advantages are usually created at home and subsidiaries are then established to exploit these competitive advantages abroad, network approaches stress that foreign subsidiaries can be a major contribution or even a source of competitive advantage. For instance, a foreign subsidiary can create a new product and later on transfer this product innovation to headquarters and sister subsidiaries. Such a product innovation is in the focus of the current research presented by Swantje Hartmann. Swantje Hartmann explores the role of the external network on product innovations in foreign subsidiaries. She aims at identifying which external business partners affect the product innovation process and which contribution the relationship to external business partners make for the innovation. However, Swantje Hartmann is not limiting herself to the absorption of knowledge from the local network; she is also interested in exploring how the foreign subsidiary transfers the product innovation to the MNC network.

Swantje Hartmann uses a case study approach, involving German subsidiaries of Swiss MNCs active in the pharmaceutical industry. The qualitative research approach allows her to identify new results. While previous studies, partially influenced by the tradition of the IMP (International Marketing and Purchasing) Group, often concentrated on buyers and suppliers in their questionnaires (and hence also in their results), Swantje Hartmann comes up with other influential business partners in her empirical setting. She succeeds in showing that innovation processes in her industry are driven by very specific, particularistic relationships, such as relationships to individual research partners.

The present research is a welcome addition to previous IB and IM literature, because it stresses the importance of multiple stakeholders on innovations and innovation processes. It also highlights that research concentrating on the result of product innovations alone falls short of explaining the influence of stakeholders. It is crucial to take the process into account that leads to innovations. In different phases of the innovation process various actors play specific roles and the relationships to these actors develop in the course of time. This is not only an important message for academics – it is also crucial for practitioners who are invited to actively manage the relationships their organizational units have with the intra-organizational as well as with the inter-organizational network.

The present research complements the research programme at my department trying to better understand subsidiaries, their roles and their relationships. I hope that the present book will find a wide audience, and I wish all readers inspiring insights from the conceptual and empirical material they can discover.

Berlin, March 2011   Stefan Schmid

Preface

Relationships are essential in most aspects of life. This insight is not only reflected in the present dissertation, it is also true for the process of writing it. Many people supported me during this time, with regards to the content and even more emotionally.

The first one to mention is, of course, Prof. Dr. Stefan Schmid who supervised the dissertation both favorably and critically and thus, had a major influence on it. He always posed the right questions to make me think further than I had done before.

Second, I want to thank Prof. Dr. Björn Walliser who did not hesitate to review the dissertation and who contributed to an interesting discussion at its defense.

An essential part of the present dissertation is the empirical study in the pharmaceutical industry. It would not have been possible without the cooperation of the two companies. I very much appreciate their interest and openness towards my research.

I also want to thank my friends at the department of International Management and Strategic Management and at the ESCP Europe. They were always open for discussions and eager to help. But more than that, we helped each other through the long and demanding process of writing a dissertation, by encouraging each other and by suffering and laughing together. These friends are: Maren Breuer, Monika Dammer-Henselmann, Tobias Dauth, Ruben Dost, Lars Dzedek, Holger Endrös, Philipp Grosche, Katharina Hefter, Nils Horch, Thomas Kotulla, Andrea Luber, Martina Maletzky, Mario Machulik, Stephan Schulze and Dennis Wurster.

Most of all, I am indebted to my partner and my family for their continuous support. My partner proved an exceptional patience to tolerate ups and downs and long working hours. And more than anyone else, I sincerely thank my parents for their constant belief in me. Thanks for always supporting and challenging me.

Thanks to all of you.

Berlin, March 2011   Swantje Hartmann

Overview of Contents

Foreword V

Preface VII

Overview of Contents IX

Table of Contents XIII

List of Figures XXIII

List of Tables XXVII

1 Introduction to the Topic of the Thesis 1

   1.1 Starting Point of the Study 1

   1.2 Research Questions 3

   1.3 Outline of the Study 7

2 Introduction to Product Innovations in the Multinational Corporation 11

   2.1 Clarifying the Understanding of Product Innovations in this Study 11

   2.2 Product Innovation and Transfer Processes in the Multinational Corporation 19

   2.3 Summary: Product Innovations in this Study 25

3 Literature Review 27

   3.1 Inter-organizational Focus: Influence of Subsidiaries' External Embeddedness on their Innovations 27

   3.2 Intra-organizational Focus: Transfer of Subsidiaries' Innovations in the MNC 46

   3.3 Summary of the Literature Review 62

4 Conceptual Background of Subsidiaries' Embeddedness 65

4.1 Systemization of Network Concepts and Selection of the Concept of the Embedded MNC 65

4.2 The Evolution of the Concept of the Embedded MNC 69

4.3 Description of the Embedded MNC Approach 72

4.4 Criticism on the Concept of the Embedded MNC 102

4.5 Extending and Refining the Concept of the Embedded MNC 109

4.6 Conclusion 126

5 Empirical Study 131

5.1 Research Design 131

5.2 Collection of Data 152

5.3 Data Analysis 155

5.4 Scientific Quality Criteria 157

6 Empirical Findings 163

6.1 Basic Case Description 164

6.2 External Business Partners in the Product Innovation Process 186

6.3 Embeddedness of Business Relationships to External Business Partners during the Product Innovation Process 205

6.4 Characteristics of Knowledge and Knowledge Transfer 250

6.5 Transfer of Knowledge between Sub-units of the MNC 291

7 Discussion	303
7.1 Contributions	303
7.2 Reflection of Results on the Concept of the Embedded MNC	309
7.3 Implications for Management Praxis	314
7.4 Limitations	316
7.5 Avenues for Further Research	317
Appendix	**321**
Appendix A: Interview Guideline	**321**
Appendix B: Final Code List as Used in this Study	**327**
References	**333**

Table of Contents

Foreword V

Preface VII

Overview of Contents IX

Table of Contents XIII

List of Figures XXIII

List of Tables XXVII

1 Introduction to the Topic of the Thesis 1

   1.1 Starting Point of the Study 1

   1.2 Research Questions 3

   1.3 Outline of the Study 7

2 Introduction to Product Innovations in the Multinational Corporation 11

   2.1 Clarifying the Understanding of Product Innovations in this Study 11

      2.1.1 Objects of Innovation 11

      2.1.2 Product Innovation as Invention, Process or Result 13

      2.1.3 Intensity of Product Innovations 15

   2.2 Product Innovation and Transfer Processes in the Multinational Corporation 19

      2.2.1 Product Innovation Process 19

         2.2.1.1 Product Innovation Process in General 19

         2.2.1.2 Geographical Scope of Product Innovation Processes in Multinational Corporations 21

      2.2.2 Transfer of Product Innovations in the Multinational Corporation 24

   2.3 Summary: Product Innovations in this Study 25

3 Literature Review ... 27

3.1 Inter-organizational Focus: Influence of Subsidiaries' External Embeddedness on their Innovations ... 27
    3.1.1 Method of the Literature Review ... 27
    3.1.2 Content of Literature ... 30
        3.1.2.1 Content of Literature with a Focus on Subsidiaries' External Embeddedness ... 30
        3.1.2.2 Content of Literature with a Focus on the Specifications of the Analyzed Innovations ... 34
    3.1.3 Research Design and Method in Literature ... 44

3.2 Intra-organizational Focus: Transfer of Subsidiaries' Innovations in the MNC ... 46
    3.2.1 Method of the Literature Review ... 46
    3.2.2 Content of Literature ... 47
        3.2.2.1 Content of Literature with a Focus on Transfer of Subsidiaries' Innovations ... 47
        3.2.2.2 Content of Literature with a Focus on the Specifications of the Analyzed Innovations ... 60
    3.2.3 Research Design and Method in Literature ... 61

3.3 Summary of the Literature Review ... 62

4 Conceptual Background of Subsidiaries' Embeddedness ... 65

4.1 Systemization of Network Concepts and Selection of the Concept of the Embedded MNC ... 65

4.2 The Evolution of the Concept of the Embedded MNC ... 69

4.3 Description of the Embedded MNC Approach ... 72
    4.3.1 Structure of the Embedded Network ... 72
        4.3.1.1 Structure of a Network ... 73
            4.3.1.1.1 Actor ... 73
            4.3.1.1.2 Relationship ... 75
            4.3.1.1.3 Network ... 82

    4.3.1.2 Structure of the Inter-organizational Network 85
    4.3.1.3 Structure of the Intra-organizational Network 87
    4.3.1.4 Network Structure from a
           Subsidiary's Perspective 89
  4.3.2 Dynamics in Business Networks 93
  4.3.3 Flows in the Network 96
    4.3.3.1 Flows of Products and Services 96
    4.3.3.2 Flows of Knowledge 97
    4.3.3.3 Social Exchange 100
        4.3.3.3.1 Flows of Trust 100
        4.3.3.3.2 Flows of Power 101

4.4 Criticism on the Concept of the Embedded MNC 102

4.5 Extending and Refining the Concept of the
     Embedded MNC 109
  4.5.1 Stakeholders 109
  4.5.2 Flows of Knowledge 112
    4.5.2.1 Characteristics of Knowledge 112
    4.5.2.2 Characteristics of Knowledge Flows 116
    4.5.2.3 Process of Knowledge Transfer 120
    4.5.2.4 Problems of Knowledge Transfer 121

4.6 Conclusion 126

5 Empirical Study 131

5.1 Research Design 131
  5.1.1 Rationale for a Case Study Approach 131
  5.1.2 Description of the Case Design 134
    5.1.2.1 Units of Analysis 134
    5.1.2.2 Selection of Cases 135
        5.1.2.2.1 Selection of Subsidiaries 135
        5.1.2.2.2 Selection of Product Innovations and
                 Business Relationships 138
  5.1.3 Operationalization of the Conceptual Framework 140

5.1.3.1 Determining the Units of Analysis 140
    5.1.3.1.1 The Intensity of Product Innovations 140
    5.1.3.1.2 The Geographical Scope of the Product
    Innovation Process 144
5.1.3.2 External and Corporate Actors in the Product
Innovation Process 144
5.1.3.3 Embeddedness and Development of Business
Relationships between Innovative Subsidiaries
and their Relevant Business Partners 145
5.1.3.4 Characteristics of Knowledge and
Knowledge Transfer 149
    5.1.3.4.1 Characteristics of Knowledge 149
    5.1.3.4.2 Characteristics of Knowledge Transfer 151

5.2 Collection of Data 152

5.3 Data Analysis 155
    5.3.1 Procedure 155
    5.3.2 Code List 156

5.4 Scientific Quality Criteria 157
    5.4.1 Construct Validity 157
    5.4.2 Internal Validity 159
    5.4.3 External Validity 160
    5.4.4 Reliability 160

6 Empirical Findings 163

6.1 Basic Case Description 164
    6.1.1 Cogis at Pharmasub 164
        6.1.1.1 Pharmasub 164
        6.1.1.2 Description of Cogis 165
        6.1.1.3 Innovation Intensity of Cogis 165
        6.1.1.4 Geographical Scope of the Product Innovation
        Process of Cogis 167
        6.1.1.5 Product Innovation Process of Medicines 167

- 6.1.2 Cantis at Diagnosub 172
  - 6.1.2.1 Diagnosub 172
  - 6.1.2.2 Description of Cantis 172
  - 6.1.2.3 Innovation Intensity of Cantis 175
    - 6.1.2.3.1 Innovation Intensity of CantisCRC 175
    - 6.1.2.3.2 Innovation Intensity of CantisPF 177
  - 6.1.2.4 Geographical Scope of the Product Innovation Process of Cantis 179
  - 6.1.2.5 Product Innovation Process at Diagnosub 179
- 6.1.3 Comparison of the Cases of Cogis and Cantis 184

6.2 External Business Partners in the Product Innovation Process 186
- 6.2.1 External Business Partners in the Innovation Process of Cogis at Pharmasub 187
  - 6.2.1.1 Pre-clinical development 187
    - 6.2.1.1.1 Pre-clinic I: In vitro tests 187
    - 6.2.1.1.2 Pre-clinic II: In vivo tests 189
  - 6.2.1.2 Clinical Development 190
    - 6.2.1.2.1 Clinical Trials Stage I 190
    - 6.2.1.2.2 Clinical Trials Stage II and III 191
  - 6.2.1.3 Summary of the External Business Partners in the Product Innovation Process of Cogis 192
- 6.2.2 External Business Partners in the Innovation Process of Cantis at Diagnosub 193
  - 6.2.2.1 External Business Partners in the Innovation Process of CantisCRC at Diagnosub 193
    - 6.2.2.1.1 Idea Generation 193
    - 6.2.2.1.2 Basic and Extended Technology Studies 194
  - 6.2.2.2 External Business Partners in the Innovation Process of CantisPF at Diagnosub 196
    - 6.2.2.2.1 Basic and Extended Technology Studies 196
    - 6.2.2.2.2 Feasibility 197
  - 6.2.2.3 Summary of the External Business Partners in the Product Innovation Process of Cantis 199

6.2.3 Comparison and Conclusion of the Most Important External Business Partners of Pharmasub and Diagnosub 201

6.3 Embeddedness of Business Relationships to External Business Partners during the Product Innovation Process... 205

6.3.1 Embeddedness of Business Relationships to External Business Partners during the Innovation Process of Cogis at Pharmasub 206

    6.3.1.1 Pre-clinical Development 206

        6.3.1.1.1 Pre-clinic I: In vitro tests 206

        6.3.1.1.2 Pre-clinic II: In vivo tests 210

    6.3.1.2 Clinical Development 215

        6.3.1.2.1 Clinical Trials Stage I 215

        6.3.1.2.2 Clinical Trials Stage II 219

        6.3.1.2.3 Clinical Trials Stage III 221

    6.3.1.3 Summary of the Embeddedness of Business Relationships to External Business Partners during the Innovation Process of Cogis at Pharmasub 224

6.3.2 Embeddedness of Business Relationships to External Business Partners during the Innovation Process of Cantis at Diagnosub... 230

    6.3.2.1 Embeddedness of Business Relationships to External Business Partners during the Innovation Process of CantisCRC at Diagnosub 230

        6.3.2.1.1 Idea Description 230

        6.3.2.1.2 Basic and Extended Technology Studies 235

    6.3.2.2 Embeddedness of Business Relationships to External Business Partners during the Innovation Process of CantisPF at Diagnosub 239

        6.3.2.2.1 Basic and Extended Technology Studies 239

        6.3.2.2.2 Feasibility 243

6.3.2.3 Summary of the Embeddedness of Business Relationships to External Business Partners during the Innovation Process of Cantis at Diagnosub 244
6.3.3 Comparison and Conclusion of the Embeddedness of Business Relationships to External Business Partners during the Innovation Process of Cogis and Cantis 248

6.4 Characteristics of Knowledge and Knowledge Transfer 250
  6.4.1 Characteristics of Knowledge Exchanged with and Knowledge Transfer to External Business Partners during the Innovation Process of Cogis at Pharmasub 251
    6.4.1.1 Pre-clinic I: In vitro tests 251
      6.4.1.1.1 Content of Knowledge Flows 251
      6.4.1.1.2 Characteristics of Knowledge 251
      6.4.1.1.3 Characteristics of Knowledge Flows 253
    6.4.1.2 Pre-clinic II: In vivo tests 254
      6.4.1.2.1 Content of Knowledge Flows 254
      6.4.1.2.2 Characteristics of Knowledge 255
      6.4.1.2.3 Characteristics of Knowledge Flows 256
    6.4.1.3 Clinical Trials Stage I 257
      6.4.1.3.1 Content of Knowledge Flows 257
      6.4.1.3.2 Characteristics of Knowledge 259
      6.4.1.3.3 Characteristics of Knowledge Flows 260
    6.4.1.4 Clinical Trials Stage II 261
      6.4.1.4.1 Characteristics of Knowledge 261
      6.4.1.4.2 Characteristics of Knowledge Flows 262
    6.4.1.5 Clinical Trials Stage III 263
      6.4.1.5.1 Characteristics of Knowledge 263
      6.4.1.5.2 Characteristics of Knowledge Flows 264
    6.4.1.6 Summary of the Characteristics of Knowledge and Knowledge Transfer of Cogis at Pharmasub 265
  6.4.2 Characteristics of Knowledge Exchanged with and Knowledge Transfer to External Business Partners during the Innovation Process of CantisCRC at Diagnosub 270

6.4.2.1 Idea Description 270
　6.4.2.1.1 Content of Knowledge Flows in Idea
　　Description 270
　6.4.2.1.2 Characteristics of Knowledge Exchanged
　　during Idea Description 270
　6.4.2.1.3 Characteristics of Knowledge Flows during
　　Idea Description 272
6.4.2.2 Basic and Extended Studies 273
　6.4.2.2.1 Content of Knowledge Flows in Basic and
　　Extended Technology Studies 273
　6.4.2.2.2 Characteristics of Knowledge Exchanged
　　during Basic and Extended Technology
　　Studies 274
　6.4.2.2.3 Characteristics of Knowledge Flows during
　　Basic and Extended Technology Studies 275
6.4.3 Characteristics of Knowledge Exchanged with and
　Knowledge Transfer to External Business Partners during
　the Innovation Process of CantisPF at Diagnosub 277
6.4.3.1 Basic and Extended Studies 277
　6.4.3.1.1 Content of Knowledge Flows in Basic and
　　Extended Technology Studies 277
　6.4.3.1.2 Characteristics of Knowledge Exchanged
　　during Basic and Extended Technology
　　Studies 277
　6.4.3.1.3 Characteristics of Knowledge Flows during
　　Basic and Extended Technology Studies 278
6.4.3.2 Feasibility 280
　6.4.3.2.1 Content of Knowledge Flows in Feasibility 280
　6.4.3.2.2 Characteristics of Knowledge Exchanged
　　during Feasibility 280
　6.4.3.2.3 Characteristics of Knowledge Flows during
　　Feasibility 282
6.4.3.3 Summary of the Characteristics of Knowledge
　and Knowledge Transfer of Cantis at Diagnosub 282

6.4.4 Comparison and Conclusion of the Characteristics of
Knowledge and Knowledge Transfer during the Product
Innovation Process of Cogis and Cantis 288

6.5 Transfer of Knowledge between Sub-units of the MNC 291

6.5.1 Organizational Structures and Processes to Facilitate the
Intra-organizational Transfer of Knowledge in the Product
Innovation Process of Cogis 291

6.5.1.1 Reasons for Integrating Foreign Subsidiaries in
the Product Innovation Process 292

6.5.1.2 Organizational Structures and Processes for
Incorporating Foreign Subsidiaries in the Product
Innovation Process 293

6.5.2 Organizational Structures and Processes to Facilitate the
Intra-organizational Transfer of Knowledge in the Product
Innovation Process of Cantis 296

6.5.2.1 Reasons of Establishing Organizational
Structures and Processes in the Product
Innovation Process 297

6.5.2.2 Organizational Structures and Processes for
Incorporating Global Marketing and Foreign
Subsidiaries in the Product Innovation Process 298

6.5.3 Comparison and Conclusion of the Organizational
Structures and Processes to Facilitate Intra-organizational
Transfer of Product Innovations at Pharmacom and
Diagnocom 301

7 Discussion 303

7.1 Contributions 303

7.2 Reflection of Results on the Concept of the
Embedded MNC 309

7.2.1 Stakeholder Groups 309

7.2.2 Embeddedness of Business Relationships 310

7.3 Implications for Management Praxis.. 314

7.4 Limitations 316

7.5 Avenues for Further Research... 317

Appendix 321

Appendix A: Interview Guideline... 321

Appendix B: Final Code List as Used in this Study.. 327

References 333

List of Figures

Figure 1-1:	Overview of the study	7
Figure 2-1:	Objects of innovation	12
Figure 2-2:	Depiction of the different understandings of product innovation	15
Figure 2-3:	Innovation process in the focus of Bartlett and Ghoshal	24
Figure 2-4:	Type of innovations analyzed in the present thesis	26
Figure 4-1:	Four levels of network research	68
Figure 4-2:	Development of the concept of the Embedded MNC	70
Figure 4-3:	Elements of networks	73
Figure 4-4:	The basic structure of business relationships	77
Figure 4-5:	Example of the breadth and depth of a particular business relationship	81
Figure 4-6:	Inter-organizational and corporate networks of MNCs	86
Figure 4-7:	Intra-organizational and corporate networks of sub-units	88
Figure 4-8:	Business network context of a focal subsidiary	90
Figure 4-9:	Flows in the network	97
Figure 4-10:	Model of intra-organizational and inter-organizational knowledge transfer	101
Figure 4-11:	Dimensions of stakeholder types	110
Figure 4-12:	Model of collaboration with external and corporate stakeholders during the product innovation process and the innovation transfer process in this contribution	111
Figure 4-13:	Business relationships and characteristics of knowledge	115
Figure 4-14:	Stages of the knowledge transfer process	120
Figure 4-15:	Summary of the research issues in this thesis	127
Figure 4-16:	Assumed relationships in this study	128
Figure 5-1:	International, global, multinational and transnational industries	137
Figure 5-2:	Interactive model of data analysis	156
Figure 6-1:	Evaluation of the innovation intensity of Cogis	166
Figure 6-2:	Product innovation process of drugs	168

Figure 6-3: Analyzed stages of the product innovation process of Cogis 171
Figure 6-4: Evaluation of the innovation intensity of CantisCRC 176
Figure 6-5: Evaluation of the innovation intensity of CantisPF 178
Figure 6-6: Product innovation process at Diagnosub 180
Figure 6-7: Analyzed stages of the product innovation process of CantisCRC and CantisPF 183
Figure 6-8: External business partners of Pharmasub during the product innovation process of Cogis 192
Figure 6-9: External business partners of Pharmasub during the product innovation process of CantisCRC and CantisPF 200
Figure 6-10: Embeddedness of the business relationship between Pharmasub and ResCog-A during in vitro tests 209
Figure 6-11: Embeddedness of the business relationship between Pharmanorth and ClinCog-A during in vivo tests 212
Figure 6-12: Development of adaptations, commitment and trust between Pharmanorth and ClinCog-A during the in vivo studies on Cogis 214
Figure 6-13: Embeddedness of the business relationship between Pharmasub and ClinCog-B in stage I of the clinical trials 217
Figure 6-14: Embeddedness of the business relationship between Pharmasub and ClinCog-C in stage II of the clinical trials 220
Figure 6-15: Embeddedness of the business relationship between Pharmasub and ClinCog-C in stage III of the clinical trials 222
Figure 6-16: Overview of the embeddedness of the business relationships to the most influential business partners during the product innovation process of Cogis 228
Figure 6-17: Embeddedness of the business relationship between Diagnosub and CustCRC-A in the stage of idea description 232
Figure 6-18: Development of mutual trust between Diagnosub and CustCRC-A 235

Figure 6-19: Embeddedness of the business relationship between Diagnosub and ClinCRC-A in the stages of basic and extended technology studies 237

Figure 6-20: Embeddedness of the business relationship between Diagnosub and SupPF-A in the stages of basic and extended technology studies 242

Figure 6-21: Overview over embeddedness of business relationships to the most influential business partners during the product innovation process of CantisCRC and CantisPF 247

Figure 6-22: Assumed determining and moderating factor of the evaluation of very important business relationships 249

Figure 6-23: Organizational structure at Pharmacom 293

Figure 6-24: Process of collecting information from the subsidiaries 295

Figure 6-25: Process of selecting medical directors for the clinical subteam 296

Figure 6-26: Organizational structure of decision making on product innovation at Diagnocom 300

List of Tables

Table 2-1:	Examples of definitions of radical product innovations	17
Table 3-1:	Literature on the influence of subsidiaries' external business network on their innovations	30
Table 3-2:	Overview of specifications of innovations analyzed in existing studies	35
Table 3-3:	Studies of the influence of subsidiaries' external business network on their innovations	43
Table 3-4:	Relevant literature on the diffusion of innovations in MNCs	47
Table 3-5:	Studies of the diffusion of subsidiaries' innovations in the MNC	59
Table 3-6:	Overview over specifications of innovations analyzed in existing studies	60
Table 4-1:	Overview over schools of network research and the network approaches	67
Table 4-2:	Measures of the embeddedness of business relationships used in existing studies on the concept of the Embedded MNC and prior concepts of the IMP-Group	107
Table 4-3:	Characteristics of knowledge	114
Table 4-4:	Characteristics of knowledge flows as applied in this study	119
Table 5-1:	Measures of product innovation intensity used in this study	143
Table 5-2:	Measures of the embeddedness and development of external and corporate business relationships applied in this study	149
Table 5-3:	Measures of characteristics of knowledge	151
Table 5-4:	Measures of characteristics of knowledge transfer	152
Table 5-5:	Respondents at Pharmacom and Diagnocom	154
Table 6-1:	Similarities between Cogis and Cantis	185

Table 6-2: Characteristics of knowledge and knowledge transfer in the case of Cogis 269

Table 6-3: Characteristics of knowledge and knowledge transfer in the case of CantisCRC and CantisPF 286

1 Introduction to the Topic of the Thesis

In this chapter, an introduction to the thesis is provided. First, the starting point of the study is explained (1.1). Then, the research questions of the study are presented (1.2) and finally, the outline of this thesis is described (1.3).

1.1 Starting Point of the Study

Product innovations[1] are known to bear a major potential for success of the innovating company (e.g. Andersson/Forsgren/Holm 2001, p. 1015, Cooper 2005, pp. 8-12, Lettl/Hienerth/Gemuenden 2008, p. 219). In the traditional view of the multinational corporation (MNC), product innovations were supposed to be created exclusively by the headquarters (HQs). HQs were considered to be superior to subsidiaries and the only center of the MNC (i.e. the "headquarters-hierarchy-syndrome", Bartlett/Ghoshal 1986, p. 88, 1998, p. 115, or center-periphery-view of the MNC, Schmid 2003, p. 278). Foreign subsidiaries were either established to gain access to cheap resources (resource-seeking motive) or to sell product innovations of HQs in the host market (market-seeking motive, Hedlund/Kogut 1993, p. 344, Dunning 1994, pp. 35-40). Thereby, subsidiaries were thought to be similar in tasks and knowledge (i.e. the "United Nations model assumption", Bartlett/Ghoshal 1986, p. 88, 1987, p. 44, 1998, pp. 114-115).

Since the 1980s the perception of subsidiaries has changed. It has been realized by researchers that subsidiaries are embedded in close relationships to external business partners. In these business relationships they gain access to specific knowledge in their host markets. Subsidiaries use the acquired knowledge to expand their knowledge stock. They do so for their own purposes, for instance to create product innovations. However, they also transfer the acquired knowledge to HQs or other subsidiaries. Thereby, they contribute to the knowledge of the whole MNC (Hed-

---

[1] In this study, product innovations are broadly understood as new products that are developed with the intent of meeting market demands (Damanpour 1991, p. 561, Ziggers 2005, p. 45). The kind of product innovation that is analyzed in this dissertation will be explained in more detail in section 2.1.

lund/Kogut 1993, p. 344, Sölvell/Zander 1995, p. 17, Kuemmerle 1999, pp. 2-4). Based on the knowledge subsidiaries have obtained from external business partners, they are able to create product innovations that meet the needs of local consumers. Thus, HQs are no longer the only unit with innovation activities. Instead, product innovations are also created in several specialized centers in some or many host countries (Cantwell/Dunning/Janne 2004, pp. 5-6, Cantwell/Mudambi 2005, pp. 1109-1110, Forsgren/Holm/Johanson 2005, p. 5).[2] Subsidiaries benefit from the knowledge they have received, for instance by adapting to customers' demands or for its product innovation processes. In addition, the whole MNC gains an advantage from the product innovation if it is transferred to other units of the MNC and used by them as well (Bartlett/Ghoshal 1998, pp. 135-136). Since subsidiaries play an important role in this view of MNCs, MNCs are not considered strict hierarchies with HQs at the top anymore. Instead they are perceived as networks of different units. Examples for network models are the heterarchy by Hedlund (1986), the transnational organization by Bartlett and Ghoshal (1987, 1998), the horizontal organization by White and Poynter (1989) and the diversified multinational corporation (DMNC) by Doz and Prahalad (1991, 2005, for a review of the concepts of the MNC see Schmid 1996a, pp. 27-31, 34-40, Kutschker/Schmid 2008, pp. 284-324).[3] MNCs which enter new markets with the intention to gain access to specific knowledge or other critical and scarce resources are called "strategic (created) asset seekers" (Dunning 1994, p. 36). This access may result in higher innovativeness of MNCs and is nowadays supposed to be one of the main competitive advantages of MNCs (Bartlett/Ghoshal 1990b, p. 216, Kutschker/Schurig/Schmid 2002, p. 230).

---

[2] Sometimes these centers are called "Centers of Excellence" (e.g. Moore 2001, Frost/Birkinshaw/Ensign 2002, Kutschker/Schurig/Schmid 2002, Schmid/Schurig 2003, p. 757) or "Centers of Competence" (e.g. Voelker/Stead 1999, Schmid 2000, Braun/Benninghoff 2003). For more details on centers of excellence see sub-section 4.3.1.4.

[3] It was as early as 1969, that Perlmutter introduced a network model of an MNC with the geocentric orientation as one of four archetypes he presented (the others being the ethnocentric, the polycentric and the regiocentric orientation). In the geocentric orientation, decisions are not exclusively made by HQs. Instead, they are reached at by the units which bear the consequences of the decision. Thus, the strategy of the MNC is not created by one center (Perlmutter 1969b, p. 12, 1969a, p. 78, 1971, p. 434; see Schmid/Machulik 2006 for a critical review of the EPRG concept).

1.2 Research Questions

Indeed, subsidiaries were found to establish strong relationships to external business partners, for instance to their customers (O'Dowd/McQuade/Murphy 2005) or to research institutions (Davis/Meyer 2004), who enhance innovations in subsidiaries. Moreover, some innovations of subsidiaries were shown to be transferred to other units of the MNC later on (e.g. Birkinshaw/Fry 1998, Birkinshaw/Ridderstråle 1999). Despite these findings and the importance of the topic, there are still many questions left to be answered.

After analyzing the existing literature (see the literature review in chapter 3), it becomes clear that researchers of the network perspective in International Business literature have not yet taken a closer look at product innovation processes within MNCs. In addition, the transfer of product innovations to other units of the MNC needs further investigation. In the present contribution, the strength[4] of the subsidiaries' business relationships to each of the most influential business partners along the product innovation process (inter-organizational perspective) and product innovation transfer (intra-organizational perspective) will be analyzed. Both perspectives are based on the concept of the Embedded MNC.

Following are the two main research questions which are presented in detail and the aims of the study are explained according to the research questions. They are also depicted in figure 1-1.

Inter-organizational perspective:
1 **How does the external business network of subsidiaries influence their product innovation process?**
    1.1 Which external business partners affect different stages of the product innovation process?
    1.2 How does the relationship between the focal subsidiary and its most influential external business partners look like?

---

[4] Later on the strength of business relationships is referred to as the embeddedness of business relationships. This will be done according to the concept of the Embedded MNC from section 4.3 onwards.

1.2.1 (How) Does the embeddedness of the relationship between the focal subsidiary and its external business partners develop during the product innovation process?

1.2.2 Which knowledge is exchanged between the focal subsidiary and its external business partners during the product innovation process?

(1.1) Which kind of external business partners are involved at which stage of the product innovation process has not been studied yet (Hallin/Kang 2008, pp. 18-19) and will be done in the present thesis. Analyzing the single stages of the product innovation process might allow valuable insights. So far, mainly customers and suppliers have been studied as influential external stakeholders (see table 4-2 in section 4.4). However, in the single stages of the product innovation process other external stakeholder groups might play an important role as well. For example, research institutions might contribute with their knowledge to develop technical solutions in later stages of the product innovation process (Ståhl 2004, pp. 38-39). Knowing which stakeholders are most influential at different stages of the process would prevent these stakeholder groups from being overlooked in both research and practice. HQs' and subsidiaries' management might take more external stakeholder groups into account, extend the business relationship to them and hence avoid conflicts with these business partners.

(1.2) The embeddedness of business relationships to important business partners will be studied in detail during the stages of the product innovation process. Here, seven measures will be employed to describe the business relationships in detail. So far, fewer measures have been used; many authors even took only one measure into account: (mutual) adaptations of business partners (e.g. Andersson/Forsgren 1996, 2000, Andersson/Forsgren/Pedersen 2001). However, examining business relationships by one or a few measures might not provide a comprehensive understanding.

Furthermore, it will be analyzed how the relationship between the innovative subsidiary and influential business partners develops during the product innovation process. So far, authors predominantly consider business relationships to be evolving slowly. Tacit knowledge is thus only exchanged after some time (Uzzi 1996, Uzzi/Gillespie 2002, Uzzi/Lancaster 2003, Forsgren/Holm/Johanson 2005). Knowing more on the development of business relationships might allow subsidiary management to control them more effectively.

In addition, knowledge flows between both the business partners will be analyzed at the stages of the product innovation process. Literature on knowledge exchange between and within MNCs already exists. However, it has not yet been investigated which knowledge is exchanged at which stage of the product innovation process between an innovative subsidiary and its external business partners (Hallin/Kang 2008, pp. 18-19). Studying both the embeddedness of business relationships and the knowledge exchanged in them might allow making more detailed propositions on the correlation between embeddedness of business relationships and knowledge transfer. Also, by knowing more about the collaboration of the innovative subsidiary with its external business partners, the subsidiary and the MNC might be able to control the product innovation process better.

Intra-organizational perspective:
2 **How does the relationship of the subsidiary with other units of the MNC affect the transfer of the subsidiary's product innovation within the MNC?**
    2.1 Which business partners are involved in the transfer of the product innovation?
    2.2 How does the business relationship between the receiving and the sending unit look like?
        2.2.1 How is the product innovation transfer organized?
        2.2.2 Which knowledge is exchanged between the focal subsidiary and the receiving unit during the innovation transfer process?

(2.1) In order to improve the intra-organizational transfer of product innovations it must be determined which units are involved in product innovation transfer. Again, knowing which stakeholders are involved in product innovation transfer might allow management to initiate the transfer process, for instance by actively involving the business partners.

(2.2) In existing literature, intra-organizational transfer of product innovations was found to be problematic (e.g. Ståhl 2004, pp. 77-78). In knowledge transfer, conflicts between units may arise. Hence, it must be specified why conflicts between units evolve or how they are avoided. Revealing the cause of problems in product innovation transfer might help management to coordinate product innovation transfer within the MNC. For instance, particular organizational structures to avoid or diminish the conflicts could be established.

In figure 1-1, the basic questions of this contribution are summarized. As a starting point of this dissertation it is assumed that the innovative subsidiary is embedded in an external business network which influences its product innovation activity. This is the inter-organizational perspective of the study in which the product innovation process is analyzed. Once the product innovation is created, it is passed on from the innovative subsidiary to other units of the MNC.[5] This corresponds to the intra-organizational perspective of the thesis in which the product innovation transfer is examined. While the inter-organizational perspective is based on the concept of external embeddedness, the intra-organizational perspective is grounded on the concept of corporate embeddedness. Since the concept of the Embedded MNC encompasses both the external and the corporate embeddedness concept, it is employed as a conceptual basis of the present contribution.

On the theoretical perspective, an aim of this contribution is to present the concept of the Embedded MNC and the knowledge on product innovations in MNCs systematically. As the concept of the Embedded MNC has evolved out of existing concepts it appears like a "patchwork"[6]. Its development and structure are explained and the concept is discussed. Further, the concept of the Embedded MNC is refined with regard to the flows of knowledge in business networks.

---

[5] Of course, both the inter-organizational perspective and the intra-organizational perspective do not apply for every product innovation. In the empirical study, product innovations will be chosen which are created with external business partners and which are intended to be passed on within the MNC.

[6] Even though there is a book which tries to summarize the concept: Forsgren/Holm/Johanson 2005.

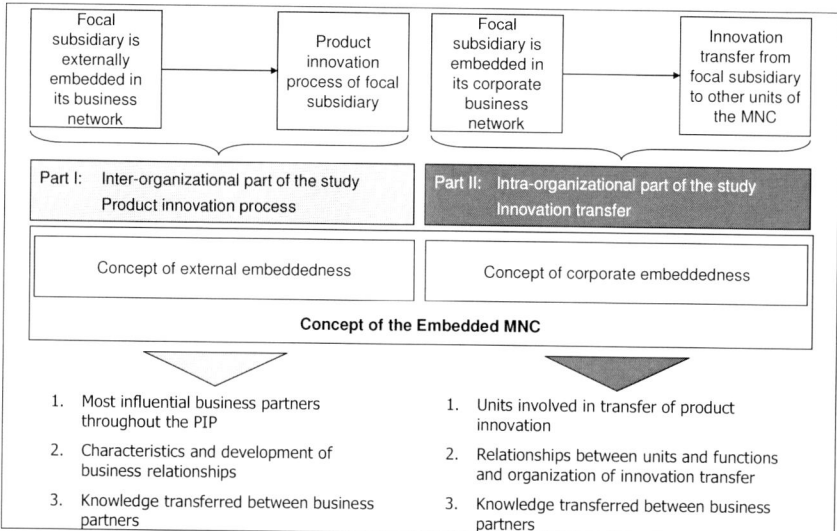

Figure 1-1: Overview of the study

1.3 Outline of the Study

Before the structure of the present thesis is introduced in this section, one remark needs to be made: This dissertation takes the perspective of a researcher in the field of International Business. The focus is on the interaction of focal subsidiaries with their environment and with other units of the MNC. The research areas of innovation and knowledge management are only considered insofar as they are essential for this study.

First, an overview of different definitions and attributes of innovations will be provided in chapter 2 in order to specify the kind of innovations analyzed in this contribution (2.1). The definition of product innovations may be found in sub-section 2.1.1 while it will be clarified in sub-section 2.1.2. The intensity of product innovations that ranges between incremental and radical innovations will be explained afterwards (2.1.3). In section 2.2, the processes of creating innovations (sub-section 2.2.1) and of transferring those inside an MNC (sub-section 2.2.2) will be described. In section 2.3, the definition of product innovations as used in this contribution will be summarized.

In chapter 3, existing literature on both research questions will be reviewed. The structure of the literature review will follow the main research questions of this study. In section 3.1, literature on the influence of external business partners on product innovations in subsidiaries will be presented while literature on the transfer of product innovations inside the MNC will be analyzed in section 3.2. The literature review aims at giving an overview of existing publications and revealing gaps in the content and method of literature. Within each section, 3.1 and 3.2, the method of the literature review will be explained first (3.1.1 and 3.2.1). Then, content (3.1.2 and 3.2.2) and methods (3.1.3 and 3.2.3) of relevant publications will be presented. In the last section of the chapter, conclusions will be drawn from the literature review (3.3).

The conceptual framework of the study will be presented in chapter 4. First, it will be explained why the concept of the Embedded MNC suits the research focus of the study (4.1). As this concept evolved out of a long tradition of network research, the roots of the concept will be reported in section 4.2. The concept of the Embedded MNC will be presented in section 4.3. The structure of networks consisting of actors, relationships and the network as a whole will be described in sub-section 4.3.1. Flows of resources, knowledge, trust and power in business networks will be described in sub-section 4.3.2 according to the concept of the Embedded MNC. The development of relationships and the network as a whole will be explained in sub-section 4.3.3. Finally, the concept of the Embedded MNC will be discussed critically in section 4.4. In section 4.5 the concept of the Embedded MNC will be refined and extended. First, in sub-section 4.5.1, knowledge on different stakeholder groups as actors will be provided. In sub-section 4.5.2, more details on characteristics of knowledge and of knowledge flows will be given. Finally, in section 4.6 the conceptual framework will be summarized.

The design and how the empirical study has been carried out will be reported in chapter 5. The research design will be presented (5.1). It will be explained why the case study design was chosen (5.1.1) and the case study design will be described (5.1.2). Details on the operationalization of the conceptual framework will be provided in sub-section 5.1.3. Information on the collection and analysis of data will be given in sections 5.2 and 5.3, respectively. In section 5.3, the procedure of data analysis will be explained first (5.3.1), and the code list will be provided afterwards (5.3.2). Scientific quality criteria will be reflected in section 5.4. Further, construct validity (5.4.1), internal validity (5.4.2), external validity (5.4.3) and reliability (5.4.4) will be discussed.

Results of the empirical study will be presented in chapter 6. In section 6.1, both cases will be described. In sub-section 6.1.1, details on the case of Cogis will be provided while in sub-section 6.1.2, the case of Cantis will be explained. Both cases will be compared in sub-section 6.1.3. In section 6.2, the external business partners that were involved in the stages of the product innovation processes of Cogis (6.2.1), CantisCRC (6.2.2) and CantisPF (6.2.3) will be analyzed.[7] In sub-section 6.2.4, the three cases will be compared and conclusions will be drawn. The embeddedness and development of business relationships to external business partners will be discussed in section 6.3. The case of Cogis will be examined in sub-section 6.3.1, the case of CantisCRC will be investigated in sub-section 6.3.2, and the case of CantisPF will be studied in 6.3.3. Again, cases will be compared and conclusions will be drawn in sub-section 6.3.4. In section 6.4, characteristics of knowledge and knowledge transfer will be examined. In sub-section 6.4.1, knowledge transfer will be studied in the case of Cogis, while that in the cases of CantisCRC and CantisPF will be analyzed in sub-sections 6.4.2 and 6.4.3, respectively. Sub-section 6.4.4 will serve to compare the cases again. Finally, the transfer of knowledge within the MNCs in product innovation and innovation transfer will be investigated in section 6.5. The case of Pharmacom (Cogis) will be examined first (6.5.1) and the case of Diagnocom (CantisCRC and CantisPF) will be analyzed next (6.5.2). In sub-section 6.5.3, both cases will be compared.

In chapter 7, contributions of the present contribution will be summarized (7.1). As parts of the results extend the concept of the Embedded MNC, they will be reflected on the concept (7.2). Results do not only have theoretical but also practical consequences. Therefore, implications for managers will be discussed (7.3). Finally, limitations of the study will be revealed (7.4) and avenues for further research will be presented (7.5).

---

[7] The case of Cantis actually includes two product innovations, CantisCRC and CantisPF that will be looked at separately.

2 Introduction to Product Innovations in the Multinational Corporation

Innovation is a term which is extensively used in research and practice. However, different definitions of innovation exist and several kinds of innovations are differentiated. Thus, in the first sub-section of this chapter, the term "product innovation" will be defined (2.1.1). Then, the understanding of product innovation as an invention, a marketed problem solution or as an innovation process is discussed (2.1.2). Finally, the intensity is presented as an important attribute of product innovations (2.1.3). In section 2.2, information on the product innovation process (2.2.1) and the innovation transfer process (2.2.2) will be provided. Within sub-section 2.2.1, general models of the innovation processes (2.2.1.1) and the geographical scope of innovation processes in MNCs (2.2.1.2) are presented. The chapter ends with a summary of the characteristics of product innovations and product innovation processes that are used in this research project.

2.1 Clarifying the Understanding of Product Innovations in this Study

2.1.1 Objects of Innovation

Innovations that are created may concern different objects. The most common differentiation is the one between product innovations and process innovations. Social innovations are sometimes also discussed.[8] The objects of innovation are depicted in figure 2-1.

(1) In the present thesis, product innovations will be examined. Product innovations[9] are new products developed with the intent of meeting market demands (Damanpour

---

[8] Apart from product, process and social innovations, marketing innovations may be studied, for instance (Ståhl 2004, pp. 47-82).

[9] Sometimes service innovations are emphasized to create an own type of innovation (e.g. Abramovici/Bancel-Charensol 2004, Jones/Samalionis 2008, Müller/Rajala/Westerlund 2008). This is done because the innovation process is fundamentally different in service than in product innovations. However, they may also be subsumed in the category of product innovations (Damanpour 1991, p. 561).

1991, p. 561, Ziggers 2005, p. 45). Product innovations may either be technology-push or market-pull innovations. In the first case, an invention is initiated inside the firm, often in the R&D department, and is then produced. Whether there is a demand for the new product is not yet clear. The marketing department is involved only at the end of the process and tries to bring the new product to the market. The customers' need is created when the product innovation has already been finished (Witt 1996, p. 7, Reichart 2002, p. 19, Khilji/Mroczkowski/Bernstein 2006). An example of this procedure is the walkman that was launched by Sony in 1979. In the case of a market-pull product innovation, the customers' need is analyzed first and then the firm initiates efforts of research and development (Reichart 2002, p. 19, Verganti 2008, p. 443). Although market-pull innovations are sometimes said to be more successful (e.g. Witt 1996, p. 7), it has been found that the probability of success is alike for technology-push and market-pull innovations (Cooper 1979, pp. 101-102). Both working on the technology and involving customer demands in the innovation process are probably needed to create successful product innovations (Specht/Beckmann 1996, pp. 32-33).

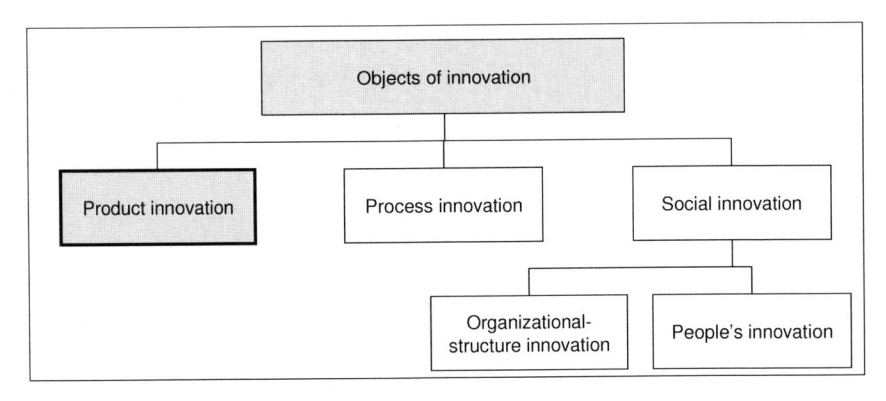

Figure 2-1: Objects of innovation
Source: Adopted from Knight 1967, p. 482.

(2) Process innovations apply to new processing techniques, for instance in production processes, or to major improvements of processing techniques within the firm. These techniques might have an impact on both the firm's equipment as well as the production. They are introduced to produce new or improved products that cannot be produced with the old traditional equipment or processing techniques, or to increase

the efficiency of the existing production system (Meißner 1989, pp. 28-29, Ziggers 2005, p. 45). Process innovations also encompass new elements in an organization's product operations like input material or work and knowledge flow mechanisms (Damanpour 1991, p. 561).

(3) Apart from product and process innovations, social innovations sometimes are differentiated (e.g. Zaltman/Duncan/Holbek 1973, p. 9, Kasper 1980, pp. 56-57). They apply to the organizational structure's innovations and people's innovations. While organizational-structure innovations include changes in authority relations or communication systems, people innovations involve changes in the staff of a firm or in the personnel's behavior (Knight 1967, p. 482).[10] They do not have a direct impact on the fundamental business activities of the firm but they often have an indirect effect on them (Damanpour 1991, pp. 560-561, Ziggers 2005, p. 45).

2.1.2 Product Innovation as Invention, Process or Result

The term "innovation" is defined in many different ways. Schumpeter introduced the concept as a possibility for growth of the firm (Schumpeter 1934, pp. 65-66). He defined it very broadly as a change in the form of the production function (Schumpeter 1939, p. 87). Thus, he said the creation of new products, technological changes in the production process, the entry in new markets, the development of new sources of supply and every "... 'doing things differently' in the realm of economic life ..." (Schumpeter 1939, p. 84) can be called innovation. Since Schumpeter many researchers have worked on innovations and many different definitions have been created. There are basically three different understandings of the term: product innovations as inventions, as marketed problem solutions or as innovation processes. The three definitions are depicted in figure 2-2.

(1) First, the terms innovation and invention can be used interchangeably. According to this understanding, a product innovation is the combination of "...two or more existing concepts or entities ... in some novel way to produce a configuration not previ-

---

[10] Organizational-structure innovations are also called administrative innovations (e.g. Van de Ven 1988, p. 105, Damanpour 1991, pp. 560-561, Ziggers 2005, p. 45).

ously known" (Zaltman/Duncan/Holbek 1973, p. 7). It is the technical realization of new scientific knowledge or a new combination of existing scientific knowledge (Specht/Beckmann 1996, p. 15). Thus, the product innovation in the sense of an invention is generated in a creative process of R&D in a laboratory but it is not necessarily produced and marketed (Zaltman/Duncan/Holbek 1973, p. 7, Garcia/Calantone 2002, p. 112). An invention that is the intended result of R&D is called "planned invention". An invention however, may also be an unplanned outcome of research and development (Brockhoff 1992, pp. 27-28).

(2) Second, an invention can also be understood as a pre-condition for a product innovation. A product innovation is then the first economic exploitation of an invention and thus includes the market launch (Smith/Barfield 1996, Vahs/Burmester 1999, p. 44). It is a novel problem solution for customers which exceeds the state of knowledge and experience till that date (Dewar/Dutton 1986, p. 1423).

(3) Third, the term "product innovation" is used to describe "... an iterative process initiated by the perception of a new market ... opportunity for a technology-based invention which leads to development, production, and marketing tasks striving for the commercial success of the invention" (Garcia/Calantone 2002, p. 112).[11] It is thus the process of development of a solution to a particular problem (Zaltman/Duncan/Holbek 1973, pp. 7-8). For the sake of clarity in this thesis, the process of innovating will be named "product innovation process". It encompasses the innovation process from the generation of the idea to the creation of the product innovation. The product innovation process is discussed in more detail in sub-section 2.2.1.1.

The interrelation of the three basic understandings of product innovation is depicted in figure 2-2. In this figure, the product innovation process is delimited after R&D activities by a dotted line because this is how far it will be analyzed in the present thesis. Why are market launch activities not considered? Of course, the innovation process is oversimplified in the figure. However, it becomes clear that the crucial and unique phase in the innovation process encompasses research and development activities. They lead to the invention as a novel combination of knowledge. Marketing

---

[11] This corresponds to the source-based perspective on the innovation process (Klein/Sorra 1996, p. 1057, see sub-section 2.2.1.1) which is taken in this study.

activities preparing the market launch of the innovative product would be basically similar whether the invention was created in the own firm or whether it was bought from another firm. Therefore, the stages of the product innovation process which involve research and development activities will be in the focus of this study. The product innovation is hence completed when the invention is made; the term "product innovation" is understood as invention. However, only product innovations will be examined that are intended to be marketed. In line with this definition, the innovation process is looked at until the invention is made.

Activity	Research & Development		Market launch
Result	Invention = Innovation as used in this study (1)		Innovation (narrow sense) (2)
	Innovation process (3)		

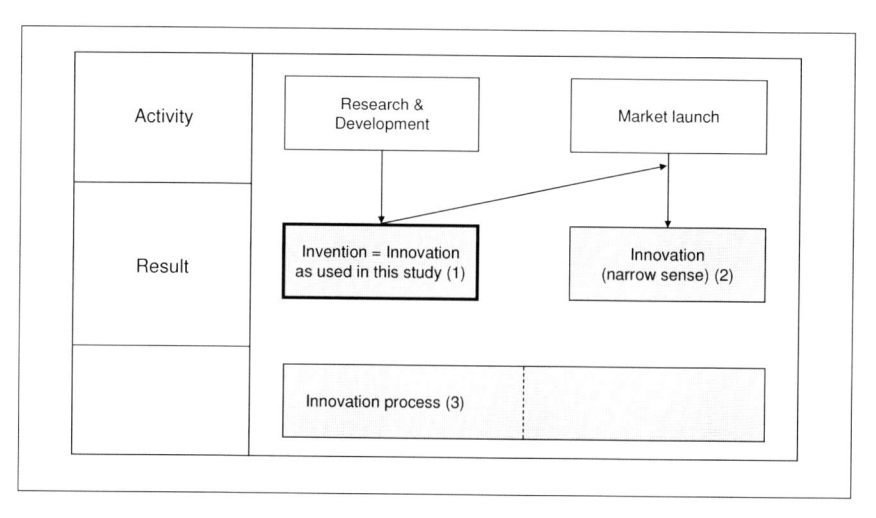

Figure 2-2: Depiction of the different understandings of product innovation
Source: Adopted from Brockhoff 1992, p. 30.

2.1.3 Intensity of Product Innovations

Product innovations are often characterized according to their degree of intensity.[12] Thereby, two perspectives may be taken: the perspective of the innovator or that of the adopter. If the perspective of the innovator is considered, product innovations are assessed on a continuum between the poles of incremental innovations at the low end and radical innovations at the high end (Zaltman/Duncan/Holbek 1973, p. 23,

---

[12] The intensity of innovations is also analyzed for process or social innovations. They are not considered in this chapter.

Dewar/Dutton 1986, pp. 1422-1423, Aboulnasr et al. 2008, p. 94).[13] If the position of potential adopters of an innovation is adopted, its degree may range from new to the person, unit or MNC to new to the world (West/Farr 1990, p. 9, Garcia/Calantone 2002, p. 113, Reichart 2002, p. 20, Cooper 2005, p. 25). In this research project, the perspective of the innovator is taken, i.e. the perspective of the innovative subsidiary in this case. The differentiation between incremental and radical product innovations is important in the present study because it has been proposed that radical product innovations rely more on inter-organizational relationships than incremental product innovations do (Ståhl 2004, pp. 168-169, Story et al. 2008, pp. 194-195).

The definitions of incremental and radical innovations differ fundamentally. Usually, radical innovations are defined and incremental innovations are the innovations that do not fit the definition. Radical innovations may be defined very generally as "...array of actions that take place suddenly, rapidly and universally" (Carrero/Peiro/ Salanova 2000, p. 504). However, definitions mainly base on one or more of the following dimensions: characteristics of the technology[14] of the innovation, of the market impact and of effects on the innovative organization. Some examples of definitions of radical innovations are given in table 2-1.

As definitions are different, the intensity of product innovations is measured quite differently. In a sophisticated study, Hauschildt and Schlaak reviewed the measures employed to identify radical product innovations. In a factor analysis, they reduced the measures to seven factors. These factors describe the intensity of product innovations: product technology, supply, production process, market and need for capital and formal and informal organization (Hauschildt/Schlaak 2001, pp. 169-170). They were then grouped into three dimensions: technology/production/supply (in the following: technological dimension), sales/need for capital (in the following: market di-

---

[13] Instead of the term radical, authors also speak of discontinuous or architectural product innovations or of emerging or disruptive technology (Garcia/Calantone 2002, p. 110, Hurmelinna-Laukkanen/Sainio/Jauhiainen 2008, p. 279). The usage of the terms is not clear-cut.
[14] Technology describes a system of means-end relations which apply to a particular application. If a technology is applied the term "technique" is used. Thus, technique is a practical element of a technology (Brockhoff 1992, p. 22).

mension) and formal/informal structure of the organization (in the following: organizational dimension; Hauschildt/Schlaak 2001, pp. 175-176).[15]

Author/s	Definition of radical innovations
Knight 1967, p. 482	"Structural radicalness" is the "extent to which the structural arrangement differs from existing ones. ... For example, with products ... the amount of change in the physical design of the product."
Zaltman/Duncan/Holbek 1973, p. 23	"Radicalness ... is closely linked to the now-familiar terms of risk, novelty, and creativity ... Innovation radicalness can be defined in terms of existing alternatives: the more an innovation differs from the existing alternatives, the higher is its degree of radicalness."
Dewar/Dutton 1986, pp. 1422-1423	"Radical innovations are fundamental changes that represent revolutionary changes in technology... The major difference captured by the labels radical and incremental is the degree of novel technological process content embodied in the innovation and hence, the degree of new knowledge embedded in the innovation."
Chandy/Tellis 1998, p. 475	"We define radical product innovation as the propensity of a firm to introduce new products that (1) incorporate substantially different technology from existing products and (2) can fulfill key customer needs better than existing products."
Simon et al. 2003, p. 17	"... we have defined a radical innovation project as one with the potential to produce one or more of the following: an entirely new set of performance features, greater than five-fold improvements in known performance features, a significant reduction in cost (> 30 percent)."
Ziggers 2005, pp. 45-46	"Radical or discontinuous innovations are causing fundamental changes in and differ to a large extent from the existing activities of the firm... Not only do they involve high risks, but it also places extensive demands on capital because of R&D spending."
Mote/Jordan/Hage 2007, pp. 358-359	"... radical innovation is defined as dramatic increases in functionality, performance ... [it; SH] typically involves higher levels of uncertainty."

Table 2-1: Examples of definitions of radical product innovations

The technological dimension (high newness of technology) is found to be the most significant indicator of radical product innovations in the study of Hauschildt and Schlaak (2001, pp. 170, 176). It is also mentioned most often to define radical product innovations (e.g. Zaltman/Duncan/Holbek 1973, p. 23, Dewar/Dutton 1986, pp. 1422-1423, Gatignon et al. 2002, p. 1112, Sarangee 2007, p. 148, Aboulnasr et al. 2008, p. 94). High newness of technology is accompanied by a large amount of new knowledge. This novelty usually leads to a high uncertainty of product innovation be-

---

[15] In the study, Hauschildt and Schlaak identified five types of product innovations: the incremental, average and radical innovation and the types of the combined product and process innovation and the technological discontinuity (Hauschildt/Schlaak 2001, pp. 171-173).

cause little experience with the new technology exists (Hauschildt/Schlaak 2001, pp. 170, 177). Furthermore, it is not clear how much R&D is required to be successful (if successful at all), how long the product innovation process will take and how much it will cost[16] (Ali 1994, pp. 56-57, Hauschildt/Schlaak 2001, p. 174, Hall/Martin 2005, p. 274, Ziggers 2005, p. 46, Johnson/Dilts 2006, p. 254, Aboulnasr et al. 2008, p. 94).

The second dimension which is used in definitions of radical vs. incremental innovations is the market aspect. While pioneering products are defined as radical innovations, improvements to existing products and additions to an existing product line are regarded as incremental innovations (Dewar/Dutton 1986, pp. 1422-1423, Sarangee 2007, p. 148). Radical product innovations are thus those product innovations that are expected to offer substantially higher benefits for the customers than incremental product innovations (Zaltman/Duncan/Holbek 1973, p. 23, Dewar/Dutton 1986, p. 1423, Aboulnasr et al. 2008, p. 94). Radical product innovations are furthermore considered to be able to create new markets and are able to cannibalize current products (Hauschildt/Schlaak 2001, pp. 170, 178, Hurmelinna-Laukkanen/Sainio/Jauhiainen 2008, p. 279). They are also assumed to contribute to a higher growth of turnover and enhance the competitiveness of the MNC more than incremental innovations do (Zaltman/Duncan/Holbek 1973, p. 24, Ziggers 2005, p. 45). However, they are also considered to involve higher uncertainty as it can not be foreseen if the product will be successful in the market (Freeman/Soete 2004, Hall/Martin 2005, p. 274).

The third dimension in definitions of radical product innovations is the organizational dimension, i.e. the effect on the innovative firm. It was identified in the study of Hauschildt and Schlaak (2001). Product innovations are defined as radical if they lead to fundamental changes in the company when they are produced, by bringing activities to the firm which differ substantially from the existing activities. As opposed to this, they are characterized as incremental when they cause only slight or modest adaptations or improvements of the current activities (Damanpour 1991, p. 561). Furthermore, radical innovations change the formal organizational structure by causing the creation of new business units, for example. They also lead to changes in the

---

[16] The need for capital is subsumed in a category with sales by Hauschildt and Schlaak (2001). However, this includes not only R&D costs but also marketing costs and investments in production technique (Hauschildt/Schlaak 2001, p. 170).

informal organization like social behavior of employees, values or the corporate culture (Hauschildt/Schlaak 2001, pp. 170, 178-179).

To sum up, in this study, the focus is on the R&D process in innovative subsidiaries (see sub-section 2.1.2). The innovation process will be analyzed till the invention is made. At this point, the market dimension can not be evaluated. The organizational dimension may also be studied only once the invention is made because mainly the effects of producing the new invention are inhered in this dimension. Hence, the technological dimension will be the basis to assess the intensity of product innovations. Therefore, the production and supply aspects of Hauschildt and Schlaak's study will be excluded for the same reasons: these aspects can only be analyzed once the product innovation is marketed. It is only from that moment on that the product innovation is produced in large scale and supplied to retailers and consumers. The intensity of product innovations is thus defined and measured as innovations with a high newness of technology which involves a large amount of new knowledge.

2.2 Product Innovation and Transfer Processes in the Multinational Corporation

2.2.1 Product Innovation Process

2.2.1.1 Product Innovation Process in General

Two fundamentally different understandings of the product innovation process exist: the source-based innovation process and the user-based innovation process. The source-based innovation process describes the creation of an innovation from the idea to the invention or the launch of the product in the innovative unit (see sub-section 2.1.2). The user-based perspective depicts the innovation process from the awareness of a need of the user until the "... incorporation of the innovation in the user's behavioral repertoire" (Klein/Sorra 1996, p. 1057). Thus, while in the source-based perspective an innovation is new to the market, in the user-based perspective it is new to the organization or unit, irrespective of the earlier use in other organizations or units. In the latter case, the innovation process encompasses the transfer and implementation of an innovation (Klein/Sorra 1996, p. 1057). In the present research project, the product innovation process is looked at from the source-based perspective, i.e. from the perspective of the innovative subsidiary. From this point of view the innovation transfer is examined as well. The implementation of innovations in the receiving unit is not investigated.

From a source-based perspective, an indefinite number of product innovation process models exist.[17] They may be grouped into different types (Reichart 2002, pp. 45-46). Some authors focus on R&D as the function in the firm that is particularly involved in the product innovation process (Specht/Beckmann 1996). A second group of product innovation process models looks at the inputs and outputs that are generated during the innovation process (e.g. Twiss 1980, pp. 1-25). Others emphasize the decisions which have to be taken during the innovation process (e.g. Cooper 2005, pp. 200-236) or they consider the innovation process as a process of reactions to external and internal stimuli of the firm (e.g. Becker/Whisler 1967, p. 468). Finally, there are models which divide the innovation process into different stages according to the activities that are managed during the creation of a product innovation (e.g. Cummings/O'Connell 1978, p. 42). This approach will also be taken in the present study.

In general, the existence of a universal innovation process model which is applicable to every industry and even within an industry is doubted (Dewar/Dutton 1986, p. 1422). In addition, it is obvious that the stages of the innovation process are not executed sequentially but are overlapping (Rothwell 1994, p. 12). This increases the complexity of the process. As the product innovation process can fail at every stage, it is highly uncertain (Sorescu/Chandy/Prabhu 2003, p. 84).

---

[17] In this sub-section, no example of an innovation process model is given. This is due to the fact that in this study, the empirical study will take place in the pharmaceutical industry (see sub-section 5.1.2.2.1). As this industry has a very specific product innovation process, it is depicted in sub-section 6.1.1.5. A general model of the product innovation process would not provide any new insights for this study.

As stated earlier (see sub-section 2.1.2), the phases of research and development as the core of the innovation process will be looked at in depth.[18] Within these phases, three fundamentally different activities take place: basic research, applied research and experimental development.[19] Basic research aims at acquiring "... new knowledge of the underlying foundation of phenomena and observable facts" (OECD 2002, p. 30). In basic research, experimental or theoretical work is done. The goal of applied research is also to gain new knowledge. However, this knowledge is clearly related to a specific practical objective. Finally, experimental development includes the usage of knowledge obtained in both stages of research or on practical experience from the production of new materials, devices or products. It may also aim at establishing new processes, systems or services or at the improvement of existing ones (OECD 2002, p. 30). The activities of R&D do not necessarily have to be completed in one firm (Brockhoff 1992, p. 35).

2.2.1.2 Geographical Scope of Product Innovation Processes in Multinational Corporations

In MNCs, the multinational organization of product innovation processes may take four different forms that Bartlett and Ghoshal reported: the center-for-global, local-for-local, locally-leveraged or globally-linked innovation process. While the first two are "classic" types of innovation processes, the latter two are called transnational innovation processes. Before explaining the four types of product innovation processes in detail it must be made clear that Bartlett and Ghoshal have a broader understanding of the product innovation process than that used in the present study. They look at the process from the generation of the idea to market launch of the product and the transfer and implementation of the product innovation to other units of the MNC.

In the center-for-global innovation process, HQs perceive a customer need in their home country market. Hence, they carry out research and development activities us-

---

[18] In this contribution, product development in the pharmaceutical industry will be analyzed (see sub-section 5.1.2.2.1). As the pharmaceutical industry has a very specific product innovation process, it will be described in the presentation of the two cases in sub-sections 6.1.1.5 and 6.1.2.5.
[19] This is a common subdivision of the R&D phase. However, the terms are not clear-cut and they are not always used in the same sense.

ing resources which are bundled in HQs. Once completed, the product innovation is marketed on a worldwide basis. This type of innovation process is often associated with a global strategy of the MNC.[20] In the local-for-local innovation process type, subsidiaries notice a customers' need in their local market and employ their own resources to create an innovation that suits this need. The product innovation is not transferred to other units of the MNC but is only used by the innovative subsidiary. The local-for-local innovation process can mainly be found in the multinational type of MNCs (Bartlett/Ghoshal 1990b, pp. 216-217, 1998, p. 132).

Apart from the two classical types of innovation processes, two new types of innovation processes, i.e. locally-leveraged and globally-linked innovation processes have evolved in the last 25 years. They are called transnational innovation processes (Bartlett/Ghoshal 1990b, p. 225, 1998, p. 133). In both types, flow of capabilities and resources runs from subsidiaries to HQs and sister units. Thus, subsidiaries play a greater role in enhancing the MNCs' capabilities and creating product innovations that are used in the whole MNC than in the center-for-global and local-for-local types of product innovation processes. In the locally-leveraged innovation process, an innovative subsidiary creates a product innovation using its own resources. In opposition to the local-for-local type, the product innovation is transferred to other units of the MNC when it is completed. It is thus exploited in more markets than the local host country market of the innovative subsidiary. However, the transfer of the product innovation might fail, for instance when the receiving unit has a not-invented-here attitude. In this case, the receiving unit generally refuses to adopt and implement innovations from outside its own unit, irrespective of the object and the particular source of innovation (Katz/Allen 1982, p. 7, Bartlett/Ghoshal 1990b, pp. 221-222). The globally-linked innovation process occurs when resources and capabilities of many different units, both HQs and subsidiaries, are bundled in order to create a product innovation jointly (Bartlett/Ghoshal 1990b, pp. 217-218). Its greatest problem, which applies to the locally-leveraged innovation process as well, are high coordination costs that

---

[20] Bartlett and Ghoshal have developed four archetypes of a MNCs' strategy of managing its international operations: the international, global, multinational and transnational type. The international MNC is very focused on its HQs which take all the strategic decisions and transfers its strategy on the foreign subsidiaries. The global strategy operates with a worldwide orientation. Products are developed centrally for a global market and are not adapted to local markets. In the multinational MNC, subsidiaries are quite autonomous and appear on their market as a local firm. The transnational type of MNC intends to combine the advantages of the other three types (Schmid 1996a, pp. 27-29).

arise because more interdependencies exist between the many units that are involved in the innovation process (Bartlett/Ghoshal 1990b, pp. 222-224). Coordination between different units is more difficult than within units. Good interpersonal relationships between the units tend to facilitate coordination (Bartlett/Ghoshal 1990b, pp. 238-239).

When analyzing the four types of product innovation processes it becomes clear that Bartlett and Ghoshal have a broader understanding of the innovation process than the one used in the present study. Locally-leveraged and globally-linked product innovation processes encompass the creation of a marketed product innovation in one or several units, its transfer to other units of the MNC and the usage of the product innovations by these units. The classic center-for-global product innovation process involves the transfer of the product innovation from HQs to subsidiaries unless the worldwide marketing involves no subsidiaries at all. The innovation process in the understanding of the present thesis, of many other authors (e.g., Garcia/Calantone 2002, p. 112) and of Bartlett and Ghoshal (1990b, pp. 216-218, 222-225, 1998, pp. 132-133) are depicted in figure 2-3. The transfer and implementation of an innovation in other units of the MNC may take place before or after the market launch. While the continuous line indicates the case that a product innovation is passed on to other units after it has been launched in one market (e.g., the home country market of the MNC), the broken line shows the case that a product innovations is transferred to other units first and is launched in several markets afterwards.

Although in this research project, the product innovation process is only defined in stages of R&D the type of product innovation process observed in the empirical study can be revealed. As in the present study, product innovations are chosen that are created in subsidiaries, product innovation processes must be either locally-leveraged or globally-linked. If the product innovation is solely developed by one subsidiary and transferred to other units afterwards, it is a locally-linked product innovation process. If several subsidiaries (and HQs) work on the development of the product innovation, a globally-linked innovation process is examined. In this thesis, either locally-leveraged or globally-linked product innovation processes will be analyzed. It will be made clear which type of product innovation process the particular product innovation runs through.

Activity	Research & Development	Market launch	Transfer and implementation of innovation to/in other units of the MNC
Result	Invention = Innovation as used in this study	Innovation (narrow sense)	Innovation (understanding of Bartlett and Ghoshal)
	Innovation process (as analyzed in this thesis)	Innovation process (narrow sense)	Innovation process (understanding of Bartlett and Ghoshal)

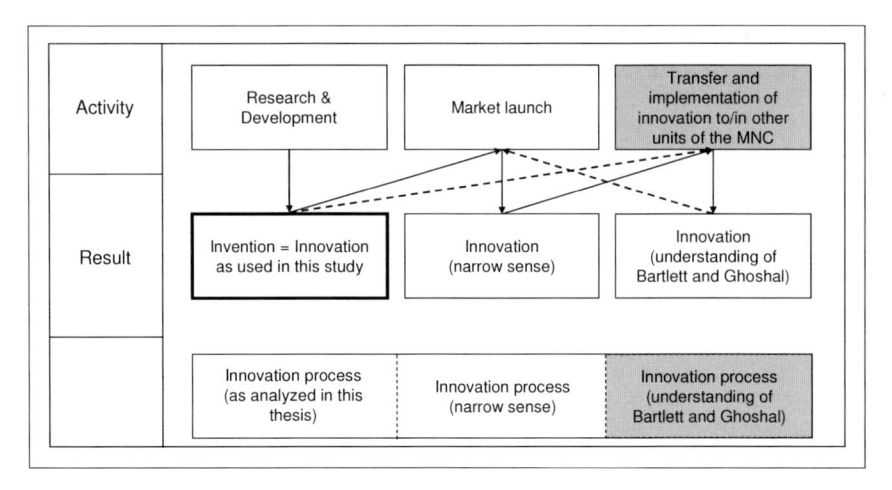

Figure 2-3: Innovation process in the focus of Bartlett and Ghoshal

2.2.2 Transfer of Product Innovations in the Multinational Corporation

Innovation transfer is the process "... whereby an innovation is shared, by means of selected mechanisms, between specific and distinct parties, i.e. senders and receivers" (Ciabuschi/Kang/Ståhl 2004, p. 5). It is "... the targeted diffusion of the innovation from the developer unit (sender) to other sister units (receivers) within the intra-firm network of subsidiaries" (Ciabuschi 2004, p. 16). In chapter 3, literature on innovation transfer in MNCs is reviewed (see section 3.2). Thereby, literature on mechanisms and antecedents of innovation transfer is found. However, in opposition to the product innovation process, a process model of innovation transfer does not seem to exist.

A comparable model of knowledge transfer in general has already been developed (see sub-section 4.5.2.3). However, during an innovation transfer process several bits of knowledge are believed to be transferred successively. This is in line with the product innovation process during which many knowledge transfers regarding different issues take place as well (e.g. the stage-gate-process; Cooper 2005, pp. 200-236). Since no model of innovation transfer process has been found it will be part of the empirical study to analyze how the product innovation transfer is organized.

2.3 Summary: Product Innovations in this Study

After having explained different aspects of product innovations, which kind of product innovations will be investigated, is summarized in this section. First, product innovations are new products developed with the intent of meeting market demands. Product innovations may be understood as inventions, i.e. the combination of knowledge in a novel way. They may also be regarded as marketed problem solutions that are based on inventions. Accordingly, the product innovation process encompasses the stages of R&D in the case of inventions while it includes additional stages of launching the product in the case of a marketed problem solution. As the unique stages in the product innovation process are the stages of R&D, the product innovation is here defined as invention. The product innovation process is thus limited to R&D stages.

The intensity of product innovations is considered to be associated with the extent of collaboration with external business partners. On a continuum between incremental and radical product innovations, those on the radical end will be chosen. The intensity may be analyzed on three dimensions that are built from seven factors: the technology/production/supply dimension, sales/need for capital dimension and formal/informal organizational structure dimension. Most of them can only be assessed once the invention is brought to the market. However, the most significant factor, the degree of technological newness can be evaluated and will be taken as the indicator of the intensity of product innovations in this study. The kind of innovations that are analyzed in this research project is summarized in figure 2-4.

The focus of this study is on the collaboration of the innovative subsidiary with external business partners throughout the product innovation process and with corporate business partners during the transfer of the product innovation to other units of the MNC. Therefore, product innovation processes were explained in this chapter. The stage models of product innovation process that are used in this study will only be depicted in sub-sections 6.1.1.5 and 6.1.2.5 though, because they are specific to the pharmaceutical firms that are analyzed there. Particular attention was paid to the geographical scope of product innovation processes in MNCs. From the four types of product innovation processes, one of the transnational types will be analyzed in the present study. In this thesis, either locally-leveraged or globally-linked product innovation processes will be analyzed. Once the product innovation is created the organization of product innovation transfer will be studied.

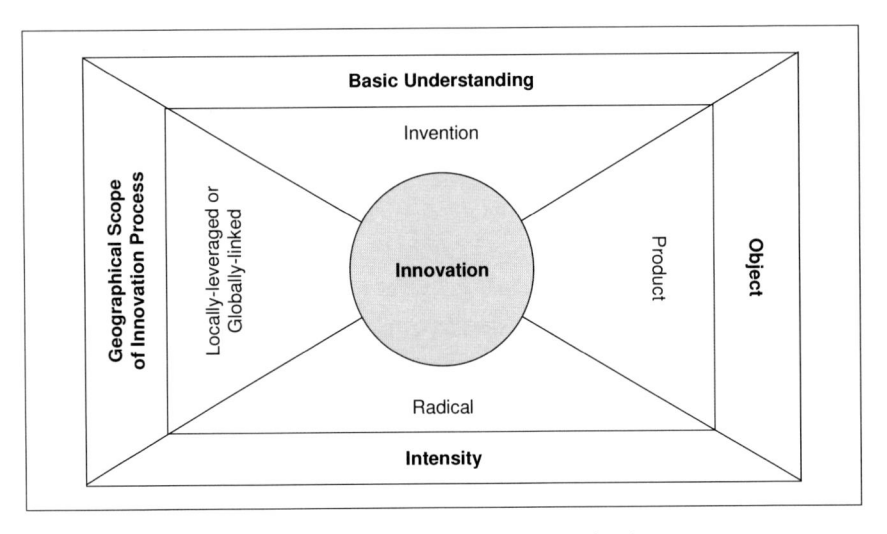

Figure 2-4: Type of innovations analyzed in the present thesis

3 Literature Review

This literature review will show which contributions to the research questions have been made in literature so far. As this study consists of both an external and a corporate dimension (see section 1.2) the literature review will be done in two parts. In section 3.1, literature on the influence of the local business environment of subsidiaries on their innovativeness will be analyzed. In section 3.2, literature about the diffusion of the focal innovation in the MNC will be explored.[21] In both sections the method of the literature review will be explained in the first sub-section (3.1.1 and 3.2.1). The content of the relevant studies will be reported in the second sub-section (3.1.2 and 3.2.2), and in the third sub-section (3.1.3 and 3.2.3), the research design of the studies will be analyzed. Finally, in division 3.3 some research gaps will be revealed which will be filled in this thesis.

3.1 Inter-organizational Focus: Influence of Subsidiaries' External Embeddedness on their Innovations

3.1.1 Method of the Literature Review

Existing literature on research question 1 was searched for in two steps. First, the databases of EBSCO and JSTOR were employed. The literature included in both databases was screened for key words. Literature that did not fit the topic was excluded. Second, additional literature was identified by looking through the references of literature that was identified in step one. In addition, literature hints were also received at a conference. Both steps are described in detail in the following.[22]

---

[21] The literature review not only includes studies on product innovations but also covers research on different kinds of innovations. This is done in order to have a broader basis for the studies. Furthermore, as can be seen in tables 3-2 and 3-5 the studies do not always specify which kind of innovations are examined.

[22] The procedure of starting the literature search with EBSCO and continuing with the references in the identified literature has been used by other authors before (e.g. Kretschmer 2008, p. 28). Other methods of searching for relevant literature are also applied by researchers, for instance analyzing specialized journals in a particular period of time (e.g. Walliser 2003b, p. 66, 2003a, pp. 6-7).

(1) Starting point of the literature review was the literature databases of EBSCO "Business Source Complete" and JSTOR. The EBSCO database is chosen because it is a comprehensive database that contains more than 1,200 journals including important journals from the fields of management and international business like the "Academy of Management Journal", "Administrative Science Quarterly" and "Journal of International Business Studies". Furthermore, it offers the possibility to search for literature on the basis of the title, abstract, publication name or keywords. The JSTOR database contains one or several journals from 542 institutions, for example the "Academy of Management" (AOM). Amongst them are 139 journals from the field of business literature. The aim of this database is to provide trustful digital archives for academics. In this database, titles and abstracts may be searched.

Both databases were employed for the search of existing literature on the research questions posed in section 1.2. In order to identify the relevant literature for the first research question on the influence of subsidiaries' external business network on their innovations, terms of the following groups: (1) "innovation" or "R&D", (2) "embeddedness", "network", "environment", "host", "business partner", or "business relationship" and (3) "subsidiary", "affiliate" or "MNC" were combined in every possible way.[23] They were sought for in titles, abstracts and keywords of the articles in EBSCO and in titles and abstracts in JSTOR. However, to limit the number of results, every search used one word of each group so that three words were always combined, e.g. "innovation" and "embeddedness" and "subsidiary" or "innovation" and "network" and "subsidiary". Furthermore, in EBSCO the search focused on the categories of academic journals, monographs and book chapters. Trade publications, newspapers, magazines, SWOT analyses, country reports, industry profiles, market research reports and product reviews which are also listed in EBSCO were excluded.

Nevertheless, with such a broad search not all of the identified literature is equally relevant for the research questions of this study. Many journal articles explore the accumulation of innovative firms in specific regions as a determinant of MNCs' decisions about the geographic dispersion of R&D sites (e.g. Janne 2002, Felker 2003, Fisch 2003, Shatz 2003, Yamawaki 2004, Pfister/Deffains 2005, Chen 2007, Sun/

---

[23] It has to be noted that EBSCO does not make a difference between singular and plural forms of nouns. Thus, it is not necessary to look for "subsidiaries" when the term "subsidiary" has already been searched for.

Von Zedtwitz/Simon 2007, Shimizutani/Todo 2008). Thus, they examine the assumption of MNCs that an innovative environment will have a positive impact on the innovativeness of its own R&D centers. Other papers focus on the consequences of the location of R&D activities on the host countries or regions (e.g. Williamson 2005, Casson 2007, Sun/Von Zedtwitz/Simon 2007) or they compare the characteristics of foreign-owned subsidiaries to local companies in a specific country (e.g. Solomon/Ingham 1977, Capon et al. 1987, Ramstetter 1999, Sadowski/Sadowski-Rasters 2006). As these studies do not contribute to the research questions of this thesis, they are not considered in the following. In addition, studies which exclusively examine the impact of the subsidiary's corporate business network on the subsidiary's innovativeness are not considered (e.g. Tsai 2001).

Special consideration has to be made about studies that include the terms "innovations" or "R&D" in the titles, keywords or abstracts but actually examine the transfer of knowledge.[24] Innovations are created through the combination of knowledge (see 2.1.2). Knowledge is an integral part of the innovation process and thus, a precondition of innovations. However, not every transfer and combination of knowledge leads to the development of innovations. Therefore, in this thesis only studies in which knowledge transfer leads to the creation of innovations are reviewed.[25]

(2) In the articles that were identified using EBSCO and JSTOR, the references were checked for more relevant literature. This was done in order to get a more complete overview of the existing literature. The journal article of Frost, Birkinshaw and Ensign (2002) which was cited in the article by Mu and his co-authors (Mu/Gnyawali/Hatfield 2007), and of Almeida (1996) cited in Phene and Almeida (2008) were perceived to be particularly relevant. The study of Håkanson and Nobel (2001) was cited by Criscuolo (2004) whose study is reviewed in section 3.2.

Additional literature was included due to the recommendations of members of the doctoral tutorial of the 34th EIBA Annual Conference held in Tallinn/Estonia in De-

---

[24] There are many studies which examine the transfer of knowledge and capabilities in a variety of contexts. It would be beyond the scope of this chapter to review all of them.
[25] Literature on knowledge transfer for innovations is not identified and reviewed if it does not include the terms mentioned above in titles, keywords or abstracts. However, as the terms are very broad it is expected that no relevant literature is missing.

cember 2008. Four dissertations from the University of Uppsala were obtained of which two are included in the review. Their references were also checked for more literature on the topic. Thus, in total 23 contributions to the first research question were detected. They are listed in table 3-1 in chronological order.

Relevant studies		
Almeida 1996	Muralidharan/Phatak 1999	Frost/Zhou 2000
Frost 2001	Håkanson/Nobel 2001	Frost/Birkinshaw/Ensign 2002
Ivarsson/Jonsson 2003	Tregaskis 2003	Almeida/Phene 2004
Britton 2004	Cantwell/Dunning/Janne 2004	Davis/Meyer 2004
Helble/Chong 2004	Hillebrand/Biemans 2004	Ståhl 2004
Ambos 2005	Boehe 2007	Chen 2007
Criscuolo/Narula/Verspagen 2005	Johnston/Paladino 2007	Mu/Gnyawali/Hatfield 2007
Hallin/Kang 2008	Phene/Almeida 2008	

Table 3-1: Literature on the influence of subsidiaries' external business network on their innovations

3.1.2 Content of Literature

3.1.2.1 Content of Literature with a Focus on Subsidiaries' External Embeddedness

The identified literature is presented in three groups. While studies of group (1) analyze the geographical sources of knowledge for subsidiaries' innovations rather abstractly, the literature in group (2) examines the actual effect of the external business network on subsidiaries' innovations. Publications in group (3) are based on the concept of the Embedded MNC (see chapter 4).

(1) A range of journal articles examines the geographical sources of subsidiaries' knowledge on which their innovations are based. They confirm that the local business environment of subsidiaries actually has an impact on their innovativeness (Almeida 1996, Frost/Zhou 2000, Frost 2001, Almeida/Phene 2004, Britton 2004, Cantwell/Dunning/Janne 2004, Criscuolo/Narula/Verspagen 2005, Phene/Almeida

2008).[26] Some of them explore whether foreign subsidiaries learn from HQs or from host country firms and find out that host country firms are more important as source of subsidiaries' innovations (Almeida/Phene 2004, Britton 2004, Phene/Almeida 2008).[27] Others differentiate between the home country of the MNC and the host country of subsidiaries as sources of knowledge which lead to innovations in subsidiaries. They find that although host country relationships have a significant influence on subsidiaries' innovations, the home country has an impact, too (Frost 2001, Criscuolo/Narula/Verspagen 2005). One study observes the development of the number of subsidiaries' innovations in a particular region over time. It detects that subsidiaries' innovativeness increases when local firms and universities escalate their innovative activity (Frost/Zhou 2000). However, as all these studies are based on patent data (see sub-section 3.1.3 for the description of the research design) they "... are unable to point to the underlying mechanisms that enable these knowledge flows" (Almeida/Phene 2004, p. 860).

(2) A second group of studies specifically analyzes the external business network of subsidiaries as one of several determinants of innovation activities of subsidiaries. Some contributions build on the concept of embeddedness. They find that tight relationships to local partners enhance the innovativeness of subsidiaries (Frost/Birkinshaw/Ensign 2002, Davis/Meyer 2004, Helble/Chong 2004, Chen 2007, Johnston/ Paladino 2007, Mu/Gnyawali/Hatfield 2007). Other articles focus on the influence of local research institutions on the innovativeness of subsidiaries (Muralidharan/Phatak 1999). Others reveal that the subsidiary's customers are most important for its innovativeness (Ivarsson/Jonsson 2003). Ambos discovered that R&D subsidiaries that enhance the knowledge stock of their MNC are particularly embedded with private research institutions and universities. On the other hand, R&D units that receive knowledge mainly from their MNC are more embedded with customers and local production units (Ambos 2005). Where the impact of subsidiaries' external network is analyzed it is discovered that their corporate business partners are also determinants

---

[26] Apart from external business partners, other external factors like the institutional environment (e.g. cultural norms, rules, regulations and social knowledge) have an impact on the behavior of firms (Descotes/Walliser/Xiaoling 2007).

[27] Opposed to these findings, Criscuolo stated that subsidiaries of U.S. based MNCs obtain their knowledge from their home country rather than from the host country. However, subsidiaries from European MNCs in the USA gained knowledge mainly from the host country (Criscuolo 2004, p. 179).

of subsidiaries' innovativeness (Håkanson/Nobel 2001, Ivarsson/Jonsson 2003, Tregaskis 2003) and interaction effects between the external and the corporate network can be identified (Hillebrand/Biemans 2004, Boehe 2007).[28]

(3) Some authors employ the concept of the Embedded MNC as a basis for their studies. They are more detailed about the innovations they investigate. One study examines product innovations and analyzes their degree of novelty. It is found that collaboration with external business partners in the product innovation process contributes to the novelty of the innovation while the involvement of corporate business partners does not have such a strong impact. Interaction effects between internal and external collaboration negatively affect the novelty of innovation (Hallin/Kang 2008, pp. 15-16). In another study, not only the novelty of a product innovation but also its importance and radicality is investigated. The involvement of the external and corporate business network in the innovation process is found to have a positive effect on the novelty, importance and radicality of the developed innovation. Thereby, novelty is positively affected by both the external and the corporate network. The importance of the innovation increases with an augmenting involvement of the corporate network while radicality increases with the amount of involvement of the external business network (Ståhl 2004, pp. 165-167).

In a comprehensive qualitative case study, Ståhl (2004) examines the development of a marketing innovation with innovative product and process elements in a foreign subsidiary (Ståhl 2004, p. 53). He detects that the impact of the external business partners on the innovation mainly had a "framing" nature. Customers passed their cost pressure on to the subsidiary and some even left the business relationship. This initiated the problem analysis in the subsidiary and led to innovative activities. Only a few business partners had an active role in the development process. Two customers served as partners to test the innovation. One supplier of the subsidiary provided knowledge and support for the development of the new product element which was a part of the whole marketing innovation. The corporate network of the innovative subsidiary hardly influences the innovation process and is declared to play an "enabling and restricting" role by Ståhl. The subsidiary obtains an informal mandate to continue

---

[28] On the corporate level, Hillebrand and Biemans do not study the collaboration of different subunits of a firm, but they look at the cooperation between different functions.

developing the innovation by HQs but the innovation process is rather passively accepted than actively supported. Other subsidiaries do not play any role in the development process. The main driver of the innovative activities comes from inside the subsidiary, from new managers and engineers who establish new business logic in the subsidiary. Thus, the role of internal drivers (of the subsidiary) of the innovation is named "defining" by Ståhl (2004, pp. 68-72).

In summary, it can be stated that that not many publications on the link between the external business network of subsidiaries and their innovations exist. In addition, many contributions analyze the external business network as only one determinant of innovation activities; the authors also examine other factors. Thus, the focal variable is studied in depth in only few papers. Characteristics of the business relationships between the innovative subsidiaries and their business partners are analyzed somewhat superficially.

While studies in the groups (2) and (3) analyze the actual influence of business partners on innovation activities, papers in group (1) only examine geographical sources of innovations. They find out whether subsidiaries' innovations are based on former innovations which were created in the MNCs' home country, the subsidiaries' local market or in other countries. Thus, the publications of groups (2) and (3) are of major relevance for this thesis. They are depicted in detail in table 3-2. The studies are listed in chronological order.[29] Thereby, the conceptual basis of the studies and definition of innovations are examined and their method and measures are studied. In case the external business network of subsidiaries is only one of several variables, the analysis of the study focuses on this variable and leaves the other variables aside. The conceptual basis is put in parentheses if it seems to be rather weak or does not concern the external business network.

---

[29] In his thesis, Ståhl (2004) conducts different studies. While the study on the radicality is a quantitative one, the study on the marketing innovation is a qualitative case study. Thus, both are listed as different studies in table 3-2.

3.1.2.2 Content of Literature with a Focus on the Specifications of the Analyzed Innovations

In this sub-section, it is presented which kind of innovations is analyzed in the relevant contributions. This is done for the three groups that were described in sub-section 3.1.2.1 on the basis of the criteria that were introduced in chapter 2. The results are summarized in table 3-2. It has to be stated that only one of the studies explicitly defines the object of innovations (Mu/Gnyawali/Hatfield 2007). Thus, this criterion is printed in bold letters in the table. For all other studies, the information on the criteria was searched in the description of the empirical study.

As stated in sub-section 3.1.2.1, studies of group (1) investigate geographical sources of subsidiaries' innovations. Most studies use patent data to find out whether subsidiaries' innovations were based on existing innovations that were created in the subsidiaries' host countries, in the home countries of their MNCs, by HQs of their MNC, or in any other country (Almeida 1996, Frost/Zhou 2000, Frost 2001, Almeida/ Phene 2004, Cantwell/Dunning/Janne 2004, Criscuolo/Narula/Verspagen 2005, Phene/Almeida 2008, for more details on the research design of the contributions see sub-section 3.1.3). Patents are approved "... to the individual or individuals who invent a new product, system, or production process" by patent offices (Zander 1994, p. 12). However, only those inventions can be patented which provide a novel technology that is " ... neither trivial nor obvious to an informed practitioner in the relevant technical field" (Frost 2001, pp. 108-109), i.e. radical innovations in the technological dimension. Thus, in line with the dimensions that were presented in chapter 2, papers of group (1) examine product and process innovations that are invented but not necessarily marketed. The innovations are radical from the technological point of view. The only exception in this group of studies is the one by Britton (2004). Britton conducted a survey on product innovations and asked for R&D and design and engineering investments of firms. Thus, both inventions and marketed problem solutions are included in his study. Details on the intensity of product innovations are not provided by the author.

Studies	Object of innovation			Basic understanding of innovation			Intensity of (product) innovation		
	Product	Process	Ad-min.	Invention	Marketed	Innovation Process	Technological dim.	Market dim.	Organizational dim.
Studies of group (1)									
Almeida 1996	+	+		+			+		
Frost/Zhou 2000	+	+		+			+		
Frost 2001	+	+		+			+		
Almeida/Phene 2004	+	+		+			+		
Cantwell/Dunning/Janne 2004	+	+		+			+		
Britton 2004	+			+	+				
Criscuolo/Narula/Verspagen 2005	+	+		+			+		
Phene/Almeida 2008	+	+		+			+		
Studies of group (2)									
Muralidharan/Phatak 1999									
Håkanson/Nobel 2001	+	+		+			+		
Ivarsson/ Jonsson 2003	+	+		+					
Tregaskis 2003	+	+		+			(+)		
Davis/Meyer 2004	+			+					
Helble/Chong 2004									
Hillebrand/ Biemans 2004	+			+					
Ambos 2005									
Boehe 2007	+			+					
Chen 2007	+	+							
Johnston/ Paladino 2007	+	+							
Mu/Gnyawali/Hatfield 2007	+	+	+	+					
Studies of group (3)									
Ståhl 2004	+				+		+	(+)	
Hallin/Kang 2008	+						+		

Table 3-2: Overview of specifications of innovations analyzed in existing studies

Contributions of part (2) are more heterogeneous. Most of them investigate marketed problem solutions (Ivarsson/Jonsson 2003, Tregaskis 2003, Davis/Meyer 2004, Hillebrand/Biemans 2004, Boehe 2007). Håkanson and Nobel (2001) and Mu, Gnyawali and Hatfield (2007) examine inventions, whether they are marketed is not specified in the papers. Many studies include both product and process innovations in their analysis (Håkansson/Nobel 2001, Ivarsson/Jonsson 2003, Tregaskis 2003, Chen 2007, Johnston/Paladino 2007). Only the studies of Davis and Meyer (2004), Hillebrand and Biemans (2004), and Boehe (2007) focus on product innovations. The publication of Mu, Gnyawali and Hatfield (2007) encompasses product, process, and administrative innovations. Only one contribution (Tregaskis 2003) addresses the intensity of the analyzed innovations. Subsidiaries are described to do R&D which leads to both radical and incremental innovation. It is not specified how radicality of innovations is defined. Thus, it can only be assumed that radicality is determined in the technological dimension because the R&D activities of subsidiaries are investigated. The papers of Muralidharan/Phatak (1999), Helble/Chong (2004), and Ambos (2005) cannot be classified with this criterion. They measure innovations with R&D expenditure and do not limit the measure to a particular object or understanding of innovations, neither do they specify the intensity of innovations.

Studies in group (3) examine marketed product innovations. They specify the intensity of innovations. Ståhl (2004) defines radicality of innovations with two criteria: technological novelty and corporate importance of the innovation. While technological novelty clearly is in line with the technological dimension of Hauschildt and Schlaak (2001, see sub-section 2.1.3), corporate importance cannot be easily classified. Since it is a way to determine the importance of the innovations, it cannot be concluded that they affected the organizational structure of the subsidiary. It could be assumed that importance means the amount of sales that is generated by the innovation. In this case, importance would be in line with the market dimension of Hauschildt and Schlaak (2001).

It can be summarized that only one contribution that is examined defines the object of innovation. In the other papers, this information is drawn from the description of the empirical study. Regarding the basic understanding of innovations, none of the authors analyze the product innovation process. Instead, all of them investigate innovations as inventions or as marketed problem solutions. Only one of the studies recommends that business relationships should be analyzed according to the single stages of the product innovation process (Hallin/Kang 2008, pp. 18-19). Finally, most contributions do not specify the intensity of innovations.

Author(s) Year	Aim of Study	Conceptual basis & definition of innovation	Research design	Measures of external embeddedness & innovation	Results
Muralidharan/ Phatak 1999	Examines which factors (market size, scientific resources, cultural distance of host country to home country, technology transfer requirement policy, intellectual property protection) influence foreign subsidiaries' investment in R&D	Eclectic theory (OLI paradigm) by Dunning (1988) R&D expenditure as an indicator of innovative activities	Secondary country level data on the R&D expenditures of MNCs from the USA in 34 countries Statistical analysis: multiple regression analysis	Local scientific resources: country's expenditure on science and technology as percent of its Gross Domestic Product (GDP) R&D investment as measure for innovativeness: aggregate R&D expenditures by all subsidiaries of U.S. MNCs in one country	Local scientific resources have an impact on the level of R&D investments in the host country
Håkanson/ Nobel 2001	Studies (1) how the external embeddedness of R&D units influences their innovativeness and (2) how it impacts the likelihood of these subsidiaries to transfer technology to their MNC (see table 3-5)	Concepts of external embeddedness No definition of innovativeness given; patents as measure: product and process innovations studied	Mail survey with CEOs of 110 R&D subsidiaries of 17 Swedish MNCs Statistical analysis: OLS regression analysis	External embeddedness: frequency of face-to-face contact and other types of contact and the number of ongoing cooperation with local universities, local customers and local suppliers Innovativeness: number of US patents subsidiary has invented	External embeddedness enhances innovations in subsidiaries
Frost/ Birkinshaw/ Ensign 2002	Studies the impact of various external (embeddedness of local "diamond", links to sources of competence) and internal factors (links to sources of competence, autonomy) on the development of centers of excellence (COE) and their performance (product innovations as one indicator)	(Centers of excellence research) No definition of innovation given, in empirical study: product innovation studied	Mail survey with CEOs of 99 Canadian subsidiaries Statistical analysis: logistic regression analysis	Impact of the following organizations on the development of the subsidiaries' competences: customers, suppliers, competitors, research institutions Performance: profitability & competitiveness (business volume of COE, profitability, competitiveness), innovation (new product introduction), learning & knowledge transfer (other units' competence development in research, development & manufacturing)	External business partners enhance the development of subsidiaries into centers of excellence Centers of excellence create more product innovations

Author(s) Year	Aim of Study	Conceptual basis & definition of innovation	Research design	Measures of external embeddedness & innovation	Results
Ivarsson/ Jonsson 2003	Examines how foreign subsidiaries gain technological competence in collaborating with local business partners in order to create product and process innovations and pass their capabilities on to other units of the firm (see table 3-5)	(As starting point of the study: eclectic theory (OLI paradigm) by Dunning (1988)) No definition of innovation given, product and process innovations studied	Mail survey with 287 Swedish subsidiaries Statistical analysis: ANOVA	Joint development of important technological competence together with the following organizations: customers, suppliers, business service firms and R&D institutions Innovations: development of new technology, improvement of existing technology, local adaptation of MNC's technology	Collaborations with external business partners enhance the creation of product and process innovations Most important partners are customers and suppliers
Tregaskis 2003	Explores which kind of learning network increases innovations in subsidiaries the most and how these networks provide knowledge which is used in the internal network of the MNC to serve as a source of power	(For knowledge as a source of power: concepts of resource dependence and legitimacy) No definition of innovation given, cases: product and process innovations	Multiple case study approach with three foreign-owned subsidiaries in the UK 28 interviews with HR directors, R&D directors, HR managers, R&D line managers and R&D employees	--	Local intra- and interorganizational networks increase the knowledge of subsidiaries on which their innovations are based
Davis/ Meyer 2004	Examines the impact of location advantages (local competition, supply conditions, scientific institutions, government support) for subsidiaries' investment in R&D	(Research on internationalization of R&D and on national systems of innovation) No definition of innovation given, R&D investments measured, discussed on the basis of product innovations	Mail survey with CEOs, financial managers, marketing managers and controllers of subsidiaries 2,109 subsidiaries in the UK, Germany, Austria, Denmark, Sweden, Norway and Finland Statistical analysis: Logit and OLS regression analysis	Evaluation of business environment regarding the availability of professionals & of supply material, quality of suppliers, level of demanding customers & of competition, government support, favorable legal environment and existence of scientific institutions R&D: existence of research and development in subsidiary & investment in both	Competition has a negative impact on the incidence of subsidiaries' R&D Supply conditions have a negative influence on the level of subsidiaries' R&D Scientific institutions have a highly positive effect on both the incidence and the level of subsidiaries' R&D Government support enhances the incidence but not the level of subsidiaries' R&D

Author(s) Year	Aim of Study	Conceptual basis & definition of innovation	Research design	Measures of external embeddedness & innovation	Results
Helble/ Chong 2004	Explores the importance of (1) external R&D networks and (2) internal R&D networks for R&D units	(Typology developed by the authors of the study which differentiates the embeddedness of external and of internal network linkages of R&D units) No definition of innovativeness given, not specified in empirical study	Multi-method research design (1) Explorative in-depth interviews which led to the development of a questionnaire (2) With this questionnaire R&D units are ought to be classified according to the typology. 71 interviews in 53 R&D units in Singapore which are owned by MNCs from Japan, America, Europe and other regions, respondents: senior R&D managers, R&D directors and managing directors (3) Further in-depth interviews to ask for management issues of the R&D units	In questionnaire: external network linkage: human resources flow (impact of external business partners on acquisition, development & training of critical human resources), innovation flow (importance of external business partners for subsidiaries' innovations), information flow (degree of freedom & importance of information transfer between subsidiaries and external partners)	Majority of R&D units have extensive external linkages but few internal linkages
Hillebrand/ Biemans 2004	Studies how corporate collaboration between different functions and external collaboration to business partners interact in product innovation projects	-- Product innovations studied but no definition provided	(1) Twelve exploratory interviews with R&D managers in eight firms (2) Six in-depth cases of product innovation projects (multi-method approach: 42 interviews, 61 questionnaires, secondary sources)	--	Four interaction patterns between external and internal collaboration in product innovation projects detected (but no evaluation of which way of collaborating is preferable): Corporate cooperation to coordinate external cooperation Corporation established norms/culture that favors external cooperation External cooperation stimulated corporate cooperation Learning from outside requires corporate cooperation

Author(s) Year	Aim of Study	Conceptual basis & definition of innovation	Research design	Measures of external embeddedness & innovation	Results
Ståhl 2004, pp. 160-169	Studies the effect of problem-solving in external and corporate collaborations on the technological novelty and corporate importance of product innovations (novelty and importance are taken as dimensions of radicality)	(Concept of the Embedded MNC, tradition of IMP Group) Product innovations studied but no definition provided	44 product innovation projects Interviews at 14 Swedish MNCs Innovations at subsidiaries in 12 European countries Statistical analysis: regression analysis	Problem-solving in (corporate or external) business relationships (degree of cooperative contact concerning technological issues, degree of adaptations) Tacitness of innovations: Innovation technology easily codifiable, Innovation technology more tacit than explicit Complexity of innovations: Innovation comprises high number of interacting subsystems/components, innovation can satisfy large number of functions Specificity of innovations: Innovation highly tailor-made for a particular user, innovation needs modification for each user	Collaboration with corporate or external business partners enhances subsidiaries' innovativeness Novelty of innovations affected by both external and corporate business relationships Importance of innovations driven by corporate business relationships Radicality of innovations significantly affected by external business relationships, only tentatively by corporate ones
Ståhl 2004, pp. 74-82	Aims at providing a thick description of capability development at the innovative subsidiary during product innovation project	(Concept of the Embedded MNC, tradition of IMP Group) Marketing innovation studied but no definition provided	In-depth case study with 18 at seven subsidiaries One MNC Interviews, demonstrations and observation	--	Due to problems with external business partners (customers), subsidiary initiated marketing innovation Few external business partners provided knowledge during innovation process Corporate business network (HQs) of the innovative subsidiary passively accepted innovation process Main driver of the innovative activities came from inside the subsidiary, from new managers and engineers who established new business logic in the subsidiary

Author(s) Year	Aim of Study	Conceptual basis & definition of innovation	Research design	Measures of external embeddedness & innovation	Results
Ambos 2005	Examines (1) the level and pace of R&D internationalization of German MNCs, (2) the motivations and mandates of overseas R&D units and (3) the embeddedness of ties to R&D units' external and internal network subject to the subsidiaries' mandate (capability augmenting vs. capability exploiting)	For (3) the embeddedness of ties to external and internal business partners: concept of embeddedness No definition of innovativeness given	Mail survey with senior R&D managers at HQs 134 R&D units of 49 German MNCs Statistical analysis: independent t-test	Type and intensity of ties to seven external business partners (i.e. competitors, suppliers, customers, other firms, private research institutions, universities, local authorities) and four internal co-operation partners (HQs, other internal R&D units, local production, other production) External and internal network density	Capability augmenting R&D units have stronger ties to private research institutions and universities compared to capability exploiting units Capability exploiting R&D units are closer linked to customers and local production units Both capability augmenting and capability exploiting units have the strongest linkages to HQs
Boehe 2007	Explains how subsidiaries' linkages to (1) internal business partners and (2) external business partners interact in influencing product innovation in subsidiaries	(For (2) linkages to external business partners: concepts of loosely and tightly coupled networks) Product innovations not defined	Online survey with CEOs 146 Brazilian subsidiaries of foreign MNCs Statistical analysis: regression and cluster analysis	Local cooperative linkages (influence of subsidiaries' relationships to customers, suppliers, research institutions & universities on the subsidiaries' product innovations and influence of these relationships on technological knowledge of subsidiaries) Local outsourcing linkages (subcontracting of research, product design, definition of product concepts, prototyping and prototype testing to local firms)	Different patterns of interaction effects exist
Chen 2007	Explores the upgrading process of innovating units in China	Global production networks approach Product and process innovations examined but no definition provided	Case studies at Motorola and Microsoft in Beijing and Shanghai Semi-structured interviews with 25 managers and experts of R&D and sales sites at Motorola and 20 managers and experts of R&D and sales sites at Microsoft	--	Units with strong knowledge transfer from HQs benefit from the access to local production and sales networks Fast knowledge accumulation in R&D site through strong relationships to universities

Author(s)/Year	Aim of Study	Conceptual basis & definition of innovation	Research design	Measures of external embeddedness & innovation	Results
Johnston/ Paladino 2007	Studies the relationship between (1) local resources (especially knowledge), (2) knowledge management techniques and (3) subsidiaries' involvement in MNCs' innovation network	For (1) local knowledge: knowledge-based view (based on Penrose (1959)) No definition of innovation provided but product and process innovations studied	Mail survey with CEOs of subsidiaries 313 Australian subsidiaries of foreign MNCs Statistical analysis: ANCOVA	Active involvement (e.g. as sources of knowledge, information, new recruits, lobbying etc.) with the following organizations: Local industry associations, local chamber of commerce, local schools & universities and local charitable organizations Involvement in innovation network: subsidiaries' ability to develop product or process innovation, degree of using and sharing innovations	Involvement with local organizations enhances the subsidiaries' involvement in the innovation network of the MNC
Mu/ Gnyawali/ Hatfield 2007	Investigates the influence of (1) subsidiaries' local embeddedness, (2) subsidiaries' top management team heterogeneity and (3) MNCs' corporate entrepreneurial culture on foreign subsidiaries' innovations	For (1) subsidiaries' local embeddedness: concept of embeddedness	Mail survey with general managers of subsidiaries 234 subsidiaries in the USA of MNCs from Japan, Germany, UK, France, Switzerland, Canada, the Netherlands, Sweden, Denmark and other countries Statistical analysis: exploratory factor analysis & structural equation modeling for confirmatory factor analysis	Licensing agreement, marketing agreement or technical assistance agreement with each of the following local institutions: customers, suppliers, universities and others	Greater local embeddedness of subsidiaries leads to higher likelihood of innovations by subsidiaries
Hallin/ Kang 2008	Studies how subsidiaries' external and corporate business relationships affect novelty of its product innovations	(Concept of the Embedded MNC, tradition of IMP Group) Product innovations studied but no definition provided	Face-to-face interviews with standardized questionnaire 64 product innovations of 54 subsidiaries of 21 MNCs Subsidiaries in 14 countries Respondents: project managers, R&D managers, engineers that were involved in product innovation project	Respondents asked for six most important business partners in product innovation project collaboration: degree of cooperative contact regarding technological issues, participation of business partner in product innovation process, level of competence provided by business partner, extent to which innovation was developed in facilities of business partner, degree of mutual adaptation for developing product innovation	Novelty of product innovation is significantly positively influenced by external business partners Novelty of product innovation is tentatively positively affected by corporate business partners Effect of both corporate and external business partners on novelty of product innovation is negative

Table 3-3: Studies of the influence of subsidiaries' external business network on their innovations

3.1.3 Research Design and Method in Literature

Three research designs have been applied in literature: quantitative studies basing on secondary data, quantitative studies based on a survey conducted personally, and qualitative or multi-method design. They are described in the following.

(1) Studies on the geographical sources of subsidiaries' knowledge for innovations (group (1) in sub-section 3.1.1) use a quantitative empirical research design. It is based on secondary data (Almeida 1996, Frost/Zhou 2000, Frost 2001, Almeida/ Phene 2004, Cantwell/Dunning/Janne 2004, Phene/Almeida 2008).[30] They work with large samples of patent data[31] which are drawn from the United States Patent and Trademark Office (USPTO; but see the study of Criscuolo/Narula/Verspagen 2005 which uses the EPO database).[32] The USPTO database has a key advantage over other patent databases which makes it very useful for research on innovation transfer. All patent databases list the basic information of patent class, assignee and inventor among others. In addition, the USPTO database provides the information of patents on which the focal patent is based. In combination with the information where the inventor lives and where the assignee (usually a company) is based it can be revealed if the innovation of the subsidiary is based on host country or home country innovations or on innovations of the MNC (e.g. Frost 2001, p. 109). Apart from patent data, another type of secondary data is employed in the study of Muralidharan and Phatak (1999). They use country level data and analyze the expenditure of U.S. based MNCs in 34 countries subject to several influences.

---

[30] One exception is the article by Britton (2004) which uses their own mail survey based on a questionnaire. The questionnaire was sent to Canadian subsidiaries.

[31] "Patents are grants issued by a national government conferring the right to exclude others from making, using, or selling an invention within the country. One of their main functions is to make it possible for inventors to appropriate the economic benefits from their inventive contributions. Patents are granted to the individual or individuals who invent a new product, system, or production process. However, ... the right to use and sell the patents has become increasingly associated with industrial firms" (Zander 1994, p. 12). An inventor has to file the patent in every country in which he wants to protect the invention. As an exception, the EPO registers patents for the region of the European Union. These patents are transformed into patents according to the national patent right of each member of the EU afterwards (OECD 1994, pp. 21-25).

[32] Both the USPTO and the „Deutsches Marken- und Patentamt" (DPMA) are patent offices of one country, the USA and Germany, respectively. The EPO registers patents for the region of the European Union (EU). These patents are transformed into patents according to the national patent right of each member of the EU afterwards (OECD 1994, pp. 21-25).

(2) The majority of the authors of explanatory studies chose a quantitative empirical research design that includes their own survey via a questionnaire (Håkanson/Nobel 2001, Frost/Birkinshaw/Ensign 2002, Ivarsson/Jonsson 2003, Davis/Meyer 2004, Ståhl 2004, pp. 160-169, Ambos 2005, Boehe 2007, Johnston/Paladino 2007, Mu/ Gnyawali/Hatfield 2007, Hallin/Kang 2008). Subsidiaries, for instance from Australia, Brazil, Canada, the USA, the UK, Germany, Austria, Denmark, Sweden, Norway and Finland, were analyzed. The number of subsidiaries taking part in the surveys ranged from about 44 to 2,109. MNCs were from Sweden, Denmark, Germany, France, Switzerland, the Netherlands, Canada, Japan and other countries.

(3) Five contributions of the literature analyzed for the first part of this thesis have a qualitative or a multi-method research design. Four studies use a case study approach. One of them examines three subsidiaries in the UK. HR managers, R&D managers and R&D employees of the MNCs and the focal subsidiaries were interviewed (Tregaskis 2003) during the study. Managers and experts of R&D and sales subsidiaries were also interviewed. Biemans and Hillebrand first conducted 12 exploratory interviews with R&D managers in eight firms. Then, they did six in-depth case studies on product innovation projects. Thereby, 42 experts were interviewed, questionnaires were used and secondary data were employed (Hillebrand/Biemans 2004). Ståhl conducted an in-depth case study with 18 employees of an MNC at seven subsidiaries of the firm. Apart from the interviews, demonstrations and observation were applied (Ståhl 2004, p. 45). Another author did case studies at Motorola and Microsoft in Beijing and Singapore (Chen 2007). The contribution of Helble and Chong (2004) used a multi-method research design and investigated 53 foreign subsidiaries in Singapore and conducted interviews with the subsidiaries' R&D managers, R&D managers of the MNCs and experts from industrial organizations and the local government (Helble/Chong 2004).

Thus, qualitative research has hardly been applied in existing studies on research question 1. German subsidiaries were only analyzed in the contribution of Davis and Meyer (2004). Interviews at German firms were not conducted.

3.2 Intra-organizational Focus: Transfer of Subsidiaries' Innovations in the MNC

3.2.1 Method of the Literature Review

As in section 3.1.1 the identification of relevant literature on the diffusion of subsidiaries' innovations in the MNC began with a search in EBSCO. This time, terms of the groups (1) "innovation" or "R&D", (2) "diffusion", "transfer" or "spillover" and (3) "subsidiary", "affiliate", "MNC", "business partner", or "business relationship"[33] were combined in every possible way using the search options: title, keywords and abstract. Again, to limit the number of results, every search used one word of each group so that always three words were combined, e.g. "innovation" and "embeddedness" and "subsidiary" or "innovation" and "network" and "subsidiary". Furthermore, the search focused on academic journals, monographs and book chapters. Trade publications, newspapers, magazines, SWOT analyses, country reports, industry profiles, market research reports and product reviews that are also offered in the database were excluded.

During this process, literature was found which is not considered to be useful for this study (e.g. Martin/Beaumont 2001, Swamy 2003). As in section 3.1, literature on the international dispersion and accumulation of R&D was found which is either descriptive (e.g. Zander 1998, Papanastassiou 1999, Pearce/Papanastassiou 1999, Pearce 1999) or examines the causes (e.g. Jones/Teegen 2000, Siler/Chengqi/Xiaming 2003, Branstetter/Fisman/Foley 2006, Sanna-Randaccio/Veugelers 2007) or the effects (e.g. Kotabe/Swan 1994, Feinberg/Majumdar 2001, Jeong 2003) of the international dispersion of R&D. Again, these studies were not analyzed in depth.

Additional literature was recommended by members of the doctoral tutorial of the 34th EIBA Annual Conference held in Tallinn/Estonia in December 2008. Like in the inter-organizational part of the literature review, two of the dissertations (Ståhl 2004, Hallin 2008a) from the University of Uppsala were included in the review.

---

[33] For research question 2, the terms "business partner" and "business relationship" were searched for in the same group as "subsidiary", "affiliate", "MNC". This was done because – due to the wording and sense of the research question – the two terms should be seeked in combination with the terms of groups (1) and (2). Contributions which do not examine MNCs or subsidiaries were excluded afterwards.

Special considerations have to be made about the studies which include the terms "innovations" or "R&D" in the titles, keywords or abstracts but actually examine the diffusion of knowledge and capabilities. There are many studies which examine the transfer of knowledge and capabilities in a variety of contexts. All of them could not be reviewed in this chapter. Innovations are built on knowledge and capabilities. Knowledge and capabilities are an integral part in the innovation process and thus, a precondition of innovations (e.g. Zaltman/Duncan/Holbek 1973, p. 7, Specht/Beckmann 1996, p. 15). However, knowledge is not always applied in innovations. It is also required before entering new markets, for instance (e.g. Erramilli/Rao 1990, Mitra/Golder 2002, Ranft/Marsh 2008). Therefore, in this thesis only those studies are reviewed in which knowledge is examined which leads to the creation of innovations. In table 3-4, literature that was found to be helpful for the present study is listed in chronological order.

Relevant studies		
Ghoshal/Bartlett 1988a	Galbraith 1990	Ensign 1999
Håkansson/Nobel 2001	Zander 2002	Ivarsson/Jonsson 2003
Tregaskis 2003	Criscuolo 2004	Ståhl 2004
Gerstlauer 2005	Harzing/Noorderhaven 2006	Hallin 2008b
Hallin/Holm/Sharma 2008		

Table 3-4: Relevant literature on the diffusion of innovations in MNCs

3.2.2 Content of Literature

3.2.2.1 Content of Literature with a Focus on Transfer of Subsidiaries' Innovations

The content of the studies that were identified as relevant for research question 2 is described briefly in the following. Most studies analyze organizational factors that affect innovation transfer within MNCs; they will be reviewed in part (1) of this subsection. Another group of studies looks at the effect of innovation transfer on the receiving sub-unit of the MNC; this group will be dealt with in part (2). All studies are listed in detail in table 3-5.

(1) Most studies examine determinants of innovation transfer in MNCs. Organizational factors dominate in these studies. Ghoshal and Bartlett (1988a) chose local slack resources, local autonomy, normative integration and intra-/inter-unit communication to study which of these factors have a positive impact on the creation and adoption of innovations in subsidiaries and on the diffusion of innovations in MNCs. Normative integration and communication were found to enhance all three levels of innovative activities whereas the effect of slack resources and local autonomy is mediated by the other two variables. Ståhl specifically examined innovations that are characterized by tacit, complex or specific knowledge and analyzed the effects of HQs' involvement, lateral transfer routines,[34] project groups, and IT systems on the cost, speed, and implementation success of innovation transfer. Costs were decreased by lateral transfer routines for tacit, complex and specific innovations. They were increased by the involvement of project groups in all three cases. Speed of innovation transfer was decreased by HQs' involvement in the cases of complex and specific innovations. None of the instruments increased the speed of innovation transfer. Level of implementation was decreased by HQs' involvement and IT systems for all innovation types. In the case of tacit innovations, project groups increased the level of implementation. Complex innovations were implemented better when lateral transfer routines and project groups were involved. Project groups also supported the implementation of specific innovations (Ståhl 2004, pp. 170-183; see also Ciabuschi/Kang/Ståhl 2004, pp. 16-17).

In an in-depth case study, Ståhl examines the efforts that were made to transfer a marketing innovation from the innovative subsidiary to other units of the MNC. Workshops were held between all subsidiary managers of the MNC in which subsidiaries could also present their innovations. The innovation was also communicated in the company newspaper and informally to particular subsidiary managers. However, only part of the innovation was transferred to one subsidiary.[35] Subsidiary managers found it difficult to explain the benefits of the innovation. Problems for innovation transfer were differences in local markets, resistance to receive knowledge from else-

---

[34] Lateral transfer routines are described as informal relationships between experts at both the sending and the receiving sub-unit. Both partners collaborated in previous transfer projects (Ståhl 2004, p. 172).
[35] The marketing innovation consisted of a machine and software.

where (not-invented-here attitude, see sub-sections 4.3.3.2 and 4.5.2.4) and a lack of support and commitment from HQs (Ståhl 2004, pp. 74-80).

Other contributions study the strategic orientation of the MNC (Zander 2002), the integration of subsidiaries (Håkansson/Nobel 2001, Ivarsson/Jonsson 2003) and instruments of human resource management such as the exchange of researchers between units (Criscuolo 2004, pp. 187-188). Above that, intra-organizational networks were found to be used to transfer knowledge and innovations (Tregaskis 2003). In his doctoral thesis, Gerstlauer (2005) discusses the potential of information and communication technologies to increase the internationality of R&D. Also on a conceptual level, Ensign (1999) draws on evolutionary, resource-based and knowledge-based perspectives to develop a comprehensive framework of knowledge transfer between the R&D units of an MNC.

Apart from organizational determinants, the geographical distance between the innovative subsidiary and HQs are found to influence the diffusion of the innovation (Harzing/Noorderhaven 2006).

(2) Several studies analyze the effects of innovation transfer on the receiving sub-units of MNCs. Hallin analyzed the usefulness of innovation transfer in MNCs for the operations of the receiving sub-unit. Thereby, novelty, specificity, and tacitness of innovations, technical and business similarity, and previous collaborations between the units and their mutual commitment to the innovation transfer were studied as influential factors. It was found that novel innovations are useful while specific innovations are not useful for the receiving unit. Mutual commitment of both business partners to the transfer project also enhanced the usefulness of the received innovation (Hallin 2008b). In another study, the influence of subsidiaries' external and corporate embeddedness and the uniqueness of the transferred innovation were studied as influential factors on the subsidiaries' business performance when they were exploiting a received innovation. It was observed that not only external embeddedness but also corporate embeddedness supported the subsidiaries' business performance when they were exploiting the innovations they received from another sub-unit of the MNC. The exploitation of unique innovations was negatively correlated with subsidi-

aries' business performance when they were highly embedded in external business relationships (Hallin/Holm/Sharma 2008).

Galbraith analyzed the impacts of the transfer of 32 process innovations (manufacturing technologies) on the receiving sub-units. He found that they suffered an average initial productivity loss of 34%. It ranged between 4% and 150%. Sub-units needed between one and 13 months to recover and reach their former productivity level. However, six sub-units never reached their prior productivity measures and four more transfers were declared to have failed. It was found that initial productivity loss after innovation transfer was increased by complexity of the innovation, training at the receiving unit and the fact that the innovation was still in an early stage of development. It was decreased by the experience of the receiving unit with innovation transfers and its commitment to the transfer. Recovery from innovation transfer was faster the less complex and young the innovation was, the lower the distance between both units was, and the more committed the receiving unit was. When the innovation was co-produced at the receiving unit, it needed less time to recover. When a team of engineers from the sending unit came to the receiving unit, time to recover was also lower. Financial success of the innovation transfer was increased by complexity of the innovation and training and documentation on it. Success was decreased by factors like the distance between sending and receiving unit, previous experience with innovation transfers and team allocation (Galbraith 1990).

To summarize, it is revealed in the literature review on innovation transfer in MNCs that there are even less contributions regarding research question 2 than concerning research question 1. Few articles analyze the impact of subsidiaries' corporate network or structure on the diffusion of innovations. Again, details of the transfer of the innovation within the MNC and of the business relationships between the innovative subsidiaries and the sub-units which receive the innovation are not analyzed.

Like in part one of this literature review (section 3.1), those studies which are considered particularly relevant are presented in detail (table 3-5). The studies are listed in chronological order. As the thesis of Ståhl comprises two studies on the topic, he is listed twice. The publications of Ensign (1999) and Gerstlauer (2005) are not presented in the table because they are conceptual. Studies are analyzed concerning their conceptual basis and definition of innovations examined and the method and the measures used. The conceptual basis is put in parentheses if it seems to be rather weak or does not concern the external business network.

Author(s)/Year	Aim of Study	Conceptual basis & definition of innovation	Research design	Measures of external embeddedness & innovation	Results
Ghoshal/Bartlett 1988b	Explores which processes lead to the creation, adoption and diffusion of innovations in MNCs, and statistically tests the impact of four processes (slack resources, subsidiaries' autonomy, normative integration and intra- & inter-unit communication) on the creation, adoption and diffusion of innovations in subsidiaries	--; Product, process or administrative innovations distinguished	Multi-method research design (1) Interviews with 184 HQs and subsidiary managers in nine MNCs about 38 cases of innovations in order to identify processes through which innovations are made in MNCs (2) Mail survey (multi-respondent survey) with 141 managers from three of the nine MNCs of the first phase (3) Mail survey (single-respondent survey) with 66 HQs from North America and Europe revealing data about 618 subsidiaries	In phase (2) and (3): intra- & inter-unit communication (frequency of communication within unit and with managers from HQs or other subsidiaries), normative integration (amount of time subsidiary manager has worked in HQs, existence of a mentor at HQs, number of subsidiary managers' visits at HQs), local autonomy (relative influence of subsidiary on decisions of introduction of new product, modification of existing product, modification of production process, restructuring of subsidiary's organization, filling of important positions at subsidiary, career development plans), level of slack resources (consequence of 10% reduction in the operating budget of subsidiaries' departments)	Positive influence of normative integration and intra- & inter-unit communication on creation, adoption and diffusion of innovations in the MNC (found in all three phases of the investigation) Slack resources at subsidiaries facilitate the creation and diffusion of innovations, but have no definite impact on the adoption The influence of local autonomy is mediated by normative integration: in case of high integration the influence of local autonomy on creation, adoption and diffusion of innovations is high whereas it is low in case of low integration

Author(s) Year	Aim of Study	Conceptual basis & definition of innovation	Research design	Measures of external embeddedness & innovation	Results
Galbraith 1990	Examines which factors (complexity of innovation, stage of development, distance between units, co-production, commitment of receiving unit, experience of receiving unit with transfer, team allocation to receiving unit, training) influence loss of productivity, time of recovery and financial success of process innovation transfer (manufacturing techniques) at the receiving unit	-- No definition of innovation provided, but process innovations were studied	Mail survey at eight US-based MNCs 32 cases of innovation transfer Statistical analysis: Regression analysis	Dependent variables: productivity loss, time to recover, financial success of innovation transfer Independent variables: complexity of innovation, stage of development, distance between units, co-production, commitment of receiving unit, experience of receiving unit with transfer, team allocation to receiving unit, training	Productivity loss: increased by complexity of the innovation, training at the receiving unit and early stage of the development, decreased by experience of the receiving unit, commitment Time of recovery: the faster the less complex and young the innovation, the lower distance between both units, the more committed the receiving unit, when innovation was co-produced at the receiving unit, when a team of engineers came to the receiving unit Financial success: increased by complexity, training and documentation, decreased by the distance between sending and receiving unit, previous experience with innovation transfers and team allocation

Author(s) Year	Aim of Study	Conceptual basis & definition of innovation	Research design	Measures of external embeddedness & innovation	Results
Håkanson/ Nobel 2001	Studies how the external and internal embeddedness of R&D units influence the propensity of subsidiaries to transfer technology to their MNC	Concepts of external embeddedness and integration (i.e. internal embeddedness) No definition of innovativeness given, patents as measure: product and process innovations studied	Mail survey with CEOs of 110 R&D subsidiaries 17 Swedish MNCs Statistical analysis: OLS regression analysis	External embeddedness: frequency of face-to-face contact and other types of contact and the number of ongoing cooperation with local universities, local customers and local suppliers Internal embeddedness/integration: number of Swedish nationals employed by R&D unit, number of personnel taking part in company rotation or training program, number of visits to or from other R&D units Innovativeness: number of US patents subsidiary has invented Technology transfer: number of occasions the subsidiary has actively transferred locally developed technology know-how to other units in Sweden	External embeddedness enhances innovations in subsidiaries Internal embeddedness enhances the transfer of technology to other units of the MNC
Zander 2002	Examines the relationship between process and structure in the evolving international innovation network	-- No definition of innovativeness given, patents as measure: product and process innovations studied	Case study research design Single longitudinal case study at ASEA and Brown Boveri and ABB (after merger in 1987) Analysis of patent data from 1890-1990	Internationalization of technological capabilities (share of US patents of ASEA outside Sweden) Technological diversity (share of US patents in particular technologies) International duplication of technological capabilities (technologies that are found in several locations)	Internationalization of technological capabilities of ASEA started in the 1920s but increased only slightly until the merger Level of technological diversity increased especially through acquisitions Duplication increased particularly after the merger After merger structure of ABB is improved dramatically but as both firms ASEA and Brown Boveri had a strong ethnocentric orientation there is little internationalization and integration of R&D

Author(s) Year	Aim of Study	Conceptual basis & definition of innovation	Research design	Measures of external embeddedness & innovation	Results
Ivarsson/ Jonsson 2003	Examines how foreign subsidiaries gain technological competence in collaborating with local business partners in order to create product and process innovations (see table 3-2) and pass their capabilities on to other units of the firm	(As a starting point of the study: eclectic theory (OLI paradigm) by Dunning (1988)) No definition of innovation given, product and process innovations studied	Mail survey with 287 Swedish subsidiaries Statistical analysis: ANOVA	Transfer of technological competence of subsidiaries which was developed by them in collaboration with their external business partners to other units of the MNC	Over two thirds of the subsidiaries pass their competencies for product and process innovations on to other units of the MNC Either through intra-firm exports or through face-to-face contacts
Tregaskis 2003	Explores which kind of learning network enhances innovations in subsidiaries the most and how these networks provide knowledge which is used in the internal network of the MNC to serve as a source of power	(For knowledge as a source of power: concepts of resource dependence and legitimacy) No definition of innovation given, cases: product and process innovations	Multiple case study approach with three foreign-owned subsidiaries in the UK 28 interviews with HR directors, R&D directors, HR managers, R&D line managers and R&D employees	--	International intra-organizational networks were used to gain resources which increase the subsidiary's credibility and to diffuse the subsidiary's knowledge and innovations in order to augment the dependence of other units on the subsidiary and thus serve as a base for subsidiary's power
Criscuolo 2004	Studies the extent to which foreign subsidiaries rely on host country knowledge and examines how researchers' mobility between units of the MNC can enhance the diffusion of innovations in MNCs	Innovations not defined but product innovations studied in cases	Multiple case study approach with six European MNCs 24 semi-structured interviews with R&D managers and scientists	--	1% of R&D staff is sent to another unit Researchers' mobility enhances the transfer of knowledge or innovations by increasing the transfer from HQs to subsidiaries and by reducing barriers between researchers of different R&D units

Author(s) Year	Aim of Study	Conceptual basis & definition of innovation	Research design	Measures of external embeddedness & innovation	Results
Ståhl 2004, pp. 74-80	Investigates efforts that were made to transfer a marketing innovation from the innovative subsidiary to other units of the MNC	(Concept of the Embedded MNC, tradition of IMP Group) Marketing innovation is defined as following: "…. it is not concerned primarily with new or adapted products in the company's traditional range, but rather with how these are sold – particularly pertaining to technical support, logistics and invoicing" (Ståhl 2004, p. 53).	In-depth case study with 18 at seven subsidiaries One MNC Interviews, demonstrations and observation	--	Efforts: Workshops between all subsidiary managers of the MNC –> innovative subsidiary presented the innovations Communication of marketing innovation in company newspaper Informal communication of innovation to particular subsidiary managers Subsidiary manager found it difficult to explain the benefits of the innovation Result: Only one subsidiary received only part of the innovation Problems for innovation transfer resulted from differences in local markets, not-invented-here attitude and lacking support and commitment from HQs

Author(s) Year	Aim of Study	Conceptual basis & definition of innovation	Research design	Measures of external embeddedness & innovation	Results
Ståhl 2004, pp. 170-183	Analyzes the effect of HQs' involvement, lateral transfer routines, project groups, and IT systems on the cost, speed, and implementation success of transfer of tacit, complex or specific innovations	(Concept of the Embedded MNC, tradition of IMP Group) No definition of innovations provided, no innovations specified, but in empirical study product innovations indicated	Interview survey about 91 innovation transfer projects of 37 innovations Respondents: Top management of subsidiaries, R&D management Statistical analysis: Multiattributable measurement model	Tacitness of innovations: Innovation technology easily codifiable, innovation technology more tacit than explicit Complexity of innovations: Innovation comprises high number of interacting sub-systems/components, innovation can satisfy large number of functions Specificity of innovations: Innovation highly tailor-made for a particular user, innovation needs modification for each user Costs: Actual costs of transfer vs. expected costs Speed: Actual first day of starting point of transfer vs. expected, actual first day of use at receiving unit vs. expected Implementation: Level of completed innovation transfer, easiness and speed of adoption	Costs of innovation transfer: Decreased by lateral transfer routines for tacit, complex and specific innovations Increased by the involvement of project groups in all three cases Speed of innovation transfer: Decreased by HQs' involvement in the cases of complex and specific innovations Level of implementation: Decreased by HQs' involvement and IT systems for all innovation types Decreased by project groups for tacit innovations Increased by lateral transfer routines and project groups for complex innovations and by project groups for specific innovations

Author(s) Year	Aim of Study	Conceptual basis & definition of innovation	Research design	Measures of external embeddedness & innovation	Results
Harzing/ Noorderhaven 2006	Examines the impact of geographical distance between HQs and subsidiaries on the role of subsidiaries in the MNCs' innovation network	Subsidiary typology of Gupta and Govindarajan (1991) on knowledge flows in the MNC. No definition of innovations provided	Mail survey with 169 subsidiaries. 59 subsidiaries from Australia and New Zealand and 110 from North America and Europe MNCs from the USA, Japan, the UK, Germany, France and the Netherlands. Statistical analysis: explanatory factor analysis & cluster analysis	Knowledge flows: according to Gupta and Govindarajan (1991, knowledge flow from focal subsidiary to HQs or other units of the MNC or vice versa) with 4 items (product design, marketing & distribution know-how and management systems and practices). Other items: autonomy, control by socialization, formal control, subsidiary capabilities, performance, intra-company flows, number of expatriates & inpatriates in top management	Subsidiaries from Australia and New Zealand are rather Local Innovators than Global Innovators compared to subsidiaries from other countries. Level of subsidiaries' capabilities are equal to that of other subsidiaries but with lower level in R&D and production
Hallin 2008b	Analyzed the effect of innovation characteristics (novelty, specificity, tacitness), characteristics of sending and receiving units (technical and business similarity), and characteristics of business relationship (previous collaborations between the units, mutual commitment to the innovation transfer) on usefulness of innovation transfer in MNCs for the receiving sub-unit's operations	(Concept of the Embedded MNC, tradition of IMP Group). No definition of innovations provided, innovations not specified; in empirical study product development addressed	Interviews at 116 sub-units of 13 MNCs. Transfer of 43 product innovations. Respondents: corporate senior management, R&D management, top management at subsidiaries. Statistical analysis: OLS regression analysis	Usefulness of innovation: easiness of adoption, extent to which knowledge on innovation was useful for basic research, technical development and marketing/sales of the subsidiary. Innovation novelty: extent of new components, new functions, new technology. Innovation specificity: development specifically for developing unit. Tacitness of innovation: codifiability and tacitness of innovation technology. Technical/business similarity: level of technical/business condition similarity between sending and receiving unit. Previous cooperation: extent of previous cooperation and knowledge sharing, existing routines for knowledge sharing between units. Mutual commitment: lack of resources for transfer at sending and receiving unit	Novel innovations are useful for receiving unit while specific innovations are. Mutual commitment of both business partners to transfer project enhances usefulness of the received innovation

Author(s) / Year	Aim of Study	Conceptual basis & definition of innovation	Research design	Measures of external embeddedness & innovation	Results
Hallin/ Holm/ Sharma 2008	Studies how subsidiaries' external and corporate embeddedness influences their business performance in exploiting an innovation received from another sub-unit of the MNC	(Concept of the Embedded MNC, tradition of IMP Group) No definition of innovations provided, innovations not specified, in empirical study product development addressed	Mail survey with 376 Swedish subsidiaries HQs outside Sweden Respondents: Subsidiary or marketing managers Statistical analysis: OLS regression analysis	External & corporate embeddedness: cooperation in product development, cooperation in marketing & sales, long-term orientation & stability of business relationships, interdependence, mutual trust Innovation uniqueness: degree to which the innovation is dissimilar from other innovations on subsidiaries local market	Especially external embeddedness but also corporate embeddedness supports subsidiaries' business performance when they exploit the innovations they received from another sub-unit of the MNC Exploitation of unique innovations was negatively correlated with subsidiaries' business performance when they were highly embedded in external business relationships

Table 3-5: Studies of the diffusion of subsidiaries' innovations in the MNC

3.2.2.2 Content of Literature with a Focus on the Specifications of the Analyzed Innovations

Most contributions on the transfer of innovations within MNCs examine product or process innovations. Only the papers of Ghoshal and Bartlett (1988a) and Harzing and Noorderhaven (2006) include administrative innovations. Bartlett and Ghoshal (1988a) are the only authors who explicitly define the innovations they study. In the other papers this information had to be searched for.

Studies	Object of innovation			Basic understanding of innovation		Intensity of (product) innovation			
	Product	Process	Admin.	Invention	Marketed	Innovation Process	Technological dim.	Market dim.	Organizational dim.
Studies of group (1)									
Ghoshal/Bartlett 1988a	+	+	+		+				
Ensign 1999				+					
Håkanson/Nobel 2001	+	+		+				+	
Zander 2002	+	+		+				+	
Ivarsson/Jonsson 2003	+	+		+					
Tregaskis 2003	+	+			+		(+)		
Ciabuschi/Kang/ Ståhl 2004	+				+		+	(+)	
Criscuolo 2004	+				+	+	+		
Ståhl 2004	+				+		+		(+)
Gerstlauer 2005	+	+		+					
Harzing/Noorder- haven 2006	+	+	+						
Studies of group (2)									
Galbraith 1990		+							
Hallin 2008b	+						+		
Hallin/Holm/ Sharma 2008	+	+							

Table 3-6: Overview over specifications of innovations analyzed in existing studies

Regarding the basic understanding of innovations, most authors focus on inventions or marketed problem solutions. Only Criscuolo (2004) analyzed the effect of researchers' mobility during the product innovation process on the future transfer of the finalized product innovations. However, the author does not examine the single stages of the product innovation process systematically but rather considers the product innovation process as a whole.

About half of the contributions specify the intensity of innovations. While Håkanson and Nobel (2001) and Zander (2002) use patent data (for more details on patents see sub-sections 3.1.2.2 and 3.1.3), Ciabuschi, Kang, and Ståhl (2004) Ståhl (2004), and Hallin (2008b) conduct a survey and measure the technological dimension of innovation intensity as novelty of the innovations. In the first two publications, the corporate importance of the innovations is also examined. The attributes of the analyzed innovations are summarized in table 3-6.

3.2.3 Research Design and Method in Literature

(1) As stated above, there is not much literature on the innovation transfer in MNCs. Most of the publications work with a quantitative research design based on their own survey. Data were collected using questionnaires (Galbraith 1990, Håkanson/Nobel 2001, Ivarsson/Jonsson 2003, Ståhl 2004, pp. 170-183, Harzing/Noorderhaven 2006, Hallin 2008b, Hallin/Holm/Sharma 2008). The examined MNCs were from the USA, Japan, the UK, Germany, France, the Netherlands and Sweden. Subsidiaries were based in Australia, New Zealand, Sweden and other countries which are not always specified (e.g. Håkanson/Nobel 2001). The number of subsidiaries analyzed ranges from 110 to 376.[36]

(2) One study has a quantitative empirical research design which is based on secondary data. It uses patent data of the USPTO (see more on patent data in sub-section 3.1.3) and focuses on the one case of ABB and watches the process of internationalization of the company's R&D in the years before and shortly after the merger (Zander 2002).

---

[36] In the publication of Galbraith, 32 cases of innovation transfer are reported. The number of subsidiaries involved is not mentioned (Galbraith 1990, pp. 61-62).

(3) Three studies have a qualitative empirical research design. Criscuolo (2004) conducted 24 interviews with R&D managers and scientists in six large European pharmaceutical companies. The other one examined three subsidiaries in the UK. HR managers, R&D managers and R&D employees of the MNCs and the focal subsidiaries were interviewed (Tregaskis 2003). Ståhl used in-depth interviews, demonstrations, and observations in his study. Interviews with 18 experts (e.g. subsidiary managers and engineers) at seven subsidiaries an HQs of five countries were conducted (Ståhl 2004, pp. 45-46). The contribution of Ghoshal and Bartlett (Ghoshal/Bartlett 1988a) uses multiple methods to explore the creation, adoption and diffusion of innovations in MNCs. Nine companies were examined with a qualitative case study method based on interviews, a survey using questionnaires for several people in the companies were used in three companies, and finally, a survey with a large sample were only one person in each enterprise in 66 North American and European MNCs.

In summary, a qualitative research design is hardly employed in publications on research question 2. Furthermore, it becomes obvious that German subsidiaries have only received limited attention in the studies.

3.3 Summary of the Literature Review

(1) Inter-organizational part – content of literature with a focus on subsidiaries' external embeddedness: The first part of the literature review (see section 3.1) reveals that there are not many studies that explain the link between the external business network of subsidiaries and their innovations. This seems stunning given the importance of the topic (see section 1.1). In addition, many contributions analyze the external network as one determinant of innovation activities amongst several others. Thus, the variable is studied in depth in only few studies. For instance, specifications of the business relationship are examined quite superficially. Furthermore, the conceptual basis of the studies is often rather weak. However, a few studies use the concept of embeddedness or are based on the concept of the Embedded MNC. This will be done in the thesis as well (see chapter 4). In the present thesis, the influence of subsidiaries' external business partners will be examined in depth. Thereby, it will be found out which stakeholders are most important. The relationships between them

will be analyzed using more criteria than were applied in the past. Also, the characteristics of knowledge and knowledge flows between the innovative subsidiaries and their business partners will be investigated (see sections 6.2 to 6.4).

(2) Intra-organizational part – content of literature with a focus on transfer of subsidiaries' innovations: The second part of the literature review shows that there are even less contributions about the transfer of innovations in MNCs. However, several mechanisms of the transfer of innovations between subsidiaries and other parts of the MNC have been studied. Amongst them were instruments of human resource management and IT. Few articles analyze the impact of subsidiaries' internal network on the diffusion of innovations. Again, details of the transfer of the innovation in the MNC as well as of the relationship between the subsidiaries and the units which receive the innovation are not examined. In this contribution, the transfer of product innovations from the innovative subsidiary to other units of the MNC will be analyzed. The receiving units will be identified and organizational structures and procedures to support the transfer of product innovations will be studied (see section 6.5).

(3) Both parts – content of literature with a focus on the specifications of the analyzed innovations: In tables 3-2 and 3-5, it was shown that hardly any of the listed studies defined the term "innovation". What was understood as an innovation tentatively became clear in the information on the empirical study. However, in some papers the information could not even be identified in this section. While most authors examined product or process innovations, some took administrative innovations into account. Almost all contributions understood innovations as inventions or marketed problem solutions. None of the publications have investigated the product innovation process in detail. However, one of the studies recommends that business partners and business relationships should be analyzed according to the single stages of the product innovation process (Hallin/Kang 2008, pp. 18-19). Finally, most contributions do not specify the intensity of innovations. As was revealed in chapter 2, in the present thesis product innovations will be analyzed. They are understood as technologically radical inventions that will be marketed but are not launched yet. In order to answer research question 1 (see section 1.2), the product innovation process will be studied in detail (see section 6.1).

(4) Both parts – research design and method: In both parts there are rather few studies which use a qualitative research design. However, qualitative research is considered to be especially useful to explore a topic in depth and understand the details of the subsidiaries' relationships to both external and internal business partners and how these relationships influence the creation and diffusion of subsidiaries' innovations. Thus, it has been recommended to employ qualitative research methods in International Business research before (e.g. Macharzina/Oesterle 2002, p. 14, Marschan-Piekkari/Welch 2004, pp. 7-8, Peterson 2004, p. 25, Wright 2004, p. 51). Furthermore, it becomes obvious that German subsidiaries have only received limited attention in the studies. In the first part, only one of the quantitative studies (Davis/Meyer 2004) analyzes German subsidiaries amongst others. None of the qualitative studies do this. However, national culture might have an impact on how external networks work. For instance, it might make a difference how much knowledge is transferred in business relationships (Sandström 1992, p. 51, Kutschker/Bäurle/Schmid 1997, p. 8). In the present publication, qualitative data will be obtained by conducting interviews within a case study approach. Thereby, German subsidiaries of Swiss MNCs will be analyzed.

(5) Conclusion: The research gaps which were identified in the literature review will be addressed in this thesis. Based on the concept of the Embedded MNC a specific product innovation of subsidiaries will be analyzed. Thereby, the product innovation process will be studied in detail. Apart from the type of business partners involved, the business relationship between the subsidiaries and their relevant business partners will be examined. It will be explored how the influence of these business partners which have an impact on the focal innovation takes place. Furthermore, it will be studied how the product innovation is transferred to other units of the MNC. Thus, product innovations will be studied from the beginning of the product innovation process to their diffusion to other units of the MNC. Choosing a qualitative case study approach with German subsidiaries and focusing on a specific innovation in subsidiaries will help to fill the research gaps.

4 Conceptual Background of Subsidiaries' Embeddedness

This thesis examines business relationships between subsidiaries and external business partners in the product innovation process. External and corporate business relationships have been the object of different network approaches. In section 4.1, a short systemization of network approaches is given and the concept of the Embedded MNC is selected. In section 4.2, the development of the concept of the Embedded MNC is described in order to explain differences in the usage of terms between authors. The concept is presented in section 4.3 and in 4.4, a critical evaluation of the concept is provided. Section 4.5 is used to extend the concept regarding stakeholder groups and refine it concerning the exchange of knowledge. In section 4.6, a conclusion of the chapter is given. The empirical study is particularly based on sub-section 4.5.1 (stakeholders; summarized in figure 4-7), sub-sections 4.3.1.1.2 and 4.3.2 (business relationship embeddedness; summarized in figure 4-4), and sub-sections 4.3.3.2 and 4.5.2 (characteristics of knowledge and knowledge transfer; summarized in tables 4-3 and 4-4 and figure 4-8).

4.1 Systemization of Network Concepts and Selection of the Concept of the Embedded MNC

Network research has led to the development of many different network approaches by several research schools which draw on different theoretical bases.[37] In 2003, Ritter and Gemünden stated: "The problem with today's body of relationship and network literature is that it is fragmented and – at least sometimes – different pieces does [sic!] not seem to fit together" (Ritter/Gemünden 2003, p. 692). Even the term

---

[37] The most comprehensive list of theories that are referred to in the field of network research seems to be Sydow's review of theories. He reveals 16 theoretical approaches which contribute to the explanation of the evolution and organization of networks. The most detailed analysis of this contribution is given of the transaction cost theory. Furthermore, economic approaches like game theory, principal agent theory, strategic, industry economic approaches and political approaches are presented. Finally, inter-organizational approaches like exchange theory, resource dependence theory, population ecology approaches, institutionalist approaches, system theory, contingency approaches, decision approaches and interaction approaches are discussed and seem to be particularly useful to examine networks (Sydow 1992, pp. 127-235). Thus, Sydow lists several rather different approaches to network evolution. However, the choice of theoretical approaches by Sydow seems to be rather arbitrary.

"network" has become imprecise (Nohria 1992, p. 3). Some authors speak of a "linguistic chaos" (Borgatti/Foster 2003, p. 996). Thus, it is a demanding task to classify network literature and identify network approaches which can exactly be described and are agreed on by several authors. Some literature tries to give an overview of the schools of network research and the network approaches developed (e.g. Grandori/Soda 1995, Araujo/Easton 1996, Renz 1998, Borgatti/Foster 2003). However, these reviews do not list the same approaches and schools. For example, the concept of the Embedded MNC is named as network approach in one of the reviews (Renz 1998, pp. 68-77) but is not in the others (Grandori/Soda 1995, Araujo/Easton 1996). The schools of network research and the network approaches are listed in table 4-1.

Overview over network literature	Object of review	Research fields and network approaches
Grandori/Soda 1995, pp. 185-193	Fields of research that contribute to network research	Industrial economics
		Historical and evolutionary approaches
		Organizational economics
		Negotiation theory
		Resource dependence theory
		Neo-institutional approach
		Organizational sociology
		Social psychology
		Social network theory
		Industrial marketing
		Economic policy
		Population ecology
Araujo/Easton 1996, pp. 67-102	Network approaches	Social network theory
		Inter-organization theory
		Actor-network theory
		Networks of innovators
		Network organizations
		Policy networks
		Networks in economic geography
		Comparative studies
		Entrepreneurship studies
		Industrial networks

Overview over network literature	Object of review	Research fields and network approaches
Renz 1998, pp. 59-330	MNCs as a network	Integrated network models
		Embedded network model
	Approaches to network research	Methodical network research
		Inter-organization theory (resource dependence theory, micropolitical approach)
		Network research in disciplines of business administration (e.g. marketing, organization structure, industrial sociology, information economy, comparative management, strategic management)
	Management in networks	Interaction theoretical approaches (e.g. interaction approach of the IMP-Group, multi-organizational model by Kirsch/Kutschker)[38]
		Swedish network approach
		Management oriented network approach
		Interaction theoretical approaches from business administration and management literature (e.g. interaction theoretical approach of the IMP-Group, multi-organizational model by Kirsch/Kutschker, Swedish network approach, concept of the Embedded MNC)

Table 4-1: Overview over schools of network research and the network approaches

Within network research, four levels of networks can be distinguished: the individual level, the intra-organizational level, the inter-organizational level and the market level (Gittell/Weiss 2004, pp. 132-133). On the individual level, networks of persons are studied. The intra-organizational and the inter-organizational level refer to the perspective of a firm. While on the intra-organizational level relationships between departments, subsidiaries and divisions may be analyzed, relationships of a firm or a firm's unit to other firms, universities, nongovernmental organizations or the government is examined on the inter-organizational level. On the market level, the structure of markets as networks is stated. This network structure dissents neoclassical theory which assumes the existence of atomistic actors (e.g. Håkansson 1982, IMP-Group 1990, Powell 1990). Markets and hierarchies may also be regarded as pure types of the organization of economic action that can nevertheless be described by network terms (Podolny/Page 1998, p. 59).

---

[38] Interaction theoretical approaches are presented by Schmid in detail (Schmid 2005, pp. 242-248).

The four levels of networks are depicted in figure 4-1. Three points need to be made clear regarding the figure: First, network approaches are used as examples for the levels of networks. Thus, the list of the network approaches in each category is not comprehensive. The list can not be comprehensive because researchers do not even agree which approaches are considered as network approaches and which are not, as stated earlier. Second, the attribution of network approaches to one of the categories is tentative. For example, the social capital concept has a clear focus on the individual's networks (Borgatti/Foster 2003, pp. 993-994; for some studies in which the social capital perspective is employed on the individual level see Belliveau/O'Reilly III/Wade 1996, Moran 2005, Thompson 2005). However, it is also transferred to the level of organizations (e.g. Burt 1992, e.g. pp. 8-13) and societies (e.g. Putnam 1995). Third, only one main publication is provided as an example for each network approach.

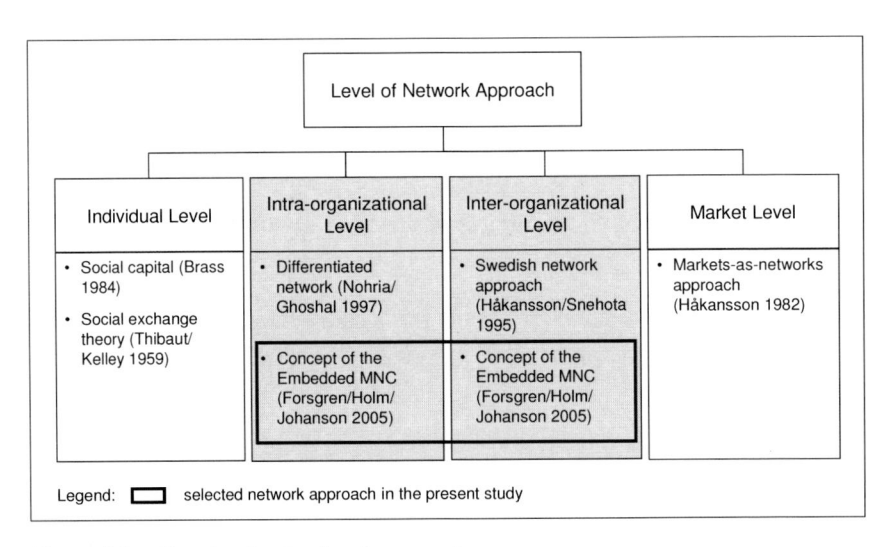

Level of Network Approach			
Individual Level	Intra-organizational Level	Inter-organizational Level	Market Level
• Social capital (Brass 1984) • Social exchange theory (Thibaut/Kelley 1959)	• Differentiated network (Nohria/Ghoshal 1997)	• Swedish network approach (Håkansson/Snehota 1995)	• Markets-as-networks approach (Håkansson 1982)
	• Concept of the Embedded MNC (Forsgren/Holm/Johanson 2005)	• Concept of the Embedded MNC (Forsgren/Holm/Johanson 2005)	

Legend: ▭ selected network approach in the present study

Figure 4-1:   Four levels of network research

As indicated in figure 4-1, the concept of the Embedded MNC is selected as a conceptual basis for the present research project. Why is this done? In this study, subsidiaries are the focal actors. It will be investigated how their external business partners support the creation of product innovations by the subsidiaries (see research question 1 in section 1.2). Furthermore, the transfer of the innovation from the focal subsidiaries to other units of the MNC will be examined (see research question 2 in section 1.2). Thus, two levels are applied in this study: the intra-organizational level and the inter-organizational study.[39] These two levels are included in the considerations of the concept of the Embedded MNC. Additionally, this concept argues on the basis of an MNC and focuses on subsidiaries and their relationships to corporate and external actors. Therefore, it seems appropriate in the context of this study and is selected.

4.2 The Evolution of the Concept of the Embedded MNC

In this section, the development of the concept of the Embedded MNC is explained. The concept emerged out of three main streams of research: the Industrial Marketing & Purchasing (IMP) Group with its concepts on dyadic relationships and networks, the concept of embeddedness, and the internationalization process model of the Uppsala school. They are depicted in figure 4-2 and are explained in detail in the following. While the first two roots play an important role in this study, the internationalization process model will not be further considered and thus will be introduced only briefly.

The concept of the Embedded MNC stems from a research stream which has a long tradition in network research. The IMP Group is a school which is regarded as one important pillar of network research by many authors (Grandori/Soda 1995, p. 192, Araujo/Easton 1996, pp. 99-102, Renz 1998, pp. 15-28, Schmid 2005, p. 245). The group was founded in 1976 and consists of researchers from many nations. Especially Scandinavian researchers have been very active developing new concepts, continuously enhancing existing ones and publishing new findings. In the stream of network research, the IMP Group first started with studies on dyadic relationships.[40] Their focus was on buyer-seller relationships in industrial markets (IMP-Group 1990, pp. 14-22, Sharma 1993). With the integration of decision theory, the interaction ap-

---

[39] On both the intra-organizational and inter-organizational level it is people who act in their unit or firm and in the relationship to business partners. However, they are assumed to act on behalf of their unit (Schmid/Daniel 2007, p. 19). For further explanations on the actors in a business network see sub-section 4.3.1.1.1.

[40] In the work on dyadic relationships researchers already acknowledged the importance of studying more than two partners (IMP-Group 1990, p. 11).

proach developed into a multi-organizational perspective (Kutschker 1990, p. 422). The Swedish network approach on which the concept of the Embedded MNC is grounded emerged from this multi-organizational view. The Swedish network approach examined relationships in a network of firms based on the resources and activities of actors. It still exclusively studied the inter-organizational perspective of the firm (Håkansson/Snehota 1995). Additionally, the kind of firm which was examined could be any kind of firm whereas the concept of the Embedded MNC focused on Multinational Corporations.[41]

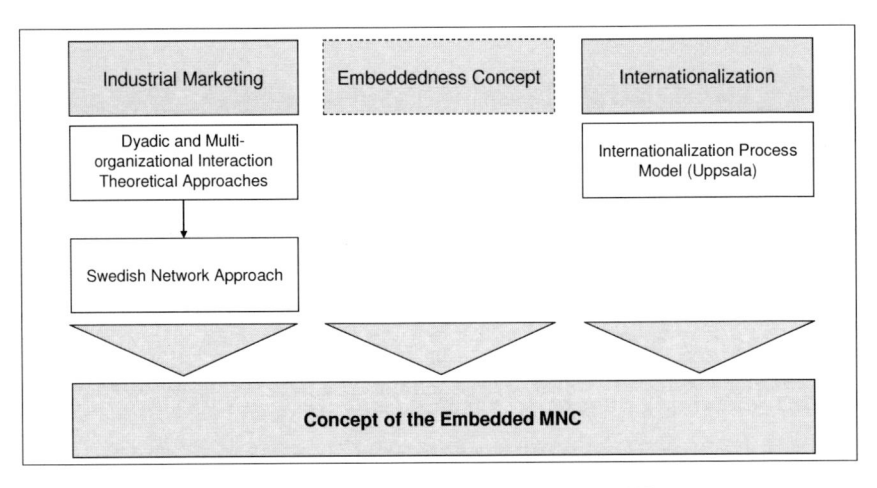

Figure 4-2: Development of the concept of the Embedded MNC
Source: Adopted from Renz (1998, p. 70).

Another concept from Swedish researchers is the internationalization process model of the Uppsala School. From this model the insight is drawn that during the internationalization process, knowledge about doing business in a particular foreign country is cumulated. This knowledge then serves as a basis for further commitment in this foreign market (Johanson/Vahlne 1977, 1978). In the concept of the Embedded MNC it is argued that knowledge about a foreign market is gained through business relationships with local actors. This fact causes barriers of doing business when a market

---

[41] Out of these interaction and network approaches the concept of the Embedded MNC has grown. Basic concepts and terms that are applied in the concept of the Embedded MNC were developed in the dyadic and multi-organizational interaction approach and the Swedish network approach. Therefore, publications from these approaches will be referred to regularly in the next sub-sections in which the concept of the Embedded MNC is explained.

is entered: Relationships to local business partners are not yet created so that knowledge can hardly be received. In the course of time, relationships are established and knowledge transfer to the entering MNC is increased. This results in a bigger commitment to the market (Johanson/Vahlne 2003, Forsgren/Holm/Johanson 2005, pp. 59-73).

Apart from Scandinavian research, the concept of the Embedded MNC draws on other approaches. One of them is the concept of embeddedness which is also suggested by the term "Embedded" MNC (Forsgren/Holm/Johanson 2005, p. 7). The concept of embeddedness emerged at about the same time as the interaction and network approaches of the IMP Group. Indeed, the embeddedness concept is often accredited to Polanyi (1957) who employed it in the context of markets to describe their structure. However, it was only decades later that Granovetter's journal article of 1985 stimulated the interest of researchers in both sociology and business research in the embeddedness concept.[42] He applied the concept of embeddedness to the context of business exchange (Granovetter 1985). The article was first and foremost a protest against the "under-socialization" of neoclassical economic theory and against the "over-socialization" of neo-institutional theories. Instead of the denial of social behavior ("under-socialization") and the assumption that actors obtain norms and habits mechanically without deciding logically ("over-socialization"), he stated that economic behavior must be analyzed in its interaction with social relations (Granovetter 1985, pp. 483-487). Granovetter stresses the importance of both dyadic relationships and networks of connected relationships for building trust in economic context (Granovetter 1985, pp. 490-491). The embeddedness of business actions affects economic action and outcomes (Granovetter 1992, p. 33, Gnyawali/Madhavan 2001, p. 431); like in the network approaches of the IMP Group (Axelsson 1992, p. 240) it may support or impede exchange processes (Uzzi 1996, p. 674).

The following description of a business network will be done according to the concept of the Embedded MNC and its preceding network concepts in this research tradition. Their terms will be used to explain basic concepts and phenomena. However, the same concepts could often be explicated by using terms of the embeddedness con-

---

[42] For a critical comment on the development of the meaning of embeddedness from Polanyi to Granovetter see Beckert (2007). For an overview over the history of the embeddedness concept see Dacin/Ventresca/Beal 1999.

cept. The embeddedness concept states similar relations between concepts like the concept of the Embedded MNC. Authors of the research tradition of the IMP Group who use network language in the main publication about the concept of the Embedded MNC (Forsgren/Holm/Johanson 2005), employ the language of the embeddedness concept in other publications (e.g. Andersson/Forsgren 1996, 2000, Andersson/ Forsgren/Holm 2001, 2002, Andersson/Björkman/Forsgren 2005, Andersson/Forsgren/Holm 2007). Although the embeddedness concept is not as detailed as the EMNC it sometimes discusses other details. Therefore, within every paragraph footnotes will reveal which term in the embeddedness concept corresponds to the one used in network research. Additions are provided whenever possible.

4.3 Description of the Embedded MNC Approach

4.3.1 Structure of the Embedded Network

The structure of a network consists of three elements: actors, dyadic relationships and the whole network as a pattern of connected relationships (e.g. Barden/Mitchell 2007, p. 1440, Schmid/Daub 2007, p. 5). When studying MNCs, each of these elements can be analyzed on two levels: the inter-organizational level and the intra-organizational level (e.g. Schmid 2005, pp. 237-239). In the following, the elements and their interplay will first be described in general according to the concept of the Embedded MNC and former concepts of this research stream (sub-section 4.3.1.1). This is done in order to explain the functionality of networks and basic terms and concepts. As this study examines both the inter-organizational and the intra-organizational network of MNCs and subsidiaries in particular, the structure of both networks will be portrayed in sub-sections 4.3.1.2 and 4.3.1.3, respectively. Thus, the concepts introduced in sub-section 4.3.1.1 will be applied to the particular context of the MNC. Finally, the network structure will be analyzed from the perspective of a focal subsidiary (sub-section 4.3.1.4).

4.3.1.1 Structure of a Network

Networks consist of three elements: actors, relationships and the network as a whole. They are depicted in figure 4-3 and are described in the following sub-sections.

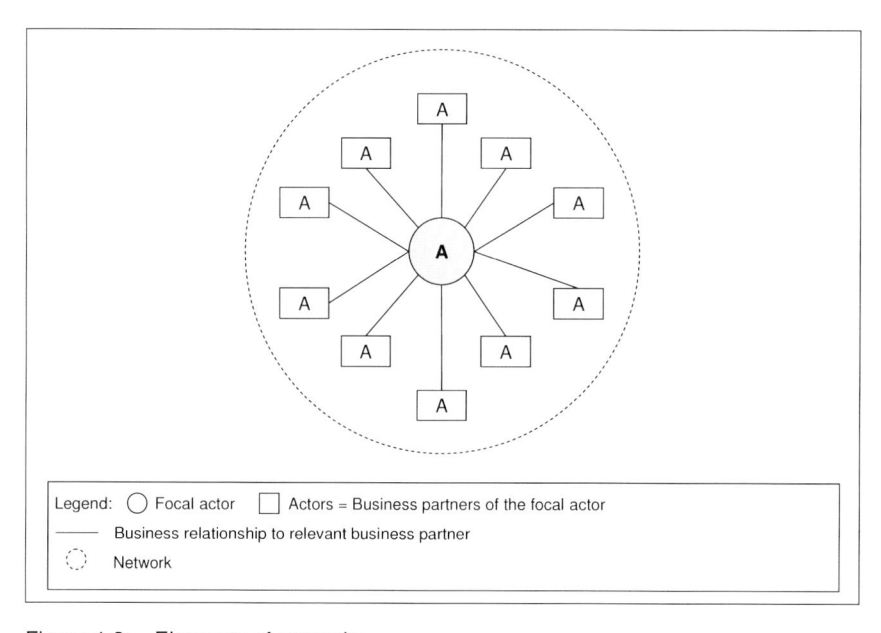

Legend: ○ Focal actor   ☐ Actors = Business partners of the focal actor
—— Business relationship to relevant business partner
⌒ Network

Figure 4-3: Elements of networks

4.3.1.1.1 Actor

Actors are individuals, groups of individuals, parts of firms, firms or groups of firms which perform activities and control resources. [43] Activities are characterized as applying resources to change other resources in some way while resources are defined as "... means used by actors when they perform activities" (Håkansson/Johanson

---

[43] The term "actors" is thus a very general one. In the present contribution, business partners are defined as actors who are in a business relationship with the focal actor. They provide the focal actor with knowledge or goods or receive knowledge or goods from the focal actor. The term "stakeholder" is used as a synonym for business partner. It stresses that different stakeholder groups exist that each have specific demands to the focal actor and provide it with specific inputs. For more details see sub-section 4.5.1.

1992, p. 28).[44] In the understanding of the network approaches of the IMP Group and following researchers, resources encompass the input and the output of an actor. Thus, not only input like raw materials, equipment and knowledge, for instance on research and development (R&D) and production, are subsumed under the term "resource", but also output like products (e.g. Håkansson/Snehota 1995, pp. 134-135). For the sake of clarity, a difference will be made between resources and products in this thesis. Resources are thus any kind of input that the firm or subsidiary acquires and uses in its operations. Products are the output of the subsidiary or firm that is sold in the market. It will also be distinguished between knowledge and other types of resources.

Researchers of the concept of the Embedded MNC and former concepts have emphasized the heterogeneity of resources. This heterogeneity results from the broad variety of possibilities to use a resource (Håkansson/Snehota 1995, p. 135). The heterogeneity of actors' resources causes interaction between the actors and hence may lead to the formation of a business relationship (Forsgren et al. 1995, p. 44). An activity constitutes the transfer (i.e. exchange) or the transformation (i.e. the combination, development or creation) of resources using other resources. While transformation activities are controlled by one actor, transfer activities encompass the transfer of control over a resource from one actor to another one and therefore include at least two actors (Håkansson/Johanson 1992, pp. 28-30).[45]

As actors exist on these different organizational levels, actors of a higher level incorporate actors of a lower level (Håkansson/Johanson 1992, p. 28). Which level of ac-

---

[44] These definitions are not conclusive. Therefore, the definition is complemented with the explanations of Barney. According to him, firm resources are all assets, organizational processes, capabilities, knowledge etc. which provide firms with the possibility to conceptualize and implement strategies for an enhanced effectiveness and efficiency. These resources may be grouped into physical capital resources (e.g. raw material, equipment), human resource capital (e.g. individual experience and knowledge) and organizational capital resources (e.g. planning and controlling systems; Barney 1991, pp. 101-102). As not all the resources of a firm are strategically relevant and enhance its competitive advantage, Barney discussed four criteria which identify resources as strategically relevant: they must be valuable, rare, hard to imitate and to substitute (Barney 1991, pp. 105-112).

[45] The Swedish network approach focuses on resources and activities. Almost the whole book of Håkansson and Snehota is about activities, resources and their connection to actors (see Håkansson/Snehota 1995). However, both concepts are hardly used in the concept of the Embedded MNC and only mentioned few times. Therefore, the concepts will not be explained here in more detail and will hardly be further used in the understanding of the Swedish network approach.

tors is investigated depends on the aim of the study.[46] In the concept of the Embedded MNC, the main focus is on parts of the MNC: on the subsidiaries and HQs as sub-units of the MNC and their relationships to each other and to external business partners (see sub-section 4.3.1.4). External business partners may be whole firms or sub-units of firms. Because the origins of the concept of the Embedded MNC were built by researchers focusing on Industrial Marketing, mostly business relationships to customers and sometimes also to suppliers are examined (see section 4.4). However, both in conceptual and empirical publications it is referred to business relationships in general. This implies that the phenomena studied in customer-supplier relationships may be transferred to other types of business relationships to other stakeholders as well.[47] For example, it is stated that in embedded business relationships with external partners more knowledge is exchanged than in less embedded ones (e.g. Andersson/Forsgren/Holm 2001, p. 1015, Forsgren/Holm/Johanson 2005, pp. 157-166). Whether this assumption applies to business relationships to other stakeholder groups, is one question of this study. In addition, other stakeholder groups might be relevant for the product innovation process as well.

4.3.1.1.2 Relationship

On every level, relationships between actors are the foundation of networks.[48] Business relationships[49] constitute relationships between autonomous business units who share common goals and interests to some extent (Håkansson/Johanson 1993, p. 14, Ford/Håkansson/Johanson 1994, p. 126). "Autonomous business units" means that they have, at least to some degree, free choice whether they want to continue the relationship with a particular business partner or not (Håkansson/Johanson 1993, p. 14). Business relationships are based on interactions between business partners

---

[46] The change of perspective between organization and individual is a typical and legitimate process in network research (Renz 1998, p. 297).
[47] More details on stakeholders are given in sub-section 4.5.1.
[48] Within the concept of embeddedness, the perspective of a dyadic relationship is called relational embeddedness (e.g. Granovetter 1992, p. 33, Gulati 1995, p. 624, Rowley/Behrens/Krackhardt 2000, Dhanaraj et al. 2004, Moran 2005, Barden/Mitchell 2007, Schmid/Daub 2007).
[49] In naming the relationships "business relationships", authors of the Embedded MNC concept emphasize that pure social relationships are not in their focus. Business relationships are based on resource interdependences. However, it is made clear that social exchange may be a part of business relationships (Forsgren/Holm/Johanson 2005, p. 7).

which are characterized as "... any set of observable behavior on the part of at least two individuals when there is reason to believe that some parts of these individuals are responding to each other" (Hallén/Johanson/Seyed-Mohamed 1991, p. 29). Interactions are the dynamic facets of relationships (Axelsson 1992, p. 8). When interacting, firms operate proactively and reactively to the actions of its business partner (Håkansson/Johanson 1993, p. 17). Thereby, these interactions are interpreted by both partners.[50] Interactions between actors are stated to consist of two processes by researchers of the IMP Group: the exchange process of which the product and service, knowledge and social exchange exist,[51] and the adaptation process[52] (Axelsson 1992, p. 8). The exchange process between business partners consists of a series of episodes. Episodes are all the interactive elements which are part of an exchange, e.g., the delivery of a product or a meeting about problems that arose during a production process (Forsgren/Holm/Johanson 2005, pp. 23-24). Adaptations may concern either the elements of exchange or the exchange process between business partners (IMP-Group 1990, p. 14). The basic structure of business relationships, as it is considered by the IMP Group, is depicted in figure 4-4.

The IMP Group and following researchers described business relationships as a mutual orientation of two business partners towards each other in a long term (Easton 1992, pp. 8-9, Blankenburg Holm/Eriksson/Johanson 1999, p. 468, Forsgren/Holm/ Johanson 2005, p. 23). Mutual orientation is defined to include knowledge about and trust[53] in each other. Each partner is aware of the other partner's interests and tries to consider them in the own actions to some degree. Products, production processes, administrative routines and contact patterns of both companies are affected by mutual orientation (Forsgren/Holm/Johanson 2005, p. 23).[54] However, these attributes have also been employed to assess the embeddedness of business relationships.

---

[50] Thus, business relationships are socially constructed phenomena (Uzzi 1997, p. 42; for social constructivism see Berger/Luckmann 1966).
[51] Exchange processes will be discussed in-depth as flows through relationships and the network in sub-section 4.3.3.
[52] The adaptation process will be discussed in more detail in sub-section 4.3.2 in which the dynamics of relationships will be explained.
[53] For a definition of trust as used in the present contribution see sub-section 4.3.3.3.1.
[54] Relationships have also been described according to the attributes of continuity, complexity, symmetry, informality, adaptations, cooperation & conflict, social interaction and routinization (Håkansson/Snehota 1995, pp. 7-10).

Therefore, in this study, relationships are simply understood as a sequence of interactions between business partners.

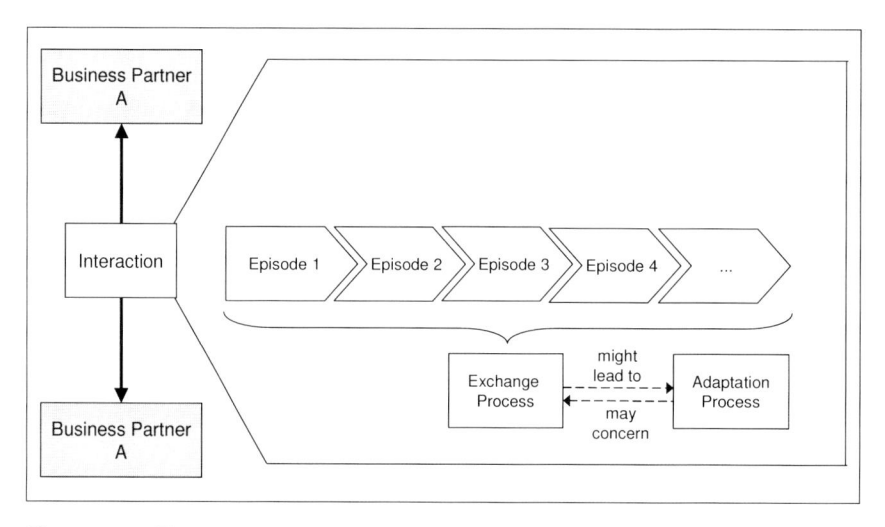

Figure 4-4: The basic structure of business relationships

Business relationships were empirically shown to be more or less strong (e.g., Andersson/Forsgren 1996, Andersson/Björkman/Forsgren 2005). As the two ends of a continuum, they can be described as arm's length (low end) or embedded (high end; Forsgren/Holm/Johanson 2005, p. 107). Researchers of the concept of the Embedded MNC consider two dimensions for the assessment of the embeddedness of business relationships: the breadth and the depth. The breadth is conceptualized as the number of functional areas that are involved in a business relationship with a particular partner (Andersson/Forsgren/Holm 2001, pp. 1016-1017). According to Porter, primary and secondary functional areas may be differentiated. While primary functional areas serve to manufacture a product and deliver it to the customer, secondary activities support primary functional areas at each step of the value chain (Porter 1999, p. 67). Primary functional areas are inbound logistics, production, marketing & sales, outbound logistics and customer service. Secondary functional areas include the infrastructure of the firm, human resources, R&D and purchasing (Porter 1999, pp. 66, 70-75). Benito, Grøgaard and Narula and Moore subsumed these functional areas to research, development, production, marketing & sales, logistics & distribution, purchasing and human resource management (Moore 2000, p. 161, 2001, p.

285, Benito/Grøgaard/Narula 2003, p. 450). In this thesis, the areas of research and development are pulled together so that six functional areas are taken into account. Often, only few functional areas deal with a business partner, for instance the sales department with a customer.

The depth of business relationships describes rather soft attributes that are more difficult to operationalize like trust and adaptations (Andersson/Forsgren/Holm 2001, pp. 1016-1017). Often, authors delimitate the embeddedness of business relationships to this dimension of depth (often, they even only consider adaptations as a measure of embeddedness; see table 4-2 in section 4.4 for the operationalization of embeddedness in empirical studies of the IMP Group and following researchers). Arm's length relationships are defined like in neoclassical theory; they are based on economic considerations and characterized by selfish, profit-seeking behavior and the exchange of knowledge about price and quantity in the buyer-seller relationship only. When conditions of the relationship or the environment change, partners are ready to leave the relationship immediately (Andersson/Forsgren/Holm 2002, p. 982, Andersson 2003, p. 428).

As opposed to this, an embedded relationship is described to be rather long-lasting. It is characterized by mutual adaptation of resources and the development of mutual dependences of activities between the business partners in different areas by the authors: technical, planning, knowledge, social, economic and legal (Håkansson/Snehota 1989, p. 191, Forsgren/Johanson 1992b, p. 4). These areas of dependence are also described as bonds between business partners (Forsgren et al. 1995, p. 21).[55] They tie business partners together and may differ in their embeddedness. They are the stronger, the more they resist disruption (Easton/Araujo 1989, p. 101).

---

[55] It is unclear why these areas were chosen to depict the level of mutual dependence between business partners. They are neither functional areas nor are they equivalent to the types of flows between the partners (products/services, knowledge, social flows; for more details see sub-section 4.3.3). Rather, they might be types of links between business partners within functional areas. For example, mutual dependences in R&D might be technical because business partners adapted to each other in their equipment. Furthermore, contracts might regulate the contributions made by each partner in the product innovation process. During the product innovation process, knowledge flows and social interaction between employees in both partners takes place. Planning steps of the innovation process has effects on the operations of each partner while the allocation of results of the product innovation process might cause economic interdependences between partner firms. The areas proposed by Håkansson and his colleagues will be employed as examples for mutual dependences in this study. If respondents describe further areas of mutual dependence they will be reported in chapter 6.

The higher the mutual dependence between partners and the stronger they are, the more important are the partners to each other. Importance means that the relationship is more critical (i.e., less substitutable) for a company than other business relationships. The end of the business relationship would have severe consequences for the business partners. Also, a large amount of mutual commitment in business operations and trust between the business partners is inhered in embedded relationships. Partners also pay more attention to each other (Hallén/Johanson/Seyed-Mohamed 1991, p. 30). This leads to further commitment, i.e. to further investments in the relationship (Andersson/Forsgren/Pedersen 2001, p. 9).[56] However, sharing a strong business relationship does not necessarily mean that there are no conflicts with the business partners. The atmosphere of a relationship may be more or less cooperative (Håkansson/Henders 1992, p. 35). Most of the features of the depth of business relationships have hardly or not at all been tested empirically (see table 4-2 in section 4.4). They were rather described on a conceptual basis.

The difference between the breadth and the depth of business relationships is not that between quantitative and qualitative attributes or structural and emotional factors. For instance, adaptations can be quantified in most cases and are a rather structural variable. If equipment is bought which is needed to manufacture products specifically for a particular customer the price of the equipment may serve as a basis to calculate the adaptation made. The same applies to adaptations in information technology, for example. Andersson and his co-authors do not discuss whether the number of functional areas is the only measure for the breadth of business relationships. Other rather quantitative attributes exist. Characteristics of exchange processes during an interaction could be examined, for instance the frequency of contact between business partners. However, the idea of the breadth of a relationship is that the business partners share many different activities and resources in their business relationship. Therefore, the involvement of different functional areas serves as a sign of a large breadth of a business relationship. If only one functional area, like the R&D department, has to contact two business partners and it has more frequent contact to one business partner than to the other this indicates a deeper relationship of the R&D department (and therefore of the firm) to the first business partner than to the second

---

[56] The dynamical development of business relationships is described in more detail in sub-section 4.3.2.

one. The same applies if different levels of one department are involved with a business partner. A business relationship is considered deeper when executive staff is involved in a business relationship in addition to functional staff.

In the present thesis, relationships will be described according to two dimensions: the breadth and the depth. While the breadth only includes the number of functional areas involved the depth encompasses both rather emotional variables like mutual trust and mutual attention and rather structural variables like mutual adaptations, mutual dependence, mutual criticality and mutual commitment.

An example of the breadth and the depth of business relationships is provided in figure 4-5. From a focal actor's perspective, the business relationship to a partner is depicted. With this partner, he collaborates in R&D and production. Thus, the number of functional areas is two out of six. Concerning both functional areas, the depth of the business relationship is described according to six criteria: mutual adaptations, mutual dependence, mutual criticality, investments, mutual trust, and mutual attention.[57] They were introduced in this sub-section and are also described in sub-section 4.3.2. While some of these criteria hardly apply for the collaboration in one functional area, other attributes of the business relationship show high values. For instance, both business partners adapted highly to each other in R&D. The (operational) dependence was medium and both criticality and investments in the business relationship are low. Trust between business partners concerning R&D is high and attention paid to the business relationship is medium. Looking at the breadth and depth this way, no final value of the embeddedness of a particular business relationship can be calculated. However, it can be assessed whether one business relationship is more embedded than another one. It can also be analyzed whether different business relationships show patterns of assessments of particular criteria.

---

[57] It has to be noticed that the criteria are not independent. Rather, as will be described in sub-section 4.3.2, the development of one criterion may influence the development of another one. However, a definite correlation between the six attributes of the depth of business relationships is not known. It is expected that not all of them show the same value in a particular relationship so that it is worth to consider all of them. A ranking of the criteria is not indicated by their sequence in figure 4-4.

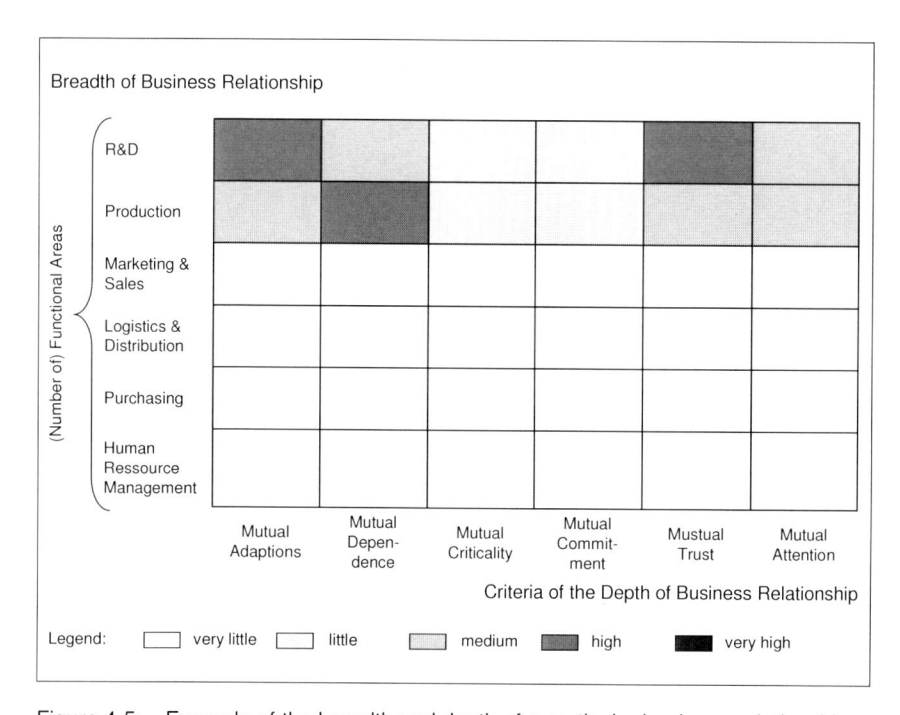

Figure 4-5: Example of the breadth and depth of a particular business relationship

Authors state that the activities of the business partners are linked to each other via exchange and adaptation processes, i.e. by building up relationships, and their resources are exchanged or related to each other. Relating resources may mean three different things: First, relationships may be built in order to control resources of a business partner to some extent. By committing own resources to the relationship with a business partner the business partner gains some control over them while the focal company gains some control over the partner's resources. This may be less costly than to obtain these resources. Second, in business relationship new resources, especially knowledge may be developed together. One way is to learn how to combine each other's resources more efficiently. The other one is that each business partner uses his own knowledge in collaborating in a particular field. The business partners then do not have to learn the other one's knowledge themselves. Third, the relationship may be considered a resource itself. Both partners have to invest in the relationship in order to keep it alive. Furthermore, the relationship is employed to support the firm's operations and thus has a purpose and a value for both business partners (Håkansson/Johanson 1993, pp. 18-19, Andersson/Forsgren 1996, p. 488).

4.3.1.1.3 Network

An actor does not only have one business relationship. Instead, plenty of relationships with actors are established for different purposes, e.g. with suppliers to purchase material, with customers to sell their products or with research institutions or competitors for common technological development. Each of the actor's business partners has business relationships to other actors as well. The relationships between the actor's business partner and another of his business partner are called the actor's connected relationships (Andersson/Forsgren 1996, p. 491, Forsgren/Holm/ Johanson 2005, p. 107). Two business relationships are defined to be connected when exchange in the focal relationship depends on the exchange in the other (Cook/Emerson 1978, p. 725, Anderson/Håkansson/Johanson 1994, p. 2). Thereby, connectedness does not only occur between embedded relationships but also between arm's length relationships. A relationship is affected by another one in a positive way when this one facilitates the exchange in the focal relationship. If exchange is impeded the focal relationship is negatively influenced by the other one (Halinen/Törnroos 1998, p. 190, Håkansson/Ford 2002, p. 134). As resources and activities of an actor and his indirect business partners are interdependent (Axelsson 1992, p. 240), a business relationship depends on relationships connected to it (Andersson/Forsgren 1996, Forsgren/Holm/Johanson 2005, p. 107).[58] On this connectedness of relationships, the network is built.[59] It is defined as "… set of connected exchange relationships between actors controlling business activities which must precede or are expected to ensue" (Forsgren/Pahlberg 1992, p. 42). Furthermore, the connectedness is the reason why the network is unbounded. Somehow each actor is assumed to be connected to each other actor (Holm/Johanson/Thile-

---

[58] The term "connected relationship" stems from the network literature. In the literature on embeddedness it is rather spoken of "indirect ties" or indirect relations (e.g. Andersson/Forsgren 1996, p. 492, Barden/Mitchell 2007, p. 1440).

[59] In embeddedness literature, structural embeddedness refers to the overall pattern of relationships in a network (see e.g. Granovetter 1992, p. 33, Uzzi 1997, Gulati 1999, Rowley/Behrens/Krackhardt 2000, Newburry 2001, Fischer/Pollock 2004, Venkatraman/Lee 2004, Moran 2005, Schmid/ Daub 2007).

nius 1995, p. 101). As arm's length relationships are created and left frequently the structure of the network is constantly changing. The complexity of the network is the reason why it can not be controlled by any firm (Easton 1992, p. 22).[60]

As this understanding of network is way too broad to work with, the business network context[61] is rather applied in empirical research. It includes the direct and connected relationships of an actor which are considered relevant by him (Forsgren/ Holm/Johanson 2005, pp. 93-94). As every actor has a different set of relationships that he considers particularly relevant, the network context is unique for each actor (Holm/Johanson/Thilenius 1995, p. 101). The business network context of an actor was found to be rather stable because relationships to relevant actors are not often broken up and new ones develop slowly (e.g. Uzzi 1996, 1997). However, the business network context is constantly changing because new interactions are made and relationships gradually evolve over time. Mutual adaptations are made and mutual trust is built (or destroyed; Uzzi 1997, pp. 44-45). In the business network context, each actor has a network position. It is defined by the actors who are directly or indirectly related to the actor. The network position itself defines the role of the actor. In an empirical study, Mattson detected that the position is path dependent and shapes future actions of the actor as it provides the norms which the related actors expect the actor to act according to (Mattson 1989, p. 122, Easton 1992, pp. 19-24, Seyed-Mohamed/Bolte 1992, pp. 215-216). It is defined by the functions an actor performs, by the importance of the actor in the network, by the embeddedness of his relation-

---

[60] This view is opposed to the perspective of the strategic network approach which considers an actor to purposefully create and control the network according to his needs and interests. Strategic networks are described as an intended organizational form to enhance the competitiveness of the firm (Miles/Snow 1986a, 1986b, Jarillo 1988). Jarillo defines strategic networks as "... networks are conceptualized as a mode of organization that can be used by managers or entrepreneurs to position their firms in a stronger competitive stance. That is why the term 'strategic' has been added to 'networks': I see strategic networks as long-term, purposeful arrangements among distinct but related for profit organizations that allow those firms in them to gain or sustain competitive advantage vis-à-vis their competitors outside the network ... Essential to this concept of strategic network is that of 'hub firm', which is the firm that, in fact, sets up the network, and, takes a pro-active attitude in the care of it" (Jarillo 1988, p. 32).

[61] Instead of the expression "business network context" the terms "network context" (Easton 1992, p. 18, Holm/Johanson/Thilenius 1995, pp. 101-102, Forsgren/Holm/Johanson 2005, p. 123) or "net" (Easton 1992, p. 18) are also used. However, this is not done consistently. In the majority of publications of the concept of the Embedded MNC, the term "business network" is used to describe the relevant business network of a focal actor (e.g. Forsgren/Holm/Johanson 2005, pp. 93-94). It has to be made clear that despite the term "context" the business network context does not encompass the general environment of business relationships or a business network. It rather includes the direct and connected business relationships of a focal actor that he considers relevant (Forsgren/Holm/Johanson 2005, pp. 93-94).

ships to other actors and by the identity of his direct and connected business partners (Mattson 1989, pp. 122-123).

The business network context may be more or less embedded. Thereby, both the direct and connected relationships of a focal actor play a role. The degree of embeddedness of the focal actor's dyadic and connected relationships determines the degree of embeddedness in a business network context. Thus, the degree of embeddedness results from the focal actor's position in the business network (Andersson/Forsgren 1996, p. 490). However, a high degree of embeddedness in a business network context does not necessarily have positive consequences. The business network context may be over-embedded (Grabher 1993, Uzzi 1997, pp. 58-60).[62] While in dyadic relationships embeddedness is found to be more detailed, holistic and tacit (see sub-section 4.3.3.2), and too much embeddedness in the business network context may impede the inflow of new knowledge into the network context. Thus, the business network may be cut-off new developments in its environment. This effect is called lock-in of the business network context (Grabher 1993).

Networks are stated to be heterogeneous. They consist of heterogeneous actors with heterogeneous resources and demands (Easton 1992, pp. 16-17). Heterogeneous products and services[63] are offered in a network and even the same product which is sold by different suppliers has different features. This is due to the intent to use the firm's own resources in the most efficient way and to diversify the own firm from competitors in the market. In choosing a supplier of a resource and adapting to him, a customer becomes dependent on him. In the course of time, mutual adaptations create interdependencies (Forsgren et al. 1995, pp. 26-35).[64] Thus, it is this heterogeneity which causes interdependencies between the actors of the network. Interdependence and heterogeneity enforce each other (Easton 1992, pp. 16-17). Like relationships, business networks may be considered a resource themselves. They are created in a path-dependent process and can not easily be imitated and substituted (Gulati/Nohria/Zaheer 2000, p. 207, Andersson/Forsgren/Holm 2002, p. 980).

---

[62] The effect of over-embeddedness stems from the embeddedness literature (Uzzi 1997, pp. 58-60).
[63] It was stated before that products and services are included in the term "resources" by the IMP Group and later researchers in this tradition (see sub-section 4.3.1.1.1).
[64] For further explanations on the dynamics in relationships see sub-section 4.3.2.

4.3.1.2 Structure of the Inter-organizational Network

Looking specifically at MNCs, the term "Embedded MNC" is explained first. The Embedded MNC is described as an MNC "...whose subsidiaries operate in business networks that, to a notable extent, are characterized by a high level of embeddedness among the relationship actors" (Forsgren/Holm/Johanson 2005, p. 97, 103). Of course, this definition is very broad. First, it is not made clear what an MNC is. Firms may be defined as multinational according to a different attributes, for instance the existence of foreign subsidiaries (Kormann 1970, p. 8, Sieber 1970, pp. 415-419) or cross-boarder activities (Sundaram/Black 1992, p. 733; for a review and comparison of various definitions of an MNC see Kutschker/Schmid 2008, pp. 242-244). Second, there is no clarity on the expression "to a notable extent'. What is "a notable extent"? How can this extent be measured and compared?

The points that were explained in sub-section 4.3.1.1 for firms in general, apply to the external context of an MNC as well. Only on the level of the actors, some specific characteristics exist for MNCs: In the external context of an MNC, the focal actor is the MNC as a whole or sub-units of the MNC, i.e. headquarters or national or foreign subsidiaries. The actors it has business relationships with are its stakeholders, e.g. suppliers, customers, competitors and research institutions (Helble/Chong 2004, p. 606). The inter-organizational network[65] thereby only encompasses external actors which are considered relevant by the focal actor.[66] It is depicted in figure 4-6. However, this does not mean that relationships to these actors have to be embedded ones. Arm's length relationships may be important for the actors as well if they count for a large part of the actor's business volume, for example. Thus, the inter-organizational network of a focal actor includes embedded and arm's length relationships which are considered relevant.

---

[65] Unfortunately, the authors of the concept of the Embedded MNC do not specify the term "inter-organizational network". In this thesis, the inter-organizational is defined to consist of the relevant business network while the external network is the unbounded network. When it is not specified in literature if only relevant actors belong to the business network, the term "external business network" or "external business partners" will be employed. The inter-organizational network and the business network are depicted in figure 4-6.

[66] In the case of an MNC, it will probably be difficult to define the inter-organizational network for the whole firm. It is doubted that even HQs have an overview over all the relationships that are relevant for the MNC. It was found that HQs do not know about all the relevant relationships of the subsidiaries (Andersson/Björkman/Forsgren 2005).

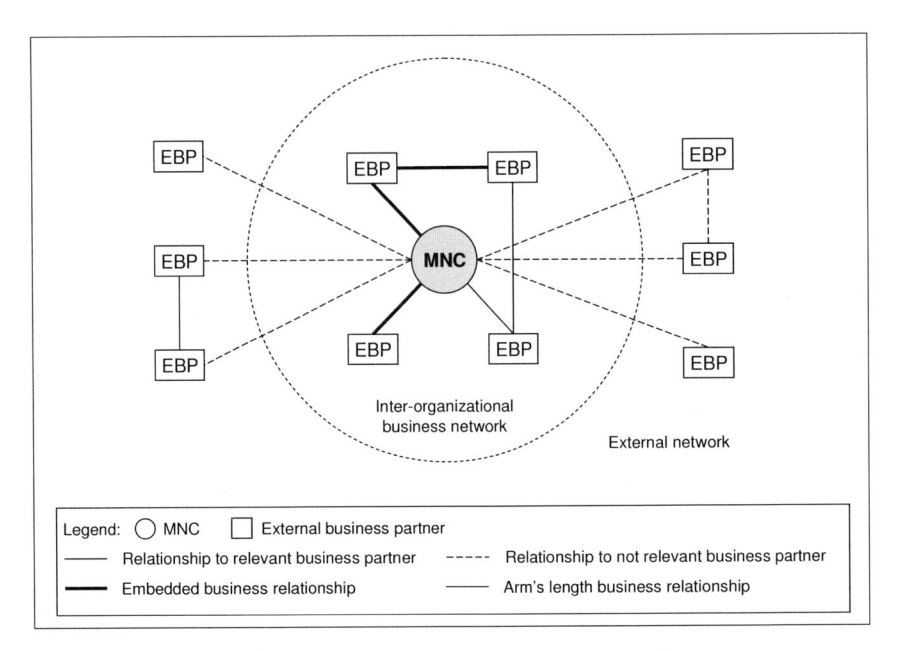

Figure 4-6: Inter-organizational and corporate networks of MNCs

Because it operates in several countries, the MNC has relevant relationships in (most of) these countries. Thus, it has a multinational inter-organizational network. The external business partners from different countries provide the MNC with resources. Some of these resources may be available in many countries but others are specific to this country and to the particular business partner. The possibility of MNCs to receive country-specific resources is regarded as one of the competitive advantages of MNCs compared to national firms (Andersson/Forsgren/Holm 2002, p. 979, Andersson 2003, p. 426).

4.3.1.3 Structure of the Intra-organizational Network

The corporate network of an MNC consists of headquarters and subsidiaries.[67] The main interest of research is on the relationship between HQs and subsidiaries (e.g. Birkinshaw et al. 2000, Young/Tavares 2004, Schmid/Daniel 2007) or subsidiaries themselves (e.g. Gupta/Becerra 2003, Schmid/Maurer 2008).[68] While no boundaries of the external network exist, as stated in sub-section 4.3.1.1.2, the corporate network has a borderline which is determined by ownership (Forsgren/Holm/Johanson 2005, p. 92). Thus, a firm belongs to the corporate network if the MNC holds more than 50.0% of its equity. This firm is then defined as a subsidiary of the MNC whereas firms are not considered to be subsidiaries if the investment is up to 50%. However, this definition is not absolutely clear-cut. It seems clear that an MNC does not only consider a unit an operational part of the MNC if it holds 50.5% but not if it holds 49.5% (Forsgren/Holm/Johanson 2005, pp. 92-93).

The relationships within MNCs can have the same characteristics like external ones (Andersson/Forsgren/Holm 2001, p. 1028). Subsidiaries do not share embedded relationships with all sister units and not even always with HQs. For example, if the MNC has a multinational orientation[69] according to the typology of Bartlett and Ghoshal, foreign subsidiaries act as local firms in the market. Headquarters and foreign subsidiaries only have little contact. Decisions are taken mainly on a local basis and little coordination takes place between sister units (Bartlett/Ghoshal 1990a, pp. 30-31, Kutschker/Schmid 2008, pp. 296-298). Although the degree of integration differs in MNCs (e.g. sub-units are described to be quite interdependent in the transnational MNC; Bartlett/Ghoshal 1990a, pp. 118-125), there is probably no MNC in which all relationships between sub-units are embedded ones. Instead, only few of its relationships are embedded (Håkanson/Nobel 2001, pp. 400-403, Schmid/Schurig 2003, pp. 760-761). Corporate actors are not equally relevant to a focal subsidiary either.

---

[67] Of course, firms which act only in their national context have a corporate network as well. On this level, relationships between employees, departments and divisions may be studied. However, the corporate level is mainly examined within MNCs because the relationships between HQs and subsidiaries as well as between sister units are of great interest.

[68] Objects of research might as well be divisions or regional HQs, for example.

[69] Note that in this case, "multinational" refers to the type of strategy of an MNC according to Bartlett and Ghoshal. Generally in this study, "multinational" refers to the fact that a firm operates in several countries.

Equivalent to the external business network, the business network of a focal actor that consists of his relevant business relationships within the MNC is called his intra-organizational business network. The network that includes all the units of the MNC is named corporate network.[70] Each unit of the MNC has a unique intra-organizational network. The intra-organizational network and the corporate network are depicted in figure 4-7.

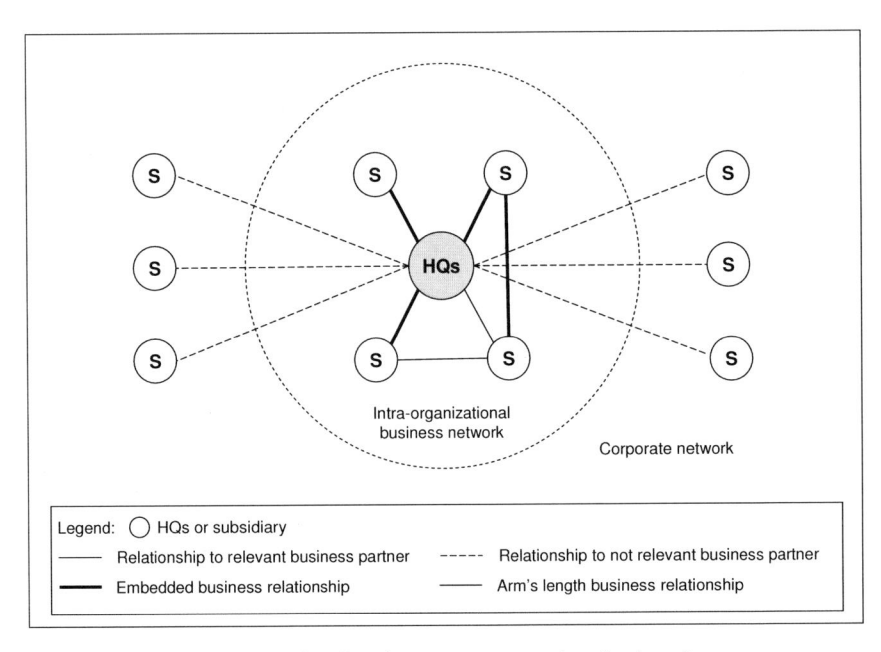

Figure 4-7: Intra-organizational and corporate networks of sub-units

The uniqueness of sub-units' business networks (regarding both their inter-organizational and intra-organizational business networks) makes sub-units heterogeneous. Other factors that are different between sub-units may be their language, culture and institutional characteristics (Forsgren/Holm/Johanson 2005, p. 92). It is a rather new view on the MNC that sub-units are heterogeneous. In the past, they have been regarded as quite homogeneous having the same responsibilities in each country. This was labeled the "United Nations model assumption" by Bartlett and Ghoshal (Bartlett/Ghoshal 1989, p. 100). However, especially since the 1980s it has been

---

[70] When it is not specified in literature if only relevant actors belong to the business network, the term "corporate business network" or "corporate business partners" will be employed in this thesis.

recognized that subsidiaries have a very different level of competences, skills and knowledge which results in very different tasks and responsibilities for the subsidiaries. Their strategic importance is expressed in the role the subsidiary is assigned to by HQs.[71]

4.3.1.4 Network Structure from a Subsidiary's Perspective

Subsidiaries are part of both a unique intra-organizational network and a unique inter-organizational network. Thus, they are embedded in two different environments: the corporate context and the business network context. Their corporate context is identified by legal and administrative links. Actors in this context are HQs and all the subsidiaries which belong to the MNC. In this context, business relationships between a focal subsidiary and HQs or other subsidiaries may, but do not necessarily need to exist. Thus, the corporate context exceeds the intra-organizational network because the latter only contains corporate actors who are considered relevant business partners by the focal subsidiary. The second environment is the business network context of the subsidiary. This context is characterized by business relationships to relevant external and corporate business partners.[72] Thus, this context encompasses both the inter-organizational and the intra-organizational network. It is depicted in figure 4-8. By comparing the corporate and business network context it can be determined if the focal subsidiary has a rather external or a corporate orientation in its business operations. If both contexts are (almost) congruent the subsidiary has a clear corporate orientation. Most of its business relationships are with corporate actors; it receives input from and delivers output to HQs and sister units in the

---

[71] Apart from HQs that assign the subsidiary's role, it is also gained by the subsidiary itself and determined by its local environment (Birkinshaw/Hood 1998, pp. 774-775). A lot of research about roles of subsidiaries has been done in the field of International Business, see for example White/Poynter 1984, Bartlett/Ghoshal 1986, D'Cruz 1986, Jarillo/Martinez 1990, Gupta/Govindarajan 1991, Birkinshaw/Morrison 1995, Forsgren/Pedersen 1996, Surlemont 1996, Ferdows 1997, Forsgren/Pedersen 1997, Taggart 1997b, 1997a. For an overview see Schmid/Bäurle/Kutschker 1998, Schmid 2004.

[72] The usage of terms in the concept of the Embedded MNC is very confusing sometimes. While the "business network context" contains relationships to both external and corporate business partners the term "business network" is often used while talking about the inter-organizational context only, e.g. in the context of local adaptation and local embeddedness (Andersson/Forsgren 1996, p. 489, Forsgren/Holm/Johanson 2005, p. 104, see also Forsgren/Holm/Johanson 1992, p. 248). In this study, the term "business network" will be applied to the whole network of inter-organizational and intra-organizational actors while mainly specifying which of these two networks is referred to.

first place. On the other hand, the subsidiary has a rather external orientation if its corporate context and its business network context contain mainly different actors (Forsgren/Holm/Johanson 2005, pp. 93-95). Both inter- and intra-organizational business relationships exist between partners in the same region, in the same country and in different countries (Andersson/Forsgren 1995, p. 79).

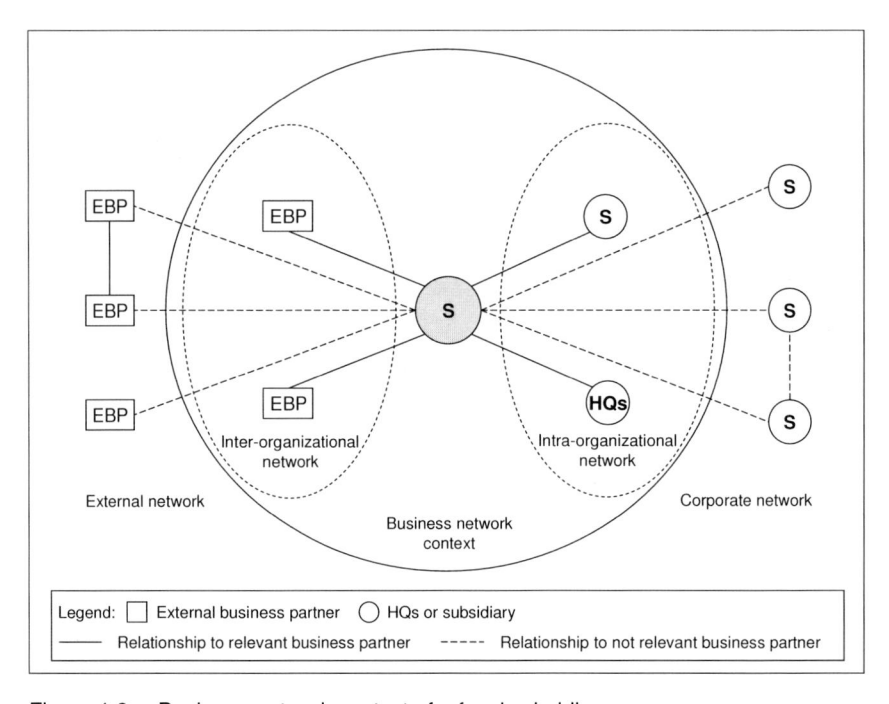

Figure 4-8: Business network context of a focal subsidiary

Apart from the number of external and corporate business relationships it can also be asked for the embeddedness of these relationships. Direct business relationships and indirectly connected business relationships which are considered relevant by the focal subsidiary play a role for its embeddedness. As explained in sub-section 4.3.1.1.2, the embeddedness can range from arm's length to embedded relationships as the two ends of a continuum (Forsgren/Holm/Johanson 2005, pp. 96-98). The embeddedness of a business relationship is defined by the breadth (i.e., the number of functional areas in which both business partners collaborate) and the depth (i.e., the mutual adaptation, mutual dependence, mutual criticality, mutual commitment, mutual trust, and mutual attention). Moreover, external embeddedness was empirically found to enhance the assessed importance of the subsidiary in its division and its influence on decision-making (Andersson/Forsgren 2000, p. 341).

Combining the number of external and corporate business partners and the embeddedness of the subsidiary's relationships to them, the subsidiary's embeddedness can be examined on the corporate and external level. Corporate embeddedness concerns exchange relationships to HQs and sister units that are more than just administrative links. Contrary to this, external embeddedness encompasses the subsidiary's exchanges with external business partners, i.e. actors outside organizational entity (Andersson/Forsgren 1996, p. 493). Thus, corporate embeddedness involves all the subsidiary's business relationships in the intra-organizational network which is part of the corporate and the business network context. External embeddedness relates to all the subsidiary's business relationships in its inter-organizational network which is part of the business network context. The terms of the intra-organizational and inter-organizational network focus on the actors whereas the corporate and external embeddedness focuses on the relationships between these actors. Both external and corporate business relationships can have a different focus regarding the functional area, e.g. purchasing, R&D, marketing, and logistics. Both inter- and intra-organizational business relationships exist between partners in the same region, in the same country and in different countries (Andersson/Forsgren 1995, p. 79). Thus, there are three dimensions which can be investigated in subsidiary's embeddedness: number of external and corporate business partners, embeddedness of business relationship to them and their location. As external business networks may be more or less embedded (see sub-section 4.3.1.2), the business networks of subsidiaries of the same MNC may be more or less embedded, too (Andersson/Forsgren/Holm 2001, p. 1016).

In both the inter-organizational network and in the intra-organizational network a subsidiary has a role. This role is determined by its position in the business network. The business network role has an impact on what a subsidiary can and will do in the relationships to its direct and connected partners. On the corporate level, the role implies how integrated the focal subsidiary is in the MNC. It also expresses how important the subsidiary is for the whole MNC and vice versa. Compared to the subsidiary's role in its inter-organizational network the intra-organizational role is assumed to be rather stable (Johanson/Pahlberg/Thilenius 1996, p. 187). Every business partner of the subsidiary has expectations of the subsidiary's behavior (see sub-section 4.3.1). If the subsidiary has mainly external business partners that it considers relevant for its own business operations it will adapt to them gradually in the course of time in order to reach local goals. Thus, it has an own strategy how to act in the local market. To do this it needs some autonomy in its operations as well as its strategy. HQs, however, have their own intentions when they create a subsidiary (Andersson/Forsgren 1996, p. 489, Andersson/Forsgren/Pedersen 2001, p. 6). They intend to coordinate the business operations of all the subsidiaries in order to achieve high profitability of the MNC as a whole. Therefore, they are often not willing to give the subsidiary as much autonomy as it wants. HQs rather tend to control the subsidiary (Andersson/Forsgren 1996, p. 489). It has been found that HQs' control over a focal subsidiary decreases when the external embeddedness of the subsidiary is high. On the other hand, control increases when the corporate embeddedness is high. The more the subsidiary's corporate and business network context deviate and the more embedded a subsidiary is in its external business relationship compared to its corporate business relationships the more probable is it that conflicts between the external and the corporate role the focal subsidiary arise (Forsgren/Holm/Johanson 2005, pp. 98-99).

Subsidiaries that have embedded business relationships both to external and corporate business partners may become centers of excellence. Researchers argue that the development of a subsidiary to a center of excellence is influenced by two factors. First, the internal resources and competences play an important role. For instance, a subsidiary may have a mandate for particular products and is responsible for the R&D, manufacturing and marketing of these products. Subsidiaries may also be specialized in R&D and have a corporate task for this functional area. It thus influences the corporate strategy in R&D. Second, the subsidiary may be embedded in an external business network of highly specialized firms with a great expertise in their field of work (Andersson/Forsgren 2000, pp. 330-331).[73] Hence, a focal subsidiary with R&D activities may have embedded relationships to highly specialized external

---

[73] Andersson and Forsgren actually discuss three factors. In addition to the two mentioned earlier, they mention the independence of subsidiaries from the other units of the MNC. If subsidiaries have enough resources to be self-sufficient, they may be defined as centers of excellence, too (Andersson/Forsgren 2000, p. 330). However, this understanding does not suit the context of the present thesis and is therefore left out.

business partners. Through these, it obtains knowledge and has the possibility to improve in its activities. When it builds business relationships to other units of the MNC and transfers its product innovations to them it becomes increasingly important for the firm. Hence, it evolves into a center of excellence.

4.3.2 Dynamics in Business Networks

Dynamics in business networks are based on dynamics in the business relationships that are part of the network. Business relationships are created for a number of reasons. Authors from the strategy research stream argue that in most cases a focal actor aims at getting access to resources like material, intellectual property or personnel via exchange. The actor does not develop these resources himself but needs them for conducting his operations. Business partners complement each other to some degree in their resources (Hardy/Phillips/Lawrence 2003, p. 324). On both the corporate and the external level, many of the business relationships probably never develop out of the arm's length level of embeddedness. They are pure exchange relationships.

On an external level, there are situations in which a certain amount of trust needs to be built before the first transaction is made. A somewhat embedded relationship is then a prerequisite for exchange. This mainly happens when the product which is exchanged is costly and is developed and manufactured specifically for a particular customer. The uncertainty that is inhered in the transaction is very high as is the case in industrial markets, for example (Forsgren/Holm/Johanson 2005, p. 96). In these transactions with high uncertainty, the focal actor often finds a business partner through his inter-organizational network. His direct and indirect business partners provide him with knowledge on potential business partners for the transaction. Apart from knowledge on resources and capabilities of potential business partners, he learns about experiences of other actors with potential business partners and thus ascertains their trustworthiness. Thus, the uncertainty of the focal actor regarding the selection of a business partner was found to be reduced through his business network (Gulati 1995, p. 627, Uzzi 1996, p. 679, Gulati/Gargiulo 1999, pp. 1444-1449, 1473, Venkatraman/Lee 2004, p. 887). Business partners also interact several times prior to the actual transaction in order to specify the details of both the product and the transaction. They intend to get to know each other better and build up mutual trust (e.g. Forsgren/Holm/Johanson 2005, p. 38). If more than one transaction is made between the partners the relationship may become even more embedded.

Another possibility is that a business relationship is created as arm's length relationship and develops into a more embedded one in the course of time (e.g. Forsgren/Holm/Johanson 2005, pp. 35-36). This may occur when the business relationship is considered important by the focal actor, for instance because of the business volume of the relationship, the financial return from that relationship or the technological development which is done in cooperation with the business partner (Håkansson/Snehota 1995, p. 11, Holm/Johanson/Thilenius 1995, p. 99). In order to improve the sequence of activities between partners, resources, products, processes, and administrative systems are modified. Thus, partners were empirically found to start to adapt to each other (e.g., Hallén/Johanson/Seyed-Mohamed 1991, Holm/Johanson/Thilenius 1995, p. 99, Andersson/Forsgren 1996). Adaptations may concern products or processes (Forsgren/Johanson 1992b, p. 4). These adaptations may be more or less specific to one particular business partner and they may refer to different areas. The more adaptations are made to each other, the more specific they are and the more functional areas they affect (depth of business relationship) the higher is the interdependence between partners, for example concerning planning, technical or economic activities (see sub-section 4.3.1.1.2; Forsgren/Olsson 1992, Holm/Johanson/Thilenius 1995, pp. 99-100). The relationship becomes more critical for the focal firm than other business relationships. Ending it would have severe consequences for the business partners (Ciabuschi 2004, Ståhl 2004, Persson 2006, Hallin 2008a).[74] When a business relationship is important for both partners, they are likely to adapt specifically to each other. This may occur quite at the beginning of the relationship in order to match the resources and products of one partner to the needs of the other one. It will especially be the case when a certain amount of embeddedness is needed before the first transaction takes place as discussed earlier. In most business relationships adaptations will only occur when several transactions have already been made. This is due to two reasons: First, adaptations involve costs of

---

[74] The measure of substitutability of a business partner was applied in the questionnaire that the thesises of the four authors used; see table 4-2 in section 4.4.

changing resources, products, processes and administrative systems. These costs will only be taken into account when both business partners are satisfied with past transactions and are sure to continue their relationship. Second, business conditions for one or both business partners may change so that adaptations become necessary (Hallén/Johanson/Seyed-Mohamed 1991, p. 138). Thus, adaptations might aim at reducing costs or the creation of innovations by linking knowledge and activities differently, for example (Håkansson/Johanson 1993, p. 17). The adaptation process is most often mutual. However, one partner may adapt more to the other one than vice versa. The depth of adaptations made by each partner is assumed to depend on the power structure of the relationship (Hallén/Johanson/Seyed-Mohamed 1991, pp. 145-146; for more details on power in relationships see sub-section 4.3.3.3.2). The sum of adaptations made by both business partners may serve as one measure for the embeddedness of the business relationship.

Increasing embeddedness of business relationships also shows in the development of trust. In the frequent interactions between business partners, resources, products and knowledge about each other regarding needs, capabilities and strategies are exchanged. If both business partners are satisfied with the interactions, the depth of the business relationship may increase. Mutual trust grows and partners are ready to make further commitments to the business relationship. Commitments are made in the form of investments in the business relationship. Researchers empirically found that commitments are made in cyclical actions; each actor's commitment depends on the perceived commitment of the partner. Thus, commitment increases in alternate little steps (Anderson/Weitz 1992, Forsgren/Holm/Johanson 1995, p. 23, Blankenburg Holm/Eriksson/Johanson 1999, p. 472). Actors pay more attention to the needs and interests of the business partner which affects future interactions. Thus, the embeddedness of a business relationship and the interactions which happen in it influence each other (Forsgren/Holm/Johanson 1995, p. 23).

Thus, changes in a business relationship happen on both dimensions of business relationships: the depth and the breadth. Within the depth, characteristics include mutual adaptations (number and specificity of adaptations), mutual commitment, mutual dependence, mutual criticality, mutual trust and mutual attention paid to the interests of each other. Of course, these characteristics are not independent. However, it is assumed that a more holistic picture of the development of a relationship can be drawn if more attributes are included in the study.

Although it seems clear that embeddedness of business relationships may also be destroyed not much has been written about it. Trust can be damaged when one partner feels abused (for an exception see Uzzi 1997, pp. 44-45).

4.3.3 Flows in the Network

As stated earlier (see sub-section 4.3.1.1.2), business relationships are built in interactions between business partners. These interactions consist of episodes in which three types of elements are exchanged between business partners. They are also called flows between the business partners: the product or service flows, knowledge flows and social flows.[75] The social flows may be differentiated into flows of power and flows of trust (e.g. Hallén/Johanson/Seyed-Mohamed 1991, pp. 30-31, Schmid/Schurig/Kutschker 2002, pp. 50-51).[76] In figure 4-9, the four types of flows are depicted and they will be presented in the following sub-sections.[77]

4.3.3.1 Flows of Products and Services

Although the exchange of products or services is the basis of business relationships (IMP-Group 1990, p. 13), not much is said on flows of products or services in the concept of the Embedded MNC. Several dimensions were proposed in order to evaluate product flows: value, frequency, complexity, homogeneity or service content (Forsgren et al. 1995, p. 23). However, they were not applied in studies of the con-

---

[75] In earlier publications, financial flows are described in addition to the three types named here (IMP-Group 1990, pp. 12-13).
[76] Sometimes, social flows are understood as flows of trust while flows of power are regarded as another type of flows (Hadjikhani/Thilenius 2005, pp. 23-31).
[77] Even if the types of flows are interdependent, a particular business network may look very differently depending on the type of flow that is focused on. For example, focusing on product exchange much more arm's length relationships will be included in the network than focusing on flows of trust. According to Thorelli (1986), flows of power and knowledge are more important for understanding a particular network than financial flows or flows of products and services (Thorelli 1986, p. 39).

cept of the Embedded MNC. The experience of business partners with this flow affects other flows as well, for instance the flow of trust and knowledge (IMP-Group 1990, p. 13).

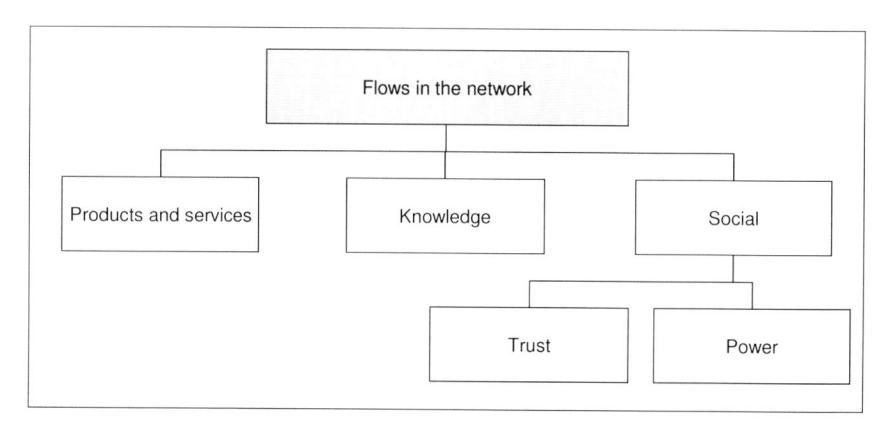

Figure 4-9: Flows in the network

4.3.3.2 Flows of Knowledge

Authors of the concept of the Embedded MNC and former concepts have done a lot of research on knowledge transfer within the MNC and between the MNC and its external business partners. Thereby, it was found that knowledge transfer is easier within MNCs than between firms. However, problems of knowledge transfer can also arise within MNCs (Andersson/Forsgren/Holm 2001, pp. 1018-1019). A central problem of knowledge transfers is the absorptive capacity of the receiving unit (Andersson/Forsgren/Holm 2001, pp. 1015-1017).[78] The absorptive capacity is necessary for the focal subsidiary to obtain knowledge from its external business partners and hence, gain an advantage from its external embeddedness (Andersson 2003, p. 426).

Within MNCs, two barriers to knowledge transfer are particularly important. The first is the relationship specificity of knowledge. Often, sending sub-units acquire their

---

[78] For more details on absorptive capacity see sub-section 4.5.2.4.

knowledge in a business relationship with an external business partner. This knowledge may be rather specific to the relationship and context of the sending sub-unit. Thus, the receiving unit may have problems applying the knowledge from the sending sub-unit. The second problem is that experts at the sending unit need to take part in the knowledge transfer between sub-units. These are most often the same experts who are involved in the development of knowledge of the sending unit. Thus, time and cost issues arise in the sending unit. It has a trade-off problem between the commitment of its experts in development and transfer of knowledge (Andersson 2003, p. 430). Inter-unit knowledge flows involve experts and managers at different levels. Knowledge flows are generated in repeated face-to-face meetings and other ways of communication (Holm/Johanson/Thilenius 1995, pp. 99-100).

In general, the transferability of knowledge depends on the codifiability of knowledge, characteristics of the sending and receiving unit and the relationship between them. Tacit, idiosyncratic, specific and non-codified knowledge is most difficult to transfer (Andersson 2003, p. 429). Acquiring tacit knowledge from a business partner that is embedded in his social context is called active learning. It is found that an embedded business relationship leads to the transfer of tacit knowledge (Johanson/Pahlberg/ Thilenius 1996, p. 186, Andersson/Forsgren/Pedersen 2001, p. 8, Andersson 2003, p. 428, Uzzi/Lancaster 2003, p. 385). Passive learning takes place when objective and observable facts like the price of products are learned. Arm's length relationships suffice to transfer this explicit kind of knowledge (Andersson/Forsgren/Pedersen 2001, p. 8, Andersson 2003, p. 428). Arm's length relationships do not require high investments to create and maintain the relationships. Thus, the focal actor can have many arm's length relationships. Thus, he may receive a lot of explicit knowledge which is not specific to him and may be hardly novel (Uzzi/Lancaster 2003, p. 385). An embedded relationship increases the amount of knowledge that is shared between business partners (Andersson/Björkman/Forsgren 2005, p. 522). An actor needs both types of knowledge in order to operate (Uzzi/Lancaster 2003, p. 385).[79] Embeddedness literature also emphasizes the effect of embeddedness of relationships on the tacitness of knowledge (Uzzi 1996, p. 678). Apart from tacitness, shared knowledge in embedded relationships is also more detailed and holistic (Uzzi 1997,

---

[79] For more details on characteristics of knowledge see sub-section 4.5.2.1.

p. 45). Further details of the characteristics of knowledge were described in literature. They are depicted in more detail in sub-section 4.5.2.1.

External embeddedness of a subsidiary enhances its capability development and also supports the development of capabilities of the whole MNC (e.g. Andersson 2003, p. 436, Schmid/Schurig 2003, pp. 773-774). Because capability development is a precondition of innovativeness, external embeddedness of subsidiaries increases their innovative potential. Furthermore, the innovativeness of a subsidiary increases when it shares knowledge with other units of the MNC (Tsai/Ghoshal 1998, p. 473). External embeddedness of a focal subsidiary is the main impact factor of its knowledge transfer to HQs. Corporate embeddedness, subsidiary's dependence on HQs and HQs' relations with subsidiary's external network were also found to affect the knowledge transfer from a subsidiary to HQs (Forsgren/Holm/Johanson 2005, p. 164).

Within the concept of the Embedded MNC a model on corporate and external knowledge transfer was developed. Referring to Richardson (Richardson 1972), similar and complementary activities of sub-units and external business partners are differentiated. Activities of business partners are defined as similar when the same capabilities are required to process them. On the corporate level, this is the case with two R&D subsidiaries, for instance. External business partners with similar capabilities are competitors. In opposition, activities are complementary when they need to be coordinated, for instance when they are undertaken at different stages of a process. External business partners with complementary activities are suppliers or customers, for instance, while corporate business partners with complementary activities are a production and an R&D subsidiary, for example (Forsgren/Holm/Johanson 2005, p. 171). As is depicted in figure 4-10, product innovations are supposed to be transferred between sub-units or external business partners with similar activities. Problems could mainly arrive because of lacking absorptive capacity and motivation of the receiving unit. In opposition, business partners with complementary activities collaborate in problem solving. Joint problem solving is supported by an embedded business relationship. Distrust is the major barrier to mutual learning (Forsgren/Holm/Johanson 2005, p. 181).[80]

4.3.3.3 Social Exchange

4.3.3.3.1 Flows of Trust

In the concept of the Embedded MNC, mutual trust[81] is one of the main characteristics of an embedded business relationship. It is mentioned as one of the basic attributes that is employed to identify an embedded relationship (see sub-section 4.3.1.1.2). However, trust is also described as one of the social flows that run between business partners (Hallén/Johanson/Seyed-Mohamed 1991, pp. 30-31). The other attributes of embedded relationships are not explicitly mentioned in exchange flows.

Not much detail is given by the authors of the concept of the Embedded MNC about the flows of trust, however. Trust between business partners is built in order to reduce uncertainty in working together and link partners on a long-term basis. The development of trust depends on experiences with the flows of products, knowledge and power (IMP-Group 1990, p. 13). It evolves over time when mutually and sequentially partners demonstrate trustworthiness. They can do so by committing themselves to the relationship (Hallén/Johanson/Seyed-Mohamed 1991, p. 139). Trust is

---

[80] This model can be criticized for a number of reasons. Above all, it seems quite arbitrary. Just two examples are discussed here. First, there is no reason why product innovations should be transferred mainly between business partners with similar capabilities. Once the product innovation is completed, it needs to be transferred to other units which market the product innovation. Second, it is also not clear why the embeddedness of business relationships is mentioned as the critical factor for learning in cases of complementary activities only. As was described, the embeddedness of business relationships encompasses several attributes like trust, mutual adaptations and mutual dependence. These factors probably play a role in collaborations between similar business partners as well. For these contradictions, the model will not particularly be considered in the empirical study.

[81] Trust is a construct that is extensively examined by social sciences. Countless definitions of trust exist. In this thesis, trust is basically understood as "...expectations, assumptions, or beliefs about the likelihood that another's future actions will be beneficial, favorable, or at least not detrimental to one's interests. ... As a general positive attitude toward another social entity, trust acts as a guideline, influencing one's interpretation of social behaviors within a relationship" (Robinson 1996, p. 576).

one precondition for collaborating in product development projects (Andersson/Forsgren/Pedersen 2001, p. 11).

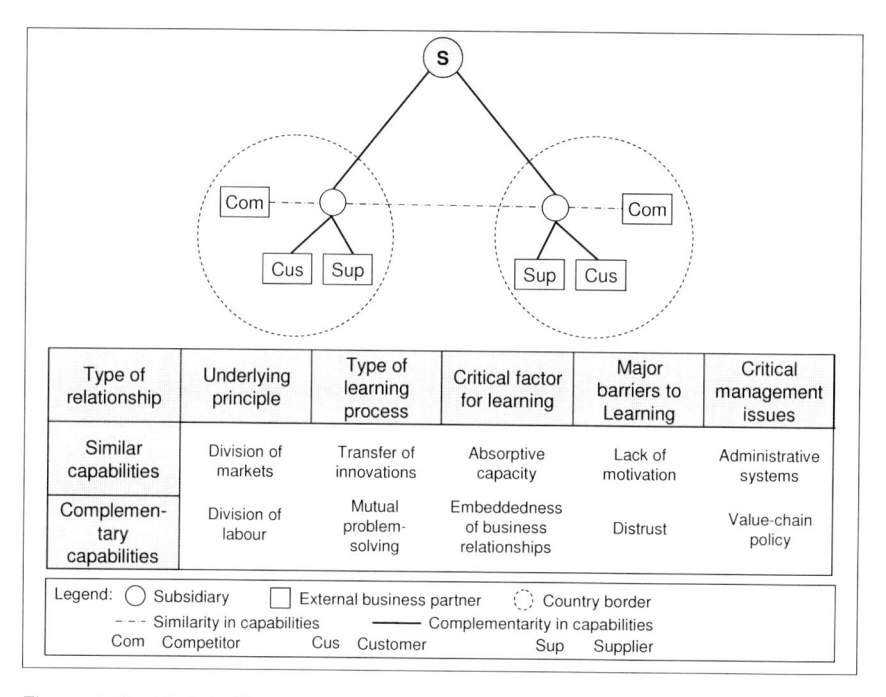

Type of relationship	Underlying principle	Type of learning process	Critical factor for learning	Major barriers to Learning	Critical management issues
Similar capabilities	Division of markets	Transfer of innovations	Absorptive capacity	Lack of motivation	Administrative systems
Complementary capabilities	Division of labour	Mutual problem-solving	Embeddedness of business relationships	Distrust	Value-chain policy

Legend: ○ Subsidiary   ☐ External business partner   ⃝ Country border
       --- Similarity in capabilities   —— Complementarity in capabilities
       Com Competitor   Cus Customer   Sup Supplier

Figure 4-10: Model of intra-organizational and inter-organizational knowledge transfer
Source: Adopted from Forsgren/Holm/Johanson 2005, pp. 179, 181.

4.3.3.3.2 Flows of Power

Power is a relational concept. Taking this view, the authors of the concept of the Embedded MNC are in line with the social exchange theory (Forsgren/Johanson 1992a, p. 24, Andersson/Forsgren 1996, p. 490). They propose three sources of power[82]: hierarchical power, structural or systemic power and resource power. Hierarchical power is only exercised within the corporate network. According to this type of power,

---

[82] In early publications, attributes of power are subsumed under the atmosphere of a business relationship (e.g. IMP-Group 1990, pp. 18-19).

HQs have more power than subsidiaries (e.g. Forsgren/Holm/Johanson 2005, p. 128). Structural and resource power concern both the inter-organizational and the intra-organizational business network of a focal sub-unit. Structural power includes the involvement of a sub-unit in the MNC and its functional interdependence with other units of the MNC. Thus, structural power is deduced from the position of the sub-unit in its inter-organizational and intra-organizational business network according to measures like centrality. Within the MNC, this position may be more important than that of units which are higher in hierarchy (Forsgren/Pahlberg 1992, pp. 42-43). Resource power draws on the resource dependence theory (Pfeffer/Salancik 1978). By controlling critical resources, a sub-unit gains power in its relationship to other sub-units or external business partners (Hallén/Johanson/Seyed-Mohamed 1991, p. 140). Resource control may also cause a high degree of independence of a sub-unit, i.e. the possibility to avoid control from higher hierarchical levels like HQs (Forsgren/ Pahlberg 1992, pp. 42-43).

The concept of the Embedded MNC draws mainly on the resource dependence theory when talking about power in business relationships (e.g. Andersson/Forsgren 1996). Some subsidiaries obtain control over critical resources in their external business relationships. This way, they may gain more power than divisional HQs, for instance. Thus, on the basis of resource control, flows within the MNC are multidirectional. As in the example, they may run from hierarchically lower to higher sub-units, between hierarchically similar sub-units (i.e. between subsidiaries) and from higher to lower sub-units, for instance from HQs to subsidiaries (Forsgren/Holm/Johanson 1992, p. 249, Forsgren/Johanson 1992a, pp. 24-25).

4.4 Criticism on the Concept of the Embedded MNC

After presenting the concept of the Embedded MNC, a critical evaluation will conclude this section. Three points will be focused on: (1) the usage of terms, (2) the theoretical basis of the EMNC, (3) the focus on Business-to-Business industries and customer and supplier relationships and (4) the measurement in empirical studies of the concept of the Embedded MNC.

(1) It has already been mentioned earlier that terms are sometimes not employed consistently by the authors of the concept of the Embedded MNC. One example is the usage of the term "business network". Conceptually, the authors state that the business network encompasses the relevant inter-organizational and intra-organizational business relationships of a focal subsidiary (Forsgren/Holm/Johanson 2005, pp. 93-94). However, the term is often employed in the inter-organizational context only, e.g. in the context of local adaptation and local embeddedness (Forsgren/Holm/Johanson 1992, p. 248, Andersson/Forsgren 1996, p. 489, Forsgren/Holm/Johanson 2005, p. 104).

Apart from the inconsistency in usage, terms are often not clearly defined. One example which was given earlier is to define which kind of firm is meant when talking about Embedded MNCs (see sub-section 4.3.1.2). Terms like mutual orientation, mutual commitment and mutual trust are used by the authors in order to describe the depth of business relationships (see sub-section 4.3.1.1.2). However, definitions of these terms are not given.

(2) From a theoretical perspective, the concept of the Embedded MNC is not well grounded in theory. For example, authors of the concept reflect on business partners of subsidiaries. However, they do not refer to stakeholder literature. This is surprising as stakeholder literature analyzes the importance of different groups of actors (e.g. customers, suppiers, stockholders, employees or the government) or discusses ways to identify relevant stakeholders for a focal actor (e.g. Mitchell/Agle/Wood 1997, Elias/Cavana/Jackson 2002). Thus, researchers from the stream of the Embedded MNC (or former concepts) could gain valuable insights from stakeholder literature.[83] In the present contribution, stakeholder literature is addressed in order to be able to describe relevant stakeholder groups in the empirical study (see sub-section 4.5.1).

(3) The concept of the Embedded MNC evolved out of former network approaches of the IMP Group. This group started by studying customer or supplier relationships in Industrial Marketing. Over the 30 years of research on business relationships and networks the authors developed their concepts further. In their publications, they now talk about business relationships in general and do not limit their considerations on

---

[83] However, it must be stated that stakeholder literature itself is not well-founded in theory either.

customer or supplier relationships or specific industries (e.g. Blankenburg Holm/Eriksson/Johanson 1999, Andersson/Björkman/Forsgren 2005, Forsgren/Holm/Johanson 2005). However, looking at the empirical studies listed in table 4-2, it becomes clear that they still almost exclusively analyze customer and sometimes supplier relationships (e.g. Andersson/Forsgren 2000, p. 337, Andersson/Forsgren/Holm 2001, p. 1021). This was even proposed by Håkansson and Henders who stated that the most important stakeholders in technological development were customers and suppliers (Håkansson/Henders 1992, p. 38).

Study	Stakeholders	Variable	Measures	Scale
Hallén/ Johanson/ Seyed-Mohamed 1991	• Customers • Suppliers	• Adaptation of firm to business partners • Dependence of firm on business partners	Adaptation of firm to customer • Adaptation regarding products • Adaptation regarding production processes • Adaptation regarding production planning Adaptations of firm to supplier • Adaptation regarding products • Adaptation regarding production processes • Adaptation regarding stockholding Dependence of firm to customer • Importance of customer as percentage of sales of the overall sales of a product • Buyer concentration (supplier's sales of a product to its three largest customers as a percentage of its total sales) Dependence of firm to supplier • Importance of supplier as percentage or purchases of the overall purchases of a product • Supplier's market share of a product in a particular country that is important to the firm	Three-level scale (none, small and large) for adaptation measures

Study	Stakeholders	Variable	Measures	Scale
Andersson/ Forsgren 1996[84]	• Customers • Suppliers • Others	• Subsidiary's embeddedness in its business network	• Adaptation of subsidiary to business partner concerning product technology • Adaptation of subsidiary to business partner concerning production technology	Five-point-Likert scale
Blankenburg Holm/ Eriksson/ Johanson 1999[85]	• Customers • Suppliers	• Mutual commitment • Mutual dependence	Mutual commitment • Investments of firm in business relationship to business partner • Investments of business partner in business relationship to focal firm Mutual dependence • Effect of loss of business partner to focal firm • Effect of loss of focal firm to business partner	
Andersson/ Forsgren 2000	• Customers • Suppliers	• Subsidiary's external technological embeddedness	• Adaptation of subsidiary to business partner concerning product and production technology	Five-point-Likert scale
Andersson/ Forsgren/ Pedersen 2001	• Customers • Suppliers • Others	• Subsidiary's external technological embeddedness	• Adaptation of subsidiary to business partner concerning product technology • Adaptation of subsidiary to business partner concerning production technology • Adaptation of business partner to subsidiary concerning product technology • Adaptation of business partner to subsidiary concerning production technology	Five-point-Likert scale
Andersson/ Forsgren/ Holm 2001	• Customers • Suppliers	• Subsidiary's external technical embeddedness	• Adaptation of subsidiary to business partner concerning product technology • Adaptation of subsidiary to business partner concerning production technology • Number of functional areas involved with business partner (sales, purchasing, production, R&D, administration and subsidiary top management)	Five-point-Likert scale

---

[84] In this study, the authors aimed at measuring structural embeddedness in addition to relational embeddedness of the subsidiary asking for interdependences between direct business partners. This could not be done in a valid and reliable way so that this aspect of embeddedness was left out (Andersson/Forsgren 1996, pp. 491-492, 497). It would not be important in the context of this study anyway because this study only considers relational embeddedness.

[85] In this study, respondents were asked about their connected business relationships as well. As this refers to structural rather than relational embeddedness, these measures are not reported here.

Study	Stakeholders	Variable	Measures	Scale
Andersson/ Forsgren/ Holm 2002	• Customers • Suppliers	• Subsidiary's external embeddedness (technical & business embeddedness)	• Adaptation of subsidiary to business partner concerning product technology • Adaptation of subsidiary to business partner concerning production technology • Adaptation of subsidiary to business partner concerning its way of doing business • Number of functional areas involved with business partner (sales, purchasing, production, R&D, administration and subsidiary top management)	Five-point-Likert scale
Andersson 2003	• Customers • Suppliers	• Subsidiary's external technical embeddedness	• Adaptation of subsidiary to business partner concerning product technology • Adaptation of subsidiary to business partner concerning production technology • Importance of business partner to subsidiary's product development • Importance of business partner to subsidiary's production process development	Five-point-Likert scale
Andersson/ Björkman/ Forsgren/ 2005	• Unspecified	• Subsidiary's external embeddedness	• Adaptation of subsidiary to business partner concerning product technology • Adaptation of subsidiary to business partner concerning production technology • Adaptation of subsidiary to business partner concerning standard operating procedure • Adaptation of subsidiary to business partner concerning business practice	Seven-point-Likert scale

Study	Stakeholders	Variable	Measures	Scale
Ciabuschi 2004, Ståhl 2004, Persson 2006, Hallin 2008a[86]	• Customers • Suppliers • Others	• External and corporate embeddedness of innovative subsidiary	Cooperative contact regarding: • Technological issues • Market potentials • Financial resources • Coordination of development process Degree of mutual adaptation for developing product innovation regarding: • Basic research, technical development, production, marketing, purchasing, service Number of functional areas involved with business partner: • General management, basic research, technical development, production, marketing, purchasing, service Others: • Participation of business partner in product innovation process • Level of competence provided by business partner • Specifying requests from business partner • Initiatives from business partner • Support from business partner • Extent to which innovation was developed in facilities of business partner • Usage of communication instruments • Close business relationship in terms of sales and purchase of goods and services • Adaptation of resources and activities to business partner • Long-term importance of business partner • Substitutability of business partner	Seven-point-Likert scale

Table 4-2: Measures of the embeddedness of business relationships used in existing studies on the concept of the Embedded MNC and prior concepts of the IMP-Group

---

[86] All four authors wrote their dissertations based on the TIME (Transfer of Innovations in Multinational Enterprises) project. Therefore, they all used the same questionnaire that includes the listed measures. However, they apply only few and varying measures in their studies (Ciabuschi 2004, p. 78, Ståhl 2004, p. 269, Persson 2006, p. 93, Hallin 2008a, p. 81).

In product development, their research also mainly limits to customer or supplier relationships. They focus on a special type of relationship development: The focal actor develops an embedded business relationship to a particular customer over time. When the focal actor starts to develop a new product this customer gives valuable input in the product innovation process, for instance by transferring knowledge to the focal actor about market demands or by testing prototypes of the new product and giving advice on necessary improvements (e.g. Forsgren/Holm/Johansson 2005, pp. 29-45). However, this mainly applies to business relationships in Business-to-Business industries. In these industries, there are a limited number of customers that play an important role for the firm. Products are quite specific and costly. In Business-to-Customer industries, however, many customers buy the same products. It is not clear whether some of them play a major role in the product innovation process. Product innovation processes consist of different stages. Probably customers do not play the most important role within each stage of the product innovation process. Rather, they might affect the first stage of the process but not be influential in the later ones. This is one of the questions that are approached in this study.

(4) The authors of the concept of the Embedded MNC describe the embeddedness of business relationships according to several attributes. They propose two dimensions: the breadth and the depth of business relationships. The breadth includes the number of functional areas that are involved with a particular business partner. The depth of business relationships encompasses the attributes of mutual trust, mutual commitment, mutual adaptations, mutual attention, mutual dependences on a technical, planning, knowledge, social, economic and legal level, criticality and investments in the business relationship. Surprisingly, in their empirical studies, the authors strongly focus on the measure of adaptations as is shown in table 4-2.[87] Mostly, they do not even measure mutual adaptations but only adaptations of the focal actor. In one article they stated that adaptation links to mutual criticality, interdependence, mutual trust and mutual commitment and hence can be taken as a measure of these variables (Andersson/Forsgren 1996, p. 497). However, the assumption is not discussed further or confirmed by an empirical study. The attributes "attention" and "commitment" are not included in the discussion. In several studies, they amend ad-

---

[87] The frequent usage of adaptations as a measure of the embeddedness of business relationships can be explained by the fact that several studies are based on the same data. Why only this measure was employed can not be clarified, though.

aptation with another measure, for instance investments, substitutability or the number of functional areas. The attribute of trust is never measured, however. This is surprising as it is proposed as the basic attribute of embedded relationships. Hence, the embeddedness of business relationships which is conceptually described as a very complex phenomenon is measured in a very simplified way, mainly by asking for one way adaptations to the business partner.

4.5 Extending and Refining the Concept of the Embedded MNC

After having presented and criticized the concept of the Embedded MNC, it is refined and extended in the following sub-sections. In sub-section 4.5.1, research on stakeholders will be presented in order to extend the view of the concept of the Embedded MNC. In sub-section 4.5.2, flows of knowledge will be described in more depth than is done by the concept of the Embedded MNC. Characteristics of knowledge (4.5.2.1) and knowledge flows (4.5.2.2) will be defined and the process (4.5.2.3) and problems of knowledge transfer (4.5.2.4) will be explained.

4.5.1 Stakeholders

Stakeholders are "... any group or individual who can affect or is affected by the achievement of the firm's objectives" (Freeman 1984, p. 46). Stakeholders provide a service to the focal actor and get something in return (Baden 2001, p. 398). The number of stakeholder groups[88] that are proposed in literature ranges from four to thirteen (Körnert 2003, p. 103). Irrespective of the number of stakeholder groups that are distinguished, two dimensions may be analyzed: corporate and external stakeholder groups and primary and secondary stakeholder groups. Regarding corporate stakeholder groups, shareholders, top management and employees of the firm are often mentioned (Schmid 1997, p. 633). Taking the perspective of a focal subsidiary,

---

[88] When talking about stakeholders, different perspectives may be taken. The term "stakeholders" may refer to single actors or groups of actors with a similar relationship to the focal actor regarding their interests, power and risk to the focal actor (Schmid 1996b, p. 6). In this thesis, the term "stakeholders" refers to single actors while a similar group of actors like customers or employees is called "stakeholder group".

other sub-units of the MNC which it affects or by which it is affected, can be considered stakeholders as well. Common external stakeholder groups are suppliers, customers, investors, universities, private research institutions and the society. Primary stakeholders are those actors that have a direct, obvious and current influence on the focal actor. Formal agreements or contracts between both actors exist. Secondary stakeholders are those that only have an indirect or weak effect on the focal actor at a given point in time (Schmid 1997, pp. 633-634). It is the task of the focal actor's top management to balance the interests of its stakeholders (Schmid 1998, p. 7). This has to be done in a way that the focal actor keeps access to critical resources and demands and performance of a business partner are balanced (Hill 1997, p. 416, Brink 2000, p. 97). The dimensions of stakeholders are depicted in figure 4-11. Few primary stakeholders, both external and corporate, are the focus of the empirical study.

Corporate Stakeholders	E.g. headquarters, other subsidiary	E.g. other subsidiary
External Stakeholders	E.g. customer, private research institution	E.g. supplier, society
	Primary Stakeholders	Secondary Stakeholders

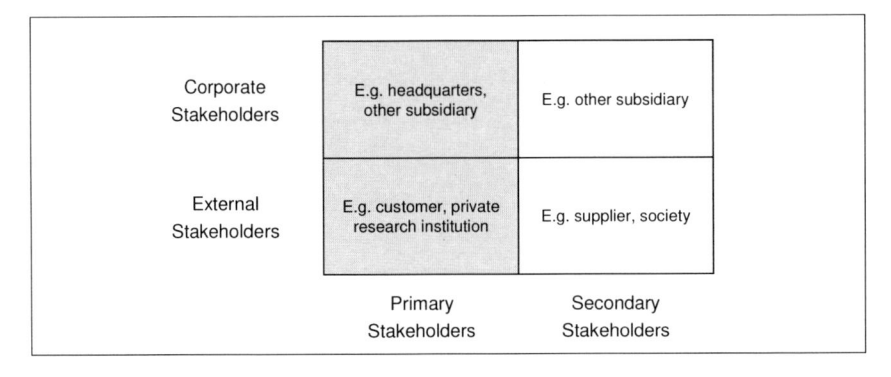

Figure 4-11: Dimensions of stakeholder types

In order to identify stakeholders of a focal actor, potential stakeholders who affect the focal actor or are affected by him are identified. Then, these actors are assessed concerning their interests, power and taken risk in relation to the focal actor. In a last step, the relevance of these groups to the focal actor is evaluated (Schmid 1998, pp. 223-224). The stakeholders may be identified concerning the focal actor in general or with respect to a particular strategic issue or project (Elias/Cavana/Jackson 2002, p. 303). In both cases, stakeholders do not stay the same but change throughout time. Thus, they can only be identified at a particular point in time. In the dynamic view of stakeholders, urgency is added to the criteria of power and legitimacy to define stakeholders that are important at the moment.[89] Urgency expresses whether potential stakeholders have an actual relationship to the focal actor (Mitchell/Agle/Wood 1997, p. 859). To these definitive stakeholders, as Mitchell and his co-authors call stakeholders that comply with all three criteria, the focal actor must give particular attention (Mitchell/Agle/Wood 1997, p. 878).

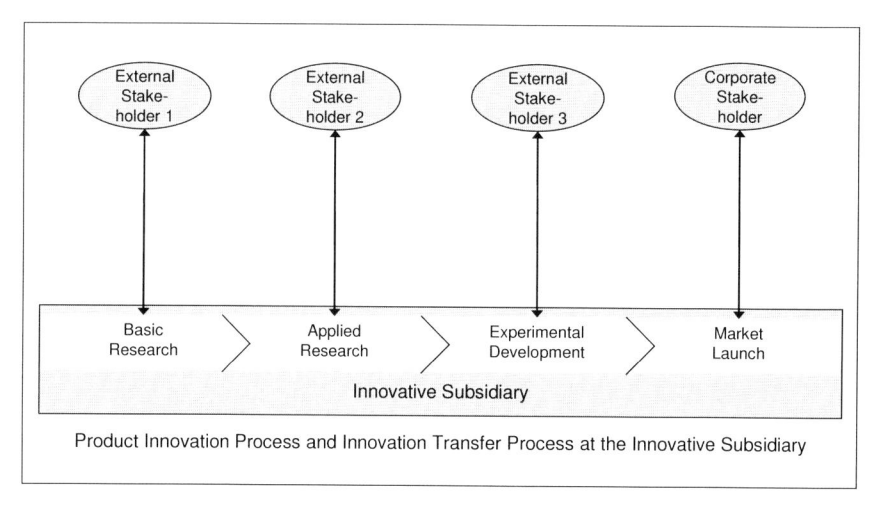

Figure 4-12: Model of collaboration with external and corporate stakeholders during the product innovation process and the innovation transfer process in this contribution

In the present thesis, the collaboration of innovative subsidiaries with their external business partners throughout the product innovation process is examined. The creation of a product innovation is a particular project in which the innovative sub-unit needs to pay attention to its external stakeholders. External stakeholder groups that may be relevant during the product innovation process are suppliers, customers, competitors, private research institutions or universities, for instance (Helble/Chong 2004, p. 606). The relevance of particular stakeholders may change throughout time when different stages of the product innovation process are subsequently gone through. The most important stakeholders in these stages may be but do not necessarily need to be the same actor. Thus, as is depicted in figure 4-12, in the empirical study it will be analyzed whether different (groups of) external stakeholders are most

---

[89] Power and legitimacy integrate the criteria of interests of a stakeholder to the focal actor and risk taken by him in the relationship to the focal actor (Mitchell/Agle/Wood 1997, pp. 861-862).

relevant to the innovative subsidiary as a partner in different stages of the innovation process. Furthermore, it will be examined which groups of external stakeholders are particularly relevant in the product innovation process. Finally, it will be revealed which corporate stakeholders play a role in the transfer of the finalized product innovation.

4.5.2 Flows of Knowledge

4.5.2.1 Characteristics of Knowledge

When looking at characteristics of knowledge, the first thing to do is, of course, to try to define the term "knowledge" and explain the difference to other terms like "information". Although (or maybe: because) the terms are extensively used and a lot of research on knowledge management has been done in the past no definition has been agreed on (Bick 2004, pp. 11-13). (1) Often, the hierarchy of data, information and knowledge is employed in order to explain the difference between the terms. Data are equalized to facts and observations. Data in a particular context are labeled information. When information is employed to make decisions, knowledge is created which serves as a basis for peoples' actions to achieve desired results (Davenport et al. 2001, pp. 119-120). However, these definitions have been criticized as not being mutually exclusive and useful in a practical context (Braganza 2004, pp. 347-348). (2) Other authors state that knowledge may be differentiated into information and know-how. Information is then a "factual statement" while know-how is a description of a process, i.e. the explanation of how activities are performed. Thus, information corresponds to declarative knowledge while know-how relates to procedural knowledge (Kogut/Zander 1993, p. 631, Zander/Kogut 1995, p. 77). (3) Yet another definition is that information is understood as flows of messages by which existing knowledge of an actor is changed, either by adding to it or by restructuring it (Machlup 1983, Nonaka 1994, p. 15). In the present study, knowledge is not subdivided into different kinds. It is not believed that they could be identified clearly. Neither is made a difference between the stock of knowledge and the flow of information. Instead, the term "knowledge" is used in every context.

Authors have categorized knowledge in different ways. The attribute which is mostly used is the tacitness of knowledge. Tacitness of knowledge means that actors "... can know more than (they; S.H.) can tell" (Polanyi 1966, p. 4).[90] Tacit knowledge involves individual experience and personal belief and values (Nonaka/Takeuchi 1995, p. viii). Thus, it is highly abstract and requires the involvement of the teacher in the learning process (Dhanaraj et al. 2004, p. 430). The other end of the continuum is explicit knowledge. It has a high degree of codifiability and can thus be easily transmitted in formal language, for instance via grammatical statements, mathematical formulas, manuals or blueprints (Nonaka/Takeuchi 1995, p. viii, Dhanaraj et al. 2004, p. 430). If knowledge is not codifiable in formal language, another possibility to transfer knowledge is to teach knowledge by showing how to carry out an activity (Polanyi 1966, pp. 4-5). Thus, tacit knowledge can not be shared as easily as explicit knowledge. More tacit knowledge may be transmitted by the exchange of specialists (Kogut/Zander 1993, p. 631).

Other authors added attributes of knowledge which influence its transferability. Winter proposed four dimensions. He suggested observability of knowledge, complexity of knowledge and system dependence of knowledge apart from tacitness. He suggests that the tacitness characteristic ranges from tacitness at one end of the continuum to articulability of knowledge at the other end. This feature may be split into teachability and the fact of knowledge being articulated (Winter 1987, pp. 170-173). The five attributes of tacit knowledge are listed and explained in table 4-3.[91] Two characteristics from embeddedness literature are added (see below).

---

[90] The differentiation between tacit and explicit knowledge goes back to Michael Polanyi (1966). As a funny note on the side, Michael Polanyi is the brother of Karl Polanyi who is considered the originator of the embeddedness concept (see section 4.2).

[91] Kogut and Zander understand the characteristics of codifiability (which is similar to Winter's articulatedness), complexity and teachability as underlying attributes of tacitness (Kogut/Zander 1993, pp. 626-627). They do not employ the observability and system dependence features in their study.

Characteristics of knowledge	Explanation
Articulability (opposition of tacitness) → split into articulatedness and teachability[92]	"Fully articulable knowledge ... can be communicated from its possessor to another person in symbolic form, and the recipient of the communication becomes as much "in the know" as the originator" (Winter 1987, p. 171).
• Articulatedness	Articulated knowledge is knowledge that is in fact articulated, i.e. that is documented in an up-to-date modus (Winter 1987, p. 172).
• Teachability	Knowledge is teachable but not articulated when it can be shown to the pupil by a teacher. The teacher performs the activity and/or watches the pupil perform and gives feedback on the performance (Winter 1987, p. 171).
Observability	Knowledge is observable when it becomes obvious by using it. An example is the design of a product which is disclosed once the product is used (Winter 1987, p. 172).
Complexity	Complexity of knowledge expresses how much knowledge is required to describe the particular piece of knowledge (Winter 1987, p. 172). It is expressed by the number of critical and interacting elements that are part of a system or an activity (Kogut/Zander 1993, p. 633).
System dependence	Knowledge is system dependent when it is only useful in combination with other knowledge (Winter 1987, p. 173).
Detailedness	Detailedness expresses how fine-grained and in depth exchanged knowledge is (Uzzi 1997, pp. 45-46).
Holisticity	When a lot of knowledge on a subject is transferred the knowledge is holistic (Uzzi 1997, pp. 45-46).

Table 4-3: Characteristics of knowledge[93]

As it is a well accepted approach, the differentiation of winter (1987, pp. 170-171) into articulatedness and teachability is applied in this study. In the empirical study (see sub-section 5.1.3.4.1 for the operationalization and section 6.4 for the results of the empirical study), the articulatedness will be asked for first. If it is found that knowledge was not articulated its teachability will be analyzed. The attributes of system dependence and complexity of the exchanged knowledge are also asked for in the empirical study. The feature of observability, however, does not suit the context of knowledge transfer in the product innovation process. In this context, knowledge is

---

[92] Kogut and Zander base the difference between codifiability (i.e. articulatedness) and teachability on the difference between information as a "factual statement" and know-how as process knowledge. Knowlegde thus is codifiable when information is articulated in documents while it is teachable when know-how is articulated (Kogut/Zander 1993, pp. 632-633).

[93] Other characteristics of knowledge were proposed. For instance, concerning market knowledge, the breadth, depth, specificity and tacitness were analyzed (De Luca/Atuahene-Gima 2007). However, in research on Strategic Management and International Business, the knowledge characteristics of Winter (1987), Kogut and Zander (1993) and Uzzi (1997) are applied by most authors. The publication of Winter (1987) is cited more than 1,600 times according to Google Scholar. The paper of Kogut and Zander (1993) is referred to more than 1,400 times and the study of Uzzi (1997) is even cited more than 2,900 times.

intentionally transferred from one actor to another in order to be used in and bring benefit to the product innovation process. Thus, knowledge is exchanged with the aim of being obvious to the business partner. It will therefore always be observed.

Embeddedness of Business Relationship to a Stakeholder		Characteristics of Knowledge
Breadth of business relationship • Number of functional areas involved Depth of business relationship • Mutual adaptations • Mutual dependence • Mutual criticality • Mutual commitment • Mutual trust • Mutual attention paid to business partner	+	Tacitness (articulatedness or teachability) Complexity System dependence Detailedness Holisticity

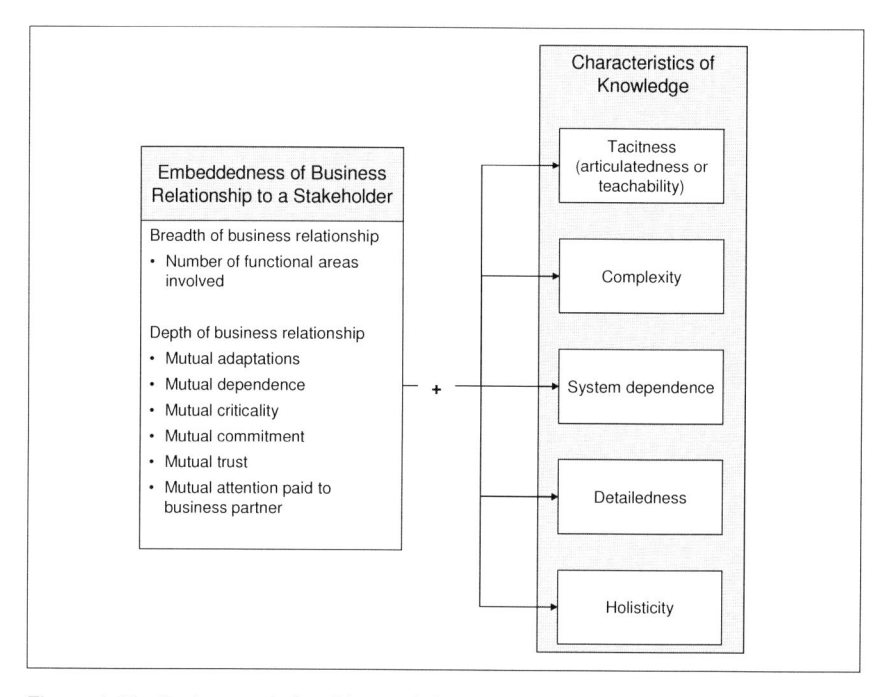

Figure 4-13: Business relationships and characteristics of knowledge

It has been stated that tacit knowledge is more valuable because it is harder to imitate. Embedded relationships support the transfer of tacit knowledge because people in both partner firms have more holistic knowledge of each other and are thus able to interpret new knowledge better. By contrast, arm's length relationships are found to transport mainly explicit knowledge (Uzzi 1997, p. 45, Hansen 1999, p. 105). However, more recently, it has also been stated that the differentiation between tacit and explicit knowledge does not always make sense. Both types of knowledge are needed to create and transfer an innovation (Persson 2006, pp. 22-23). Nevertheless, it is intended to investigate the characteristics of knowledge transferred. Apart from the tacitness of knowledge, it was also found that the knowledge shared was more detailed and more holistic (Uzzi 1997, pp. 45-46). The assumed correlation between the embeddedness of business relationships and characteristics of is depicted in figure 4-13.

4.5.2.2 Characteristics of Knowledge Flows

Flows between external and corporate business partners can be analyzed according to the following attributes: (1) content, (2) domain, (3) genesis, (4) basis, (5) nature, (6) frequency, (7) criticality, (8) provider, receiver and coordinator and (9) coordination of flows (Schmid/Schurig/Kutschker 2002, pp. 50-56). The characteristics refer to all four types of flows in the corporate business network. However, they can be applied to analyze a particular type of flow which is the knowledge flow in this case. Most features apply to inter-organizational flows as well. In table 4-4, the attributes of knowledge flows that are examined in the present research project are listed.

(1) The content of flows in this study is knowledge which is an immaterial resource.

(2) The domain of flow may be inter-functional, inter-business and cross-border (Schmid/Schurig/Kutschker 2002, pp. 50-51). In this study, the functional area of research and development is examined. Inter-business flows of knowledge refer to flows between strategic business units of an MNC and therefore concern only corporate flows (Schmid/Schurig/Kutschker 2002, p. 51). A particular product innovation is mostly created by one business unit so that inter-business flows of knowledge will probably not occur. If knowledge flows between external or corporate actors who are situated in different countries, cross-border flows take place (Schmid/Schurig/Kutschker 2002, p. 51). On both the corporate and external level, this may be the case in this study. Therefore, cross-border knowledge flows will be asked for in the empirical study. However, this will be done in the section on business partners and not in the knowledge section.

(3) Like strategies, flows are not always planned but they also emerge in an unplanned way (Schmid/Schurig/Kutschker 2002, p. 52). During an innovation process, some flows of knowledge will definitely be planned, between corporate business partners as well as between external business partners. In the process of working

together on a product innovation, tasks are allocated to a business partner. The knowledge on the results of these tasks will be a planned flow of knowledge. During the fulfillment of tasks, emergent flows of knowledge can occur, for instance when a problem arises. Even if it is expected that most knowledge flows between external and corporate business partners are planned, this will be asked for in the empirical study.

(4) The basis of flows may be tangible and intangible assets, responsibilities or innovations that were created by a subsidiary (Schmid/Schurig/Kutschker 2002, pp. 52-53). In this study, the innovation process is examined. According to the concept of the Embedded MNC, the reason for a subsidiary to collaborate together with corporate or external business partner in an innovation process is heterogeneity of resources and demands of different actors (Easton 1992, pp. 16-17, Forsgren et al. 1995, pp. 26-35). Thus, business partners are chosen because they control tangible and intangible resources that the subsidiary does not control but are needed to manage the innovation process successfully. In this study, the basis of flows will not be asked for in the context of knowledge flows. Rather, it will be asked why particular business partners were selected. Thus, the basis of flows will be subsumed in the category of actors in the empirical study.

(5) Flows cause dependence between the actors. Different types of dependence exist: an actor is independent from his business partner when other actors can generate the same activity like he does. Business partners are hence exchangeable. When a business partner is the only one to perform an activity the way the focal actor needs it, the actor depends on his business partner. When this business partner can replace the focal actor, this dependence is one way. When dependence is both ways, interdependence occurs (Schmid/Schurig/Kutschker 2002, p. 53). In the perspective of the concept of the Embedded MNC, interdependence is the consequence of exchange (Håkansson/Snehota 1989, p. 191, Forsgren/Johanson 1992b, p. 4). This interdependence is symmetrical when both business partners depend on each other equally. If one business partner depends more on the other than vice versa, the interdependence is asymmetrical. Apart from the type of interdependence, its degree can be analyzed. The degree may be pooled, reciprocal or sequential (Schmid/Schurig/Kutschker 2002, p. 53).

(6) The frequency can range between once over several times, but irregularly to frequently and regularly (Schmid/Schurig/Kutschker 2002, p. 54). If contact occurs more than once it is interesting to analyze which content of knowledge is transferred between business partners every time. Some contacts might serve to transfer knowledge about the object of collaboration while others might serve to pass on other information in order to build trust or solve problems. The frequency of contact will be analyzed as one measure of the embeddedness of relationships in the empirical study. The content of knowledge that flows during single contacts will be analyzed in the knowledge section, as stated earlier.

(7) The criticality of flows is related to the substitutability of business relationships. Both variables refer to the consequences for the focal actor if a particular business relationship – and the knowledge he obtains in this relationship – is terminated for some reason (Schmid/Schurig/Kutschker 2002, p. 54). The substitutability of the business relationship as a whole will be asked for in the relationship section of the empirical study. Also, the criticality of knowledge flows will be examined specifically.

(8) The provider and receiver of flows are the actors who transfer knowledge in their business relationship provider (Schmid/Schurig/Kutschker 2002, p. 53). The coordinator of flows can be the provider, receiver or a third actor, for instance HQs in corporate flows (Schmid/Schurig/Kutschker 2002, p. 55). Provider, receiver and coordinator of knowledge flows will be investigated in the actor section of the empirical study. Knowledge flows can be coordinated using different mechanisms. Process-based (e.g. by formalization, standardization), behavior-based (values, norms), output-based coordination (reports, budgets) and self-organization may be distinguished.

(9) In the context of International Business research, different possibilities to coordinate business activities in MNCs have been proposed. Structural, technocratic, personal, and other coordination instruments can be distinguished. Structural coordination instruments concern the establishment of organizational structures and processes to facilitate business activities. In order to coordinate knowledge flows a particular position for communication with an external or corporate business partner can be established, for instance. Technocratic coordination instruments are standardized

solutions for recurring issues, for instance rules and programs. Frequent knowledge flows can be organized efficiently by instituting rules of how to handle the particular knowledge flow. Personal coordination instruments refer to the mechanisms that require personal involvement of employees, for instance visitations at the business partner (Kutschker/Schmid 2008, pp. 1033-1062). They also support knowledge flows. Finally, other coordination instruments include transfer prices, knowledge transfer and self organization. To apply the instruments of this category to the context of knowledge flows is difficult. Knowledge can hardly be valued so that transfer prices will hardly be employed. Even more digressive is the coordination instrument of knowledge transfer to organize knowledge flows. Finally, self organization may take place in some processes. However, the product innovation and transfer process is crucial for firms so that it is most likely well organized. Thus, structural, technocratic, and personal coordination mechanisms will be looked at briefly in the empirical study while the category of "other coordination mechanisms" will not be considered.

Characteristics of knowledge flows	Explanation
Cross-border flows	Knowledge may be exchanged between different countries when the business partners of the innovative subsidiary are located in another country.
Planned versus emergent knowledge flows	Some knowledge flows are planned but others occur in an unplanned way. They are called emergent flows.
Frequency	Knowledge flows between the innovative subsidiary and its business partners may occur regularly or irregularly, only few times or often.
Criticality	Knowledge flows may be more or less critical for the innovative subsidiary and its business partners. The more severe the consequences of the loss of the knowledge flow are the more critical is the knowledge flow.
Coordinator	Knowledge flows between the innovative subsidiary and its business partners may be coordinated by the subsidiary, the business partner or a third actor like HQs.
Coordination	Knowledge flows may be coordinated using different mechanisms. Structural, technocratic, and personal coordination instruments may be distinguished.

Table 4-4: Characteristics of knowledge flows as applied in this study

4.5.2.3 Process of Knowledge Transfer

The process of knowledge transfer[94] is divided into four sequential stages that are depicted in figure 4-14: (1) initiation, (2) implementation, (3) ramp-up and (4) integration. (1) The initiation stage begins when a deficiency of knowledge in one unit and the knowledge needed is present in another unit. Thereby, it does not matter whether the need is diagnosed and a search for knowledge is initiated or the existence of best practice is discovered and is decided to be transferred to other units with the same task. If both the need and the knowledge are found, the feasibility of knowledge transfer is verified. (2) When a decision about the transfer of knowledge between two units is made the implementation stage begins. Resources flow between the source unit and the recipient unit. Social ties between both units are established and the transferred practice is adapted to meet the specific needs of the recipient unit. The transition to the next stage is smooth. (3) The ramp-up stage starts when the recipient unit starts using the obtained knowledge. In this stage, unexpected problems are identified and solved by the unit. The usage is rather inefficient at first but performance is gradually improved. (4) Once satisfactory results are achieved with the transferred knowledge the final stage of integration begins. During this stage, routines of usage develop. In the recipient unit, a shared history of usage evolves and actors and actions connected to the usage of the knowledge are exemplified. After a while, new practices are regarded as standard and are thus taken for granted (Szulanski 1996, pp. 28-29, 2000, pp. 12-16).

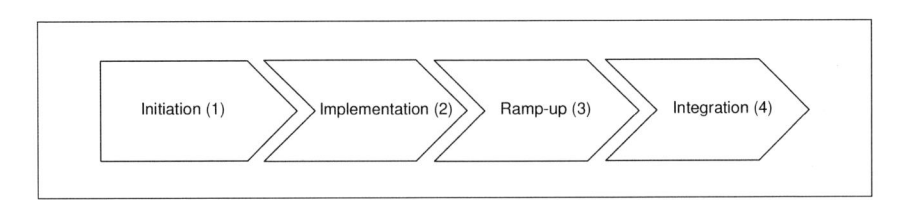

| Initiation (1) | Implementation (2) | Ramp-up (3) | Integration (4) |

Figure 4-14: Stages of the knowledge transfer process
Source: Szulanski 2000, p. 13.

---

[94] This process is described on an intra-organizational level by Szulanski (1996, pp. 28-29, Szulanski 2000, pp. 12-16). However, the stages of initiation, implementation, ramp-up and integration are so basic that they occur in inter-organizational knowledge transfer as well. Only the specific instruments of transfer might differ. For instance, for intra-organizational knowledge transfer more cross-unit-teams might be employed than in inter-organizational transfer.

4.5.2.4 Problems of Knowledge Transfer

Transferring knowledge from one actor to another one is not an easy process. In the empirical study of the present contribution, experts are asked about problems of knowledge transfer in the sub-section on characteristics of knowledge transfer. Therefore, possible issues are presented in this sub-section. A special focus is laid on the absorptive capabilities as a problem of the recipient unit because it has been identified to be particularly relevant for business unit innovation in past studies (Tsai 2001). Many difficulties may arise which lead to the notion of knowledge being sticky. The transfer of knowledge is defined to be sticky when it is worthy to be noticed, i.e. when it is an "event". If the transfer proceeds without problems it will hardly be re-marked and in this case knowledge is not said to be sticky. The stickiness is higher the more effort is needed to detect and handle difficulties, the costlier knowledge transfer is, the more time it takes and the more expectations and realizations of knowledge transfer diverge, i.e. the less successful it is (Szulanski 1995, p. 437, 1996, pp. 29-30, Szulanski/Cappetta 2003, p. 514).[95] However, the difficulty of knowledge transfer is not an objective fact but it is subjective to the evaluation of the individuals who are involved in the transfer process. Their effort in the process depends on their perceived difficulty (Szulanski 1996, p. 30). Drawing on the communication model of Shannon and Weaver (1949), five categories of potential problems are recognized: (1) the knowledge itself, (2) the context of knowledge transfer, (3) the source unit, (4) the recipient unit, and (5) the transfer channel (Szulanski 2000, p. 11). Szulanski focuses on the categories (1) to (4) and identifies two or three characteristics of these category which may hamper knowledge transfer (Szulanski 1996, pp. 30-32).

(1) Regarding knowledge itself either causal ambiguity or unprovenness may be attributes of sticky knowledge. Causal ambiguity occurs when individuals involved in the transfer are not able to identify the factors of success or failure of knowledge transfer, even ex post. This may happen when a lot of tacit knowledge needs to be transferred. In this case, the uncertainty that is connected to knowledge transfer can not be reduced. In the case of unprovenness the knowledge to be transferred has not

---

[95] Von Hippel who introduced the term 'sticky information' only referred to the cost of information transfer (Von Hippel 1994, p. 430).

been proven to be helpful in another unit than the original one yet. This may cause the recipient unit to refuse to invest resources and time in the transfer. If the transfer proceeds and difficulties arise the transfer is more likely to be stopped (Szulanski 1996, pp. 30-31).

(2) Two features of the context of the knowledge transfer may hamper it: an arduous relationship and a barren organizational context. An arduous relationship may be characterized by aloofness or hostility. In any kind of knowledge transfer, especially in the transfer of tacit knowledge, a lot of interaction is needed. If the source unit and the recipient unit do not want to interact for aloofness or hostility reasons the transfer will be very problematic (Szulanski 1996, p. 32). As stated by network and embeddedness concepts the transfer of knowledge will be much more easy, detailed and holistic in an embedded relationship than in an arm's length relationship. Also, more tacit knowledge is transferred in an embedded relationship (Johanson/Pahlberg/Thilenius 1996, p. 186, Andersson/Forsgren/Pedersen 2001, p. 8, Andersson 2003, p. 428, Uzzi/Lancaster 2003, p. 385). The lack of a shared language, both in national language and in terminology also impedes transfer of knowledge (Bendt 2000, p. 56). Therefore, when the terminology and expertise of source and recipient unit differ significantly a boundary spanner in the recipient unit is necessary. He looks for useful knowledge in other units of the MNC and translates this knowledge into the terminology of his own unit (Cohen/Levinthal 1990, p. 132). A barren organizational context may result from different factors. For example, a high degree of standardization and formalization in communication processes decreases the necessary flexibility in transferring knowledge. Hierarchy, specialization and centralization, strong role pressures and unfavorable systems of evaluation and rewarding also lead to less attempts to transfer knowledge from one unit to another one (Szulanski 1996, pp. 31-32, Bendt 2000, pp. 57-58). A lack of resources and of transparency about sources and deficiencies of knowledge may also impede knowledge transfer. The corporate culture may hinder attempts to transfer knowledge when trust is lacking and mistakes are not accepted and when the importance of knowledge (transfers) is not acknowledged (Bendt 2000, pp. 57-58).

The attributes of the source and recipient unit of knowledge that may impede knowledge transfer can be categorized as motivational factors and ability factors (see Bendt 2000, pp. 52-56).

(3) Within the source unit the fear of losing its position of power is one motivational reason why knowledge transfers may fail. Superior knowledge is a crucial source of power. It often is a critical resource that may be decisive for the success of a unit. One example is a unit which possesses best practice in manufacturing a particular product or in the development process of new products. The knowledge of best practices makes this unit more successful than other ones with similar tasks. This will probably result in a powerful position of this unit in the MNC. If the unit shares the knowledge of best practices with other ones, the criticality of this resource will fade and the power of the source unit will decrease (Pfeffer/Salancik 1978, Szulanski 1996, p. 31, Hansen/Nohria 2004, p. 25). Another reason for little motivation to transfer knowledge to other units is missing rewards for the transfer (Szulanski 1996, p. 31, Bendt 2000, p. 53). A third motivational barrier within the source unit is an attitude of superiority of the source unit. If it does not expect the recipient unit to understand the knowledge or be able to use it the source unit will not be willing to share the knowledge (Szulanski 1996, p. 31).

Apart from deficient motivation, the source unit may not have the ability to transfer knowledge. Reasons can be incapability of communicating in general, lacking of experience in transferring knowledge, a high spread of knowledge among individuals of the source unit and little trustworthiness[96] of the source unit. A high capability of communicating and interacting is particularly necessary when tacit knowledge is about to be transferred. As tacit knowledge can not be articulated via language other possibilities to explain have to be developed. This requires high skills of communication of the source unit. Lacking experience results in a higher complexity and need of coordination of a transfer process in the source unit. A high spread of knowledge among individuals in the source unit increases the complexity of transfer (Heppner

---

[96] Trust is also found to be important in another context. It enhances the "absolute" absorptive capacity of the recipient firm because it increases the willingness of source firm to help the recipient firm to understand the knowledge transferred (Lane/Salk/Lyles 2001, p. 1141). For more details on the absorptive capacity of firms see below (same sub-section).

1997, pp. 207-210). Little trustworthiness or reliability again results in the unwillingness of the recipient unit to engage in the transfer process (Szulanski 1996, p. 31).

(4) Motivational factors of the recipient unit that impede knowledge transfer are: unwillingness to accept new knowledge from outside the own unit ("not invented here" syndrome), ambition to save the face and a feeling of superiority (Szulanski 1996, p. 31, Bendt 2000, pp. 54-55). Apart from deficient motivation, the recipient unit may not be able to absorb or maintain the knowledge that is transferred to it by the source unit. This phenomenon is discussed as (limited) absorptive capacity.^{97} The absorptive capacity is defined as "... ability to recognize the value of new information, assimilate it, and apply it to commercial ends" (Cohen/Levinthal 1990, p. 128). Thus, the recipient unit does not only have to assimilate the new information but also needs to apply it to the aim it was transferred for in order to improve the performance of the MNC. Absorptive capacity of a unit was stated to build on prior knowledge including basic knowledge, skills, a shared language or specific technical knowledge in the field alike. Because of its character of being cumulative, the absorptive capacity of a unit and thus its knowledge only increase gradually. For a knowledge transfer to be successful, the knowledge of source unit and of recipient unit needs to be overlapping to a certain degree. Otherwise, the cognitive capacity of the recipient unit will not be enough to obtain the new knowledge. However, some diversity in knowledge is also needed. Otherwise, learning is not necessary and innovations which result from the combination of knowledge will not be created. As stated earlier, the recipient unit needs to learn not only substantive knowledge but also knowledge about the location of expertise within the MNC. Both are critical knowledge for the recipient unit. While substantive knowledge like technical capabilities can be enhanced by R&D and manufacturing investments and efforts and training of the staff, knowledge on potential sources of expertise can only be increased by establishing relationships in the MNC (Cohen/Levinthal 1990, pp. 128-133). Both absorptive capacity (measured as R&D investment) and network centrality have been found to enhance innovations in

---

[97] Absorptive capacity is explained here in more detail than the other characteristics of sticky knowledge because it was found to be the most important predictor of stickiness (Szulanski 1996, pp. 35-37). Causal ambiguity and an arduous relationship between source and recipient unit are also barriers of knowledge transfer (Szulanski 1996, pp. 35-37). Thus, ability factors were found to be more important barriers than motivational factors in the context of "absolute" absorptive capacity. In addition, the concept of absorptive capacity has been picked up by many authors (e.g. Minbaeva et al. 2003, Van den Bosch/Van Wijk/Volberda 2003, Björkman/Stahl/Vaara 2007, Abecassis-Moedas/Mahmoud-Jouini 2008, Hongwu 2008).

sub-units. Thereby, absorptive capacity has a direct effect on the sub-units innovativeness as well as an indirect effect by mediating the influence of network centrality on innovation (Tsai 2001).

While Cohen and Levinthal (Cohen/Levinthal 1990) focus on the absorptive capacity of the recipient unit the interest later shifted to the learning dyad between two firms[98] and then was labeled relative absorptive capacity (Lane/Lubatkin 1998). Thereby, it is stated that interactive learning is needed to answer the question of "how and why" in opposition to other forms of learning.[99] When interactive learning proceeds, more tacit knowledge is transferred. This tacit knowledge is embedded in the specific context of the source firm. It is unique and hardly imitable and hence provides a higher strategic value for the recipient firm (Lane/Lubatkin 1998, pp. 462-463). Thus, interactive learning is the basis for a competitive advantage of the recipient firm (Andersson/Forsgren/Pedersen 2001, p. 8). Furthermore, it was emphasized that a firm can not learn from any other firm equally well. Instead, the recipient firm's absolute absorptive capacity depends on the type of knowledge that the source firm is about to transfer, on the similarity between both firms regarding organization structures and compensation practices and on the recipient firm's familiarity with the source firm's set of organizational issues. At this stage, "know-what" is learned. The recipient firm's ability to identify and evaluate new knowledge increases when its basic knowledge[100] is similar to the source firm's knowledge while their specific knowledge differs. In order to assimilate the new knowledge and learn the know-how from the source firm, the knowledge processing systems of both firms should be similar. Similar types of problems in both firms facilitate the recipient firm's attempts to commercialize the newly learned knowledge. The know-why is learned in this stage (Lane/Lubatkin 1998, pp. 461-466).

---

[98] Opposed to the original concept of the 'absolute' absorptive capacity, the relative absorptive capacity is discussed and studied on the inter-organizational level (see Cohen/Levinthal 1990 for "absolute" absorptive capacity and Lane/Lubatkin 1998, Lane/Salk/Lyles 2001 for relative absorptive capacity).

[99] Lane and Lubatkin differ between three methods of learning: the passive, active and interactive learning. When learning in a passive way, firms obtain explicit knowledge about technical and managerial processes, for example from journals or consultants. Active learning encompasses a broader view of competitors' capabilities. Questions on 'what, who, when and where' are asked and a kind of benchmarking is made (Lane/Lubatkin 1998, p. 462).

[100] Basic knowledge encompasses "… general understanding of the traditions and techniques upon which a discipline is based" (Lane/Lubatkin 1998, p. 464).

After the knowledge has been absorbed by the recipient unit it has to maintain it. Szulanski names this ability "retentive capacity" (Szulanski 1996, p. 31). Knowledge is maintained by institutionalizing it within the unit. Therefore, this barrier of knowledge transfer will mainly occur in the final stage of the knowledge transfer, the integration stage (Szulanski 1996, p. 31, Bendt 2000, p. 56, Szulanski 2000, p. 16). Surprisingly though, retentive capacity was found to be significant in the ramp-up stage (Szulanski 2000, p. 22). This indicates problems of measurement in the study of Szulanski.

Stickiness of knowledge is mainly studied on the intra-organizational level. Knowledge transfer is generally assumed to be easier than on the inter-organizational level. However, as the identified predictors for stickiness were deducted from the general communication model and a literature review that includes studies from several levels of knowledge transfer it may also be applied to the inter-organizational level. This is done in some studies (e.g. Abecassis-Moedas/Mahmoud-Jouini 2008). Stickiness of knowledge was found to have an impact on the location of innovation. If an innovation is created at the supplier, manufacturer or customer depends on the stickiness of the innovation-related knowledge. If the knowledge on user needs is sticky, innovations related to the user need design will be done by the user. If knowledge on technology is sticky the innovation will be mainly done by the manufacturer. In this case, users will not play a big role (Von Hippel 1994, Ogawa 1998, p. 778).

4.6 Conclusion

In this chapter, the concept of the Embedded MNC was presented. The summary of the research questions is depicted in figure 4-15.

With the research questions 1.1 and 2.1 in mind, the concept was extended regarding the actors. As was stated in the critical evaluation of the concept of the Embedded MNC (see section 4.4), the authors of the concept of the Embedded MNC still mainly look at customers and suppliers as business partners of the focal MNC or subsidiary. They do so even though they refer to business partners in general in their conceptual considerations. Thus, stakeholder groups were discussed in sub-section

4.5.1 and the issue of different stakeholders collaborating with the focal subsidiary during the product innovation process was depicted in figure 4-12. Several stakeholder groups will probably be found as external business partners in the product innovation process.

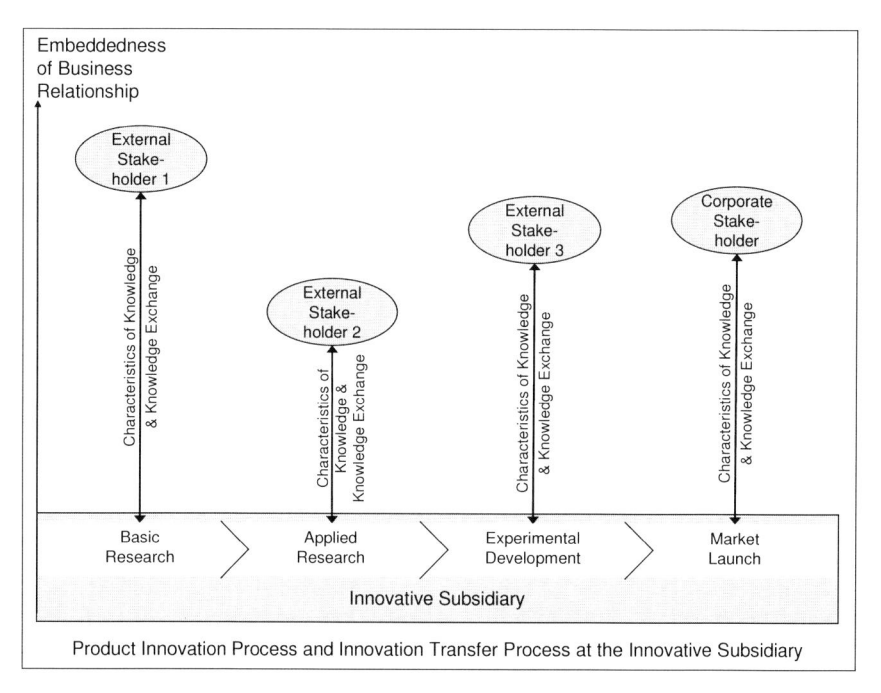

Figure 4-15: Summary of the research issues in this thesis

Following research questions 1.2 and 2.2, a special focus was on the description of the state and development of the embeddedness of business relationships (subsections 4.3.1.1.2 and 4.3.2, respectively). The embeddedness of business relationships is evaluated on two dimensions, the breadth and the depth. Both dimensions were subsumed in figure 4-5.

Embeddedness of Business Relationship to a Stakeholder		Characteristics of Knowledge	
Breadth of business relationship • Number of functional areas involved Depth of business relationship • Mutual adaptations • Mutual dependence • Mutual criticality • Investments in business relationship • Trust • Attention paid to business partner	→	Tacitness	
	→	Complexity	
	→	System dependence	
	→	Detailedness	
	→	Holisticity	
	+ ?	**Characteristics of Knowledge Flows**	
	→	Cross-boarder flows	
	→	Planned flows	
	→	Frequency	
	→	Criticality	
	→	Coordinator and coordination	
	−	**Problems of Knowledge Flows**	

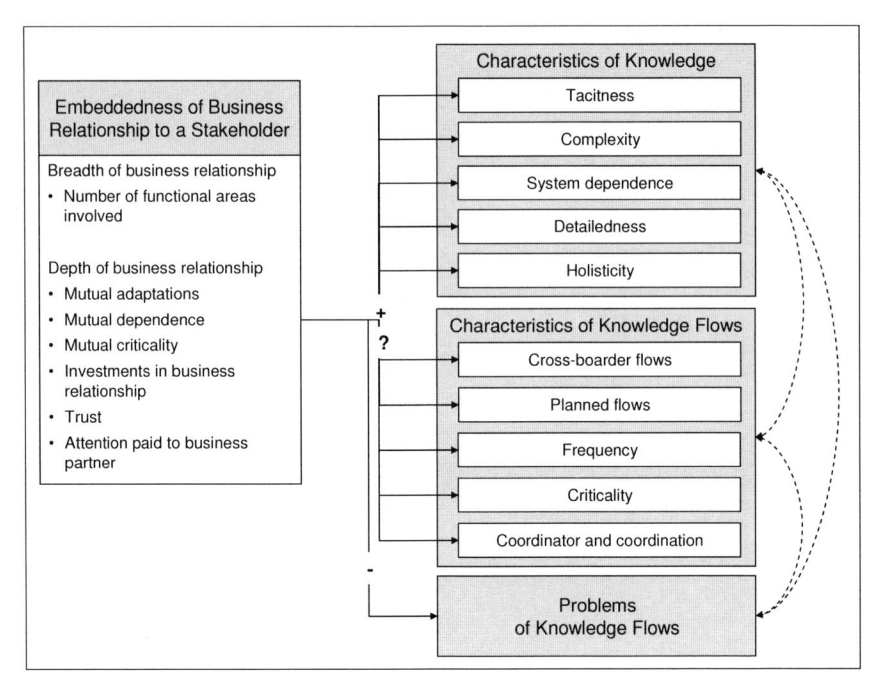

Figure 4-16: Assumed relationships in this study

Finally, research questions 1.2.2 and 2.2.2 lead to research on knowledge and knowledge transfer. The concept of the Embedded MNC and the embeddedness concept include research on tacitness and stickiness in their own research. However, they do so in a shortened way so that research on knowledge transfer was presented in a more extended way. In sub-section 4.5.2, more details were given on characteristics of knowledge and knowledge transfer. They were complemented by explanations of potential problems that might arise in knowledge transfer. The concept of the Embedded MNC proposes an effect of the embeddedness of business relationships on the tacitness of knowledge that is exchanged between business partners. The assumed effect of the embeddedness of business relationships on the characteristics of knowledge and knowledge flows and problems of knowledge flows is illustrated in figure 4-16. Thereby, it has to be noted that characteristics of knowledge and attributes of knowledge transfer are not independent. For instance, it might be assumed that the transfer of complex knowledge is rather planned while flows of simple knowledge emerge. Or it might be proposed that holistic knowledge is passed on in more frequent instances of knowledge transfer than rather non-holistic knowledge. However, interdependences between the characteristics of knowledge and of knowledge transfer are not examined in the present thesis. Instead, the impact of the embeddedness of business relationships on attributes of knowledge and of knowledge transfer is studied.

5 Empirical Study

5.1 Research Design

Researchers have recommended to lay the conceptual framework open as that serves as a basis of a study before conducting the actual empirical work (Cepeda/Martin 2005, p. 858). So, after having explained the conceptual framework, the empirical study is presented. In the first section of this chapter, the research design will be described (5.1). The research design must make clear which kind of data are acquired using which method of data collection within which research strategy (Yin 1981, p. 58). This study aims at obtaining qualitative data using interviews within a case study approach. First, it will be explained why a case study approach is employed (5.1.1) and how it is set up (5.1.2). The units of analysis are presented (5.1.2.1) and the choice of the cases that were studied is described (5.1.2.2). The operationalization of constructs is explained in sub-section 5.1.3. Following this, operationalizations regarding the unit of analysis are provided in sub-section 5.1.3.1. Operationalizations concerning the business partners are given in sub-section 5.1.3.2, those concerning the embeddedness of business relationships in 5.1.3.3 and finally those concerning the characteristics of knowledge and knowledge transfer in 5.1.3.4. Then details on the process of data collection and analysis are presented (5.2 and 5.3, respectively). Finally, the empirical study will be evaluated according to scientific quality criteria (5.4).

5.1.1 Rationale for a Case Study Approach

As was shown in sub-sections 2.1.3 and 2.2.3 of the literature review, existing studies on the research questions of the present thesis (see section 1.2) have hardly applied qualitative case study designs. Instead, they have collected quantitative data in large scale surveys. However, it has been recommended to employ qualitative research methods in International Business research before (e.g. Macharzina/Oesterle 2002, p. 14, Marschan-Piekkari/Welch 2004, pp. 7-8, Peterson 2004, p. 25, Wright 2004, p. 51). Thus, it will be discussed in this sub-section if qualitative data from a case study design are helpful to explore the creation of product innovations in subsidiaries in collaboration with external business partners and the transfer of product innovations within the MNC.

A case is defined as "... a phenomenon of some sort occurring in a bounded context" (Miles/Huberman 1994, p. 25). Case studies are a research strategy like experiments, histories, archival analyses or surveys (Yin 2009, p. 8). One case corresponds to one unit of analysis that is discussed in sub-section 5.1.2.1 for this study (Miles/Huberman 1994, p. 25). The decision for a research strategy has to be taken carefully. Some criteria for the application of case studies have been compiled in literature. Case studies should be employed when the research issue meets the following criteria:

- Kind of research questions: Case studies should be employed when "how" and "why" questions are asked (Wrona 2005, pp. 16-17, Yin 2009, pp. 9-11).
- Control over behavioral events: Case studies are a suitable approach for studying social phenomena that are not under control of the researcher (Yin 2009, pp. 11-13).
- Complexity: Related to the control over events is the issue of complexity. Case studies are suitable when the phenomenon under research is broad and complex, when it is sticky and practice-based, when experiences of the actors are important and the phenomenon cannot be clearly isolated from its context (Yin 1981, p. 59, Bonoma 1985, p. 207, Cepeda/Martin 2005, p. 852).
- Contemporary versus historical events: Case studies can only be used when potential respondents are alive. Thus, the phenomenon must be contemporary (Yin 2009, pp. 11-13).
- Processes as phenomena: Case studies are helpful when processes and dynamics of a phenomenon are studied (Gummesson 1991, p. 75, Creswell 2003, p. 106, Siggelkow 2007, p. 22).

In the present thesis, both the research questions are "how" questions. They look at business relationships that contribute to the creation and transfer of product innovations. As was suggested in section 4.3.1.1.2, business relationships are social phenomena with a very high complexity. In order to answer the research questions, both the product innovation process and the mechanisms of product innovation transfer will be studied. In addition to that, the dynamics of relationships between innovative subsidiaries and their business partners are examined. In the pharmaceutical industry which will be examined (see sub-section 5.1.2.2.1), product innovation processes with a duration of 15 to 20 years are normal (Fischer/Breitenbach 2007, p. 29). The product innovation processes of the cases examined here are in an advanced stage but have not been completed yet. Those stages of the innovation process will be studied that are already finished. The greatest part of the innovative work will be done though. Thus, they will mainly be examined in retrospect. However, product innovations are selected whose creation has only been a few years ago because business relationships and networks change in the course of time (Gulati 1995). The study is thus based on contemporary events. In summary, following the criteria listed above, the case study approach seems suitable in this study.

Case studies are a helpful research strategy because they allow "... investigators to retain the holistic and meaningful characteristics of real-life events" (Yin 2009, p. 4). Their goals are manifold. They provide the opportunity of exploring a research question, making rich descriptions of the research issue and explaining causes, effects and processes of research questions (Gummesson 1991, pp. 75-76, Eisenhardt/ Graebner 2007, p. 25). Studying an exceptional case in reality may serve as a motivation to ask a particular research question and as an illustration of conceptual contributions (Siggelkow 2007, pp. 21-22). Furthermore, case studies are employed when there is no profound theoretical basis for the particular research question. Thus, they are a mainly inductive research strategy. They help to generate new concepts. Existing research serves as an orientation but theory is built on the basis of the empirical findings. However, they are also applied in order to revise established theoretical concepts. Empirical findings then serve to extend theory. Thus, qualitative case studies are mainly inductive but have deductive elements as well (Wrona 2005, pp. 19-21Bonoma 1985, p. 207, Eisenhardt 1989, p. 535, Miles/Huberman 1994, p. 1, Keating 1995, p. 69, Cepeda/Martin 2005, pp. 852-853, Siggelkow 2007, p. 21).

The present research project aims at revising existing concepts and extending them using case studies. It includes both inductive and deductive elements. As stated in the conceptual part of the thesis, the concept of the Embedded MNC is applied as a basis concerning the state and development of business relationships (see sub-sections 4.3.1.1.2 and 4.3.2, respectively). This concept suggests that more tacit, detailed and holistic knowledge is exchanged in more embedded business relationships (see sub-section 4.3.3.2). In the present thesis, this assumption will be checked empirically. Also, the concept is enriched by a more detailed information on stakeholders (see sub-section 4.5.1), characteristics of knowledge (see sub-section 4.5.2.1) and knowledge transfer (see sub-section 4.5.2.2). Whether the extensions to the concept of the Embedded MNC are correct and helpful will be checked in the empirical study as well.

5.1.2 Description of the Case Design

5.1.2.1 Units of Analysis

Within the case study approach, different case designs exist. Two attributes of case designs must be considered. The first one is the difference between holistic and embedded case studies. Embedded case studies contain more than one unit of analysis. Within the main unit of analysis, several sub-units of analysis can be identified. A holistic case design is indicated when no logical criteria exist to divide the main unit of analysis. Then, there is a danger of lacking specificity in research (Yin 2009, pp. 50-52). In this study, a holistic case design is chosen.[101] Within the inter-organizational part of the study, the unit of analysis is the business relationship between the innovative unit and the influential business partner at each single stage of the product innovation process. The unit contains the embeddedness of business relationships, knowledge flows and type of actors. In the intra-organizational part of the study, the unit of analysis is the organizational structure and processes that enhance the product innovation transfer from the innovative subsidiary to corporate business partners.

The second dimension is the decision between a single and a multiple case design. A single case design may be suitable in different situations. For example, it is indi-

---

[101] It could be argued that an embedded case study design is preferable because product innovations could be considered the main unit of analysis within which business relationships (inter-organizational part) and organizational structure and processes (intra-organizational part) are sub-units. However, the main focus of this contribution is not on product innovations but on business relationships between and within firms. This was already stated in section 1.3 when it was made clear that this thesis is written from the perspective of a researcher of International Business.

cated when a unique or extreme case or, the opposite, a representative case is examined. It may also be sufficient when a longitudinal study takes place which includes observations at two or more points in time. Then, change of a phenomenon over time is examined. However, a single case always bears the danger of not fitting the research questions perfectly (Yin 2009, pp. 47-50). Above that, it is regarded as less robust than multiple cases. In order to replicate findings and attain a higher level of robustness, multiple case studies may be conducted. The cases will be chosen from the same industry. Thereby, an industry with a transnational nature will be focused on because innovations are created by subsidiaries and transferred to other units in the MNC in the transnational type of MNCs (Bartlett/Ghoshal 1998, pp. 135-136). The number of cases that is needed can not exactly be defined (Miles/Huberman 1994, p. 30, Yin 2009, p. 58). In this study, two case studies are conducted.

5.1.2.2 Selection of Cases

5.1.2.2.1 Selection of Subsidiaries

Before selecting subsidiaries, it must be defined which units are regarded as foreign subsidiaries. Here, a definition by Birkinshaw gives a hint. He describes foreign subsidiaries as "… any operational unit controlled by the MNC and situated outside the home country" (Birkinshaw 1997, p. 207). The concept of the Embedded MNC is more explicit regarding the ownership structure of subsidiaries. A subsidiary is only considered a part of the corporate network if the MNC holds at least 50% of the unit's equity (Forsgren/Holm/Johanson 2005, pp. 92-93). In this study, a foreign subsidiary is defined as an operational unit of which at least 50% of the equity is owned by the MNC and the unit is situated outside the home country of the MNC.

Having defined foreign subsidiaries, some characteristics of the subsidiaries which are approached must be refined. First, since sociological issues like the embeddedness of relationships may be evaluated differently across national cultures (Sandström 1992, p. 51, Kutschker/Bäurle/Schmid 1997, p. 8), subsidiaries from one country, i.e. Germany, were examined.[102] German subsidiaries were chosen for easier access to experts in the subsidiary for face-to-face interviews (Merkens 2007, p. 166). Second, subsidiaries were selected which developed a radical product innovation. The focus on radical product innovations was made clear in the research outline which was sent to suiting subsidiaries. In the first interview at the subsidiary, an appropriate product innovation was chosen and discussed.

Third, an industry had to be chosen. In this study, locally-leveraged or globally-linked product innovations are examined (see section 3.2.1.2). They are created by one or several subsidiaries and then transferred to other units of the MNC (Bartlett/Ghoshal 1990b, pp. 221-222). As at least one subsidiary is the originator of the product innovation and the innovation is not only used in the subsidiary's local market, both locally-leveraged and globally-linked innovations belong to transnational innovation processes (Bartlett/Ghoshal 1990b, p. 233, see sub-section 3.2.1.2 for more details and a discussion on transnational innovation processes). Thus, industries with transnational MNCs were an ideal choice. Hedlund (1986)[103] and Ghoshal and Nohria (Ghoshal/Nohria 1993) have suggested some industries to be international, global, multinational or transnational.[104] However, they propose different industries. In figure 5-1, all these industries are listed. While the ones found by Ghoshal and Nohria are printed in bold letters, the industries named by Hedlund are printed in italic letters.

In this study, the pharmaceutical industry is chosen. This is due to a number of reasons: First, the development of new products, i.e. new diagnostic tests, instruments and especially drugs, takes several years. High investments in R&D are needed. Therefore, firms in pharmaceutical industry collaborate a lot with other firms that are specialized in particular fields of biotechnology, with private research institutions and universities. With these external partners they engage in research and development (R&D) activities (Powell/Koput/Smith-Doerr 1996, Orsenigo et al. 1998, Belsey/Pav-

---

[102] National cultures do not always match country boundaries; see the discussion in Schmid 1996a, pp. 230-236.
[103] Naming the industries, Hedlund cites the doctoral thesis of Bartlett (1984) but gives no information on the page.
[104] The categorization of industries as international, global, multinational and transnational was made by Hedlund and Ghoshal/Nohria about 20 years ago, in 1986 (based on Bartlett (1984)) and 1993, respectively. Of course, industries might change because the forces for global integration or local responsiveness increase or decrease. However, recent literature showed that the pharmaceutical industry still has a transnational character (e.g. Rygl 2008).

lou 2005). Thus, the possibility of identifying cases in which the innovative subsidiary collaborated with external business partners during the product innovation process was high. Second, as the development of new diagnostic products and drugs is very costly, they are likely to be transferred within the MNC so that other units make use of the product innovation. The receiving units may be sales units which distribute the new drug in their local markets. This results in higher profits from the new product. The receiving unit may also be another R&D unit of the MNC which develops another new product on the basis of the technology of the focal product innovation. Third, the stages of the product innovation process in pharmaceutical industry are very well defined. This makes it easy to discuss the innovation process systematically with respondents. Furthermore, the results of this study are likely to be transferrable to other drug development processes in pharmaceutical corporations.

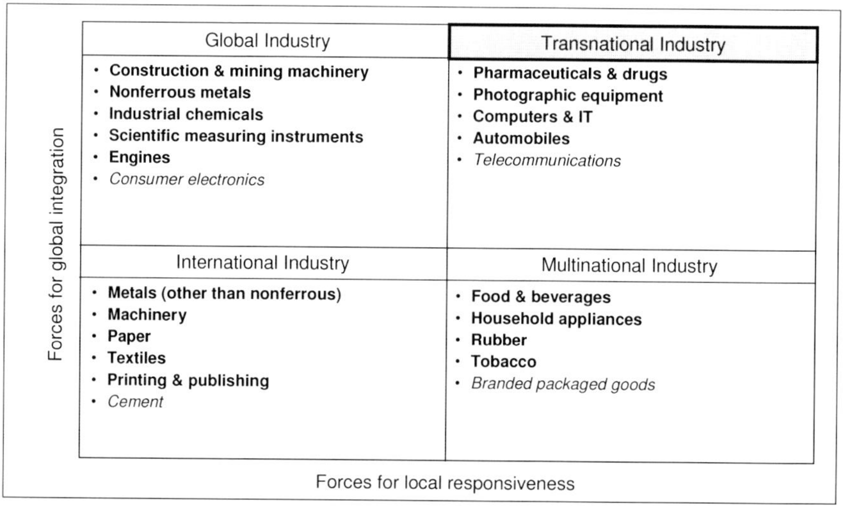

	Global Industry	Transnational Industry
Forces for global integration	• Construction & mining machinery • Nonferrous metals • Industrial chemicals • Scientific measuring instruments • Engines • *Consumer electronics*	• Pharmaceuticals & drugs • Photographic equipment • Computers & IT • Automobiles • *Telecommunications*
	International Industry	Multinational Industry
	• Metals (other than nonferrous) • Machinery • Paper • Textiles • Printing & publishing • *Cement*	• Food & beverages • Household appliances • Rubber • Tobacco • *Branded packaged goods*
	Forces for local responsiveness	

Figure 5-1:   International, global, multinational and transnational industries
Source: Hedlund 1986, p. 21, Ghoshal/Nohria 1993, p. 27.

Innovative German subsidiaries were identified by searching the websites of MNCs in the pharmaceutical industry which are involved in research and development (R&D). A first hint was given by the website of the industry association "Pharma Documentation Ring" (P-D-R, http://www.p-d-r.com/index.shtml) which aims at supporting knowledge flows between its corporate members and help in finding network partners. The

"Verband forschender Pharmaunternehmen" (VFA, http://www.vfa.de/de/index.html) provides helpful information as well. It offers a map of locations of its corporate members in Germany and information on the activities done there. Once promising subsidiaries had been identified, experts from the areas of innovations and R&D were contacted in social networks. They were given a short description of the research project. On the basis of the proposal, they were asked whether they were interested in a more detailed description of the research project. If they agreed the research proposal was sent to them via mail. Two German subsidiaries of Swiss MNCs agreed to take part in the study. One of them works on the development of drugs and is referred to as "Pharmasub" in the thesis. The analyzed product innovation is called Cogis. The other one develops diagnostic test and platforms. This subsidiary is called "Diagnosub" in this thesis and the respective product innovation is named Cantis. The MNCs to which these subsidiaries belong are called "Pharmacom" and "Diagnocom", respectively. The cases were selected in order to give a comprehensive picture of the pharmaceutical industry by presenting different business areas. Although Pharmacom develops drugs and Diagnocom develops diagnostics tests and platforms, both cases are comparable as is demonstrated in sub-section 6.1.3.

5.1.2.2.2 Selection of Product Innovations and Business Relationships

The main units of analysis in this study are product innovations (see sub-section 5.1.2.1). As business relationships and networks change in the course of time (Gulati 1995), product innovations had to be chosen which are still in the process of innovation. However, it was necessary that the innovative part was completed. Hence, the product innovation process needed to be at a rather late stage.

In the first interview, experts at both subsidiaries were asked whether they are in the process of developing a product innovation which is later supposed to be transferred to other units of the MNC. They were requested to explain the product innovation. This was done to fully understand the specifications and benefits of the new product. Furthermore, respondents assessed the product innovation they had in mind according to eight criteria about the intensity of the product innovation (see table 5-1). This was done in order to assure that radical product innovations were studied. It was also clarified that the product innovation the experts had in mind was created either in a locally-leveraged or in a globally-linked product innovation process. The respondents were invited to describe the innovation process briefly. They were asked whether any other sub-unit apart from their subsidiary was involved in the product innovation process. In the case of Cogis, the product innovation process took place mainly at Pharmasub. The stage of in vivo tests (pre-clinic II) was conducted at another German subsidiary, Pharmanorth. Thus, the product innovation process of Cogis was a globally-linked process although most of the R&D activities were conducted at Pharmasub. The product innovation process of Cantis was fully done at Diagnosub. Thus, it is a locally-leveraged product innovation process.

Within the main unit of analysis, two types of sub-units were defined. The first type was the business relationships to external business partners of the innovative subsidiary within the product innovation process. In this sub-unit, the type of stakeholder, embeddedness and development of business relationship and knowledge flows between business partners were analyzed. This sub-unit contained the embeddedness of business relationships, knowledge flows and type of actors. Nine sub-units of this type were examined.[105] The second type of sub-units included the business relationships to corporate business partners of the R&D function at the innovative subsidiary within product innovation transfer of subsidiaries. In these sub-units, organizational structures and processes that facilitate the transfer of product innovations were studied. Two sub-units were analyzed.

It was stated before that relevant business partners are best identified by the focal actors. They are also the most suitable respondents for attributes of the relationship to these actors (Andersson/Forsgren 1996, p. 491). Therefore, the experts were asked whether they collaborate with external business partners in different stages of the product innovation process. They were also asked to identify the sub-units within the MNC which received product innovations from the focal subsidiary after creation.

---

[105] In one of the nine sub-units, selection of business partners is not finished yet. Hence, not all the objects can be analyzed (see sub-sections 6.2.2.2.2, 6.3.2.2.2, and 6.4.3.2).

5.1.3 Operationalization of the Conceptual Framework

In this sub-section, the operationalization of constructs is explained. First, operationalizations regarding the unit of analysis are provided in sub-section 5.1.3.1. The intensity of product innovations is operationalized in sub-section 5.1.3.1.1 while measuring the type of product innovation process is explained in sub-section 5.1.3.1.2. Operationalizations concerning the business partners are given in sub-section 5.1.3.2 and those regarding the embeddedness of business relationships in 5.1.3.3. Finally, in sub-section 5.1.3.4, it is explained how the characteristics of knowledge (5.1.3.4.1) and knowledge transfer (5.1.3.4.2) were measured.

5.1.3.1 Determining the Units of Analysis

5.1.3.1.1 The Intensity of Product Innovations

As stated in sub-section 3.1.3, radical product innovations are studied. Thus, the intensity of product innovations needs to be determined. Researchers have stated the difficulty to assess the intensity of product innovations (e.g. Hurmelinna-Laukkanen/ Sainio/Jauhiainen 2008, p. 279). Two methods are usually employed (Sorescu/Chandy/Prabhu 2003, p. 83): First, managers may serve as assessors of product innovations of their own unit or firm. They are provided with a definition of radical innovations and are asked to evaluate the innovativeness of their firm or unit on this basis (e.g. Gatignon/Xuereb 1997, Emsley/Nevicky/Harrison 2006). Of course, this method bears the risk of self-report bias. Responding managers might evaluate their unit or firm to be more innovative than experts from outside the firm would do. This does not have to be intentional, managers might not even be aware of the bias (Sorescu/ Chandy/Prabhu 2003, p. 83). Second, retrospective coding may be applied to measure the intensity of product innovations. Here, experts are given a definition of radical innovations and a list of products which were launched in the past. The experts are asked to evaluate which of the products are radically innovative (e.g. Dewar/Dutton 1986, Golder/Tellis 1993). However, the second method can not be employed in this study as the examined product innovation processes are not completed yet. A retrospective evaluation of the product innovation is thus not possible. Furthermore, in this study, respondents are not managers of the innovative subsidiary but R&D experts. They are asked about the product innovation and details of the innovation process. This procedure hopefully diminishes the self-report bias.

Measures of product innovation intensity differ in their specificity. In sub-section 3.1.3, it was defined that radical product innovations are pioneering products with a new technology while incremental product innovations are improvements of existing products or extensions of a product line. In line with this definition, past studies simply asked whether a product launched by a firm or unit was completely new or whether it was a new generation of an existing product (e.g. Garcia/Calantone 2002, Hurmelinna-Laukkanen/Sainio/Jauhiainen 2008, p. 283). In the present study, the examined product innovations are not launched yet. However, experts in the innovative subsidiary are asked if the new technology[106] will end in a completely new product or if it is developed in order to complement an existing product line. In most cases, new technologies are integrated in completely new products in the pharmaceutical industry. This criterion is taken as a precondition to further evaluate product innovations concerning their intensity according to other criteria.

However, this measure is considered too general and singular. Therefore, other criteria will also be used. In the publications of Hauschildt and Schlaak (2001) and Lettl and his co-authors (2008), more detailed measures of the intensity of product innovations were chosen. In both studies three dimensions of the intensity of product innovations are examined: the market dimension, the technological dimension and the organizational dimension (Hauschildt/Schlaak 2001, p. 176, Lettl/Hienerth/Gemuenden 2008, p. 229). From these three dimensions, only the technological dimension will be adopted.[107] Within this dimension, the following measures are proposed in the

---

[106] In the present study, the term "technology" does not perfectly suit the context of drug development. Technology describes a system of means-end relations which apply to a particular application (Brockhoff 1992, p. 22). In a short note, Hauschildt and Schlaak (2001) equalize this term with "mode of action" which rather fits the drug development case. This term was hence used in the communication with the subsidiary which developed a drug. However, in the case on the development of a diagnostic test and a platform to process this test, the term "technology" is more suitable. For the sake of uniformity, the term "technology" is used in the thesis.

[107] In the study of Hauschildt and Schlaak (2001, pp. 175-176), the factors of technology, supply and production are grouped into the dimension technique/production. From this factor, only the factor of technology is relevant here because supply and production only take place once the innovation is launched in the market. The innovations studied here are not marketed yet. For more details on the three dimensions and a discussion of selecting the technological dimension as relevant dimension for this study see sub-section 3.1.3.

paper of Hauschildt and Schlaak (2001): the degree of newness of technology, the degree of substitution of the formerly used technology for the newly developed technology, the degree of new knowledge in the technology, the amount of well-known techniques that are inhered in the new product innovation and the amount of experience with technique of the product innovation (Hauschildt/Schlaak 2001, p. 177).[108] In the study of Lettl and his co-authors (2008), the degree of newness of the technological principle, degree of the complexity of technology, degree of the technological uncertainty for the firm, uncertainty about the feasibility of technology, uncertainty about the development time, and uncertainty about the development costs are used as measures for technological dimension of the intensity of product innovations (Lettl/ Hienerth/Gemuenden 2008, p. 229).

Not all of the measures of the two papers are taken into account for the present thesis. From the study of Hauschildt and Schlaak (2001), the degree of newness of technology, the amount of new knowledge that is obtained during the innovation process and the amount of past experience with the technology are taken into account. The degree of substitution of existing technologies with the new one is left out in this study. This is done because in drug development new technologies are usually developed for the creation of completely new drugs and not for the improvement of existing ones. The amount of well-known techniques is also not considered because the development of new drugs is a process which most often starts in the very beginning of discovery research. For the sake of comparability, both criteria are also left out in the case of the diagnostic test and platform. From the study of Lettl and his co-authors (2008), the measures of the degree of uncertainty of the feasibility of technology and the degree of uncertainty about the development time and about the development costs are drawn. This is done because radical product innovations are known to include higher levels of uncertainty (see sub-section 3.1.3). Above that, the product innovation process is examined. Therefore, criteria on the intensity of product innovations according to the innovation process should be taken into account. The authors also use the degree of newness and complexity of the technology as a measure. The uncertainty about the technology is excluded in this study because in the pharmaceutical context it means the same as the uncertainty of the feasibility of

---

[108] The degree of past experience with the technology is reciprocal to the other measures. If the degree of past experience with the technology of the product innovation is low the product innovation is more radical.

technology. The measures are not always mutually exclusive. For example, if the innovative subsidiary can build on a large amount of past experience the uncertainty of the mode of action is likely to be smaller. However, by using the eight criteria, a quite reliable picture of the intensity of the product innovation may be depicted.

The eight criteria are assessed by the first respondent of the subsidiary with whom it is decided which product innovation suits the research and verified with other respondents. As the measures only serve to identify suitable product innovations, a five-point Likert scale is considered sufficient to evaluate the intensity of product innovations. In table 5-1, the measures of the intensity of product innovations as used in this study are summarized and some studies which use these measures are listed.

Measure	Scale	Author
Active ingredient is designed for completely new product? (precondition)	Yes/No	Hurmelinna-Laukkanen/Sainio/Jauhiainen 2008, p. 283
Degree of newness of the technology	Five-point Likert scale	Hauschildt/Schlaak 2001, p. 177, Gatignon et al. 2002, p. 1112, Lettl/Hienerth/Gemuenden 2008, p. 229
Amount of new knowledge obtained in the innovation process	Five-point Likert scale	Hauschildt/Schlaak 2001, p. 177
Amount of experience with innovative technology at the beginning of the innovation process	Five-point Likert scale	Hauschildt/Schlaak 2001, p. 177
Degree of the complexity of technology	Five-point Likert scale	Lettl/Hienerth/Gemuenden 2008, p. 229
Degree of the uncertainty of feasibility of technology for firm	Five-point Likert scale	Lettl/Hienerth/Gemuenden 2008, p. 229
Degree of uncertainty about the development time	Five-point Likert scale	Lettl/Hienerth/Gemuenden 2008, p. 229
Degree of uncertainty about the development costs	Five-point Likert scale	Lettl/Hienerth/Gemuenden 2008, p. 229

Table 5-1: Measures of product innovation intensity used in this study

5.1.3.1.2 The Geographical Scope of the Product Innovation Process

After determining the intensity of the product innovation, the geographical scope of product innovation process needs to be clarified. In sub-section 3.2.1.2, it was stated that locally-leveraged or globally-linked product innovation processes will be studied here. Both types of product innovation processes take place in innovative subsidiaries. Subsidiaries employ their own resources to develop a product innovation. In opposition to the local-for-local type, the product innovation is transferred to other units of the MNC once it is completed (Bartlett/Ghoshal 1990b, p. 217). The innovation process typology of Bartlett and Ghoshal has hardly been applied in studies (for an exception see Cantwell/Iammarino 1998). However, the operationalization is rather easy. For each case, the product innovation process will be reconstructed in the interviews. This way it will be revealed which steps of the product innovation process were conducted in the focal subsidiary and whether several sub-units provided their resources to develop a product innovation.

5.1.3.2 External and Corporate Actors in the Product Innovation Process

In order to answer the research questions 1.1 and 2.1, each subsidiary that is involved in the product innovation process will be asked about the most influential external and corporate business partners in its stage of the innovation process. It will also be inquired where the business partners are located. This is in line with the concept of the Embedded MNC and other network approaches. They state that the focal actor can best assess his most influential business partners (Forsgren/Holm/Johanson 2005, pp. 95-96). Respondents will be asked which type of stakeholder the most important business partner is. Furthermore, they will be asked whether other functional areas of the focal subsidiary or MNC work with the same business partners in order to specify the type of stakeholder. In line with Benito, Grøgaard and Narula and Moore, production, marketing & sales, logistics & distribution, purchasing and human resource management will be taken into account apart from R&D (Moore 2000, p. 161, 2001, p. 285, Benito/Grøgaard/Narula 2003, p. 450). Thus, six functional areas are asked for.

Another interesting question will be whether a particular business partner is involved in other stages of the product innovation process as well. In addition, it will be examined whether the focal subsidiary chose the business partners in its stage of the innovation process or whether it was the R&D management of the MNC. Finally, it will be investigated who coordinated the collaboration with a particular business partner at the stage of the innovation process.

5.1.3.3 Embeddedness and Development of Business Relationships between Innovative Subsidiaries and their Relevant Business Partners

Several publications on the concept of the Embedded MNC or earlier concepts of the IMP Group are conceptual or describe anecdotes of collaboration in a business network. The empirical studies that have been done in the past were analyzed in section 4.4 for the measures that have been employed. Most studies examine a subsidiary's or firm's relational embeddedness which is calculated as average of the embeddedness of all relevant business relationships. Some studies focus on the embeddedness of particular relationships and do not sum them up. As is demonstrated in table 4-2, most studies from researchers of the Embedded MNC concept and former concepts use adaptation as the main measure of embeddedness and add a few variables: number of functional areas that are involved with a business partner, importance of the business partner, mutual dependence and mutual commitment. Mutual commitment is measured as investments made in the business relationship. Trust is only applied once as a measure. The strong focus on adaptations and little variety of variables is surprising as the same researchers describe the embeddedness of relationships as a complex multidimensional construct.

In this thesis, the following seven criteria are employed to evaluate the embeddedness of the business relationship. They are summarized in table 5-2.

(1) Number of functional areas: As was depicted in sub-section 4.3.1.1.2, business relationships may be described according to their breadth and their depth. The breadth is assessed according to the number of functional areas involved in the relationship with a particular business partner. Past studies of the IMP Group and follow-

ing researchers focus on one functional area (i.e. technological development) and hence do not investigate the breadth of business relationships. Only two studies take the number of functional areas that are involved in a business relationship into account. They ask for six possible functional areas (Andersson/Forsgren/Holm 2001, 2002). In this study, the number of functional areas will be examined. As the business relationship between a focal subsidiary and relevant business partners are investigated, it will be examined how many functional areas of the focal subsidiary are involved with a particular business partner. According to Benito et al. and Moore, R&D, production, marketing & sales, logistics & distribution, purchasing and human resource management are taken into account (Moore 2000, p. 161, 2001, p. 285, Benito/Grøgaard/Narula 2003, p. 450). Thus, the number may range from one (the R&D department) to six. Of course, subsidiaries do not necessarily have all six functional areas so a small number does not imply a loose relationship. Therefore, if other functional areas (apart from R&D) are involved with a business partner the subsidiary will be asked which of the six functional areas they inhere. This is done in order to be able to evaluate the number of functional areas involved with a business partner.

(2) Mutual adaptations: The depth includes attributes of mutual adaptation and the development of interdependencies, mutual trust and mutual commitment made in it. In past studies the depth of relationships is mainly assessed through the variable of adaptations. Subsidiary's adaptations in product and production technology to particular business partners are assessed. Mutual adaptations are only considered in one study (Andersson/Forsgren/Pedersen 2001). In this study, mutual adaptations regarding the product will only be considered in the case of diagnostic products. In this case, customers like doctor's practices, hospitals or laboratories might affect the product innovation. Thus, the diagnostics subsidiary will be asked for both adaptations in the product innovation and in the product innovation process. In the development of drugs however, adaptations in the product innovation itself are not possible due to two reasons: First, medicine is not a modular product. It is not possible to change one ingredient to adapt to a business partner because the whole mode of action would change. Second, the experts at pharmaceutical firms know very well about the specifications the product needs. Specifications are determined by the purpose of the drug. Thus, the questions on mutual adaptations regarding the product innovation will be left out in the case study on subsidiaries that develop drugs.

(3) Mutual dependence: Mutual dependence or mutual independence has only been studied once. Mutual independence is measured as substitutability of the business partner. However, in theory, substitutability and mutual dependence have been treated as two interrelated but distinct variables. This will be done here accordingly. Mutual dependence has been conceptualized as technical, planning, knowledge, social, economic and legal bonds throughout the business relationship (see sub-section 4.3.1.1.2; Håkansson/Snehota 1989, p. 191, Forsgren/Johanson 1992b, p. 4). These bonds will be used as examples in the empirical study. Mutual dependence considers the operational dependence of business partners, for instance during a particular project like the product innovation process.

(4) Mutual criticality: The criticality looks at the long term dependence of business partners. It evaluates the consequences of the termination of a business relationship for the focal firm and its business partner (Blankenburg Holm/Eriksson/Johanson 1999, p. 477). It is the variable converse to substitutability.

(5) Mutual commitment: The level of mutual investments is a sign of mutual commitment and hence, another sign of an embedded relationship (Andersson/Forsgren/Pedersen 2001, p. 9). Respondents will be asked for the level of investments made in the business relationship. This will not be measured by numbers alone but on a five-point scale.

(6) Mutual trust is only included once in past papers. This is really surprising because trust is always mentioned when embedded relationships are described. One study asked for the trust between business partners. Other publications use closeness of the business relationship (Ciabuschi 2004, p. 78, Ståhl 2004, p. 269, Persson 2006, p. 93, Hallin 2008a, p. 81). Reading closeness, respondents probably have a more diffuse imagination of what is asked. Therefore, in this research project, respondents will be asked how trustful they think the relationship is from their own perspective and from that of the business partner.

(7) Mutual attention: In the concept of the Embedded MNC and former concepts one indicator of an embedded relationship is the attention that partners pay to each oth-

ers' needs. However, past studies have ignored this fact. In this thesis, the characteristic of mutual attention will be included in the empirical study.

Measure	Scale	Author
Number of functional areas of the focal subsidiary that are involved with a particular business partner	1-6 (R&D, production, marketing & sales, logistics & distribution, purchasing and human resource management)	Moore 2000, p. 161, Andersson/Forsgren/Holm 2001, pp. 1023-1026, Moore 2001, p. 285, Andersson/Forsgren/Holm 2002, p. 987, Benito/Grøgaard/Narula 2003, p. 450[109]
Degree of adaptations in the product innovation by the focal subsidiary specifically to its business partner	Five-point Likert scale	Andersson/Forsgren 1996, pp. 497-498, 2000, p. 339, Andersson/Forsgren/Pedersen 2001, p. 15, Andersson/Forsgren/Holm 2002, p. 987, Andersson 2003, pp. 434-435, Andersson/Björkman/Forsgren 2005, p. 528
Degree of adaptations in the product innovation process by the focal subsidiary specifically to its business partner	Five-point Likert scale	Andersson/Forsgren 1996, pp. 497-498, 2000, p. 339, Andersson/Forsgren/Pedersen 2001, p. 15, Andersson/Forsgren/Holm 2002, p. 987, Andersson 2003, pp. 434-435, Andersson/Björkman/Forsgren 2005, p. 528
Degree of adaptations in the product innovation by the business partner specifically to the focal subsidiary	Five-point Likert scale	Andersson/Forsgren/Pedersen 2001, p. 15
Degree of adaptations in the product innovation process by the business partner specifically to the focal subsidiary	Five-point Likert scale	Andersson/Forsgren/Pedersen 2001, p. 15
Degree of technical, planning, knowledge, social, economic and legal bonds as dimensions of dependence of the subsidiary	Five-point Likert scale	Håkansson/Snehota 1989, p. 191, Forsgren/Johanson 1992b, p. 4 (conceptual)
Degree of technical, planning, knowledge, social, economic and legal bonds as dimensions of dependence of the business partners	Five-point Likert scale	Håkansson/Snehota 1989, p. 191, Forsgren/Johanson 1992b, p. 4 (conceptual)
Degree of criticality of focal subsidiary	Five-point Likert scale	Andersson/Forsgren 1996, p. 497 (conceptual)
Degree of criticality of business partner	Five-point Likert scale	Andersson/Forsgren 1996, p. 497 (conceptual)

---

[109] The two publications by Andersson and his colleagues additionally asked for administration and top management but left out logistics and distribution and human resource management.

Measure	Scale	Author
Height of investments made in the business relationship by the focal subsidiary	Five-point Likert scale	Andersson/Forsgren/Pedersen 2001, p. 9 (conceptual)
Height of investments made in the business relationship by the business partner	Five-point Likert scale	Andersson/Forsgren/Pedersen 2001, p. 9 (conceptual)
Degree of trust of the subsidiary in the business relationship	Five-point Likert scale	Uzzi 1996, p. 678, 1997, pp. 43-45, Andersson/Forsgren/ Holm 2001, pp. 1016-1017 (conceptual or without details about operationalization)
Degree of trust of the business partner in the business relationship	Five-point Likert scale	Uzzi 1996, p. 678, 1997, pp. 43-45, Andersson/Forsgren/ Holm 2001, pp. 1016-1017 (conceptual or without details about operationalization)
Degree of attention paid by the focal subsidiary to the partner's needs	Five-point Likert scale	Forsgren et al. 1995, p. 23
Degree of attention paid by the partner to the focal subsidiary's needs	Five-point Likert scale	Forsgren et al. 1995, p. 23

Table 5-2: Measures of the embeddedness and development of external and corporate business relationships applied in this study

As stated earlier, mutual adaptation of resources, the development of mutual dependence, mutual criticality, mutual commitment, mutual trust and mutual attention are not independent. Rather, they are mutually dependent as was described in sub-section 4.3.1.1.2. However, by delimitating an empirical study on one or two variables will not allow a comprehensive picture of the business relationship. Therefore, each of these variables will be addressed in this study.

5.1.3.4 Characteristics of Knowledge and Knowledge Transfer

5.1.3.4.1 Characteristics of Knowledge

As stated in sub-section 4.5.2.1, different characteristics of knowledge will be analyzed: tacitness, complexity of knowledge and system dependence. Tacitness is mainly checked by the question if (and how) exchanged knowledge was articulated. If it was not articulated it will be asked how knowledge has been taught, i.e. the question of teachability of knowledge. Apart from these characteristics of knowledge that are based on Winter (Winter 1987, pp. 171-173), it will be evaluated how detailed and holistic the knowledge has been. Both dimensions go back to Uzzi who found that more tacit, detailed and holistic knowledge is exchanged in embedded business relationships as compared to arm's length business relationships (Uzzi 1997, pp. 45-46).

Uzzi (1996, 1997, Uzzi/Lancaster 2003) found the effect of embedded business relationships on the degree of tacitness, detailedness and holisticness of knowledge in exploratory case studies in which he did not use a particular operationalization of these variables. In a study on manufacturing processes, Kogut and Zander measured the codifiability, teachability and complexity of knowledge;[110] each of them with four or five measures. Concerning the codifiability it will be asked whether manuals, software (standard or specific) or documentation was produced and applied in the manufacturing process. Regarding teachability it will be enquired whether new manufacturing personnel could easily learn the manufacturing process from more experienced personnel or from blueprints. Furthermore, it will be determined whether training of new personnel is an easy task, whether new personnel could manufacture the product with knowledge from high school or from vocational training. Complexity will be measured by looking at the importance of four different processes that occur in manufacturing (Kogut/Zander 1993, p. 641). As Kogut and Zander analyze manufacturing processes, operationalization can not be adopted. Therefore, the definitions of the dimensions are taken as a starting point for the operationalization. As stated in sub-section 4.5.2.1, knowledge is articulated when it is expressed in documents like manuals, presentations, blueprints or templates. If knowledge is found not to be articulated, it will be asked how the source of knowledge taught the knowledge to the receiver (Winter 1987, pp. 171-172). Complexity has been defined as the number of critical and interacting elements that are part of a system or activity (Kogut/Zander 1993, p. 633). It is asked how much knowledge is required to describe a particular piece of knowledge. System dependence asks whether the receiver of knowledge is able to understand pieces of knowledge without being an expert in the field (Winter

---

[110] It has been seen earlier that Kogut and Zander regard these three variables as a basis of tacitness of knowledge (see footnote 90 in sub-section 4.5.2.1).

1987, pp. 172-173). These definitions will be applied as a basis of the empirical study.

Apart from articulatedness, teachability, complexity and system dependence of knowledge, it will be asked how detailed and holistic the knowledge that was exchanged between business partners was. Respondents will be required to give examples of detailed and holistic knowledge in order to illustrate the difference. Furthermore, it will be found out whether the exchanged knowledge was more articulated, complex, system dependent, detailed and holistic than in other business relationships which are less embedded. The operationalization of characteristics of knowledge is listed in table 5-3. Not only will the degree of the characteristics be asked for but also explanations and examples of exchanged knowledge.

Dimension of knowledge	Author
Articulatedness	Winter 1987, p. 172 (conceptual)
Teachability	Winter 1987, p. 171 (conceptual)
Observability	Winter 1987, p. 172 (conceptual)
Complexity	Winter 1987, p. 172 (conceptual)
System dependence	Winter 1987, p. 173 (conceptual)
Detailedness	Uzzi 1997, pp. 45-46 (details on operationalization not provided)
Holisticity	Uzzi 1997, pp. 45-46 (details on operationalization not provided)

Table 5-3:   Measures of characteristics of knowledge

5.1.3.4.2 Characteristics of Knowledge Transfer

Regarding the flows of knowledge, the dimensions were introduced in sub-section 4.5.2.2. Again, no empirical studies that apply these dimensions are known to the author. Therefore, similar to the characteristics of knowledge, operationalization of the dimensions will be drawn from the definitions of the dimensions. First, it will be found out whether knowledge exchange was cross-border (Schmid/Schurig/Kutschker 2002, pp. 50-51). For this, it will simply be asked where the business partner of the innovative subsidiary is located. If it collaborated with an MNC, respondents will specify with which subsidiary they worked. Second, knowledge flows can be planned or emergent (Schmid/Schurig/Kutschker 2002, p. 52). It will be asked which incidents of knowledge exchange were planned. Third, the frequency of knowledge transfer will be analyzed. In addition, it will be inquired which knowledge is transferred during single incidents of knowledge transfer (Schmid/Schurig/Kutschker 2002, p. 54).[111] Fourth, the criticality of knowledge flows is analyzed. This topic is closely related to the criticality of the business relationship (Schmid/Schurig/Kutschker 2002, p. 54). Fifth, it will be asked who coordinated the knowledge flows. This may be the innovative subsidiary, its business partner or a third party, for instance HQs (Schmid/Schurig/Kutschker 2002, p. 55). Sixth, the mechanisms of coordination will be analyzed (Schmid/Schurig/Kutschker 2002, p. 56). Finally, problems that occurred during knowledge transfer will be asked for (Szulanski 1996, pp. 30-32). The measures are listed in table 5-4.

Dimension of knowledge flows	Author
Cross-border flows	Schmid/Schurig/Kutschker 2002, pp. 50-51 (conceptual)
Planned versus emergent knowledge flows	Schmid/Schurig/Kutschker 2002, p. 52 (conceptual)
Frequency	Schmid/Schurig/Kutschker 2002, p. 54 (conceptual)
Criticality	Schmid/Schurig/Kutschker 2002, p. 54 (conceptual)
Coordinator	Schmid/Schurig/Kutschker 2002, p. 55 (conceptual)
Coordination	Schmid/Schurig/Kutschker 2002, p. 56 (conceptual)
Problems	Szulanski 1996, pp. 30-32 (conceptual)

Table 5-4: Measures of characteristics of knowledge transfer

5.2 Collection of Data

The empirical study pursues several objectives. First, it aims at analyzing which kind of stakeholders are the most important external business partners of the focal subsidiary at different stages of the product innovation process. Second, it is investigated how embedded the business relationship between the innovative subsidiary and its business partners is. Third, it is examined whether and how the embeddedness of business relationships develops. Fourth, characteristics of knowledge and of the knowledge transfer are analyzed. Fifth, the sub-unit within the MNC that receives the

---

[111] The content of knowledge transfer will not be described in the sub-sections on the characteristics of knowledge transfer but will be depicted in separate sub-sections in the next chapter.

product innovation is identified and organizational structures and processes which facilitate the transfer of product innovations within the MNC are analyzed.

In order to answer these questions, semi-structured interviews were conducted and supplemented by documents that were provided by the MNCs.[112] This type of interview combines characteristics of non-standardized interviews and standardized interviews (Healey/Rawlinson 1993, pp. 342-344, King 1994, pp. 15-16). Semi-structured interviews are appropriate when only a rather small number of respondents exist (Daniels/Cannice 2004, p. 186). They are particularly helpful because respondents are given the opportunity to explain their views on the research questions (King 1994, p. 14). Apart from the explicit answers to the questions, the respondent can transport additional information (Scapens 1990, p. 274). Thus, the researcher may gain a precise picture of the respondent's views and opinions (Ghauri/Grønhaug 2005, p. 133). Due to concerns about sensitive issues like the product innovation process, questions asked in questionnaires may be neglected. In interviews, the researcher can alleviate the concerns of respondents (Peterson 2004, pp. 34-35). Furthermore, data obtained from interviews are more reliable than those from questionnaires because the researcher may explain the questions to the respondent (Healey/Rawlinson 1993, p. 341). For interviews, an interview guide is necessary. It was constructed according to the operationalization depicted in sub-section 5.1.3. The interview guideline is presented in appendix A.

Once a suitable product innovation was chosen, it was decided with the contact person which experts in the subsidiary could be interviewed. As a necessary precondition, they needed to be well informed about the product innovation process and the collaboration with external business partners and/or the innovation transfer process and the business relationship with corporate business partners. In addition, they had to be available and willing to participate in the study. Following the "snowballing" method, first interviewees were asked for additional interview partners (Welch et al. 2002, p. 620). As it has been recommended that both the sender and receiver of knowledge be asked about the process of knowledge transfer (Ciabuschi 2004, p. 55), contacts to experts in the external and corporate business partners of the sub-

---

[112] Case studies may use different methods of data collection, for example interviews, group discussions, content analysis or observations (Lamnek 1995, 2005, pp. 292-640).

sidiary that were involved in one of the processes had to be found. This was done in order to get a more comprehensive view of the innovation and the transfer process, and the relationship between the innovative subsidiary and its partners who were important for the product innovation and the innovation transfer. Unfortunately, these contacts could not be found. Both subsidiaries had confidential disclosure agreements (CDA) with their business partners. Thus, business partners were not named and could not be approached. The experts in the subsidiaries and in the business partner firms were interviewed between March and June 2009. Among them were the inventor(s) of the product innovation as well as the general innovation management of the focal subsidiary and management of other units of the MNC. An overview of the interview partners is given in table 5-5. The table includes the company, sub-unit, respondent and identification of the respondent in the empirical study.

Company	Sub-unit	Respondent	Appellation
Pharmacom	Subsidiary Northern Germany (Pharmanorth)	Head of Pharmacology and Pharmaceutical Drug Safety	A-R1
Pharmacom	Pharmasub	Head of Exploratory Clinical Development	A-R2
Pharmacom	Pharmasub	Director Strategic Planning and Business Support[113]	A-R3
Pharmacom	Subsidiary Austria[114]	Senior Director LOC (Local Operating Company) Medical Relations	A-R4
Diagnocom	Diagnosub	Head of Innovation & IP Management	B-R1 & B-R6[115]
Diagnocom	Diagnosub	Coordinator R&D & Workflows	B-R2
Diagnocom	Diagnosub	Head of Test Development	B-R3
Diagnocom	Diagnosub	Head of Technological Development	B-R4
Diagnocom	Diagnosub	R&D Project Manager	B-R5

Table 5-5: Respondents at Pharmacom and Diagnocom

---

[113] The Head of Exploratory Clinical Development and Director Strategic Planning and Business Support were interviewed together.
[114] The Senior Director LOC Medical Relations is located at the subsidiary in Austria but belongs to the corporate organization of Pharmacom.
[115] Two interviews were conducted with the Head of Innovation & IP Management.

Nine interviews were conducted as part of the study. Most of them were done face-to-face. Personal interviews have several advantages. They take place in the normal surroundings of the respondent. Because of this contextual naturalness, respondents are thought to give more precise and faithful answers. Also, interviews are preferred when complex topics are involved. Personal interviews are also recommended when talking about sensitive issues like product innovations. Telephonic interviews were also conducted because of cost and time reasons (Shuy 2001, pp. 540-544). Interviews were mainly conducted in German as this was the mother tongue of the author of this study and the interviewees.

5.3 Data Analysis

5.3.1 Procedure

All interviews were recorded. Interviewees were asked before the interview if recording was permitted, to which they agreed. Later, the interviews were transcribed. This is suggested by researchers in order to preserve the data in an exact way (Bogdan/Biklen 1992, p. 128, Silverman 2000, pp. 148-151). Transcriptions helped improve the interviewing process. Where possible, interviews were tentatively analyzed immediately after transcription so that first results of the data analysis affected further interviews. This is recommended by researchers (Miles/Huberman 1994, p. 50). Thus, data collection and data analysis were interrelated in a circular process (Glaser/Strauss 1979, pp. 94-95, Eisenhardt 1989, p. 539).

Once the data are obtained and transcribed, qualitative data analysis starts. It consists of three parts: data reduction, data display and conclusion drawing and verification. In the data reduction process, data are selected, focused, simplified, abstracted and transformed. They are sharpened and sorted. Data reduction activities, for instance are coding, clustering or writing summaries. In the data display process, data are systemized so that they can be presented in an organized and compressed way afterwards. Presentation may include graphs, charts or networks. Data reduction is done because the cognitive capabilities of human beings can not process large amounts of information. It is the precondition for drawing conclusions. Conclusion drawing starts right from the beginning of data collection. During and after the process of data collection the researcher takes notes on regularities, patterns, explanations, causal flows and propositions. Final conclusions are mostly drawn only after the data collection process is terminated. Conclusions are verified when they are tested for their plausibility and validity. Data reduction, data display and conclusion drawing and verification take place in cyclical and interactive processes (Miles/Huberman 1994, pp. 10-12). The interactive process is depicted in figure 5-2.

```
┌─────────────────┐         ┌─────────────────┐
│ Data Collection │────────▶│  Data Display   │
└─────────────────┘         └─────────────────┘
        │  ╲               ╱         │
        │    ╲           ╱           │
        ▼      ╲       ╱             ▼
┌─────────────────┐   ╳     ┌─────────────────┐
│ Data Reduction  │◀────────│Conclusion Drawing│
│                 │         │  or Verification │
└─────────────────┘         └─────────────────┘
```

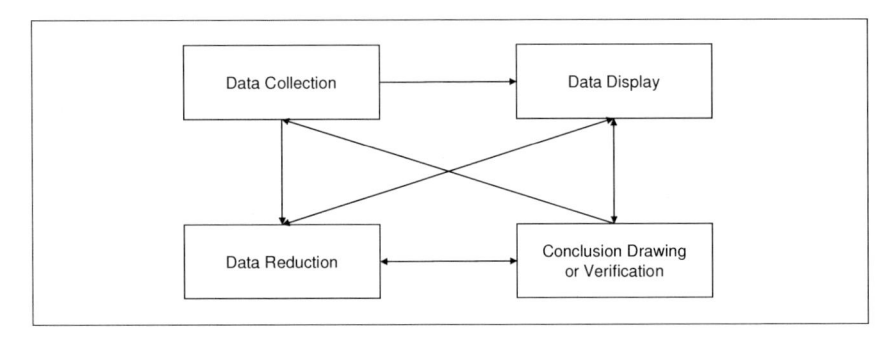

Figure 5-2:   Interactive model of data analysis
Source: Miles/Huberman 1994, p. 12.

In this study, data are reduced by coding the transcribed interviews. The code list is provided in the following sub-section. The code list is already a form of data display. Data are also displayed in graphs in the following chapter on empirical findings of the study. In the following chapter, conclusions are drawn and they are summarized in the final chapter.

5.3.2   Code List

As stated above, coding is a way to reduce data. Codes are defined as "... tags or labels for assigning units of meaning to the descriptive or inferential information compiled during a study" (Miles/Huberman 1994, p. 56). They can encompass few words, sentences or whole paragraphs.[116] Researchers employ codes in order to find and cluster units of texts which refer to the same construct, hypotheses or research ques-

---

[116] Not every piece of text has to be coded, however (Miles/Huberman 1994, p. 65).

tion. Codes can either be descriptive or interpretive. Furthermore, pattern codes are used when patterns of behavior become obvious throughout the research (Miles/Huberman 1994, pp. 56-58). Each code has to be clearly defined so that it is applied consistently by the researcher (Miles/Huberman 1994, p. 63). Clustering and displaying condensed text units is the basis of drawing conclusions later on (Miles/Huberman 1994, p. 57).

In order to decide which data should be taken into account codes should be derived from the conceptual framework, research questions or hypotheses. In the course of data analysis new codes are added (Miles/Huberman 1994, p. 58). The final code list is provided in appendix B.

5.4 Scientific Quality Criteria

Different criteria may be applied to evaluate the scientific quality of a study. However, there is no final agreement among researchers about which criteria apply for qualitative research. Some authors recommend using the same criteria as in quantitative research (e.g. Brühl/Buch 2006). Others defined varying criteria (e.g. Steinke 2004, Cepeda/Martin 2005). Construct validity, internal validity, external validity and reliability are criteria often used (Cepeda/Martin 2005, p. 862, Yin 2009, pp. 40-41). These criteria will be employed to discuss the empirical study.

5.4.1 Construct Validity

With construct validity the operational measures of the study are tested. It is evaluated whether the measures used actually reflect the phenomena that are intended to be examined. The problem thus arises mainly during the data collection phase. The issue of construct validity may be decreased by defining indicators, using multiple data sources like interviews with several respondents, documents or observations, establishing chains of evidence and having key informants review the draft (Bryman 1989, pp. 164-165).

In the present research project, operationalizations of constructs were presented in sub-section 5.1.3. They were mainly derived from literature. For instance, operationalizations of radical product innovations were employed in existing studies already. Other measures were described in literature conceptually but were not used in studies yet. They have been employed according to the description. In addition, the author was very attentive whether the respondents understood the measures. For instance, this was assured by asking the respondents to give examples for adaptations that were made between the business partners during the collaboration on the product innovation. All measures were defined thoroughly in the final code list and that has been provided in appendix B.

In this study, interviews were the main source of evidence. However, for the specification and description of the product innovation processes at both firms, other sources were included. In the case of drug development at Pharmasub, stages of the product innovation process were identified in literature. On this basis, it was discussed with respondents whether these stages apply to the product innovation process of Cogis. In the case of Cantis, graphs of the product innovation process at Diagnosub were provided to the author by the subsidiary. They were employed to discuss the development of Cantis. More sources of evidence were asked for by the author, which included information about the organizational structure and processes of integrating foreign subsidiaries in the product innovation process at Pharmacom. However, due to confidentiality of the information these sources were not provided. Apart from other types of sources respondents were also asked for contacts to their business partners. This was done in order to look at both perspectives of the business relationship. However, contacts to business partners of Pharmasub and Diagnosub could not be found because of reasons involving confidentiality. Both firms make CDAs with their external business partners that prohibit naming them.

Construct validity may also be assured by establishing chains of evidence. This is done by making the whole research process very transparent, from posing the research question in the beginning to explaining the results of the study in the end. In the chapter on results of the empirical study, adequate parts of the database have been cited. Discussion and interpretations of results are made as transparent as possible. Circumstances of data collection are obvious in the database (e.g. location and time of the interviews; Yin 2009, pp. 122-124).

Finally, construct validity is enhanced when key respondents read drafts of the empirical study. This affects the stage of reporting the case study. The empirical findings of this analysis were provided to Pharmasub and Diagnosub. Hence, this demand of scientific quality was met as well.

5.4.2 Internal Validity

Internal validity is a concern of explanatory or causal studies only (Yin 2009, p. 40). It is about the credibility and authenticity of the study (Miles/Huberman 1994, pp. 278-279). Internal validity is assured when the researcher correctly concludes from the study that one event causes another event. Differing explanations of the observed effect are excluded (Bortz/Döring 2002, pp. 56-57, Yin 2009, pp. 42-43). To assure internal validity, the instruments of pattern matching, explanation building,[117] addressing of rival explanations and usage of logic models may be applied (Yin 2009, p. 41). In the present study, most parts are rather descriptive in nature (see the research questions in section 1.2). Which type of stakeholder is most influential in stages of the product innovation process (research question 1.1) and is the receiver of the product innovation within the MNC (research question 2.1) are descriptive questions. The embeddedness and development of business relationships between firms and within the MNC (research questions 1.2.1 and 2.2.1, respectively) and the characteristics of knowledge and knowledge exchange (research questions 1.2.2 and 2.2.2) are mainly descriptive as well. Only in the end, explanations of the embeddedness of relationships and of the relationship between the embeddedness and characteristics of knowledge and knowledge exchange are developed. Here, explanations regarding the embeddedness of business relationships depending on different measures like criticality or trust are drawn in pattern matching and results from both cases are synthesized. Relationships between the embeddedness of business relationships and characteristics of knowledge are explained in theory and confirmed and refined by the results of the empirical study. In the sub-sections of organizational structures

---

[117] Explanation building is a special case of pattern matching (Yin 2009, p. 141).

and processes to facilitate corporate product innovation transfer, pattern matching is done again.

5.4.3 External Validity

External validity refers to the generalizability of results of the empirical study. The question is whether results can be transferred to other contexts and in which domain the results of the case study can be generalized (Miles/Huberman 1994, p. 279). When it comes to external validity, qualitative research is often criticized for not producing generalizable results. In quantitative study design, statistical generalizability is aimed at. This is not possible for research with a limited number of cases like in this study. However, qualitative case study research relies on another type of generalization: analytical generalization. A strategy to ensure analytical generalization is the replication of findings. This is achieved in the present publication by conducting two case studies. In these two case studies, the characteristics of embeddedness, knowledge and knowledge flows and the relationships between them are examined on an inter-organizational and intra-organizational level. Only the influential stakeholders on the single stages of the product innovation process cannot be replicated because different product innovation processes are analyzed in the cases. In addition, results are linked to theory in order to reach analytical generalization (Yin 2009, pp. 43-44). Theory is presented in chapter 4 in which the concepts of stakeholders, embedded business relationships, knowledge and knowledge flows are explained. The results are linked to theory in the discussion (chapter 7).

5.4.4 Reliability

Finally, the test of reliability has to be done. With this it is ensured that another researcher could do the same case studies and obtain the same results (Yin 2009, p. 45). While exact replication can hardly be achieved, inter-subject comprehensibility is aimed at in this study (Steinke 2004, pp. 186-188). This goal is approached by several instruments. First, this chapter about the empirical study serves to reconstruct the study for readers. Second, transcripts of the interviews are provided to the supervisor of the thesis. They are coded to make the assignment of text passages to analyzed constructs obvious. It is required that the coding of transcripts is done thoroughly. This can be assured by having two or more persons code the transcript. If they apply the same codes at the same text passages, inter-coder reliability is achieved (Schnell/Hill/Esser 2005, p. 405). As the author of the thesis is the only person that has coded material, intra-coder reliability must be guaranteed. This is done by coding more than half of the transcripts twice. The second coding takes place about two weeks after the first coding of the transcripts. More than 90% of the codes were the same as in first codification. This percentage is adequate (Miles/Huberman 1994, p. 64). Third, interpretations of the coded transcripts in the following chapter can not be made very comprehensible for readers. However, providing the theoretical framework that leads to pre-assumptions of the researcher is regarded as a way to enhance comprehensibility (Lamnek 2005, p. 170). Further, results of the interviews are discussed and conclusions are explained so that interpretations of material hopefully become obvious.

6 Empirical Findings

In this chapter, the findings of the empirical study are presented. The chapter starts with a description of the two cases, Cogis and Cantis (6.1.1 and 6.1.2). Furthermore, the innovative subsidiaries and product innovations are introduced and the intensity of innovation of Cogis and Cantis are assessed. Then, the geographical scope of both product innovation processes is described and product innovation processes are explained.

The following sections are organized according to the research questions of this dissertation.[118] In section 6.2, external business partners during the product innovation processes are presented. Then, the embeddedness of the business relationships to the most important external business partners is analyzed (6.3). In section 6.4, characteristics of knowledge and knowledge transfer between the innovative subsidiaries and their most important external business partners are explained. Finally, in section 6.5, the organization of product innovation transfer from the innovative subsidiaries to the global marketing organization is described. Within the sections, findings are presented according to the cases. In section 6.2, 6.3 and 6.4, which deal with the inter-organizational perspectives, findings are presented in cases and within the cases they are presented according to stages of the product innovation processes of Cogis and Cantis.

---

[118] The research questions are specified in section 1.2 on pages 3-5.

6.1 Basic Case Description

6.1.1 Cogis at Pharmasub

6.1.1.1 Pharmasub

Pharmasub is a German subsidiary of a Swiss based MNC.[119] The MNC to which the subsidiary belongs is called "Pharmacom" in this study. Pharmacom employed about 11,500 people in 2008. Its turnover amounted to € 3.3 billion. It has subsidiaries in over 50 countries; its products are sold in more than 100 countries. Pharmacom focuses on the development, production and marketing of medicines. It offers branded medicines for gastroenterology, respiratory and inflammatory diseases, pain and osteoporosis and tissue management. The MNC also sells over-the-counter (OTC) products.[120]

Pharmacom mainly licenses drug candidates in. This used to happen at late stages of the product innovation process until a few years ago but now it is done at earlier stages of the product innovation process as well. In addition, Pharmacom increasingly gets involved in developing drugs on its own, conducting all stages of the product innovation process from discovery to market launch. In order to obtain expertise in the whole product innovation process, Pharmacom bought other firms in the past. The biggest acquisition was done in 2006 and included the whole strategic business unit (SBU) of pharma of a German MNC from the chemical and pharmaceutical industry (referred to as "Pre-Pharmacom"). Part of this SBU was Pharmasub which is now the central R&D subsidiary of Pharmacom. It is involved at almost each stage of the product innovation process of new drugs.

---

[119] Information on Pharmasub was gathered from the website of the firm. It cannot be cited for confidentiality reasons.
[120] Over-the-counter products are non-prescription medicines.

6.1.1.2 Description of Cogis

Cogis is a drug which medicates Chronic Obstructive Pulmonary Disease (COPD) or smoker's cough. Despite the common name, this disease does not concern only people who smoke or have smoked. It is a complex fatal disease which cannot be simply reduced to a bacterial or viral infection. Instead, it has several causes and thus is a multifactorial disease. The disease causes the contraction of bronchial tubes, reduced active volume of the lungs, chronic bronchitis and an increased secretion of phlegm. Patients feel that they cannot breathe normally and also have problems with their skeletal muscles. This leads to serious problems with walking normal distances (A-R2&3 §59-61).

Until now, medicines only treat the symptoms of COPD. Their aim has been to relax the lungs in order to enable the patients to breathe normally. However, the causes for the disease have not been medicated yet. Cogis is the first drug which targets the causes and intends to modify the disease progression. It reduces or even stops the inflammation and in this way, not only relieves the symptoms but also modifies the course of the disease. Patients not only feel significantly better because they can breathe more easily but they do not acquire the dramatic stages of the disease that have to be treated in hospital. This not only benefits the patients but also reduces costs for national health systems. Thus, the drug has both an innovative mode of action and a new result. Third, the pharmaceutical form is very convenient. With existing medicines, patients mainly need to inhale. With Cogis, one capsule per day is sufficient (A-R2&3 §61-78).

6.1.1.3 Innovation Intensity of Cogis

The Head of Exploratory Clinical Development and the Director Strategic Planning and Business Support, were asked to evaluate the intensity of Cogis.[121] They as-

---

[121] Both respondents were interviewed jointly. They were the first respondents at Pharmasub. They were also particularly able to assess the intensity of Cogis because both the Head of Exploratory Clinical Development and Director Strategic Planning and Business Support have a very good insight into the product. As the Head of Exploratory Clinical Development is focused on the final

sessed Cogis undoubtedly as a radical product innovation. The evaluation of the intensity of Cogis is depicted in figure 6-1.

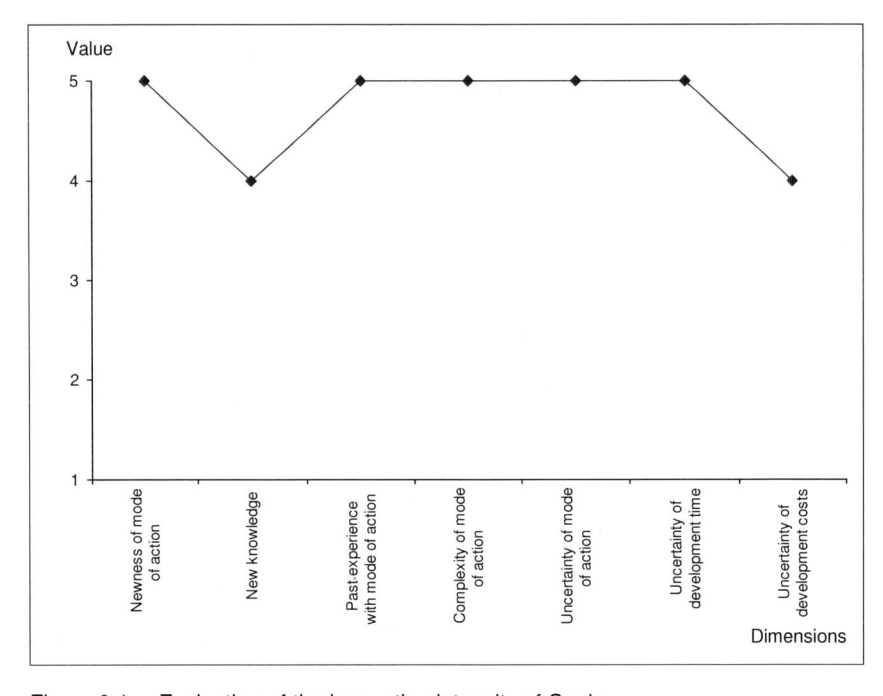

Figure 6-1: Evaluation of the innovation intensity of Cogis

The innovative mode of action will be integrated in a completely new drug (A-R2&3 §81). Newness, complexity and uncertainty of mode of action were assessed as very high (A-R2&3 §84-93, 142-146, 148-152). The newness of mode of action is so high that even experts at Pharmasub do not perfectly understand each step of the chemical chain that Cogis causes in the body of patients (A-R2&3 §125). The uncertainty of the duration of the product innovation process is very high until the end (A-R2&3 §157-159). The costs also cannot be predicted at the beginning of the project. Only the approximate cost of the innovation is known. Therefore, the uncertainty concerning this dimension was regarded as high (A-R2&3 §162-164). The amount of new knowledge which was obtained during the product innovation process was evaluated

---

stages of the product innovation process he knows about the whole product innovation process from the stages before clinical trials to the end.

as high, too (A-R2&3 §109-125). Pharmasub had no experience with the mode of action before the project (A-R2&3 §136-141).[122]

6.1.1.4 Geographical Scope of the Product Innovation Process of Cogis

Cogis was mainly but not solely developed at Pharmasub (for details on the product innovation process see the next sub-section 6.1.1.5). The lead development took place at Pharmasub and the lead was refined and developed to a substance. In vitro tests were conducted at Pharmasub or, in case of an external business partner proceeding them, they were coordinated by Pharmasub (A-R2&3 §184-194). In vivo studies (pre-clinic II) were coordinated by Pharmanorth which is a subsidiary situated in the north of Germany. Clinical trials I to III were conducted by Pharmasub. Once the innovation process of Cogis is finished, the drug will be transferred to HQs and foreign subsidiaries to sell the product on a worldwide basis. The product innovation process of Cogis thus is a globally-linked process even though Pharmasub plays the greatest role by far.

6.1.1.5 Product Innovation Process of Medicines

The pharmaceutical innovation process of new drugs is very specific concerning R&D activities. This is mainly because of strict legal regulations that apply to the industry. Broadly, the process may be divided into the stages of pre-clinical research and clinical trials. After the clinical trials are completed successfully, the drug enters the certification stage with legal authorities in different countries, for example the US Food and Drug Administration (FDA). Once the drug is approved, it may be launched in the market (Reiss/Hinze 2000, p. 53). The research and development process is presented here as a basic structure for the empirical study on the first research question. The product innovation process of medicines is depicted in figure 6-2.

---

[122] In figure 6-1, the reciprocal value of past experience with the mode of action is depicted as explained in sub-section 5.1.3.1.1.

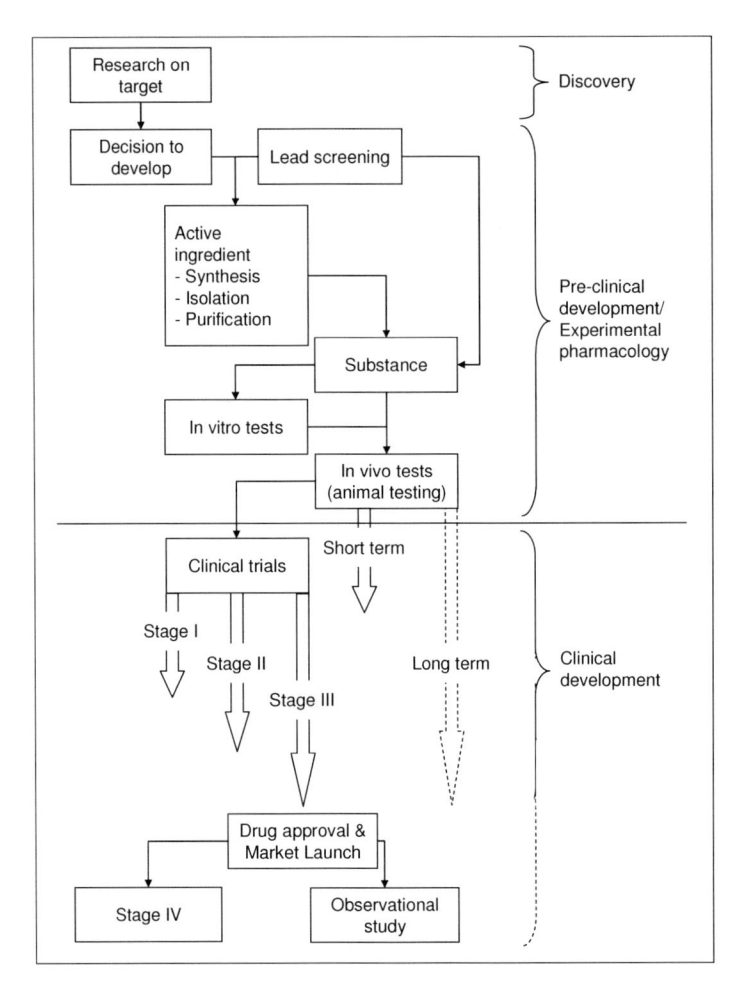

Figure 6-2: Product innovation process of drugs
Source: Adopted from Fischer/Breitenbach 2007, p. 69 and B-R2&3 §180-182.

At the beginning of the process, a protein, molecule or other substance in the body must be identified which serves as a target for curing a disease. This basic research is done in the discovery stage that is often carried out in universities. After a target has been found a pharmaceutical industry may decide to try and develop a drug based on this target. It starts with pre-clinical research that proceeds in three stages. After a target is defined, chemists screen up to 10,000 substances from the combinatory library of the firm in pre-clinic 0. They try to find some that interact with the target. About 20 substances are found during the screening process. They are called "hits" or "New Chemical Entities" (NCEs). These hits are taken as an indicator to look for similar chemical structures that might interact even better with the target. This way, an attempt is made to find causal relationships between target and hit. Furthermore, the effect of hits is intended to be improved by modifying their chemical structure.

The best fitting substances are called "leads" (Reiss/Hinze 2000, p. 53, Fischer/Breitenbach 2007, p. 49). These leads must be tested for their effectiveness, selectivity, toxicity and metabolizability. In order to optimize these specifications, the lead must be easy to synthesize and modify (Fischer/Breitenbach 2007, p. 56). This is done in pre-clinic I and II. In pre-clinic I, leads are examined in vitro with cells, tissues and organs. Pre-clinic I is also called chemical development. After this, the chemical structure of the hits is improved and its interaction with auxiliary substances is analyzed. In this stage, the first toxicological tests are made. Poisoning indication after a single application of the substances is investigated (acute toxicity). In pre-clinic II, the pharmacological and toxicological effects of the improved hits are studied in vivo with bacteria and animals. In this stage, chronic toxicological indications are analyzed which develop after a daily dose over one to three months. Reproduction toxicity encompasses tests of the effect on fertility, the impact of the substance on the embryo and deformation of newborns. Mutagenity and cancerogenity of the substances are then tested. After about four years of pre-clinical research approximately ten NCEs enter the stage of clinical trials. At this point in time, they may be spoken of "drugs" (Reiss/Hinze 2000, pp. 53-55).

Clinical development is usually subdivided into three stages as well. In all stages, tests with human beings are conducted. They serve to choose the best active ingredient and to improve it and its interplay with other components. Furthermore, clinical trials must be conducted in order to prove and document the quality, effectiveness, pharmacology and safety of the drug (Fischer/Breitenbach 2007, p. 87). Pharmacology includes pharmacokinetics and pharmacodynamics. In pharmacokinetics, it is observed how the concentration of the drug in the body changes over time. In pharmacodynamics, it is investigated how the drug works in the body of human beings (Fischer/Breitenbach 2007, p. 68). National approval authorities are provided with documentation of clinical trials. If the drug is not approved by national authorities, it cannot be sold in the country. In the first stage, clinical trials I, groups of about 10 healthy people are given the drugs that were selected through pre-clinical stages 0 to II. Special focus is on the safety and tolerability of the drugs that are tested. As the drug is tested with humans for the first time, proof of concept is made (Fischer/ Breitenbach 2007, p. 35). Special focus in stage I is on tolerability, pharmacokinetics and the definition of a range of doses for the following clinical studies (Fischer/ Breitenbach 2007, p. 93). Studies at clinical trials II and III are conducted with patients who have the disease that the drug intends to treat. In stage II, experts intend to prove the effectiveness of the drug for the indications that are supposed to be approved. Therefore, exploratory studies are conducted. 50 to 300 patients are involved in these studies. The form of application and the dose rate of the drug are defined in these studies. In stage III, findings of stage II are supposed to be confirmed with a large database. Up to several thousand patients are tested. Studies take several years. Apart from the effectiveness of the drug, side effects are examined. However, very rare side effects are only discovered in stage IV of the clinical studies. This stage begins after the approval of the drug. As there is no time pressure for the studies anymore, large numbers of patients are tested and rare side effects can be detected (Fischer/Breitenbach 2007, pp. 94-95).

There are some specifics about the product innovation process in the pharmaceutical industry. First, the pharmaceutical industry is regulated much more than other industries. Medicines must be approved by legal authorities of all countries. Legal authorities are the Food and Drug Administration (FDA) in the USA or the European Agency for the Evaluation of Medical Products (EMEA) which approves medicines for the 25 countries of the EU. If medicines are not approved by authorities, they cannot not be sold in the particular country or region (Fischer/Breitenbach 2007, pp. 36-37). Approval authorities get many documents about the quality, toxicity, pharmacology of the medicine, reports from clinical and non-clinical studies and the design of the package and package insert from the pharmaceutical firms (Fischer/Breitenbach 2007, pp. 125-127). Second, unlike most other industries, drugs are not modular products. If a compound of the drug does not suit others it can not simply be replaced by another compound. Rather, the system of the technology has to be changed (A-R2&3 §128-131, 160-161). This makes development of medicines very complex.

Discovery	Pre-clinical Development				Clinical Development		
Target	Lead screening	In vitro tests (cells, tissues)	In vivo tests (animal testing)		Clinical trials I (healthy test persons)	Clinical trials II (exploratory study on patients)	Clinical trials II (confirmatory study on patients)

Respondent: Head of Pharmacology and Pharmaceutical Drug Safety (A-R1)	Respondents: Head of Exploratory Clinical Development (A-R2), Director Strategic Planning and Business Support (A-R3)

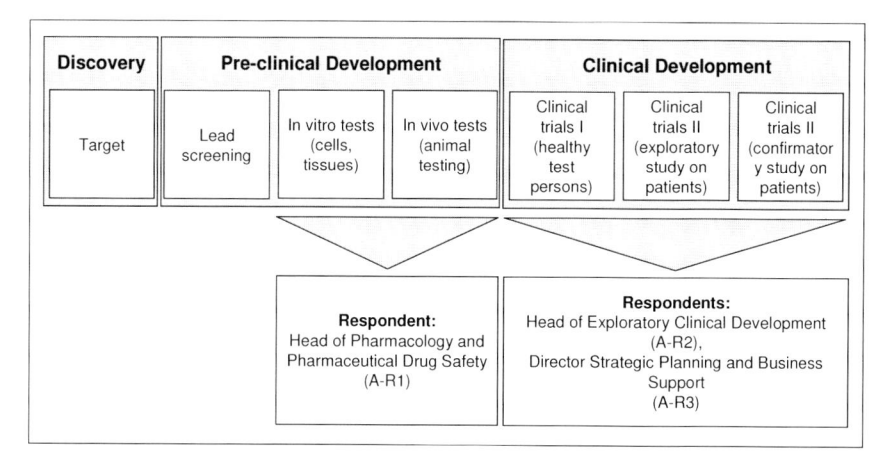

Figure 6-3: Analyzed stages of the product innovation process of Cogis

The model of the product innovation process in medicine development is idealized, of course. For example, stages I to III of the clinical trials are not conducted gradually. Instead, stages overlap (Fischer/Breitenbach 2007, pp. 92-93, A-R2&3 §202-204). Also, the innovative activity does not necessarily take place in discovery or pre-clinical development. Much of the innovation is created in clinical development (A-R2&3 §95-101).

In the case of Cogis, the product innovation process has gone through the stages of discovery, pre-clinical development and stage I to III of the clinical development. The innovation process of Cogis took about 20 to 25 years. It started in the 1980s. Experts of Pharmasub came up with the idea of developing a drug that is anti-inflammatory (A-R2&3 §63-65).[123] The drug is now on the edge of the approval stage. Cogis will presumably be approved and launched in 2010 (A-R2&3 §171-175). For the case study, experts were asked about the stages of in vitro and in vivo tests and clinical trials.[124] In figure 6-3, the stages that were examined and respondents in these stages are depicted.

---

[123] Respondents said that the idea of developing an anti-inflammatory medicine against COPD was developed internally at Pharmasub. Whether this is true or not can not be verified anymore because the experts who had the idea where no longer in the firm. The stage of lead screening could not be analyzed for the same reason.

[124] The Head of Pharmacology and Pharmaceutical Drug Safety was interviewed about the stages of in vitro and in vivo studies. He is located in a subsidiary in Northern Germany. However, in vitro studies were coordinated from Pharmasub. There, the contact to the most important business

6.1.2 Cantis at Diagnosub

6.1.2.1 Diagnosub

Diagnosub is a German subsidiary of a Swiss based pharmaceutical MNC which is referred to as "Diagnocom" in this study.[125] The turnover of the MNC was about € 30.5 billion in 2008. About 80,000 people worked in the MNC. Diagnocom operates in development, production and marketing of both medicines and diagnostic products for products on cancer, autoimmune and inflammatory diseases and virology. Accordingly, it is organized in two divisions: pharmaceuticals and diagnostics. Each division is sub-divided into different business areas. In the diagnostics division, five business areas exist of which one is professional diagnostics. Diagnostics had a turnover of about € 6.5 billion in 2008. About 25,000 people were employed at the diagnostics division in 2008.

Diagnosub is one of the R&D centers of Diagnocom. 4,500 people work in the subsidiary which is involved in the development and production of both diagnostic and pharmaceutical products. Personalized healthcare is a special focus of the subsidiary. In diagnostics, tests to identify diseases and technical platforms that read these tests are developed and produced.

6.1.2.2 Description of Cantis

The case is on the development of a test for colorectal cancer (CRC) and the platform which analyzes this test. The test is called CantisCRC in this thesis while the platform to read the test is called CantisPF. CantisCRC is innovative regarding two specifications. First, it is a multi-parametric test. So far, only one parameter (i.e. one marker) is used in tests in order to identify a disease. A one parameter test is positive

---

partner ResCog-A was made and kept. The Head of Pharmacology and Pharmaceutical Drug Safety received the results from this collaboration and he was also involved in the business relationship. In vivo studies were coordinated by him and thus, by the subsidiary in Northern Germany and not by Pharmasub.

[125] Information on Diagnosub was gathered from the website of the firm. It cannot be cited for confidentiality reasons.

if a particular protein is detected in the blood. The higher the concentration of the protein, the higher is the resulting value of the test. The multi-parametric test searches for several proteins in the blood. The intensity of each marker is identified and a final value for all markers is calculated on the basis of a formula. The test now is so sensitive and specific that the result predicts colorectal cancer with a very high certainty (B-R1 §14-16).

Second, the disease can be diagnosed on the basis of blood. Until now, colorectal cancer could only be diagnosed applying a stool test or a coloscopy. In the case of a stool test, the patient gets the instrument to do the test himself. However, many patients do not do the test, only 2-3% of them return to the doctor. If they return, the doctor sends the specimen to a laboratory which takes a few days to get the result. In the case of a coloscopy, the patient needs to take an extra appointment for the coloscopy. Many patients refuse to go to the coloscopy because it is an unpleasant procedure. If they go, a little piece of tissue is cut out of the intestine. The tissue is then sent to a laboratory which cuts the tissue in pieces and does several tests with these pieces. This procedure is quite costly. With the identification of the disease on the basis of serum, any doctor can immediately take blood from the patient. Thus, if the patient visits his general practitioner for any reason, he can take a blood sample which is an easy, quick and cost-efficient procedure. Patients are used to this procedure and normally do not oppose it. They do not need to be active themselves in any way and there is no fear of the examination that could make them miss their appointment with the doctor. The blood sample is tested directly at the premises of the physician or it is sent to a laboratory which does the test. The test itself takes about 30 minutes. Thus, it yields fast results and is cost-efficient compared to the coloscopy. Second, as patients do not need to become active, the test on the serum basis might help to identify colorectal cancer in an earlier stage which minimizes costs for the national health system (B-R1 §14-16, B-R2 §25-27).

The innovation actually consists of two product innovations: the test CantisCRC and the system platform CantisPF which analyzes the test.[126] For the multi-parametric

---

[126] The differentiation between CantisCRC and CantisPF is not always clear-cut because it is a system solution. The difference is defined here according to the activity. While CantisCRC is about the chemical work on the test, CantisPF includes both the chip on which the markers of the test

test, suitable markers needed to be identified and a formula to bring them together needed to be developed (B-R3 §23, 157). The markers were applied to a protein chip in which the serum is filled. The system platform takes the chip, fills it with the serum and with different reagents, takes a fluorescent picture of the chip and calculates the result on the basis of this picture.[127] An early version of the platform was developed in 1999 but the innovation process was not taken to the stage of design goal[128] because, at that time, there were no applications (B-R1 §52). Diagnosub knew that it could develop the platform and chips to analyze multi-parametric tests but no tests were developed so far. In the meantime, in addition to CantisCRC two tests for other diseases have been developed (B-R1 §18).

The product innovation processes of CantisCRC and CantisPF will be looked at separately. This is due to the following reason: The innovation process of CantisCRC and CantisPF run through the same stages of the product innovation process. However, the innovation activities with both products are very different. The innovation process of CantisCRC involves mainly chemical processes. Researchers who developed the test needed to identify markers in literature which react to proteins in the blood that indicate the existence of CRC. Then, they needed to prove that the marker actually reacts to CRC. Finally, they had to find the formula to calculate the final result (B-R3 §23, 157). In the product innovation process of CantisPF, mainly engineering activities are involved. CantisPF takes many different steps to analyze multi-parametric tests. The protein chip with the serum must be taken, filled with different reagents, they must be mixed and a fluorescent photo of the chip must be taken.[129] Also, the protein chip had to be developed on which the test is applied (B-R4 §9). Hence, different teams of experts were involved in the product innovation process of CantisPF and CantisCRC. Different types of external business partners are needed in the product innovation processes of CantisCRC and CantisPF.[130] However, the

---

are applicated and the platform that reads the test. Thus, CantisPF encompasses the engineering part of the system innovation.

[127] This was explained while the breadboard of CantisPF was demonstrated in the laboratory at Diagnosub.

[128] For details on the innovation process at Diagnosub see sub-section 6.1.2.5.

[129] This was explained while the breadboard of CantisPF was demonstrated in the laboratory at Diagnosub. Of course, it is a very simplified abstract of the analysis process.

[130] Even though it makes sense to look at CantisPF and CantisCRC for the reasons explained above, it is an artificial separation of both product innovations when looking at the product innovation process. In the stages of research, clearly different activities are done regarding CantisCRC and

internal process of passing on the product innovation is the same for both CantisCRC and CantisPF. The organizational structures and processes apply for both product innovations. Therefore, the intra-organizational aspects of both product innovations are explained together.

6.1.2.3 Innovation Intensity of Cantis

The intensity of CantisCRC and CantisPF were evaluated by the first two respondents at Diagnosub who were the Head of Innovation Management at Diagnosub and the Coordinator R&D and Workflows.[131]

6.1.2.3.1 Innovation Intensity of CantisCRC

Both respondents affirmed that the innovation would result in a completely new product (B-R1 §16, B-R2 §182).[132] The newness of technology and the gain in new knowledge during the product innovation process were both explained to be very high (B-R1 §16, B-R2 §20). Technology of the test was new because no multi-parametric protein tests existed before (B-R1 §14, 16, 24). A lot of knowledge was learnt about the validation of markers and the development of the formula to calculate the proportion of each marker during the product innovation process of CantisCRC (B-R1 §18). The degree of past experience with the technology that was used in the Cantis test was low. They had experience with developing one parameter tests from antibodies. However, they did not have experience with the particular markers in CantisCRC. Neither did they have experience with developing multi-parametric tests

---

CantisPF. However, when asked about development stages of CantisCRC, respondents mainly talk about the development of CantisPF (B-R1 §46, B-R3 §161). The innovation of CantisCRC is mainly done after research. Markers are identified and the formula is developed. The only problem of development that may arise is the upscaling of marker production (B-R1 §36). Applying markers on the chip, however, is done by the CantisPF team (B-R4 §9).

[131] In the first discussion with the Head of Innovation Management at Diagnosub he described the product innovation and assessed its intensity. When it became clear that the innovation of Cantis actually consists of two radical product innovations, CantisCRC and CantisPF, the intensity of CantisCRC was assessed separately. The intensity of CantisPF was clear from the discussion with the Head of Innovation Management.

[132] As stated in sub-section 5.1.3.1.1, this criterion was taken as a precondition to further consider product innovations and evaluate their intensity according to other criteria.

(B-R1 §24).[133] The complexity of the technology of CantisCRC and the uncertainty of development costs were assessed to be high (B-R1 §24-26 and B-R1 §42). The uncertainty of costs not only refers to R&D costs but also to costs for pre-marketing and marketing activities (B-R1 §34). Uncertainty also concerns the problem of keeping the price of CantisCRC low so that it is bought by doctors and reimbursed by health insurance (B-R1 §28, 30, 34). The uncertainty of technology was evaluated as medium (B-R1 §26). Both the success in research and in development, i.e. in upscaling for production, are uncertain (B-R1 §34-36). Finally, the uncertainty of development time was evaluated as low by the Head of Innovation Management (B-R1 §42) while it was assessed as high by the Coordinator R&D and Workflows. This was due to the fact that the development time depends heavily on the acceptance of the project at Diagnocom (B-R2 §183-191). Thus, the uncertainty of costs is set as medium in this thesis.

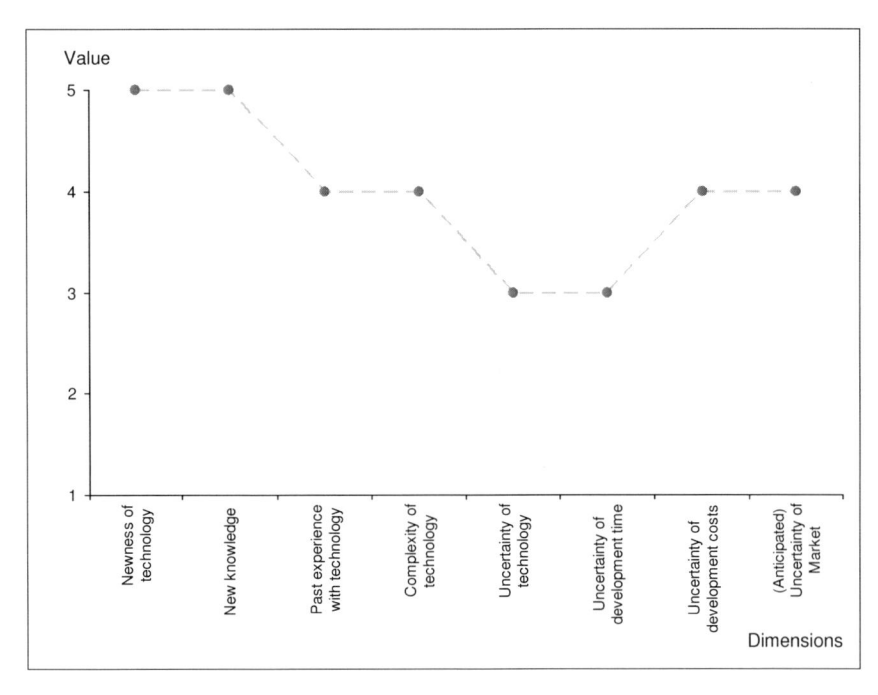

Figure 6-4: Evaluation of the innovation intensity of CantisCRC

---

[133] As stated earlier (see footnote 90 in sub-section 4.5.2.1), the value of past experience is taken reciprocally because less past experience means a higher radicality of product innovations.

A new criterion was added during the study: The Head of Innovation Management spoke of the uncertainty of the market several times. This included the acceptance of the new test with new technology in the market. Both doctors and health insurance systems have to be convinced that the new test has benefits compared to other diagnostic methods for colorectal cancer (B-R1 §26). In order to prove these benefits to doctors and health insurances and make the higher price of the new test legitimate, clinical tests have to be conducted and documented in a detailed way. Mostly, they need to be more detailed than the documents which are required by governmental institutions which approve new diagnostic products. The studies have hence become an increasingly important part in the product innovation process in the diagnostic pharma industry (B-R1 §30-32). This criterion was not included in the study from the beginning and it is not part of the technological dimension of product innovations. Uncertainty of market acceptance is an unanticipated phenomenon in this case as Cantis is not yet launched in the market. Looking at the other dimensions which were identified in the study of Hauschildt and Schlaak (sales market, purchasing, production process, formal and informal organization, Hauschildt/Schlaak 2001, p. 175), the new criterion fits the market dimension. However, none of the questions asked by the authors in this dimension suits the issue described here. In the case of CantisCRC, the uncertainty of market was evaluated as high (B-R1 §26). The intensity of CantisCRC is depicted in figure 6-4.

6.1.2.3.2 Innovation Intensity of CantisPF

CantisPF is a completely new product. It is needed to analyze multi-parametric tests (B-R1 §16). The technology of both the platform to read multi-parametric tests and of the protein chips for the CRC test is completely new (B-R1 §16, 24). Throughout the product innovation process of CantisPF, Diagnosub gained a lot of new knowledge. They were asked about the platform and the multi-parametric chips by competitors and the innovation was proposed for a science prize by the "Kurt-Eberhard-Bode Stiftung" (B-R1 §18). Diagnosub had no past experience with the innovative technology. Both the chip technology and the platform were brand new (B-R1 §20-22). Complexity of CantisPF was assessed as high and uncertainty of technology was assessed as medium (B-R1 §24-26, 42). Uncertainty of development time was low

(B-R1 §42). The development of instruments usually takes five to six years (B-R6 §25). Uncertainty of costs is medium. On the one hand, uncertainty of technology, time and cost were described to be rather low (B-R1 §39-40). On the other hand, cost pressure on Diagnosub is big. A pharmaceutical product is only reimbursed by health insurance when the insurers accept the cost benefit ratio. Hence, costs must be kept low (B-R1 §28). The uncertainty of the market was assessed as high for the whole system of Cantis that includes both the test CantisCRC and the platform CantisPF. Hence, the uncertainty of the market is high for CantisPF as well (B-R1 §25-26). In summary, the uncertainties of technology, time and costs are medium or low in the case of CantisPF. The other attributes though, were evaluated as high or very high. Thus, CantisPF is not as radical as Cogis or CantisCRC. Still, it is a clearly radical innovation. The intensity of CantisPF is depicted in figure 6-5.

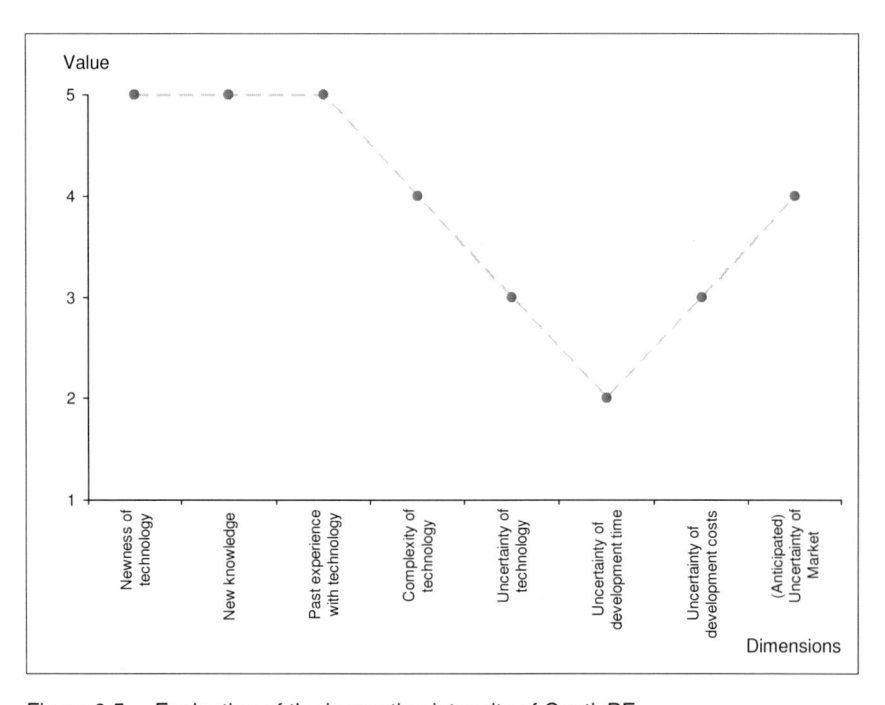

Figure 6-5: Evaluation of the innovation intensity of CantisPF

6.1.2.4 Geographical Scope of the Product Innovation Process of Cantis

CantisCRC and CantisPF are developed by Diagnosub. In this subsidiary, the idea of both the test and the system platform came up. All the stages of the product innovation processes which are completed have been conducted at Diagnosub. The following stages will be proceeded there as well (B-R6 §9). Once Cantis is in a stage to be marketed, it will be transferred to HQs in Switzerland. The global marketing organization is located there. From Switzerland, Cantis will be passed on to foreign subsidiaries of Diagnocom. They will carry on with local marketing activities (B-R2 §139-141). CantisCRC will be produced at Diagnosub. The platform system will be manufactured by an external partner but the production will also be coordinated by Diagnosub (B-R5 §14).

6.1.2.5 Product Innovation Process at Diagnosub

The product innovation process at Diagnosub is a stage gate process which consists of two sub-processes (B-R1 §8).[134] The first sub-process consists of research activities and encompasses three stages: idea description, basic technology studies and extended technology studies (B-R2 §10-13). The second sub-process involves development activities and includes four stages: analysis, feasibility, development and implementation. An overview of the product innovation process at Diagnosub is provided in figure 6-6.

For the development of tests, a particular indication is chosen at the stage of idea description, for instance here it is for the indication colorectal cancer. For this indication, the whole workflow from diagnosing the disease to the aftertreatment of an operation, for example, is analyzed. Steps in the workflow that are problematic are identified. For these gaps, the market is screened for products of competitors. Then ideas are developed as to how a gap could be filled with an own product. After specifications of the product have been defined experts at hospitals are approached. They are asked to evaluate the product idea and its specifications. Doctors assess whether

---

[134] The product innovation process is explained according to the example of Cantis. However, it is the general process model which is applied in each product innovation process of the site.

they would buy the product and which attributes are missing in the idea description (B-R2 §21). When the function of the potential new product can be explained in terms of the workflow of doctors or laboratories and its basic specifications can be described, the technology and marker board of Diagnocom discusses the idea and decides if the project should be continued and more research activities are conducted (B-R6 §55).

Research				Development			
Idea	Basic Technology Studies	Extended Technology Studies	Analysis	Feasibility	Development	Implementation	

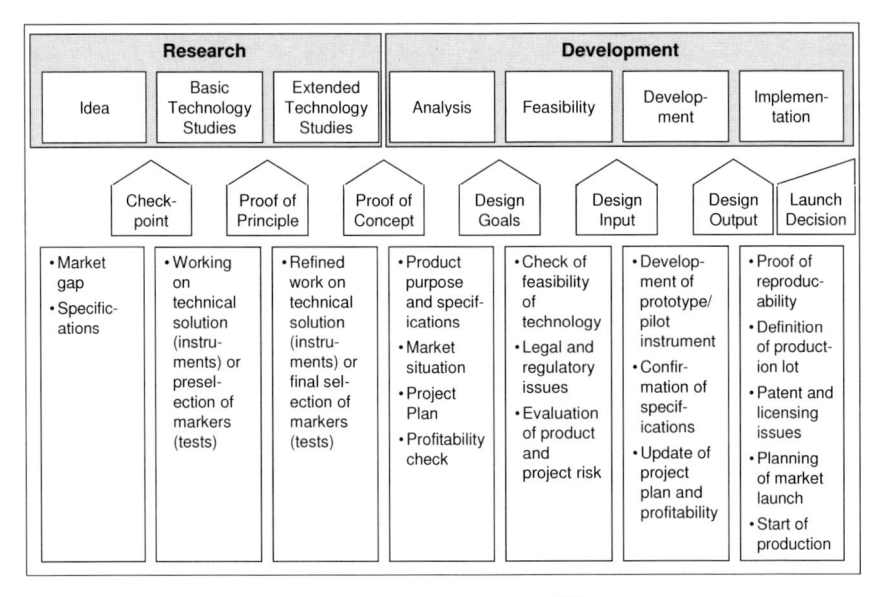

Checkpoint	Proof of Principle	Proof of Concept	Design Goals	Design Input	Design Output	Launch Decision
• Market gap • Specifications	• Working on technical solution (instruments) or preselection of markers (tests)	• Refined work on technical solution (instruments) or final selection of markers (tests)	• Product purpose and specifications • Market situation • Project Plan • Profitability check	• Check of feasibility of technology • Legal and regulatory issues • Evaluation of product and project risk	• Development of prototype/ pilot instrument • Confirmation of specifications • Update of project plan and profitability	• Proof of reproducability • Definition of production lot • Patent and licensing issues • Planning of market launch • Start of production

Figure 6-6: Product innovation process at Diagnosub[135]

At the stage of basic technology studies, marker candidates are tested for their performance in the diagnosis of colorectal cancer. Marker candidates are identified from different sources, screening literature, participating in conferences or buying them from other firms.[136] Experts at Diagnosub also develop markers themselves (B-R3 §23-27). They are tested by using tissue probes of patients with colorectal cancer. Markers are applied to these probes and evaluated according to their performance.

---

[135] Figure 6-6 is based on two illustrations that were provided by the Head of Innovation Management. One showed the research activities and the other one depicted the development activities.

[136] Markers respond to substances in the blood (e.g. proteins) that indicate a particular disease (or the amount of the substances does). These substances are called targets and like in the product innovation process of medicines, they are mostly identified in basic research by scientists at universities. Thus, the stage of basic research is rarely done in the firms.

Non-performers are not considered further (B-R3 §23-27, 35). At the end of basic technology studies, the milestone reached is called "proof of principle". At this milestone, the basic technological principle can be affirmed and it can tentatively be stated that a product can technologically be developed. The technology and marker board meets again and decides whether to continue with the project. This decision is based on opportunities and risks of the project. In extended technology studies, the test procedures are refined. Apart from the criterion of colorectal cancer, other diseases of the patients, the drugs they consume and demographic facts are taken into account. The number of tissue probes is a lot larger than in the basic studies. Marker candidates that survived the basic technology studies are tested in more detail and in combination with each other (B-R3 §151-157).[137] In the case of CantisCRC which is a multiparametrical test, the formula for calculating the selected markers is also developed during the extended technology studies. At the end of this stage, the technology and marker board meets again and the product portfolio board is also consulted. They decide whether the project is taken into the development stages which constitute the second sub-process (B-R6 §55). The development of CantisCRC is mainly done after the stages of research. Markers are identified and the formula is developed. The only problem in development stages that may arise is the upscaling of marker production (B-R1 §36). Applying markers on the chip, however, is done by the CantisPF team (B-R4 §9). Hence, from the R&D perspective there are very few development activities. Thus, it is not a problem that development stages of the test can not be analyzed.

For the development of CantisPF, the idea description was done during the research on the predecessor of CantisPF. Diagnosub thought that multi-parametric tests would be successful diagnostical products. However, at that time no tests had been developed yet so the project of the platform remained stagnant. According to the respondent, no external business partners were involved at this stage (B-R4 §9-11).[138] At the stage of basic technology studies, experts tried to find technical solutions for the identification of few basic markers and first developed breadboards. Sometimes,

---

[137] The activities that are undertaken in basic and extended technology studies are very similar. Therefore, Diagnosub collaborates mainly with the same business partners in both stages. Thus, they will be merged in the present research project.

[138] The Head of Technological Development stated that the idea for CantisPF came from an expert at Diagnosub. This expert had since left the firm and hence could not be interviewed.

markers could not be identified. In these cases it was evaluated whether this was due to the manual procedure. At this stage, a lot of the work is done manually so the work steps are not as precise as they would be if done by an automated instrument. Thus, the basic technology may be able to identify markers when work steps are automated. This is evaluated in the proof of principle (B-R4 §17-19). At the stage of extended technology studies, technological solutions for work steps of the platform are refined and breadboards are developed further (B-R4 §17). Like in the case of development of tests, work in the basic and extended technology studies is similar but it is more fine-grained in extended studies. Thus, both stages are analyzed jointly.

The second sub-process encompasses development activities of Diagnosub. It starts with the analysis stage where design goals are determined. Market gaps that have already been identified in the idea description are evaluated again. Specifications of the test and platform system are refined and are cross-checked with market demands in a more detailed way. The conceptual and scientific knowledge that was obtained during the first sub-process is now substantiated into a concept of an actual product. In the next stage, feasibility of the technology and profitability of the product are assessed and confirmed. Product and project risks are evaluated and regulatory issues are considered in order to make a detailed project plan. At the development stage, development activities are nearly finished. A prototype is built. It is checked if specifications are met by the pilot test and platform system. At the implementation stage, scale up of the product is planned. Parts of the product and materials used are defined; production and logistics are planned. The project plan and profitability evaluation are updated. After implementing the decisions and proving that the product can be manufactured in large quantities, the launch is finally decided. The external validation of the product performance is completed. Production and logistic processes are validated and the production lot is agreed upon. Marketing activities are prepared. After the product is launched and sold for some time, a post launch review is made. Customer feedback and complaints and manufacturing and quality control experiences are analyzed. Sales volume and profitability of the product are checked and countermeasures are implemented if necessary. The project account is finally closed.[139]

---

[139] This description is based on a figure that was provided by the Head of Innovation Management.

The product innovation process of CantisCRC has taken about five to six years at the time of the interviews (June 2009) (B-R3 §18-19).[140] The research on CantisCRC has been terminated. Markers are identified that diagnose CRC. The formula to combine the markers has been developed, too. Feasibility has already been demonstrated and confirmatory studies of the effectiveness of the test have been conducted with large populations of patients. Feasibility and confirmatory studies are usually done at the developmental stages only. However, as CantisCRC is such an important project some work steps have been done earlier. Now, the project enters the development stages and approaches the design goals (B-R2 §15-19). In the upcoming stages of development, mainly upscaling of marker production is done. Hence, the innovative activities of the product innovation process are finished. All three stages of research (idea, basic and extended technology studies) are analyzed in this thesis as depicted in figure 6-7.

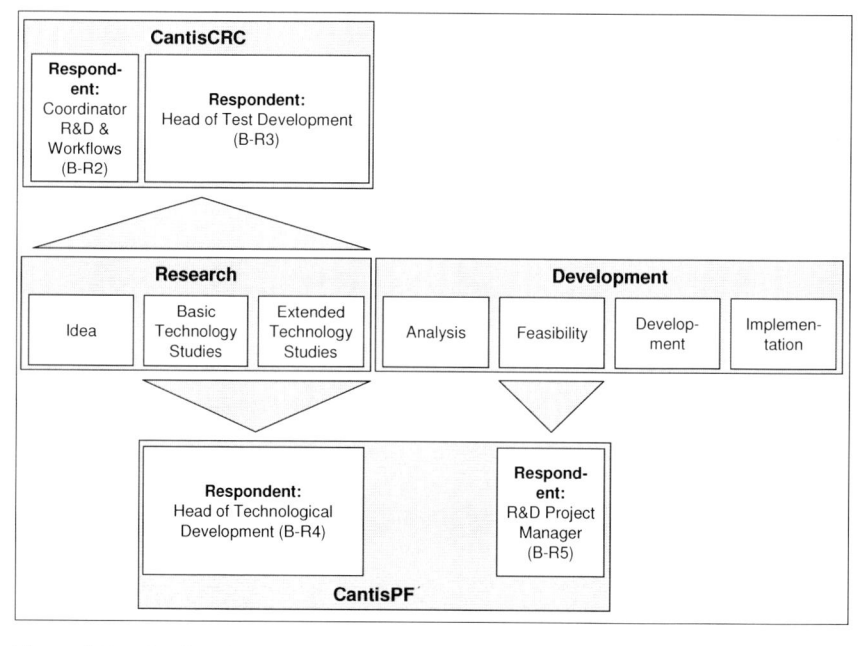

Figure 6-7: Analyzed stages of the product innovation process of CantisCRC and CantisPF

---

[140] Another respondent talked about two years (B-R6 §25).

The engineering team develops both the chips that carry the dots of markers and the instrument to read the tests, CantisPF. CantisPF is based on an earlier project (B-R4 §11). Diagnosub knew that a platform to conduct multiparametrical tests would be a successful product. However, as they did not yet have any tests for the instrument, the project was put on hold. It was picked up about seven years ago. Due to the stagnation of the project, there has been a long time gap since the idea description stage. The expert who was in charge for this stage and had the idea of the project was also no longer with the firm. Thus, this stage could not be analyzed. CantisPF now approaches the design input. Breadboards are developed and technical solutions for each work step of the instrument are found. Thus, the innovative part of the product innovation process is done. Further, external business partners are selected to build the final product. The final version of CantisPF must be producible in large amounts, it must be able to handle about 12,000 chips per day and it must be producible at low cost. As depicted in figure 6-7, the stages of basic and extended technology studies and of feasibility are analyzed.[141]

6.1.3 Comparison of the Cases of Cogis and Cantis

While Cogis is a medicine, Cantis is a diagnostic product that consists of CantisCRC and CantisPF. Cogis and Cantis are therefore different and their comparability must be proven. This is done in the present sub-section. The arguments are summarized in table 6-1.

(1) First, in both cases, **firms collaborate heavily with external business partners** of different stakeholder groups. Universities and private research institutions play an important role in the product innovation process of both firms because specialization is high in the industry and work is divided among business partners for reasons concerning expertise and cost.

---

[141] At the stage of analysis, work is done internally without the participation of external business partners. At this stage, the evaluation of market gaps and product specifications is re-assessed and refined. The expert that was responsible for this stage is no longer in the firm and hence could not be interviewed (B-R5 §10).

Criteria	Cogis	Cantis
Collaboration with external business partners	• Collaboration with various stakeholder groups, e.g. universities and private research institutions	• Collaboration with various stakeholder groups, e.g. universities and private research institutions
Product innovation process include idea, basic research, advanced research, and development	• Basic research: discovery of target • Idea: decision to develop • Advanced research: lead screening, in vitro tests, in vivo tests • Development: clinical trials I, II, and III	• Basic research: targets for markers • Idea: idea description • Advanced research: basic and extended technology studies • Development: analysis, feasibility, and development
Capabilities in the product innovation process	• Mainly biochemical knowledge involved • Special focus on extensive legal requirements and on marketing studies for reimbursement authorities	• Mainly biochemical (CantisCRC) and engineerial (CantisPF) knowledge involved • Special focus on extensive legal requirements and on marketing studies for reimbursement authorities

Table 6-1: Similarities between Cogis and Cantis

(2) Second, **both product innovation processes are grounded on the same basic activities** of basic research, advanced research and development that were presented in sub-section 2.2.1.1. In sub-sections 6.1.1.5 and 6.1.2.5, the product innovation processes of both firms are explained. With drug development, basic research takes place when a target for the treatment of a disease is searched for and identified. In the case of the development of diagnostic tests, the target is a substance that indicates a disease. In both medicine and test development, basic research is rarely done in pharmaceutical firms. Rather, scientists at universities do research on a disease and identify targets. After the idea of developing a medicine or a diagnostic test based on a target is approved by the management of a pharmaceutical company, R&D experts of the company begin with applied research. In drug development, these stages are called preclinical development and include lead screening, in vitro and in vivo tests. Development activities encompass three stages of clinical trials. This is called clinical development in pharmaceutical industry. In the development of diagnostic products, applied research encompasses the stages of basic and extended technology studies. In these stages, the specifications of the product are defined and the feasibility of the product is proved. Indicators of the disease are identified and combined to the product. Development takes place in the stages of analysis,

feasibility and development. In these stages, the final product that can be produced at a large scale is developed.[142]

(3) Third, **both product innovation processes involve similar capabilities.** Analysis and a study of biochemical activities are core activities in both firms. Business activities like marketing studies and legal activities like the consideration of legal requirements are done in both product innovation processes as well. Apart from regulatory issues, both firms deal a lot with administrative questions concerning the national health systems. The market success of both drugs and diagnostic tests and platforms depends to a very high degree on reimbursement. Health insurance providers need to be convinced that the benefits of the new drugs or diagnostic systems outweigh their costs. Therefore, benefits and problems of the product that are specified throughout the innovation process need to be documented in a very detailed way. Thus, basic activities are comparable.

6.2 External Business Partners in the Product Innovation Process

In this section, it is examined which types of stakeholders[143] were most influential in the product innovation processes of Cogis (6.2.1) and Cantis (6.2.2). A summary of the most important business partners will be provided after each of the product innovation processes has been analyzed (6.2.1.3 and 6.2.2.3). At the end of the section, both cases are compared and conclusions are drawn.

---

[142] For more details on the stages of the product innovation processes see sub-section 6.1.2.5.
[143] As explained in sub-section 4.3.1.1.1, business partners are defined as actors who are in a business relationship with the focal actor in the present contribution. They provide the focal actor with knowledge or goods or who receive knowledge or goods from the focal actor. The term "stakeholder" is used as a synonym for business partner. It stresses that different stakeholder groups exist each with specific demands for the focal actor and which provide it with specific inputs. For more details see sub-section 4.5.1.

6.2.1 External Business Partners in the Innovation Process of Cogis at Pharmasub

As part of the product innovation processes of Cogis, the stages of in vitro tests, in vivo tests and clinical trials I to III were analyzed. The most influential business partners in each stage of the product innovation process will now be described. Specifically, it will be clarified which stakeholder groups are important at each stage of the process. The most influential business partner at each stage of the innovation process of Cogis will then be presented and reasons for the selection of the particular business partner will be provided.

Generally, during the innovation process of medicines, external business partners are needed mainly for two reasons: First, pharmaceutical firms do not have the expertise and capacity to carry out all the processes that are part of the product innovation process. Second, external business partners are helpful in the contact to governmental institutions. For instance, reports from external experts are required in the approval process in order to increase the credibility of results and prove that the process was carried out correctly (A-R2&3 §200).

6.2.1.1 Pre-clinical development

6.2.1.1.1 Pre-clinic I: In vitro tests

In vitro tests start when the target for the drug has been identified in discovery and leads developed in pre-clinic 0. At the stage of in vitro tests, leads are tested with cells, tissues and organs (Reiss/Hinze 2000, pp. 53-55).

At the stage of in vitro tests, Pharmacom usually collaborates with service contractors, universities or private research institutions that conduct studies for Pharmasub. Studies serve to clarify open questions regarding the effectiveness of the active compounds or of excluding risks for animals that are provided with the substance in the in vivo tests. Of course, effectiveness and risks are optimized for the test persons in clinical trials. In some rare cases, Pharmacom also works with other pharmaceutical firms to use their instruments (A-R1 §19-22, 115-116).

In the case of Cogis, the most influential business partner was a researcher and his team in the USA. This researcher works at a private research institution. His primary interest is in science. He collaborates with pharmaceutical firms on single projects but this is not his core business. Therefore, he is called ResCog-A in this thesis. He conducted studies and consulted Pharmasub concerning the problem of the olfactory toxicity of Cogis. In in vivo studies, the active compound of Cogis was found to be toxic to rodents like mice or hamsters.[144] With rodents, Cogis caused changes in the epithelium of the nose. Cells mutated, inflammations developed and after some time, tumors were caused. Of course, these risks had to be thoroughly excluded for humans before tests with humans could begin (A-R1 §34-38, 115-116, 228). ResCog-A proved the non-toxicity of Cogis to humans. Pharmasub received the results from the studies on olfactory toxicity of Cogis to humans from ResCog-A. The results consisted of data from the study and the interpretation of the data. They were accompanied by the documentation of the study. The documentation is needed for approval authorities of medicine (A-R1 §98, 104, 134). In return, ResCog-A received money from Pharmasub for the studies he conducted. Furthermore, he might have used the findings of the studies in his publications. However, this was doubted by respondents (A-R1 §70, 72).

ResCog-A was selected as a business partner by Pharmasub because he was one of very few experts in the field of olfactory toxicity. He was by far the most experienced and best equipped scientist. He specialized in enzymes, tissues like the olfactory epithelium and different species of which he tested cells and tissues (A-R1 §40). He was approached by experts at Pharmasub. They identified him in scientific literature. ResCog-A was also recommended to them by another scientific consultant (A-R1 §40-42).

---

[144] This example shows that the ideal model of the product innovation process in drug development does not always apply to reality. In vitro and in vivo studies were not conducted gradually but in parallel in the case of Cogis.

6.2.1.1.2 Pre-clinic II: In vivo tests

At the stage of in vivo tests, Pharmacom generally worked with the same kind of actors as during in vitro tests. It's mainly service contractors that conduct studies for Pharmanorth. Other business partners are universities or private research institutions. In rare cases, Pharmanorth also collaborates with other pharmaceutical firms to use their instruments (A-R1 §19-22). In addition, scientific consultants advise Pharmanorth about matters concerning in vivo studies (A-R1 §145-146).

In the case of Pharmanorth, the most influential business partner was a service contractor. It is called ClinCog-A in the present study. ClinCog-A is an MNC. Pharmanorth worked with the German subsidiary of ClinCog-A. As a study center, its business model is to carry out in vivo studies for pharmaceutical firms. For Pharmanorth, it conducted in vivo studies with Cogis with apes. These studies included investigations on side effects like toxicity, tolerability and genetic effects of Cogis. ClinCog-A transferred the data of the studies to Pharmanorth and also delivered its own interpretations of these data. For these studies, they were paid by the pharmaceutical firm (A-R1 §154-162, 198, 223-224). Pharmasub received the results and documentation of the studies (A-R1 §220).

ClinCog-A was selected by Pharmanorth to conduct the studies because they had great expertise in the field of toxicity studies. ClinCog-A had up-to-date equipment to conduct the studies and the infrastructure to guarantee a smooth process. Further, past collaborations between Pharmanorth and ClinCog-A were perceived as very pleasant and successful. The business relationship got more embedded during the Cogis project (A-R1 §154-162). Coordination between both partners was not very formal but uncomplicated. If an issue arose one partner called the other and they discussed the problem. Furthermore, they were located rather near to Pharmanorth which made visitations easy (A-R1 §163-166, 171-172).

6.2.1.2 Clinical Development

6.2.1.2.1 Clinical Trials Stage I

During the three stages of clinical trials, private research institutions, service contractors and university hospitals are the most important external stakeholders (A-R2&3 §200). Service contractors in the form of specialized study centers are the most important external business partners. They recruit healthy test persons for clinical studies (A-R2&3 §208, 671).

Most private study centers are specialized in particular diseases. They recruit healthy participants for clinical studies in stage I (A-R2&3 §216-223). Often, test persons participate repeatedly in clinical studies of stage I. They know the study center and go there to take part in clinical trials. If each pharmaceutical firm carried out the clinical trials themselves, test persons would need to go to the different firms (A-R2&3 §216-233). Apart from the access to participants, private study centers for clinical trials have special process knowledge on conducting clinical trials. They know how to proceed with the clinical tests quickly, precisely and reliably (A-R2&3 §313-317). This is very important because time is a critical issue in conducting clinical trials (A-R2&3 §222). Delays are costly for Pharmasub (A-R2&3 §305).

In the case of Cogis, the business partner who was particularly influential in stage I of the clinical trials of Cogis is called ClinCog-B. Respondents described the capabilities of the study center as operationally excellent (A-R2&3 §318). In opposition to ClinCog-A, ClinCog-B only delivered data of the studies but no interpretations. This is due to the fact that ClinCog-B did not know which test persons they provided with Cogis or a non-effective substance (A-R2&3 §369-373, 673). Thus, Pharmasub had the scientific, conceptual and strategic knowledge while the contract service providers like ClinCog-B had the operational knowledge on carrying out clinical trials (A-R2&3 §313-320).

ClinCog-B was selected by the R&D management of Pharmasub for two reasons (A-R2&3 §241-244): At the time of the studies on Cogis, Pharmasub had an agreement with ClinCog-B and the study center was chosen because it was located near Pharmasub (A-R2&3 §235-240).

6.2.1.2.2 Clinical Trials Stage II and III

In stage II and III of the clinical trials, patients who have the disease that the medicine intends to treat take part in the studies. The external business partners are mainly hospitals, often university hospitals that carry out the study. The patients are under medical treatment in that hospital for the particular disease and are asked to participate in the study and to help in testing the new medicine by their doctor (A-R2&3 §222). Often, the study is carried out in several hospitals so that data are delivered from multiple partners (A-R2&3 §573). Although study nurses are staffed specifically for a study, university hospitals are less specialized and experienced in conducting studies than service contractors in stage I of clinical trials (A-R2&3 §671). The most important business partner was a university hospital and it was the same in stage II and III of the clinical trials (A-R2&3 §520-521, 625). This partner is called ClinCog-C.

ClinCog-C is a university hospital. In opposition to ClinCog-A and ClinCog-B, it is not the primary activity of ClinCog-C to conduct studies for pharmaceutical firms. University hospitals treat their patients and conduct studies as side projects only. However, benefits and rewards are the same as in the business relationships with ClinCog-A and ClinCog-B. For the studies, ClinCog-C was paid by Pharmasub (A-R2&3 §670-671). Pharmasub received the data and documentation of the studies. ClinCog-C only delivered data of the studies but no interpretations because ClinCog-C did not know which test persons they provided with Cogis or a non-effective substance (A-R2&3 §673).

6.2.1.3 Summary of the External Business Partners in the Product Innovation Process of Cogis

In the earlier sub-sections, business partners of Pharmasub and Pharmanorth in the product innovation process of Cogis were reported. The most important business partners were described in detail. In the stage of in vitro tests, the most important business partner was ResCog-A. He was a scientist at a private research institution. In the stages of in vivo tests and clinical trials I, the most important business partners were service contractors, ClinCog-A and ClinCog-B. The main difference between the two was that ClinCog-A delivered interpretations with the data while ClinCog-B provided Pharmasub with data only. In clinical trials II and III, the same actor was the most important business partner, ClinCog-C. ClinCog-C was a university hospital that conducted studies for pharmaceutical firms as side projects. The business partners are depicted in figure 6-8.

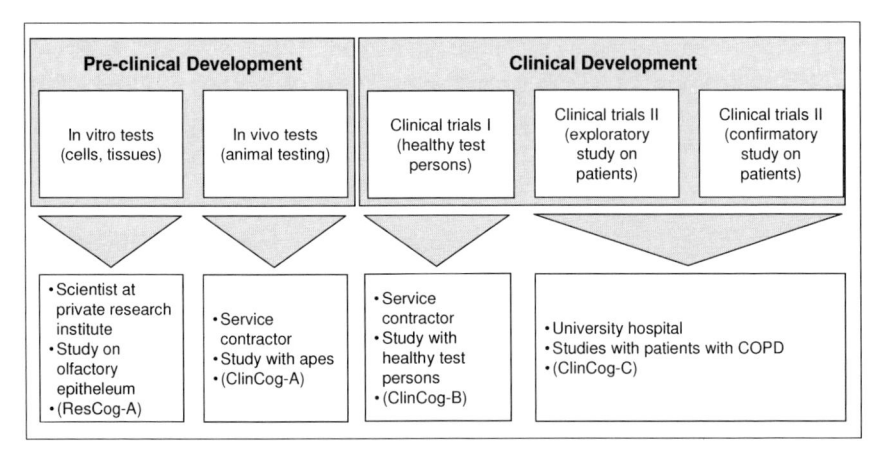

Pre-clinical Development		Clinical Development		
In vitro tests (cells, tissues)	In vivo tests (animal testing)	Clinical trials I (healthy test persons)	Clinical trials II (exploratory study on patients)	Clinical trials II (confirmatory study on patients)
• Scientist at private research institute • Study on olfactory epitheleum • (ResCog-A)	• Service contractor • Study with apes • (ClinCog-A)	• Service contractor • Study with healthy test persons • (ClinCog-B)	• University hospital • Studies with patients with COPD • (ClinCog-C)	

Figure 6-8: External business partners of Pharmasub during the product innovation process of Cogis

Through the whole product innovation process of Cogis, ResCog-A was the most influential business partner. If he had not proven that Cogis is not toxic to humans, it would not even have entered the stage of clinical trials. Further, ResCog-A was the only scientist who could conduct the studies. In contrast, ClinCog-A, ClinCog-B, and ClinCog-C conducted important but not critical studies. Of course, the studies had to be conducted and properly documented for approval authorities. But the business partners could have been replaced by other service contractors and university hospitals. Especially results of studies of stages II and III were not as uncertain as the in vitro study.

6.2.2 External Business Partners in the Innovation Process of Cantis at Diagnosub

6.2.2.1 External Business Partners in the Innovation Process of CantisCRC at Diagnosub

6.2.2.1.1 Idea Generation

At the stage of idea generation of new diagnostic products, the input of experts at Diagnosub is higher than in other stages of the product innovation process. They screen the market of diagnostic products systematically for market gaps. Ideas for radically new products seldom come from external sources. Marketing only passes on ideas for the improvement of existing products or the extension of a product line. Congresses may draw the attention of Diagnosub on popular themes. However, experts at R&D and Business Development often decide to develop a diagnostic product for an indication according to other criteria, for instance the frequency of particular diseases. Then they analyze the workflow of doctors, hospitals and laboratories along the whole process of detecting the disease to the aftercare. The experts look for processes in the workflow that are not managed perfectly and define the specifications of a product which would solve this situation in a better way. They also consider new products of competitors. Only when they have an idea of how the product should be and at which step of the workflow the product would approach they discuss their idea with a doctor, often of university hospitals (B-R2 §21).

Doctors at university hospitals are often chosen as first external partners to discuss a new product idea. As against doctors at other hospitals they are involved in research. Thus, they are particularly interested in new solutions for problems in diagnosing and treating diseases. They are able and willing to imagine other solutions than the ones that are employed at the moment. Therefore, they are helpful partners to critically discuss new product ideas. As potential customers of the product, doctors tell Diagnosub whether they would buy the product. Further, they can identify specifications that the new product needs in order to improve existing processes. This helps professionals at Pharmasub to push the product idea internally (B-R2 §33).

In this case of CantisCRC, the most influential business partner was a doctor at a university hospital in the UK. She is specialized in CRC and hence, was a potential customer of CantisCRC. Therefore she is called CustCRC-A in this study. For the evaluation of CantisCRC in the stage of idea description, she was not paid by Diagnosub and did not get any other reward. In this particular case, the business relationship ended after this stage. Usually, she would have been approached for conducting studies in later stages of the product innovation process. If these studies would have been successful, she would have been named as one of several authors in publications of the study results (B-R2 §33, 43, 83, 91). Diagnosub benefited from the knowledge of CustCRC-A (B-R2 §159, 117).

CustCRC-A was chosen as a business partner at this stage for several reasons. First, an expert in the UK was needed because the UK is a very important market for the pharmaceutical industry and its health care system is different from that of other European countries. Second, she had many publications in the field of colorectal cancer. Third, professionals at another business partner of Pharmasub were asked whether they knew experts in this field. They also recommended CustCRC-A to Diagnosub (B-R2 §43).

6.2.2.1.2 Basic and Extended Technology Studies

During the stages of basic and extended technology studies, the innovative activities of identifying marker candidates and evaluating them are done at Diagnosub. Both the identification of marker candidates and the evaluation are done according to criteria that are specific to Diagnosub. Furthermore, the collection of markers for the final test is also developed by the experts of Diagnosub (B-R3 §21-31). For the tests of marker candidates, sample material from patients is needed. It is delivered by state or university hospitals. They were the most important business partners for Diagnosub at the stages of basic and extended technology studies of the innovation process of CantisCRC because they provided much of the sample material (B-R3 §37).[145] 20 to 25 sites collected material for the control group i.e. from persons who do not suffer from CRC.

ClinCRC-A, a German university hospital (B-R3 §53), was the most important business partner for Diagnosub at this stage (B-R3 §37). ClinCRC-A provided Diagnosub with sample material. The sample material was processed at the university hospitals already. In addition to the sample material, the hospital transferred knowledge to Diagnosub (B-R3 §41-43). Knowlegde included demographic data on the patients, for instance their age and sex. Furthermore, knowledge on the CRC disease was also passed on, for instance on the size of the tumor, whether it was metastatic and how it was operated. Without this knowledge, the sample material could not have been used by Diagnosub (B-R3 §77). In addition, ClinCRC-A brought their knowledge on the processing of studies in the business relationship. For instance, Diagnosub discussed with them how patients should be grouped (B-R3 §111).

In return, ClinCRC-A got the amount spent for the study from Diagnosub. As the studies are part of ClinCRC-A's research, Diagnosub funds part of their research. Apart from payment, potential publications in later stages of the product innovation process are a reward for the study doctor. At the end of the product innovation process CantisCRC is tested in clinical trials. Hence, the collaboration of the early stages might be continued. The university hospital might earn more. If the product innovation process on CantisCRC is successful and the product gets launched publications on the mode of action of the test are written. The professor who managed the study would be listed as one of the authors (B-R3 §87).

It was selected by the project team of CantisCRC at Diagnosub for five reasons: First, ClinCRC-A is a well-known university hospital. This is important because it signals that the university hospital has up-to-date therapies. Above that, professors at well-known hospitals act as opinion leaders. Once the product is launched, they can be asked to talk about CantisCRC at conferences (B-R3 §57). Second, ClinCRC-A

---

[145] In other cases, the most important business partners might be firms or universities doing research. If they identified and developed new markers for a particular protein, for instance, Diagnosub might license the marker. It could be integrated in a test (B-R3 §13-15).

does a lot of research and publishing. Professors of the hospital are invited to conferences. Third, ClinCRC-A has many patients with CRC. Of course, hospitals which do not have many CRC patients would not be able to deliver enough sample material. Fourth, ClinCRC-A has the infrastructure to collect the data. Medical staff at hospitals is very busy with every day work with patients. Thus, a study nurse is needed who solely cares about collecting samples and information. Fifth, reliability is a criterion. In the case of ClinCRC-A, this could hardly be assessed before the beginning of the business relationship. However, in other cases the team from clinical trials at Diagnosub is asked about their experience with a hospital (B-R3 §55).

6.2.2.2 External Business Partners in the Innovation Process of CantisPF at Diagnosub

6.2.2.2.1 Basic and Extended Technology Studies

At the stage of basic and extended technology studies, Diagnosub collaborated with several firms to develop different parts of the platform for serial maturity. For the proof of principle a rough version of the breadboard was sufficient. In this rough version, more work steps were done manually than in the final product, and several parts of the breadboard were very expensive. However, for serial production the platform needed to be low cost (B-R4 §79). Furthermore, it must be possible to produce the platform at a large scale and to handle tests in large numbers (B-R4 §11).

In basic and extended technology studies, business partners were mainly involved for two reasons. First, engineers of different fields work at Diagnosub. They are able to develop some solutions for different technical problems. They can also evaluate solutions presented to them by external business partners. However, engineers in the R&D of Diagnosub are not as specialized as in firms that focus on the fields of optical instruments or mixture procedures, for instance. Thus, external business partners are integrated in the stage of basic and extended technology studies because they have specific knowledge and competences that Diagnosub does not have (B-R4 §25-27). Second, professionals at Diagnosub looked for different solutions for a particular problem in order to find the optimal solution for CantisPF. Especially in critical issues like the mixing procedure of chemicals in this case, Diagnosub tried to identify as many solutions as possible. If one solution did not work in the manual version of the breadboard it could still have been the best solution for the automated breadboard (B-R4 §9).

The most important business partner in both stages was SupPF-A. The firm was specialized in optical instruments and collaborated with Diagnosub in the development of a photodetector (B-R4 §27). SupPF-A did contract research for Diagnosub. The firm was paid by Diagnosub for the development of a detector and for producing a small number of detectors for the breadboards of Diagnosub. However, if Diagnosub could have given SupPF-A a perspective SupPF-A would probably have produced detectors for Diagnosub in larger scale and thus, would have been the supplier of photodetectors for CantisPF (B-R4 §25, 33).

In order to find the best business partner for the development of the photodetector, several firms in the field were contacted (B-R4 §27). The process of identifying potential business partners and selecting SupPF-A was coordinated by professionals of the project team of CantisPF at Diagnosub. Though, they needed to get the funding for the collaboration from the corporate Technology and Marker Board that meets at HQs of Diagnocom (B-R4 §31, see sub-section 6.5.2.2 for details on the organization structure).

6.2.2.2.2 Feasibility

Diagnosub currently enters the stage of feasibility. When the thesis was being written (June 2009), the R&D project manager of CantisPF and the program manager were in the process of selecting a business partner to develop the final product of CantisCRC. Instrumentation of CantisPF could be done by an instrumentation team of Diagnocom. However, program management decided to look for an external business partner (B-R5 §14). The selection process is not completed yet (B-R5 §14). It will be described in depth later.

The selection process started when the R&D project manager of CantisPF got an appointment from program management to search for external business partners for the instrumentation. First, R&D and business professionals developed a list of specifications that the final product needed to fulfill (B-R5 §14). Experts at Diagnosub had a lot of experience with CantisPF already. Several versions of the breadboard of CantisPF had been developed by Diagnosub. Technical specifications were drawn from these breadboards. However, while in the breadboards a lot was done manually, with the final product almost every step in the work flow had to be automated. Also, the final product must be producible in large scale (B-R1 §46-48). Furthermore, it must be as low cost as possible to enhance the market potential of the product (B-R4 §79, B-R5 §16).

Having clarified the specifications of CantisPF, the market was screened for firms that could develop the product. Four firms were selected that were considered to have the technological and logistic capabilities to develop CantisPF. R&D experts from Diagnosub visited the candidates in order to inform them about the project and to get a better impression of the firm (B-R5 §14-16). All four candidates entered the competition (B-R5 §20). All candidates were invited to a joint meeting to present CantisPF in more detail. They were also demonstrated the breadboard of the platform and provided with technical details of the platform. Further conditions were clarified: the timeline of the development of final CantisPF and the fact that the firms must prefinance the development. No price limit was provided. However, Diagnosub was very clear about the price being one of the most important criteria for the selection of the business partner (B-R5 §14-16, 22).

In order to find out more about the technical competence of the firms and get the best technical solution possible, the candidates were asked to develop a detailed concept of the platform. They were also supposed to present a well-grounded estimation of costs (B-R5 §18). Based on the concept and estimation of costs, two candidates were excluded from further process. The main criterion for this decision was the estimation of costs that was significantly higher than that of the other two firms. Diagnosub gave them feedback on their concept and estimation of costs. The other two firms were still in the selection process. They updated their concept and estimation regarding some technical specifications. Some of the new technical specifications were not presented by Diagnosub in the first meeting due to outstanding patent application. Others were suggested by one of the candidates and integrated in the concept specifications (B-R5 §30-34).

Diagnosub now chooses which candidate they will work with. This decision is based on four criteria: First, the firm should have competences regarding in vitro diagnostics which is the field of CantisPF. Second, while one of the candidates already is a tight business partner Diagnosub has not yet collaborated with the other candidate. Business management will decide whether they intend to intensify the business relationship to the familiar business partner or diversify with a new one. Third, the price of final CantisPF is a main criterion. Fourth, Diagnosub is now entering negotiations with both candidates. For instance, they will talk about intellectual property arrangements with both candidates. It might be that one of the business partners does not agree with Diagnosub concerning this issue. In this case, the other business partner would be selected (B-R5 §36-38).

The final choice will be made by the R&D project management and by business management of Diagnocom (B-R5 §39-40). While one of the candidates has more expertise in the field of in vitro diagnostics the other one is already a well-known business partner of Diagnocom (B-R5 §46). Irrespective of the final decision, the business relationship will be a customer-supplier-relationship. After the specific development of the final version of CantisPF by the business partner, he will produce CantisPF in large scale and deliver it to Diagnocom (B-R5 §14). The business partner is thus called SupPF-B.

6.2.2.3 Summary of the External Business Partners in the Product Innovation Process of Cantis

In the earlier sub-sections, the external business partners of both CantisCRC and CantisPF were described. In the idea description stage of CantisCRC, CustCRC-A, a potential customer was the most important business partner. She was a doctor at a university hospital in the UK and advised Diagnosub regarding the product specifications of CantisCRC. In the basic and extended technology studies of CantisCRC, the most influential business partner was ClinCog-A. ClinCog-A was a university hospital that provided Diagnosub with sample material for tests on marker candidates.

The idea of CantisPF came up inside Diagnosub and was developed further there. The most important business partner in basic and extended technology studies was SupPF-A. This was a firm that specialized in optical instruments and developed a detector for the breadboard of CantisPF. In the stage of feasibility, the selection process of the most important business partner is not completed yet. However, the business partner will be a supplier (SupPF-B) who develops the serial version of CantisPF and then manufactures it. The business partners of Diagnosub during the product innovation processes of CantisCRC and CantisPF are depicted in figure 6-9.

CantisCRC				
• Doctor at hospital • Potential customer of Diagnosub • (CustCRC-A)	• University hospital • Supplier of sample material and information on patients for studies on marker candidates • (ClinCRC-A)			
	Research		**Development**	
Idea	Basic Technology Studies	Extended Technology Studies	Analysis	Feasibility
	• Firm • Contract research on a detector for the breadboard of CantisPF • (SupPF-A)		• Firm • Development and production of final CantisPF • (SupPF-B)	
		CantisPF		

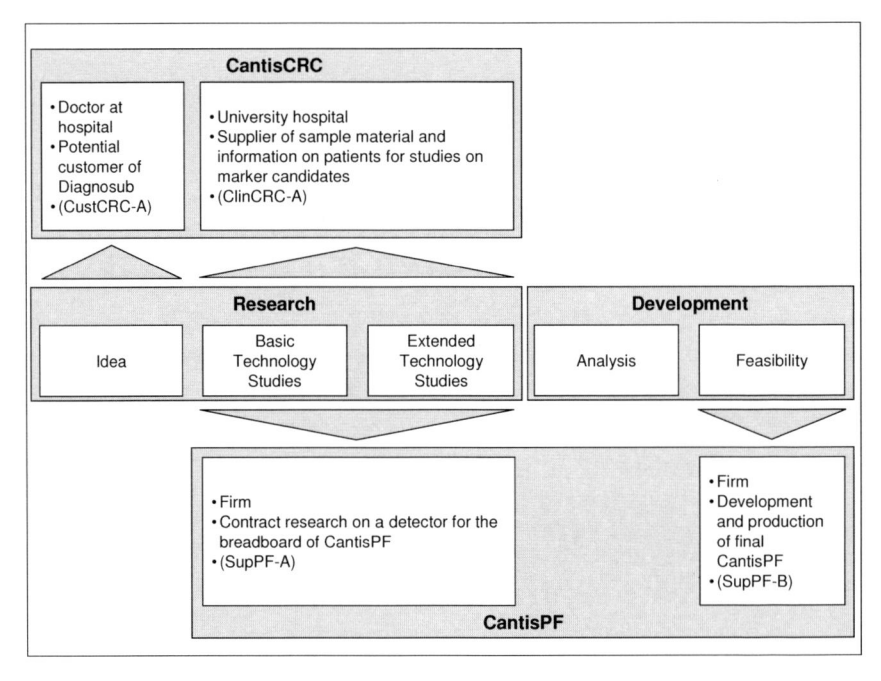

Figure 6-9: External business partners of Pharmasub during the product innovation process of CantisCRC and CantisPF

In the product innovation process of CantisCRC, the most influential business partner in the product innovation process was CustCRC-A. She gave Diagnosub advice on the product idea and product specifications of CantisCRC. Thus, she had a significant impact on the product development. At the stages of basic and extended technology studies, ClinCRC-A delivered sample material and information on the material. This was necessary to test the marker candidates. However, ClinCRC-A did not actively influence the product of CantisCRC.

In the product innovation process of CantisPF, the most important business partner can not be determined. At the stage of idea description, one particular expert at Diagnosub had the idea of CantisPF and developed its specifications. Regarding basic and extended technology studies, SupPF-A was quite influential even though they do not produce the detector for CantisPF in serial production. However, in this collaboration Diagnosub learned that a detector could be developed according to their requirements and that it could be produced at a low cost. At the stage of feasibility, another supplier will be the business partner of Diagnosub. This supplier will develop the prototype of CantisPF and manufacture it in serial production. For the whole product innovation process, this might be the most influential business partner.

6.2.3 Comparison and Conclusion of the Most Important External Business Partners of Pharmasub and Diagnosub

After having analyzed the most important business external business partners in the product innovation processes of Cogis, CantisCRC and CantisPF, the three cases are compared and findings are interpreted. This is done according to the stages first. Basic research is not reported as it is rarely done by pharmaceutical firms, as stated in sub-section 6.1.3.

(1) **Idea**: The idea generation (i.e. decision to develop in figure 6-2) of Cogis could not be analyzed in depth. This is due to the fact that the experts who were involved in idea generation had left the firm. However, respondents stated that the idea of Cogis came up inside Pharmasub. Whether customers were involved in the first stage of idea is not clear. However, this can be seriously doubted. Customers of Cogis will be patients with COPD. As they are single persons without medical or pharmaceutical knowledge they most likely were not asked to assess specifications of the drug. Doctors and health insurance providers might be considered customers as well because

they prescribe the drug and reimburse it. It is also doubted that they exerted influence on Pharmasub in the product innovation process. This is due to two reasons: First, the disease of COPD is well known and the need for a medicine to stop or modify the progress of the disease is clear to pharmaceutical firms. Thus, Pharmasub did not need the affirmation that the product idea of Cogis is a good one. Second, Pharmasub has special expertise in respiratory infections and knew which specifications the product needed. Specifications are determined by the purpose of the drug. Therefore, it can be doubted that customers, doctors or health insurances are involved in the stage of idea finding.

As opposed to this, customers were involved in the stage of idea description in the product innovation process of CantisCRC. In the case of diagnostic products, customers are doctors in practices or hospitals. They ask laboratories for a particular product that they want to use. In the case of CantisCRC, doctors in hospitals were involved. The most important one was CustCRC-A, who was a doctor at a university hospital in the UK. She gave a lot of input on the basic interest in the potential product, on desired product specifications and on development projects by competitors of Diagnosub. Thereby, she influenced CantisCRC very much.

In the case of CantisPF, the stage of idea description could not be analyzed in depth because the idea stems from a preceding project of CantisPF. This project was started over ten years ago. The expert who had the idea and was responsible for the idea description had left the firm. It was stated by another respondent that this expert developed the idea without the collaboration of external business partners.

(2) **Research**: In the product innovation process of drug development, research is done in discovery when a target is identified. The target is then addressed by the medicine in order to cure or modify the disease. However, discovery is very often done at universities and not at pharmaceutical firms. In the case of Cogis, research was also done at the in vitro stage in pre-clinical development. It is also done in the stage before in vitro studies. In pre-clinic 0, substances that approach the target are screened and their chemical structure is improved. Thus, in spite of the name, stages of pre-clinical development are regarded as research. Pre-clinic 0 was not analyzed here in depth because no experts of this stage were available. In pre-clinic I, the

most important business partner for in vitro tests was ResCog-A. He was a scientist who worked at a private research institute. He had a great influence on the product innovation process of Cogis because he proved the non-toxicity of Cogis to the olfactory epithelium of humans. In an in vivo study it had been found that Cogis was toxic to the olfactory epithelium of rodents. If ResCog-A would not have been able to prove the non-toxicity of Cogis to humans, Cogis would not even have entered the clinical trials. For this task, ResCog-A was virtually the only expert in this field. Hence, he had a huge impact on the product innovation process. In pre-clinic II, the most important business partner for the in vivo tests was the service contractor ClinCog-A. They conducted studies with Cogis on apes. Thereby, a broad range of study objects were included.

In the case of CantisCRC, research included basic and extended technology studies. The most important business partner was ClinCog-A. ClinCog-A was a university hospital that provided Diagnosub with sample material and information on the material. With the sample material Diagnosub tested the effectiveness of marker candidates.

The most influential business partner in basic and extended technology studies in the case of CantisPF was SupPF-A. SupPF-A was a firm that developed and produced optical instruments. It developed a detector for the breadboards of CantisPF. SupPF-A ended the business relationship after this stage because Diagnosub could not guarantee SupPF-A that they would be allowed to produce and sell CantisPF. Hence, SupPF-A was not sure that they could produce the detector on a large scale.

(3) **Development**: In the case of Cogis, clinical development is split into three stages. In stage I, the most important business partner of Pharmasub was ClinCog-B. ClinCog-B was a service contractor that conducted studies on Cogis with healthy test persons. In stages II and III, the most influential business partner was ClinCog-C. ClinCog-C was a university hospital that conducted studies on patients with COPD.

In the product development process of CantisCRC, no stages of development were analyzed because the product only enters the stage of development now. However, as was stated earlier, in these stages, the development of CantisCRC and CantisPF is intermingled. The chemical work on CantisCRC is mainly done at the end of research. The stages of development in which the test is applied on chips and chips are developed for large scale production is subsumed under development of CantisPF in which engineerial work is done.

In the product innovation process of CantisPF, Diagnosub is in the stage of feasibility. The most influential business partner in this stage will be a supplier who will produce CantisPF in serial production. The business partner is not selected yet.

As stated in sub-section 6.2.1.3, ResCog-A was the most important business partner in the product innovation process of Cogis. Although not the whole product innovation process could be analyzed, it can be assumed that no other business partner in earlier stages was as influential as ResCog-A. This is due to the fact that the idea of Cogis was born internally and customers of Cogis cannot be asked about the product idea. Customers as patients are single persons without medical or pharmaceutical knowledge. They are unable to give an input on the product idea. Doctors and health insurance providers might be considered customers as well because they prescribe the drug and reimburse it. However, their input in the product innovation process probably was not required either, because the disease of COPD is well known and the need for a medicine to stop or modify the progress of the disease was clear to Pharmacom. Also, Pharmasub knew which specifications the product needed because the subsidiary had special expertise in respiratory infections. Specifications are determined by the purpose of the drug. Therefore, there is little doubt that customers, doctors or health insurance providers are involved in the stage of idea finding. Thus, ResCog-A can be assumed to be the most influential business partner in the whole product innovation process.

In the product innovation process of CantisCRC, the most influential business partner in the product innovation process was CustCRC-A. She gave Diagnosub advice on the product idea and product specifications of CantisCRC. Thus, she had quite an impact on the product development. On the other hand, ClinCRC-A delivered sample material and information on the material. This was necessary to test marker candidates. However, ClinCRC-A did not actively influence the product of CantisCRC.

Thus, CustCRC-A clearly was the most influential business partner in the whole product innovation process.

In the product innovation process of CantisPF, the most important business partner cannot be determined. Business partners in the idea description process could not be analyzed. However, it was stated that one particular expert at Diagnosub had the idea of CantisPF and developed specifications. SupPF-A was quite influential even though they do not produce the detector for CantisPF in serial production. However, in this collaboration Diagnosub learned that a detector could be developed according to their requirements and that it could be produced at low cost. In the stage of feasibility, another supplier will be business partner of Diagnosub. This supplier will develop the prototype of CantisPF and manufacture it in serial production. For the whole product innovation process, this might be the most influential business partner.

Hence, while in the product innovation process of Cogis, the most influential business partner was a scientist at a private research institution, it was a potential customer in the product innovation process of CantisCRC. Main business partners in the product innovation process of CantisPF were suppliers.

6.3 Embeddedness of Business Relationships to External Business Partners during the Product Innovation Process

As was stated in the conceptual part of the thesis, business relationships may be evaluated on two dimensions: the breadth and depth. While the breadth addresses the number of functional areas that are involved with a particular business partner the depth includes several attributes: mutual adaptations,[146] mutual dependence, and mutual criticality of each partner for the other, commitment of both partners in the business relationship, mutual trust and mutual attention paid to the business partners. For each stage of the product innovation processes at Pharmasub and Diagno-

---

[146] As stated in sub-section 5.1.3.3 adaptations of the product are only considered in the cases of CantisCRC and CantisPF. Mutual adaptations concerning the process will be assessed in all three cases.

sub, these criteria were assessed. The results are presented in the following sub-section.

6.3.1 Embeddedness of Business Relationships to External Business Partners during the Innovation Process of Cogis at Pharmasub

The product innovation process at Pharmasub starts with screening of substances that the target responds to in pre-clinic 0. As was stated earlier (see sub-section 6.1.1.5), pre-clinic 0 could not be analyzed. Thus, the analysis of embeddedness of business relationship starts with in vitro tests in pre-clinic I. In this stage, the most important business partner was a scientist at a private research institution, ResCog-A. He proved the non-toxicity of Cogis to humans. In pre-clinic II, the most important business partner was ClinCog-A. ClinCog-A was a service contractor that conducted studies with Cogis on apes. In clinical trials I, the most influential business partner was a service contractor as well. ClinCog-B conducted studies on healthy test persons with Cogis. In the next two stages, clinical trials II and III, the most important business partner was the same. ClinCog-C was a university hospital that conducted the exploratory and confirmatory studies with Cogis on patients with COPD. In the following parts that are mentioned, business relationships in the stages of preclinical development (6.3.1.1) and clinical development (6.3.1.2) are analyzed.

6.3.1.1 Pre-clinical Development

6.3.1.1.1 Pre-clinic I: In vitro tests

The Head of Pharmacology and Pharmaceutical Drug Safety was interviewed about collaborations during the in vitro tests. He assessed the breadth and depth of the business relationships to the most important external business partner, ResCog-A, from the perspective of Pharmasub and of ResCog-A. The attributes of the depth of business relationships are depicted in figure 6-10.

In general, the business relationship between Pharmasub and ResCog-A was described as excellent and extraordinarily trustful (A-R1 §49-56). It was also a key collaboration for the development of Cogis. The project would probably have failed if ResCog-A had not proven the non-toxicity of Cogis to humans. At least it would have taken much longer and would have been more costly (A-R1 §63-66, 114-116).

(1) Number of functional areas involved with the business partner (breadth of business relationship): Pharmasub and ResCog-A worked together only in R&D. They only collaborated in the question of the non-toxicity of Cogis to humans (A-R1 §45-48).

(2) Mutual adaptations:
(a) Adaptations of Pharmasub: The adaptation of Pharmasub to ResCog-A in the product innovation process of Cogis was assessed to be very high. ResCog-A decided how to proceed with the tests and how to document the studies. Pharmasub did not provide ResCog-A with guidelines about these issues as his way of conducting the study and documenting the results was alright for Pharmasub (A-R1 §60).
(b) Adaptations of ResCog-A: The adaptation of ResCog-A regarding his work was evaluated to be very high, too. When Pharmasub gave suggestions to ResCog-A, he acted on them. He could have neglected the ideas because he might have worked differently in past projects but did not do so (A-R1 §62).

(3) Mutual dependence:
(a) Dependence of Pharmasub: Pharmasub and ResCog-A collaborated for about three to four years. The study on toxicity took two years. After the study, ResCog-A consulted Pharmasub regarding the in vivo tests. Particularly during the in vitro tests, Pharmasub was highly dependent on ResCog-A. ResCog-A had the equipment and the expertise that was required for proving the non-toxicity of Cogis to humans (A-R1 §72).
(b) Dependence of ResCog-A: ResCog-A also depended on Pharmasub to a very high degree. Pharmasub had to provide the material for the tests and pay for the study (A-R1 §72).

(4) Mutual criticality:

(a) Criticality of the business relationship for Pharmasub: For Pharmasub, the collaboration with ResCog-A was crucial for the product innovation process of Cogis. If ResCog-A had not proven that Cogis is not toxic to humans, Cogis would not have entered the stage of clinical trials. The project of Cogis would have ended unsuccessfully. Only one scientist could have been approached if ResCog-A had not collaborated with Pharmasub. However, this scientist did not have a comparable expertise and equipment in this particular issue of olfactory toxicity. The innovation process of Cogis would have taken much longer and would have been much more costly (A-R1 §64-66).

(b) Criticality of the business relationship for ResCog-A: The criticality of the collaboration with Pharmasub on Cogis was assessed as low for ResCog-A. As he is virtually the only expert in this field, several firms are interested in his expertise and compete for his knowledge. He had the option to choose between business partners. The collaboration could only have enhanced his scientific reputation as a result of subsequent publications. However, this was doubted by the respondent (A-R1 §70).

(5) Mutual commitment:

(a) Commitment of Pharmasub: The investments of Pharmasub in the business relationship with ResCog-A were evaluated as very high. Pharmasub reacted to requests of ResCog-A immediately. When ResCog-A approached Pharmasub they always responded and did not put him on hold. Furthermore, Pharmasub worked on the topic as fast as possible so that their results and those of ResCog-A could be exchanged and compared. They even visited him in the USA without any particular reason other than to stay in contact. This was done for two reasons: First, the issue of olfactory toxicity was a very critical one for the project of Cogis. Second, the business relationship to ResCog-A was perceived as very pleasant (A-R1 §80, 90).

(b) Commitment of ResCog-A: ResCog-A also invested a lot of time and personal capacity in the project with Pharmasub. Most often he provided Pharmasub with partial results before the deadline (A-R1 §80). Although he flew less to Pharmasub than vice versa it was not perceived as a signal of less interest. Flying to Germany was simply not necessary to collaborate because everything could be discussed on the phone or in USA (A-R1 §92).

(6) Mutual trust:
(a) Pharmasub's trust in ResCog-A: Trust of Pharmasub in ResCog-A was very high. This included both the work of ResCog-A and his personality (A-R1 §83-88).
(b) ResCog-A's trust in Pharmasub: Trust of ResCog-A in Pharmasub was assessed to be very high as well (A-R1 §83-88).

(7) Mutual attention:
(a) Attention paid by Pharmasub to ResCog-A: Attention of Pharmasub to the interests of ResCog-A was assessed to be very high. Pharmasub responded immediately to his needs. They also went out of their way to maintain contact (A-R1 §90).
(b) Attention paid by ResCog-A to Pharmasub: The attention that ResCog-A paid to Pharmasub was high, too. As stated earlier, he was always before time with results and implemented the ideas provided by Pharmasub (A-R1 §62, 80).

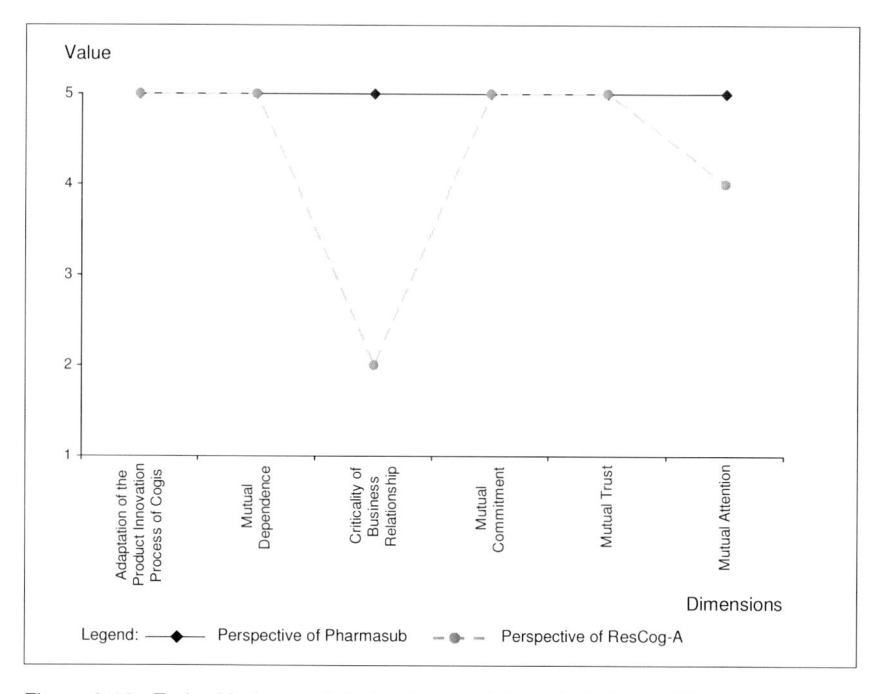

Figure 6-10: Embeddedness of the business relationship between Pharmasub and ResCog-A during in vitro tests

6.3.1.1.2 Pre-clinic II: In vivo tests

The Head of Pharmacology and Pharmaceutical Drug Safety was interviewed about collaborations during the in vivo test, again. He assessed the breadth and depth of the business relationships to the most important external business partners from the perspective of Pharmanorth and of ClinCog-A. The attributes of the depth of business relationships are depicted in figure 6-11.

The business relationship between Pharmanorth and ClinCog-A was perceived as very good (A-R1 §176). The relation between the contact persons at Pharmanorth and ClinCog-A was such that they were on first-name basis during the project on Cogis (A-R1 §244). ClinCog-A was very reliable during the project (A-R1 §206).

(1) Number of functional areas involved with the business partner (breadth of business relationship): Pharmanorth collaborated with ClinCog-A only in R&D. As depicted in figure 6-2 in sub-section 6.1.1.5, in vivo studies may continue during the whole innovation process (A-R1 §182).

(2) Mutual adaptations:
(a) Adaptations of Pharmanorth: Adaptations of Pharmanorth in the product innovation process of Cogis were evaluated as low. Adaptations were mainly made concerning the time line of the studies. ClinCog-A did not always have available capacities when Pharmanorth wanted to start a study. However, protractions did not occur often (A-R1 §183-188).
(b) Adaptations of ClinCog-A: The adaptations of ClinCog-A during the in vivo studies were assessed as high. Although ClinCog-A could not always stick to the timeline of Pharmanorth, they started the studies of Pharmanorth as early as possible. Also, they followed the guidelines of Pharmanorth on how to conduct the studies (A-R1 §190).

(3) Mutual dependence:
(a) Dependence of Pharmanorth: Operational dependence of Pharmanorth was perceived as high. If the collaboration had failed during the studies, the product innovation process would have taken more time and would have been more costly. Phar-

manorth would have needed to select another service contractor and start studies with him, again (A-R1 §198).

(b) Dependence of ClinCog-A: Dependence of ClinCog-A was perceived as low. Many pharmaceutical firms conduct studies with them. Hence, if the collaboration had been terminated they would have used their resources in another study. Though this could not have happened immediately but it would not have taken too long either. ClinCog-A depended on Pharmanorth to conduct the studies because Pharmanorth explained to them how to take the olfactory epithelium, for instance. Though they could have learned that from literature as well (A-R1 §180, 192, 198, 232).

(4) Mutual criticality:
(a) Criticality of the business relationship for Pharmanorth: The business relationship to ClinCog-A was evaluated as very low for Pharmanorth. There are four comparable service contractors and if ClinCog-A and Pharmanorth did not collaborate anymore after the Cogis project, Pharmanorth would work with one of their competitors (A-R1 §192-194).

(b) Criticality of the business relationship for ClinCog-A: For ClinCog-A, the business relationship with Pharmanorth is not critical in the long run either. As they conduct studies for many pharmaceutical firms they will not have any problem if Pharmanorth does not work with them. They are always fully booked (A-R1 §192-196).

(5) Mutual commitment:
(a) Commitment of Pharmanorth: Commitment of Pharmanorth in the business relationship with ClinCog-A were assessed as high. Usually, pharmaceutical firms provide service contractors with the substance and tell them how to conduct the studies. Pharmanorth additionally explained ClinCog-A what Cogis is for, at which stage the project is and what they already know about the substance. They were the first customers of ClinCog-A who behaved in this way (A-R1 §190, 199-202).

(b) Commitment of ClinCog-A: Commitment of ClinCog-A was evaluated as rather low. However, Pharmanorth is a preferred customer of ClinCog-A. They try to make things possible for Pharmanorth that they probably do not do for other customers (A-R1 §190, 203-204).

(6) Mutual trust:

(a) Pharmanorth's trust in ClinCog-A: Pharmanorth had a lot of trust in ClinCog-A. This was due to the way ClinCog-A handled the mistakes they made and the problems that arose. In any in vivo study, there are always problems and mistakes. ClinCog-A was very open about them so that Pharmanorth could assess and deal with their faults. Less reliable business partners would have tried to cover their mistakes (A-R1 §206-208).

(b) ClinCog-A's trust in Pharmasub: ClinCog-A's trust in Pharmasub was very high as well. Pharmasub behaved very cooperatively with ClinCog-A and explained to them much more about the substance and the study than other business partner would have done. In addition, they were very open with data from other studies after having signed the CDA (A-R1 §190, 206).

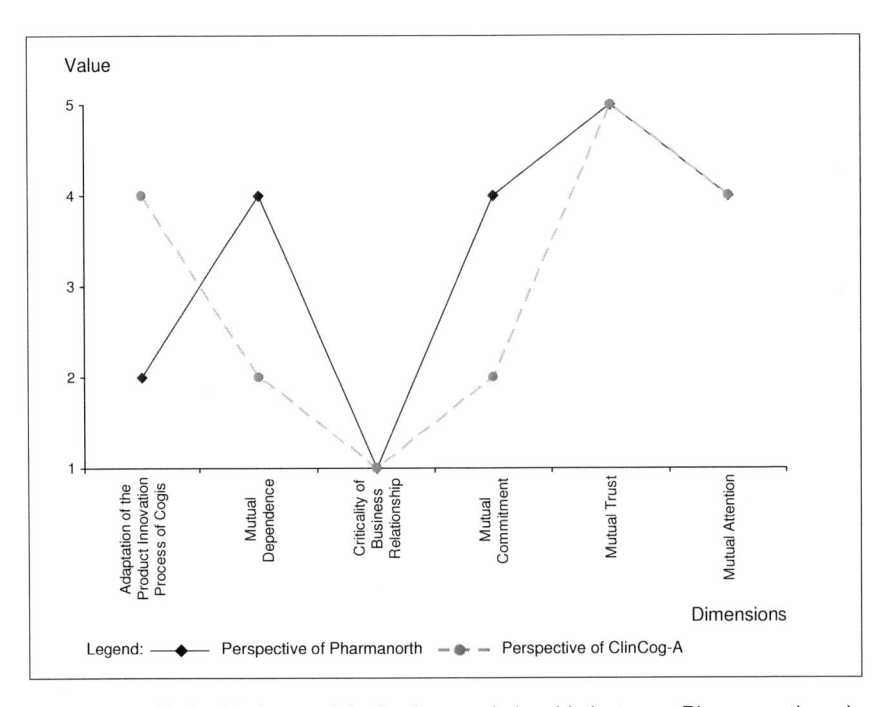

Figure 6-11: Embeddedness of the business relationship between Pharmanorth and ClinCog-A during in vivo tests

(7) Mutual attention:
(a) Attention paid by Pharmanorth to ClinCog-A: Pharmanorth paid a lot of attention to ClinCog-A during the study. They visited them several times to discuss issues or results and talk about the next steps (A-R1 §210).
(b) Attention paid by ClinCog-A to Pharmanorth: The attention paid by ClinCog-A to Pharmanorth was evaluated as high, too. For instance, they provided Pharmanorth with information on the progress of the study without being asked to do so (A-R1 §212-214).

The Respondent stated that the business relationship between Pharmanorth and ClinCog-A developed during the collaboration in pre-clinic II of Cogis. Both partners had worked together before. However, the personal relationship between the main contact persons of both firms grew tighter during this collaboration. While the attributes of mutual dependence, criticality and attention did not change during the collaboration on Cogis, adaptations of ClinCog-A, commitment of Pharmanorth and mutual trust increased (A-R1 §256-262).[147] The development of the latter three dimensions is depicted in figure 6-12.

ClinCog-A adapted to Pharmanorth particularly when Pharmanorth wanted to renew the contract for three more months from six months to nine months. They asked ClinCog-A to renew the contract shortly before the contract ended. Although ClinCog-A certainly had planned their resources for other purposes already, they renewed the contract. The Respondent thought that they probably would not have done so in an earlier collaboration. Also, ClinCog-A offered Pharmanorth additional service without billing it. Of course, it was only regarding small amounts of money. However, they did not do that before. Hence, adaptations of ClinCog-A increased from low to high (A-R1 §260).

Commitment of Pharmanorth increased as well. Contacts got a lot more frequent. Pharmanorth continued to work with ClinCog-A in other projects without bargaining with other possible business partners. Prior to the collaboration on Cogis, Pharman-

---

[147] In figure 6-11, adaptations of ClinCog-A, commitment of Pharmanorth, and mutual trust are depicted as they were perceived in the end of the business relationship.

orth used to solicit offers from other service contractors before selecting one of them (A-R1 §258).

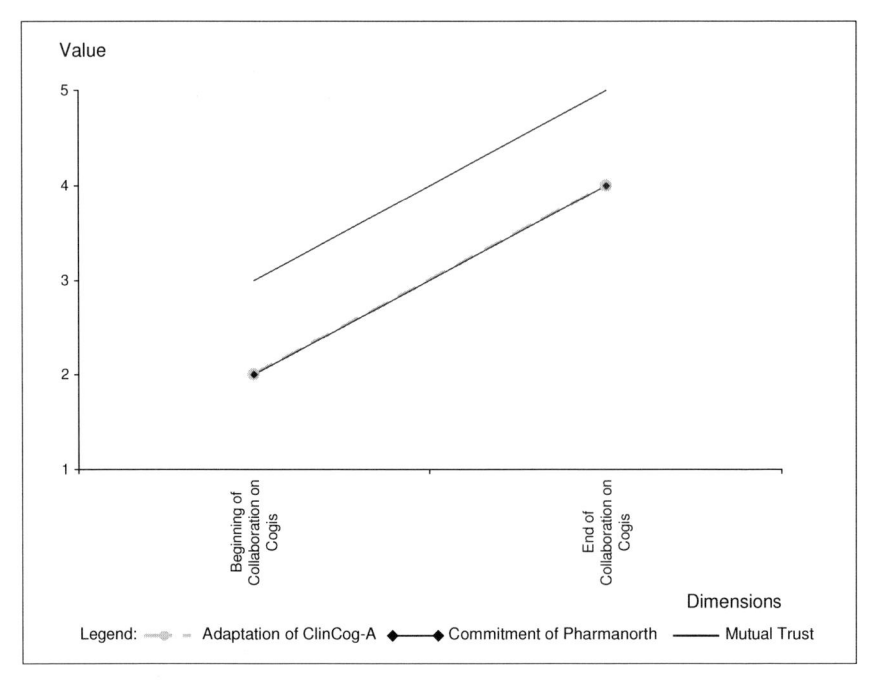

Figure 6-12: Development of adaptations, commitment and trust between Pharmanorth and ClinCog-A during the in vivo studies on Cogis

During the collaboration of Pharmanorth and ClinCog-A in the in vivo studies of Cogis, personal trust increased a lot. Prior to this collaboration, the relationship was a normal trustful business relationship. During this collaboration however, contacts got more frequent and personal. The main contact persons on both sides are now on first-name terms with each other (A-R1 §254).

6.3.1.2 Clinical Development

6.3.1.2.1 Clinical Trials Stage I

For the three stages of clinical trials, two experts at Pharmasub were interviewed together. One was the Head of Exploratory Clinical Development and the other one was the Director Strategic Planning and Business Support. They assessed the breadth and depth of the business relationships to the most important external business partners from the perspective of Pharmasub and ClinCog-B. The attributes of the depth of business relationships are depicted in figure 6-13.

The business relationship between Pharmasub and ClinCog-B was described rather unemotionally. Respondents stated that trust in the expertise of ClinCog-B was necessary to collaborate in clinical studies. Reliability of the business partner must be expected. Otherwise, the service contractor is not chosen as a business partner (A-R2&3 §264-266). Reliability obviously was expected because Pharmasub and ClinCog-B had created a legal contract before the collaboration on Cogis began (A-R2&3 §236). As the legal regulations for clinical trials are very strict the tasks of ClinCog-B were clear. Hence, business partners at this stage were selected for their expertise. The embeddedness of the business relationship is not a reason to select a particular business partner. However, collaborations in clinical trials can fail for "soft" embeddedness reasons (A-R2&3 §264-266).

(1) Number of functional areas involved with the business partner (breadth of business relationship): With ClinCog-B, Pharmasub only worked in R&D. No other functional area was involved with this business partner. Also, they only collaborated in stage I of the clinical trials (A-R2&3 §271-272).

(2) Mutual adaptations:
(a) Adaptations of Pharmasub: Adaptations of Pharmasub to ClinCog-B in stage I of the clinical trials of Cogis were assessed as low by the respondents. The adaptations were done rather unwillingly and concerned the duration of the study (A-R2&3 §274-280). Studies take longer when test persons are not recruited as quickly as expected. Recruiting of test persons is a critical issue in clinical studies. One day of delay costs

the sponsor of the study (i.e. Pharmasub in this case) about 23 million US Dollars (A-R2&3 §305). The competition between study centers for test persons is high. Even within the study centers, different studies compete for test persons. Thus, the recruiting of people who take part in studies is not an easy task. This applies to stage I but even more so to stage II and III (A-R2&3 §326-329).

(b) Adaptations of ClinCog-B: The adaptations of ClinCog-B to Pharmasub in stage I of the clinical trials were evaluated as high. Like any study center, ClinCog-B got the guidelines for the study from Pharmasub (A-R2&3 §281-284). They determined the specifications in protocols of the study. For instance, it was specified which kind of people are to be included in the study as test persons. Further, it was determined how the study would proceed, e.g., when to provide test persons with Cogis or when to test which parameter of the test persons. These guidelines were defined within strict legal regulations on clinical trials (A-R2&3 §265).

(3) Mutual Dependence:

(a) Dependence of Pharmasub:[148] During the study, dependence of Pharmasub was high. They depended on ClinCog-B in terms of recruiting enough test persons in a limited duration of time. Furthermore, they had to rely on ClinCog-B to follow the guidelines of Pharmasub and proceed with the study while maintaining the expected quality. If the collaboration with ClinCog-B had been aborted and another partner had been selected, stage I of the clinical trials would have taken more time than had been planned. The duration of the whole project would have been protracted (A-R2&3 §295-300).

(b) Dependence of ClinCog-B: The dependence of ClinCog-B was assessed to be high again. ClinCog-B depended not only on the payment but also on the planning and knowledge input from Pharmasub. They required the guidelines from Pharmasub about what to do, when to do it and how to do it. They also needed to know the timeline of the study (A-R2&3 §295-299).

---

[148] The dependence of Pharmasub on ClinCog-B in stage I of the development process of Cogis was subdivided by the respondents in two dimensions: strategic and operational dependence. In line with the operationalization (see sub-section 5.1.3.3), operational dependence is described here as dependence while strategic dependence actually concerns the criticality of the business relationship.

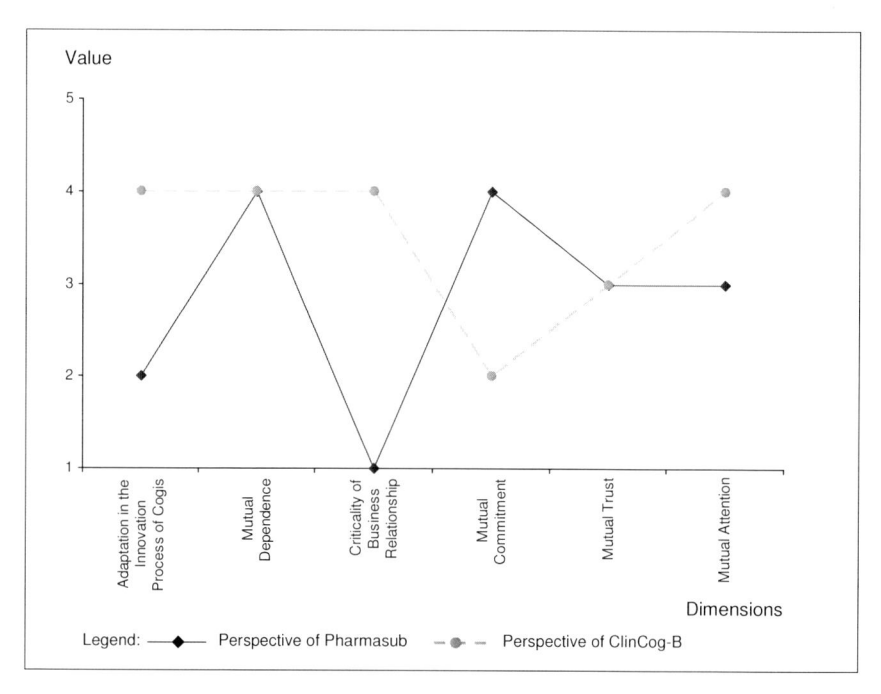

Figure 6-13: Embeddedness of the business relationship between Pharmasub and ClinCog-B in stage I of the clinical trials

(4) Mutual criticality:

(a) Criticality of the business relationship for Pharmasub: Criticality from the perspective of Pharmasub was evaluated as very low. As was stated earlier, study centers like ClinCog-B are substitutable. If the collaboration had not been successful because ClinCog-B did not work according to the expectations of Pharmasub they would have been substituted by another study center. As Pharmasub had a frame agreement with ClinCog-B, they would have had to incur costs if they had terminated the business relationship. However, these costs would have been acceptable (A-R2&3 §295-299, 322).

(b) Criticality of the business relationship for ClinCog-B: Criticality was assessed to be high. ClinCog-B was dependent in an economic way because they were paid by Pharmasub for the study. To lose the contract for a study and not get mandates for further studies would have caused a severe economic damage to ClinCog-B. It would also have caused a decrease in their reputation. They also got an opportunity to learn from Pharmasub about the scientific basis of the study (A-R2&3 §295-299, 343-345).

(5) Mutual commitment:
(a) Commitment of Pharmasub: Pharmasub's investments in the business relationship were assessed as high. They spent time and resources to teach ClinCog-B the know-how that the study center needed in order to proceed with the clinical study. They transferred knowledge to them about the quality expectations, processes involved in conducting the study and methods of testing for several parameters (A-R2&3 §347-349).
(b) Commitment of ClinCog-B: The investments of ClinCog-B in the business relationship were lower. They also spent time, of course, and let Pharmasub train them. Their main investment was to obtain and accept knowledge from Pharmasub (A-R2&3 §351).

(6) Mutual trust:
(a) Pharmasub's trust in ClinCog-B: The trust of Pharmasub in the business relationship with ClinCog-B was assessed as medium. It was described as stable but used to be higher before the frame agreement was made. Thus, trust evolved over time. Respondents differentiated two dimensions of trust: trust in competence and quality and trust in delivery. Trust in competence and quality remained the same but trust in delivery diminished a bit. It decreased when difficulties with the recruiting of test persons arose and the timeline of the study was protracted (A-R2&3 §353).
(b) ClinCog-B's trust in Pharmasub: Trust from ClinCog-B in Pharmasub was estimated to be medium, too (A-R2&3 §353).

(7) Mutual attention:
(a) Attention paid by Pharmasub to ClinCog-B: Pharmasub evaluated its attention to ClinCog-B as medium. Attention referred to considering ClinCog-B when new studies were planned and when thinking about the management of processes in the past (A-R2&3 §355).
(b) Attention paid by ClinCog-B to Pharmasub: On the other hand, the attention that was achieved by Pharmasub from ClinCog-B was assessed to be high. This was due to the economic dependence of ClinCog-B from Pharmasub (A-R2&3 §359-361).

6.3.1.2.2 Clinical Trials Stage II

For stage II of the clinical trials, the breadth and depth of the business relationship to the most important external business partner was evaluated again. The most important business partner is called ClinCog-C. Attributes of the depth of business relationships are depicted in figure 6-14.

The business relationship between Pharmasub and ClinCog-C was evaluated by the same respondents who evaluated it for ClinCog-B. Compared to ClinCog-B, ClinCog-C was reported to be more professional in conducting studies (A-R2&3 §541-543). After the collaboration on Cogis, a frame contract was signed between Pharmasub and ClinCog-C (A-R2&3 §644-645).

(1) Number of functional areas involved with the business partner (breadth of business relationship): With ClinCog-C, Pharmasub only collaborated in R&D. No other functional area was involved with this business partner. However, with this business partner Pharmasub also collaborated in stage I and stage III of product innovation processes. In the case of Cogis, Pharmasub worked with ClinCog-C in stage II and III of the clinical trials (A-R2&3 §528-531).

(2) Mutual adaptations:
(a) Adaptations of Pharmasub: The degree of adaptations of Pharmasub to ClinCog-C in the innovation process of Cogis was assessed as low. The need to adjust to unforeseen problems was lower than in stage I. ClinCog-C did not have more expertise concerning the content of the study but it had a higher degree of professionalism in organizing the study. They had more process know-how than ClinCog-B. Thus, fewer problems arose in the course of the study (A-R2&3 §533, 541-549).
(b) Adaptations of ClinCog-C: The adaptations were evaluated as low again (A-R2&3 §265).

(3) Mutual Dependence:
(a) Dependence of Pharmasub: The dependence of Pharmasub on ClinCog-C in stage II of the innovation process of Cogis was evaluated as low. This is surprising as the mechanisms are the same (A-R2&3 §551). Pharmasub also depended on

ClinCog-C to recruit enough test persons in the given time. Again, if ClinCog-C had not delivered data as expected, the collaboration would have been terminated. This would have led to additional costs and the protraction of the study (A-R2&3 §295-300). Maybe, the dependence was perceived lower because ClinCog-C was more reliable regarding the delivery of data in time (A-R2&3 §543-545).

(b) Dependence of ClinCog-C: The dependence of ClinCog-C on Pharmasub in stage II of the innovation process of Cogis was assessed as low as well (A-R2&3 §551). Thus, compared to stage I dependence of the business partner was lower. This may be because not that many adaptations to each other were necessary and hence, ClinCog-C did not need the input of Pharmasub as much (A-R2&3 §533).

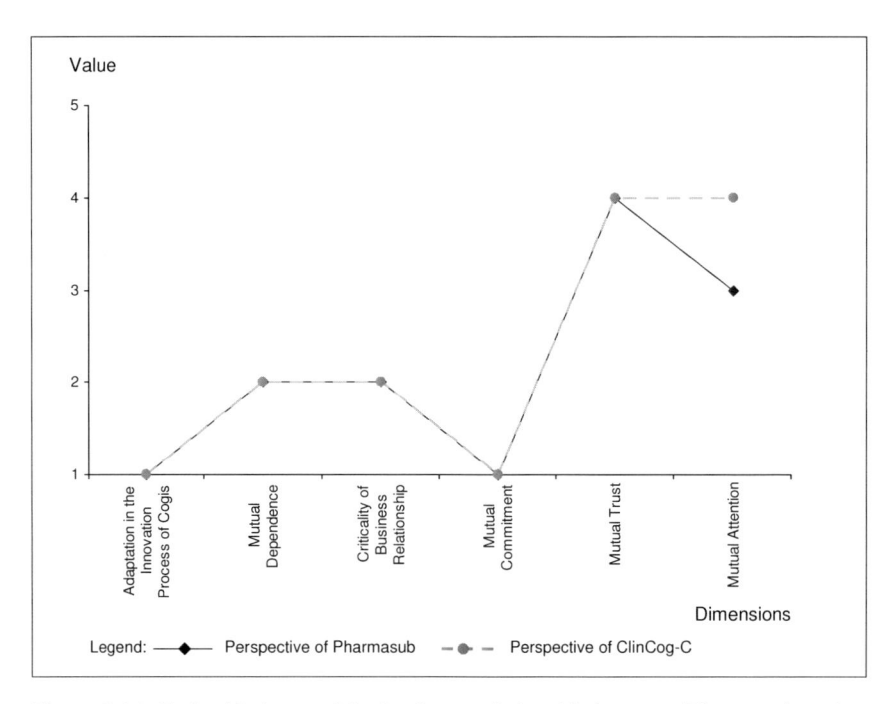

Figure 6-14: Embeddedness of the business relationship between Pharmasub and ClinCog-C in stage II of the clinical trials

(4) Mutual criticality:

(a) Criticality of the business relationship for Pharmasub: Criticality of the business relationship to ClinCog-C for Pharmasub was evaluated as low but not very low like in stage I. Consequences of a termination are higher the more the product innovation process progresses (A-R2&3 §555). Studies take longer and costs of the whole product innovation project are higher (A-R2&3 §647).

(b) Criticality of the business relationship for ClinCog-C: Criticality of the business relationship of ClinCog-C to Pharmasub was also evaluated as low (A-R2&3 §555).

(5) Mutual commitment:

(a) Commitment of Pharmasub: Because adjustments and coordination were not that essential with ClinCog-C, the investments in the business relationship were assessed as very low (A-R2&3 §556-559).

(b) Commitment of ClinCog-C: The investments of ClinCog-C in the business relationship were evaluated as very low for the same reasons (A-R2&3 §556-559).

(6) Mutual trust:

(a) Pharmasub's trust in ClinCog-C: Because of the reliability of ClinCog-C in operational processes trust was high (A-R2&3 §560-565).

(b) ClinCog-C's trust in Pharmasub: Trust from ClinCog-C was assessed equally high (A-R2&3 §561).

(7) Mutual attention:

(a) Attention paid by Pharmasub to ClinCog-C: The attention paid to ClinCog-C by Pharmasub in the course of the study was assessed as medium because it was not that necessary (A-R2&3 §567).

(b) Attention paid by ClinCog-C to Pharmasub: The attention that ClinCog-C paid to the business relationship to Pharmasub in stage II of the clinical trials was assessed as high. The reason is the economic dependence of ClinCog-C (A-R2&3 §359-361, 567).

6.3.1.2.3 Clinical Trials Stage III

For stage III of the clinical trials, the breadth and depth of the business relationship to the most important external business partner was evaluated again. As has been stated earlier, the most important business partner is ClinCog-C again. Attributes of the depth of business relationships are depicted in figure 6-15.

(1) Number of functional areas involved with the business partner (breadth of business relationship): As this is the same partner like in stage II, the same applies to stage III of the clinical trials, of course. Pharmasub worked with ClinCog-C only in R&D. They collaborated with ClinCog-C also in stage I and stage III of product innovation processes (A-R2&3 §528-531).

(2) Mutual adaptations:
(a) Adaptations of Pharmasub: Like in stage II, adaptations from Pharmasub concerning the innovation process of Cogis were very low (A-R2&3 §631-633). As ClinCog-C was a competent and reliable business partner and was already involved in stage II of the clinical trials, little adaptations were necessary (A-R2&3 §541-545, 631-633).
(b) Adaptations of ClinCog-C: The same explanation applies to the adaptations of ClinCog-C for Pharmasub (A-R2&3 §631-633).

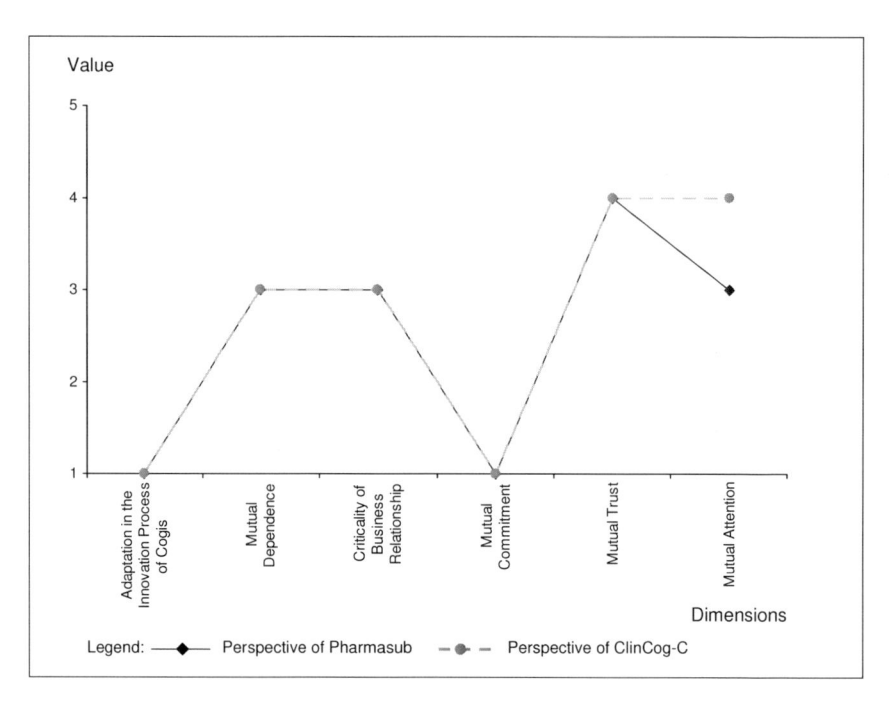

Figure 6-15: Embeddedness of the business relationship between Pharmasub and ClinCog-C in stage III of the clinical trials

(3) Mutual Dependence:

(a) Dependence of Pharmasub: The dependence of Pharmasub on ClinCog-C increased in stage III as the study was more extensive and there was more at stake at this late stage of the product innovation process. Investments during the process were high so that the study would not have been given up easily. Dependence was thus evaluated as medium (A-R2&3 §635).

(b) Dependence of ClinCog-C: The dependence of ClinCog-C on Pharmasub is higher in stage III as well because the budget is higher. It was set medium, too. If this study would have been terminated without success the loss of money would not have been easy to compensate (A-R2&3 §635).

(4) Mutual criticality:

(a) Criticality of the business relationship for Pharmasub: Criticality of the business relationship to ClinCog-C for Pharmasub in stage III of the innovation process of Cogis was also evaluated as medium (A-R2&3 §647). It was higher than in stage II because the study takes longer. Thus, it would have been costly to replace ClinCog-C with another actor. Again, the investments in the whole project had been very high at this stage of the process. About ten years of research and development had passed successfully. If the project had failed in the last few years the loss would have been tremendous (A-R2&3 §635).

(b) Criticality of the business relationship for ClinCog-C: The criticality of the business relationship of ClinCog-C to Pharmasub also increased because the study took a lot of time. If it had been terminated suddenly, ClinCog-C would have had many resources that could not have been used immediately (A-R2&3 §649). Furthermore, the reputation of ClinCog-C would have been seriously damaged if they had not completed the study successfully (A-R2&3 §641).

(5) Mutual commitment:

(a) Commitment of Pharmasub: Investments of Pharmasub in the business relationship to ClinCog-C in stage III of the clinical trials were very low. Again, this is due to the fact that no adjustments were necessary (A-R2&3 §559, 651).

(b) Commitment of ClinCog-C: Like for Pharmasub, the investments in the business relationship were very low from the perspective of ClinCog-C (A-R2&3 §559, 651).

(6) Mutual trust:

(a) Pharmasub's trust in ClinCog-C: Pharmasub's trust in ClinCog-C in stage III of the innovation process of Cogis was evaluated as high. It is the same value as in stage II because the business relationship is the same and no specifics of the stage exist (A-R2&3 §653, 561-565).

(b) ClinCog-C's trust in Pharmasub: Trust from the perspective of ClinCog-C was high again (A-R2&3 §653, 561-565).

(7) Mutual attention:

(a) Attention paid by Pharmasub to ClinCog-C: The attention paid to ClinCog-C by Pharmasub in the course of the study was assessed as medium (A-R2&3 §567, 654).

(b) Attention paid by ClinCog-C to Pharmasub: The attention that ClinCog-C paid to the business relationship to Pharmasub in stage II of the clinical trials was assessed as high again due to the economic dependence (A-R2&3 §359-361, 654).

6.3.1.3 Summary of the Embeddedness of Business Relationships to External Business Partners during the Innovation Process of Cogis at Pharmasub

In the past sub-sections, the embeddedness of the business relationships of Pharmasub and Pharmanorth to external business partners was analyzed. To do this, a qualitative evaluation of the respondents was provided. The breadth and the depth of the relationships were assessed by respondents on a five-point Likert scale. In this sub-section, the qualitative description of the business relationship is compared to the evaluation of the depth of the business relationships.[149] An overview of the embeddedness of business relationships is presented in figure 6-16 that summarizes figures 6-10, 6-11, 6-13, 6-14 and 6-15. In figure 6-16, relationships to business partners are arranged from left to right and top to bottom. In the first row, business relationships to ResCog-A (in vitro studies) and ClinCog-A (in vivo studies) are depicted. In the second row, business relationships to ClinCog-B (clinical trials I) and ClinCog-C (clinical trials II) are shown and finally, business relationship to ClinCog-C

---

[149] The breadth of the business relationship is not considered because all the business partners collaborated in R&D only.

in clinical trials III is listed. The criteria are arranged as follows from left to right: mutual adaptations concerning the innovation process, mutual dependence, mutual criticality of the business relationship, mutual commitment, mutual trust and mutual attention.

(1) In **pre-clinic I**, Pharmasub collaborated with ResCog-A, who was a scientist at a private research institute in the USA. In in vitro studies, he proved the non-toxicity of Cogis to human olfactory epithelium. This business relationship was crucial for the development of Cogis. If he had not proved the non-toxicity of Cogis, the drug could not have been tested in clinical trials with humans. The product innovation process would have failed. Also, ResCog-A could have hardly been substituted by another scientist. No other business relationship was that crucial in the product innovation process of Cogis. No other business relationship was described as enthusiastically as this one either. Asked to describe the business relationship in own words the respondent stated that it was excellent. Experts at Pharmasub were enthusiastic about the collaboration. This was explained by the fact that ResCog-A was very reliable, delivered studies and documents with very good quality and even delivered part results before the deadline. The quantitative assessments of the depth of the embeddedness of the business relationships show very high values for almost all criteria. Mutual adaptations, mutual commitment and mutual trust was evaluated as very high from both Pharmasub's and ResCog-A's perspective. Mutual dependence during the study was very high from both sides as well. Criticality of the business relationship in the long run, too was assessed as very high for Pharmasub because the product innovation process of Cogis would have been terminated without success at the stage of pre-clinic I without the collaboration to ResCog-A. However, the business relationship was hardly critical for ResCog-A. The attention paid to the business relationship by Pharmasub was very high while it was high from ResCog-A. For instance, Pharmasub even flew to ResCog-A to the USA to maintain contact without any particular occasion. In total, Pharmasub valued very high on all six criteria of the depth of the business relationship. For all business relationships that were analyzed, only here, this was found. It is likely that the immense criticality of the collaboration for Pharmasub had an impact on the evaluation of the business relationship. ResCog-A was a very reliable partner who provided part results even before deadline. Pharmasub was thankful and relieved that they had such a trustful partner for

this crucial collaboration. Thus, in this case, the criticality of the business relationship probably has an impact on the evaluation of the other criteria. Trust that includes reliability probably has a moderating effect on this correlation.

(2) In **pre-clinic II**, Pharmanorth collaborated with ClinCog-A. ClinCog-A was a service provider that conducted studies on apes with Cogis. The business relationship was described as very good. Pharmanorth and ClinCog-A had collaborated in other projects before but the business relationship became more embedded and personal during the collaboration on Cogis. ClinCog-A was perceived as very reliable. They were very open with problems and mistakes during the studies. Further, they were very cooperative. For instance, they extended the contract at short notice and offered extra services without any payment required from Pharmanorth. Mutual trust was evaluated as very high both from the perspective of Pharmanorth and of ClinCog-A. Mutual attention was high from both sides. The commitment of Pharmanorth was assessed as high, too, while that of ClinCog-A was perceived as low. This is because Pharmanorth taught them how to conduct particular studies and also told them a lot about the Cogis project. ClinCog-A did their job very well but did not need to invest a lot in the business relationship. As ClinCog-A conducted the studies like Pharmanorth demanded and was very cooperative in sticking to the time line of the collaboration they adapted highly to Pharmanorth. In contrast, Pharmanorth only adapted its product innovation process slightly for ClinCog-A. Adaptations of Pharmanorth only concerned the time line of the project. The procedure of the studies and documentation is regulated by authorities quite strictly. The dependence of Pharmanorth during the studies was perceived as high because they needed high quality results and documentation from ClinCog-A. Substituting ClinCog-A would have taken time. Dependence of ClinCog-A on Pharmanorth was assessed as low because they only needed the material and information on how to conduct studies. The criticality of the business relationship in the long run was perceived as very low from both sides. Pharmanorth could have worked with other service providers and ClinCog-A was booked by many other pharmaceutical firms. Hence, in total, the picture looks quite diverse. Three of the six criteria were assessed with same values for Pharmanorth and ClinCog-A. The other three criteria were always assessed low for one partner and high for the other one. Values ranged from very low to very high.

(3) In **clinical trials I**, Pharmasub collaborated with ClinCog-B. ClinCog-B conducted studies on Cogis with healthy test persons. The business relationship between Pharmasub and ClinCog-B was described rather unemotionally. Pharmasub obviously had trust in ClinCog-B before the collaboration started because both partners already had a frame contract (A-R2&3 §236). As the legal regulations for clinical trials are very strict it was clear how ClinCog-B had to execute studies and how they should behave. Respondents stated that this is the reason why business partners at this stage are selected for expertise reasons and not for embeddedness reasons. Problems at ClinCog-B in recruiting test persons were reported. They were not recruited as quickly as expected. The criteria of the depth of business relationship were evaluated very differently for Pharmasub and ClinCog-B. Only two criteria had the same values for both partners. Mutual dependence was evaluated as high and mutual trust was evaluated as medium. Commitment from Pharmasub was high while that of ClinCog-B was low. This is because Pharmasub had to train ClinCog-B on how to conduct the study. The adaptations to the business partner and the attention paid to the business partner were higher from ClinCog-B because ClinCog-A had to act in accordance with the requests of Pharmasub during the study. The criticality of the business relationship was assessed as higher for ClinCog-B than for Pharmasub because it is the business model of ClinCog-B to conduct studies for pharmaceutical firms.[150] From all the analyzed relationships, this was the one with most diverging values between Pharmasub and ClinCog-B. Criticality of the business relationship was low and trust was only assessed as medium. It was also described less emotionally and positively than the other business relationships of Pharmasub and Pharmanorth during the Cogis project. Maybe perceiving a difference in values between business partners in many criteria of the depth of relationships indicates disharmony between the partners.

---

[150] In the case of ClinCog-A, the criticality was assessed as very low although they have the same business model as ClinCog-B. Probably, they are booked by more firms than ClinCog-B.

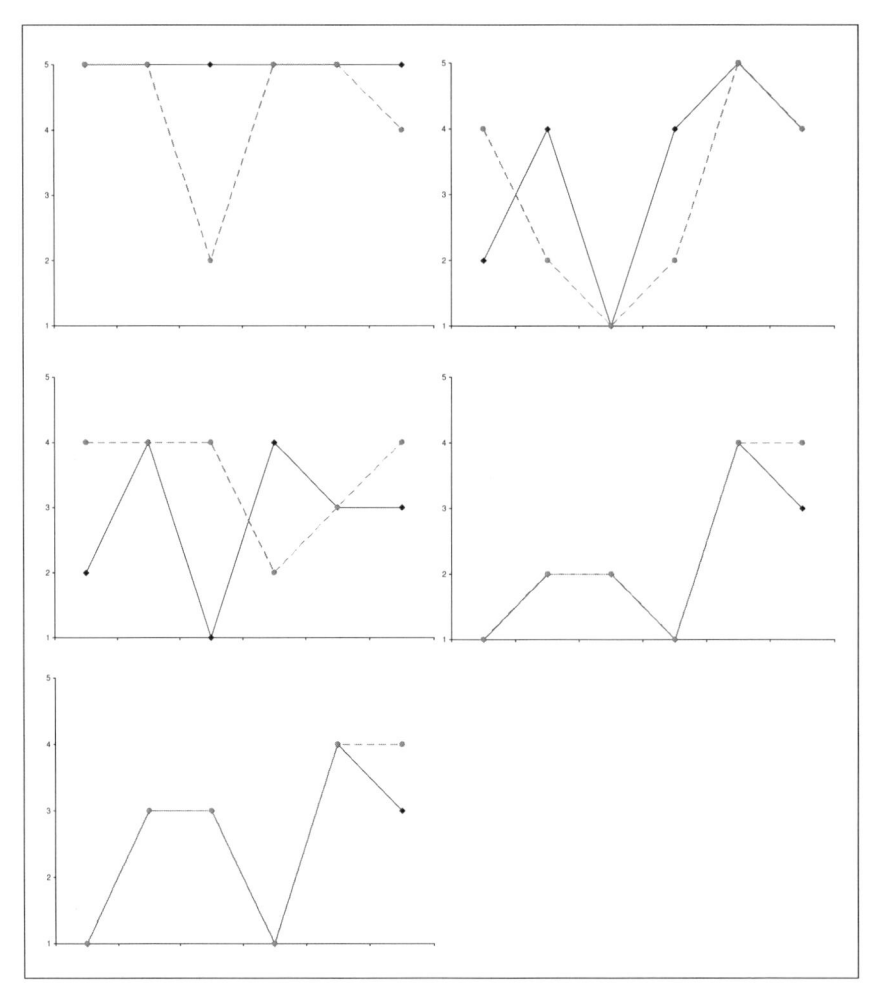

Figure 6-16: Overview of the embeddedness of the business relationships to the most influential business partners during the product innovation process of Cogis

(4) In **clinical trials II**, Pharmasub collaborated with ClinCog-C. ClinCog-C was a university hospital that conducted exploratory studies of Cogis on patients with COPD. The business relationship between Pharmasub and ClinCog-C was described as very good. ClinCog-C was reported to be more professional in conducting studies. After the collaboration on Cogis, a frame contract was signed between Pharmasub and ClinCog-C. Almost all criteria were assessed with the same values for both busi-

ness partners. Only little adaptations were necessary because ClinCog-C was very professional. Investments in the business relationship were very low as well because both partners knew each other already. Mutual dependence and criticality of the business relationship were low for both partners. Business partners acted quite independently and could be substituted in the long run. Mutual trust was high on both sides. Only the value of mutual attention diverged. For Pharmasub the attention was assessed as medium while for ClinCog-C it was a high. The business relationship to ClinCog-C was assessed by the same respondents as the one to ClinCog-B. It was described as more uncomplicated than the one to ClinCog-B. ClinCog-C was described as more professional in conducting studies. Criteria of the depth of business relationships were assessed with the same values for both partners. This supports the assumption that if respondents provide same values it might indicate a more harmonic business relationship than for diverging values.

(5) In **clinical trials III**, Pharmasub collaborated with ClinCog-C as well. Hence, the description of the business relationship applies here, too. There were some differences in values compared to clinical trials II but these were caused by differences between the studies. In clinical trials III confirmatory studies are conducted that confirm the findings of stage II with many patients. This costs a lot of money. A lot of money has already been spent in the product innovation process before clinical trials III. Hence, the pressure which increases with each stage culminates in stage III of the clinical trials. Thus, the mutual dependence is medium instead of low like the criticality. The other criteria were evaluated equally as in stage II. Again, all criteria have been evaluated with the same values for both partners. The only exception is mutual attention.

Comparing the evaluations of business relationships in the case of Cogis, the business relationship to the most influential business partner, ResCog-A, was evaluated as the best business relationship. The respondent rated the business relationship as excellent regarding all criteria from the perspective of Pharmasub. He also assessed four of six criteria as similar for Pharmasub and ResCog-A. The business relationship to ClinCog-A in the in vivo studies was evaluated as very good both on a professional and on a personal level. From Pharmanorth's point of view, almost all the criteria were evaluated as high. Only the criticality of the business relationship and the adaptations of Pharmanorth were low. Three out of six criteria were rated similar for both business partners. ClinCog-B was described as the least professional and trust was lowest of all business relationships. Only two of six criteria were assessed as similar for both business partners. The business relationship to ClinCog-C at the stages of clinical trials II and III was evaluated as very good again. ClinCog-C was assessed as more professional than ClinCog-B. Trust in ClinCog-C was hence high. Apart from attention, the other criteria were evaluated as similar for both business partners.

6.3.2 Embeddedness of Business Relationships to External Business Partners during the Innovation Process of Cantis at Diagnosub

6.3.2.1 Embeddedness of Business Relationships to External Business Partners during the Innovation Process of CantisCRC at Diagnosub

The product innovation process at Diagnocom starts with the idea description. As was stated earlier (sub-section 6.1.2.2), Diagnosub actually created two product innovations that are applied together. For the CRC test, the most influential business partner at the stage of idea description was a doctor at a university hospital in the UK. In the stages of the basic and extended technology studies, the same business partner was regarded as most important. It was a university hospital that delivered sample materials for the trials. In the following, business relationships in the stages of idea generation (6.3.2.1) and basic and extended studies (6.3.2.2) are described.

6.3.2.1.1 Idea Description

The first stage of the product innovation process of CantisCRC is the idea description. For this stage, CustCRC-A was the most influential business partner. The breadth and depth of the business relationship to her was evaluated again. The attributes of the depth of business relationships are depicted in figure 6-17.

The business relationship between Diagnosub and CustCRC-A was described as very good. Both business partners were very open and business relationship was trustful (B-R2 §57). CustCRC-A gave a lot of input on the idea of CantisCRC. Thereby, she took the perspective of Diagnosub and pointed Diagnosub's experts to questions they had not considered before. Diagnosub was very thankful for the valuable input and good relationship (B-R2 §171). However, even if the business relationship was perceived as very open and trustful, it was made clear that there is no tight personal relationship between the contact person at Diagnosub and CustCRC-A. It is still a formal business relationship. The rare relationships with tight personal contact need some time to develop and are particularly valuable (B-R2 §123-125).

(1) Number of functional areas involved with the business partner (breadth of business relationship): Diagnosub and CustCRC-A only collaborated in R&D at the stage of idea description. The business relationship ended after the project of CantisCRC was temporarily stopped at Pharmasub because of budget issues (B-R2 §47). In other cases, Diagnosub and the business partner at the stage of idea description collaborated in later stages of the R&D process as well. The business partner then conducted studies on the test and published the results together with experts of Diagnosub. Only in these later stages, the collaboration brings benefits for the business partner. Apart from other stages of the product innovation process, CustCRC-A could later have been involved in marketing activities of Diagnocom on CantisCRC. For instance, she could have been invited to conferences to speak about CantisCRC (B-R2 §62-63).

(2) Mutual adaptations:
(a) Adaptations of CantisCRC of Diagnosub: The adaptations of Diagnosub to CustCRC-A regarding CantisCRC were assessed as very high. The idea of developing a test on CRC from serum came from Diagnosub. However, CustCRC-A gave a lot of input on specifications of the test. Specifications encompass the specificity and sensitivity of the test, for instance. Diagnosub and CustCRC-A also discussed whether the test should detect pre-stages of cancer (B-R2 §67).
(b) Adaptations of the innovations process of CantisCRC at Diagnosub: The product innovation process of CantisCRC at Diagnosub was not affected by the collaboration with CustCRC-A (B-R2 §71).
(c) Adaptations of the work of CustCRC-A: The collaboration of Diagnosub and CustCRC-A had little impact on the work of CustCRC-A (B-R2 §74-75).

(3) Mutual Dependence:

(a) Dependence of Diagnosub: The dependence of Diagnosub on CustCRC-A was evaluated as very low and rather indirect. The confirmation of CustCRC-A that the product idea was promising was needed by R&D experts at Diagnosub in order to push the project in Diagnocom. External business partners are used in order to specify and confirm the product idea (B-R2 §76-79).

(b) Dependence of CustCRC-A: The dependence of CustCRC-A on Diagnosub was also very low (B-R2 §81-82).

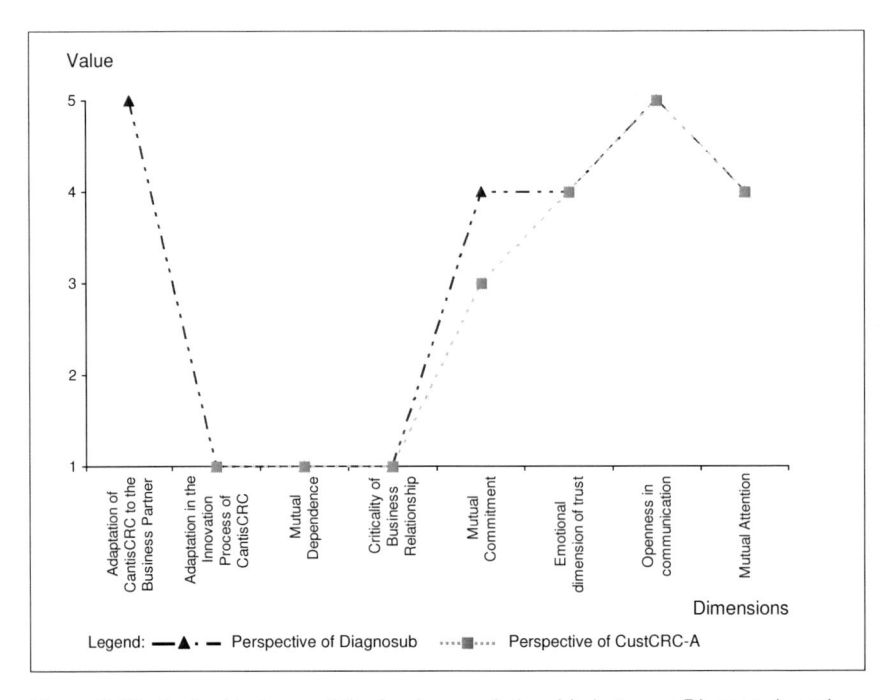

Figure 6-17: Embeddedness of the business relationship between Diagnosub and CustCRC-A in the stage of idea description[151]

(4) Mutual criticality:

(a) Criticality of the business relationship for Diagnosub: The criticality of the business relationship to CustCRC-A was evaluated as very low. If CustCRC-A had not

---

[151] The emotional dimension of trust and the openness in communication evolved in the course of the business relationship; see section (6) and figure 6-18. It is depicted on the peak of the business relationship in this figure.

been willing to discuss the product idea with the experts of Diagnosub, they would have selected another doctor. As the questions had a rather general scientific and clinical nature other clinical doctors would have been able to answer the questions as well (B-R2 §85).

(b) Criticality of the business relationship for CustCRC-A: The business relationship actually ended after the stage of idea description because at Pharmasub the project was interrupted for some years. When the project was revived and Pharmasub got back to CustCRC-A she did not continue the business relationship. The reason was that she was involved in projects on imaging procedures to detect CRC meanwhile (B-R2 §47, 86-87, 91).

(5) Mutual commitment:

(a) Commitment of Diagnosub: The investments of Diagnosub in the business relationship with CustCRC-A were assessed as high. Experts from Diagnosub approached the doctor and maintained contact with her. In order to discuss their product idea with her they flew to her about three times (B-R2 §88-89, 117).

(b) Commitment of CustCRC-A: CustCRC-A's investments in the business relationship were evaluated as medium. When discussing the product idea and later the results of studies, CustCRC-A invests time that she would otherwise spend on her clinical work (B-R2 §89).

(6) Mutual trust:

(a) Diagnosub's trust in CustCRC-A: Diagnosub and CustCRC-A collaborated for the first time during the project of CantisCRC (B-R2 §40-41). Thus, before the first contact trust did not exist. Diagnosub's trust in CustCRC-A was assessed as high. The respondent described two dimensions of trust: the emotional dimension and the openness in communication. This dimension evolved during the course of the collaboration. Diagnosub and CustCRC-A had not worked together before. Nevertheless, the emotional trust and the openness were quite high from the beginning. There is no doubt that Diagnosub needed to provide CustCRC-A with information on the product idea. Otherwise, CustCRC-A could not have given valuable input on the product idea. After the first contacts, the project stagnated at Diagnosub. During this time Diagnosub did not have any contact with CustCRC-A. When they resumed the innovation process, Diagnosub got back to CustCRC-A. However, CustCRC-A was not able to discuss the data of studies on CantisCRC anymore because she had made contracts with other firms. Her research now involved imaging diagnostic procedures. When the experts of Diagnosub contacted her again after the project was resumed in the firm, the relationship was immediately very good, again. They flew to her to discuss results of a study on the test. However, she had not signed the Confidentiality and Disclosure Agreement (CDA) of Diagnosub and informed the professionals of Diagnosub about her new partnerships. Of course, the experts did not show CustCRC-A the data of the study. In this unpleasant and unexpected situation, the emotional perspective of trust between the business partners remained and the situation was explained very openly. Despite the unexpected ending of the business relationship, Diagnosub would approach CustCRC-A again. However, they would not show her any data. Hence, the openness decreased between Diagnosub and CustCRC-A, but trust remained (B-R2 §47, 91-99). The evolution of trust and openness is depicted in figure 6-18.

(b) CustCRC-A's trust in Diagnosub: The trust of CustCRC-A in Diagnosub was evaluated as high as well. She experienced the same trustful atmosphere in the critical situation as Diagnosub (B-R2 §101).

(7) Mutual attention:
(a) Attention paid by Diagnosub to CustCRC-A: The attention paid to CustCRC-A by Diagnosub was evaluated as high. Diagnosub already selected the business partner with great care. They looked at the publications of potential business partners in the field of CRC, checked collaborations with other pharmaceutical firms and also the business background. For instance, if a potential business partner has changed university few months ago he probably needs to establish himself at the university first. Thus, selection of the business partner was done carefully (B-R2 §33, 104-109). Second, contacts to CustCRC-A were prepared accurately. Experts at Diagnosub had a clear idea of the purpose of CantisCRC. Furthermore, they had some ideas on the specifications of the product. Otherwise, discussing the product idea would not have made sense. Diagnosub would have wasted CustCRC-A's time (B-R2 §89).

(b) Attention paid by CustCRC-A to Diagnosub: The attention of CustCRC-A to Diagnosub was assessed high, too. Before the collaboration started, CustCRC-A gathered information about Diagnocom. She checked whether the firm was able to implement the product idea (B-R2 §110-113). Furthermore, she anticipated the position of Diagnosub and informed them about potential competitors. Thus, she also made up her mind on issues that Diagnosub did not ask her about explicitly (B-R2 §171).

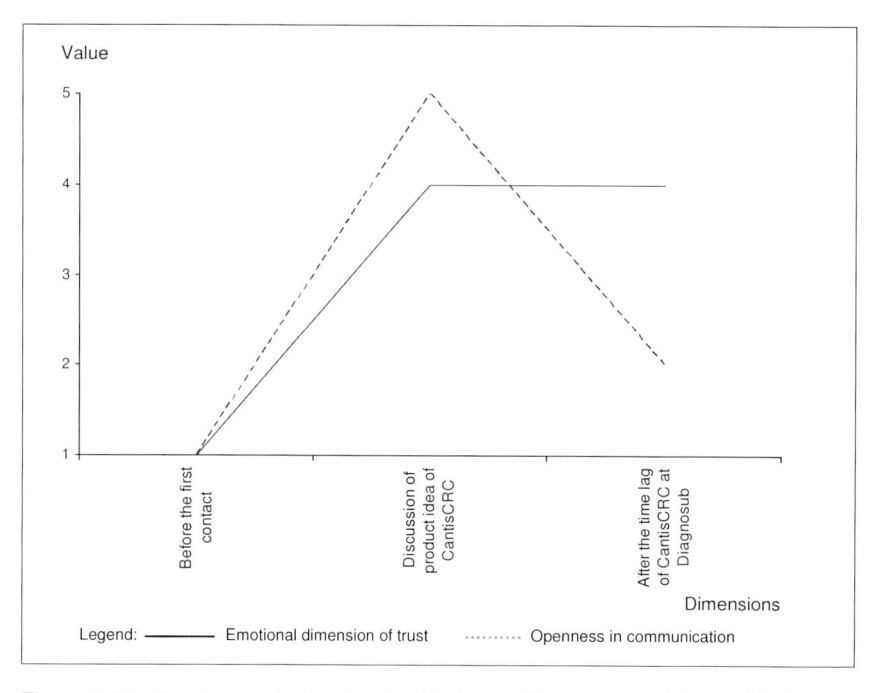

Figure 6-18: Development of mutual trust between Diagnosub and CustCRC-A

6.3.2.1.2 Basic and Extended Technology Studies

The second and third stages of the product innovation process of CantisCRC are basic and extended technology studies. For both stages, ClinCRC-A was the most influential business partner.[152] The breadth and depth of the business relationship with the hospital was evaluated again. The attributes of the depth of business relationships are depicted in figure 6-19.

---

[152] As was described in sub-section 6.1.2.5, basic and extended studies merge. In both stages, marker candidates are tested for their effectiveness for diagnosing colorectal cancer. Only the degree of fineness differs between the stages.

The business relationship between Diagnosub and ClinCRC-A was described as intense. They have frequent contact and discuss studies. ClinCRC-A is also very interested in the state of the product innovation process of CantisCRC after the collaboration on the studies was finished. Some of the professors of the university hospital also worked as consultants in later stages of the project or in other projects (B-R3 §67).

(1) Number of functional areas involved with the business partner (breadth of business relationship): Diagnosub collaborated with ClinCRC-A in R&D. So far, ClinCRC-A was only involved in stages of basic and extended technology studies. However, she might also get concerned with later stages of the product innovation process of CantisCRC. At the end of the development process, the product will be tested with patients in clinical trials. Then, Diagnosub might return to ClinCRC-A (B-R3 §51). In addition, ClinCRC-A might be integrated in marketing activities. For instance, the professor who managed the clinical study in basic and extended technology studies and clinical trials might talk at conferences about the results of the study (B-R3 §57, 71). But at the moment, Diagnosub and ClinCRC-A only collaborate in basic and extended technology studies.

(2) Mutual adaptations:
(a) Adaptations of CantisCRC of Diagnosub to ClinCRC-A: Adaptations of CantisCRC to ClinCRC-A were assessed as medium. Diagnosub had a concept of CantisCRC. However, in discussions with ClinCRC-A Diagnosub was confirmed about the viability of this concept. This was an important signal for internal negotiations at Diagnosub (B-R3 §73-75).
(b) Adaptations of the innovations process of CantisCRC at Diagnosub to ClinCRC-A: The product innovation process of CantisCRC was not adapted to ClinCRC-A (B-R3 §79).
(c) Adaptations of the work of ClinCRC-A: Regarding the process of taking the sample material from patients, ClinCRC-A completely acted according to the guidelines of Diagnosub (B-R3 §77). Experts of Diagnosub wrote guidelines about the taking of sample material. They also went to ClinCRC-A in the beginning of the collaboration and trained them how to take the sample material (B-R3 §131).

(3) Mutual Dependence:

(a) Dependence of Diagnosub on ClinCRC-A: The dependence of Diagnosub on ClinCRC-A was evaluated to be high. Dependence is twofold. First, ClinCRC-A must deliver the sample material and information in time as expected. Second, the sample material and especially the information must have the expected quality (B-R3 §81).

(b) Dependence of ClinCRC-A: The dependence of ClinCRC-A was very low. The every day work of the hospital was not affected by the study. ClinCRC-A received money for the study. They might also have got a research budget. If the product innovation process is successful and CantisCRC is launched someday the professor may also be listed as an author in the publications on the test (B-R3 §87-89).

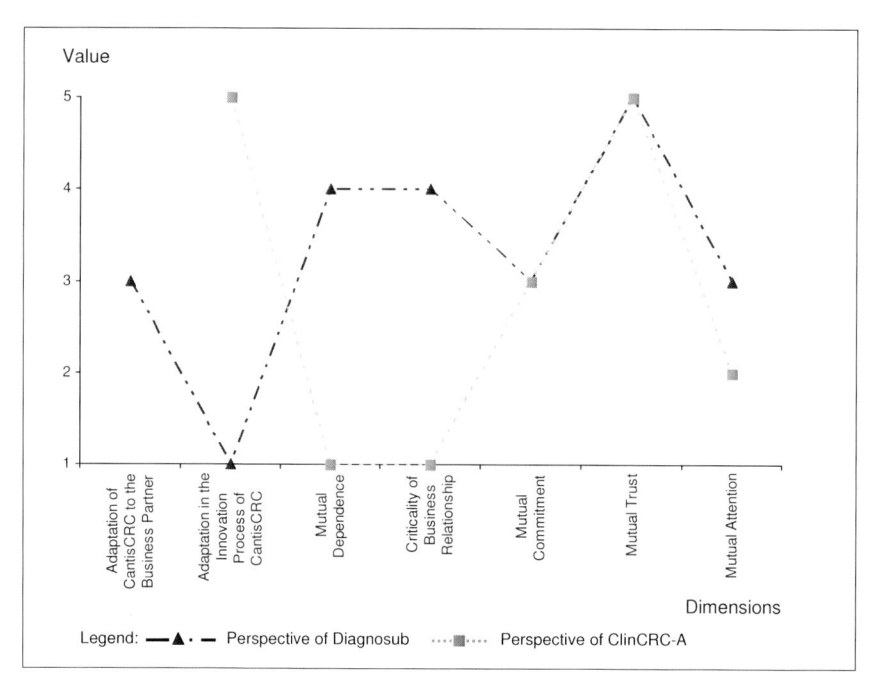

Figure 6-19: Embeddedness of the business relationship between Diagnosub and ClinCRC-A in the stages of basic and extended technology studies

(4) Mutual criticality:

(a) Criticality of the business relationship for Diagnosub: If the business relationship with ClinCRC-A had been terminated Diagnosub would have needed another hospital to get the sample material and the information for the stages of basic and extended technology studies. However, ClinCRC-A couldn't have been replaced quickly. Studies have to be approved by the ethics committee of the university or federal state; this takes about six months (B-R3 §93).

(b) Criticality of the business relationship for ClinCRC-A: The criticality of the business relationship of ClinCRC-A to Diagnosub was evaluated as very low. Each firm that develops diagnostic products or medicine needs university hospitals as partners to get sample material or conduct clinical trials. ClinCRC-A is a business partner that is known for scientific excellence and reliability. Hence, several firms in pharmaceutical industry would probably have liked to collaborate with ClinCRC-A (B-R3 §97).

(5) Mutual commitment:

(a) Commitment of Diagnosub: Investments of Diagnosub in the business relationship to ClinCRC-A were perceived as medium. Time was spent to maintain contact with ClinCRC-A and to discuss upcoming issues and answer questions by ClinCRC-A on the study (B-R3 §101).

(b) Commitment of ClinCRC-A: Investments by ClinCRC-A in the business relationship to Diagnosub were medium as well. While the professor only spent little time to take part in meetings the study nurse worked full time for the study with Diagnosub. As it often happens, a study nurse was staffed particularly for this study. She was paid from the funds that ClinCRC-A received from Diagnosub. Hence, the overall investment in the business relationship was medium (B-R3 §103).

(6) Mutual trust:

(a) Diagnosub's trust in ClinCRC-A: Diagnosub had a lot of trust in ClinCRC-A. This trust was described according to three dimensions. First, they trusted the quality of the sample material and information that they received from ClinCRC-A. The information was complete and both sample material and information were delivered in time. Second, ClinCRC-A had up-to-date technologies and therapies. Third, the personal relationships between the professor and the study nurse at ClinCRC-A and the project team at Diagnosub were very good (B-R3 §104-109).

(b) ClinCRC-A's trust in Diagnosub: ClinCRC-A's trust in Diagnosub was perceived as very high, too (B-R3 §109).

(7) Mutual attention:
(a) Attention paid by Diagnosub to ClinCRC-A: The attention paid by Diagnosub to ClinCRC-A was assessed to be medium. As ClinCRC-A was involved in discussions on how to conduct the study (e.g. on the grouping of patients), Diagnosub contacted them several times (B-R3 §111).
(b) Attention paid by ClinCRC-A to Diagnosub: The attention paid by ClinCRC-A to Diagnosub in the collaboration during the stages of basic and extended technology studies was evaluated as lower than vice versa (B-R3 §113).

6.3.2.2 Embeddedness of Business Relationships to External Business Partners during the Innovation Process of CantisPF at Diagnosub

The product innovation process at Diagnocom starts with the idea description. As was stated earlier (sub-section 6.1.2.2), Diagnosub actually created two product innovations which are applied together. The idea for the platform which proceeds multi-parametric tests was developed internally by an expert at Diagnosub without the participation of external business partners (B-R4 §3).[153] The idea was developed in a project about 10 years before CantisPF was started. In the stages of basic and extended studies, the most influential business partner was a firm for optical instruments. This business partner is named SupPF-A in this thesis. In the stage of feasibility, Diagnosub is still in the process of selecting a business partner who develops and manufactures CantisPF for Diagnocom. In the following, the business relationship to SupPF-A in the stage of basic and extended studies (6.3.3.1) is analyzed. In sub-section 6.3.3.2, the selection process of business partners in the stage of design goals is described.

6.3.2.2.1 Basic and Extended Technology Studies

The business relationship between Diagnosub and SupPF-A was described as very good, pragmatic and uncomplicated. This was true especially for engineers who

---

[153] The expert who developed the idea in the earlier project on a platform for multiparametrical tests left Diagnocom. Thus, unfortunately he could not be asked about the stage of idea description.

worked on the project both at Diagnosub and SupPF-A (B-R4 §65, 73). When SupPF-A needed a business perspective, the business relationship ended (B-R4 §27).

(1) Number of functional areas involved with the business partner (breadth of business relationship): Diagnosub repeatedly collaborated with SupPF-A in R&D projects (B-R4 §17). Diagnosub told SupPF-A the specifications of the photodetector they needed. SupPF-A developed cameras accordingly (B-R4 §21).

(2) Mutual adaptations:
(a) Adaptations of CantisPF of Diagnosub to SupPF-A: Adaptations of CantisPF to SupPF-A were low. The product idea and concept were already developed at Diagnosub. Hence, Diagnosub was able to specify the desired attributes of the photodetector. The main aims were to enhance the dynamic range of measurement and to minimize costs. Diagnosub primarily collaborated with SupPF-A in order to find basic approaches to solve this problem and a few others (B-R4 §33). The business relationship was terminated by SupPF-A during the process because Diagnosub could not assure them that CantisPF would be launched in the market. SupPF-A was not sure that they could produce the photodetector in large scale (B-R4 §27). Thus, now Diagnosub uses the photodetector of another firm. However, in the collaboration with SupPF-A Diagnosub learned that the problem of the dynamic range of measurement could be solved by developing a software (B-R4 §37, 55). Furthermore, they learned at which points of the photodetector costs could be saved (B-R4 §29).
(b) Adaptations of the innovations process of CantisCRC at Diagnosub to SupPF-A: The product innovation process of CantisPF was not affected by the collaboration with SupPF-A (B-R4 §39).
(c) Adaptations of the photodetector of SupPF-A to Diagnosub: SupPF-A was strongly influenced by Diagnosub in their work on the photodetector. They got the desired specifications of the photodetector from Diagnosub and were told that one of the main goals was to keep costs low. According to these guidelines SupPF-A started developing the photodetector (B-R4 §37).

(d) Adaptations of the innovation process of the photodetector at SupPF-A to Diagnosub: The product innovation process of the photodetector at SupPF-A was not affected by Diagnosub (B-R4 §41-43).

(3) Mutual Dependence:
(a) Dependence of Diagnosub on SupPF-A: The dependence of Diagnosub on SupPF-A during the work on photodetector in the basic and extended studies was high (B-R4 §51-55).
(b) Dependence of SupPF-A on Diagnosub: During the collaboration on the photodetector, the dependence of SupPF-A on Diagnosub was low. SupPF-A committed some of their experts to the development of the photodetector who were available when the project ended. However, it was SupPF-A who decided to terminate the project. Hence, their dependence was obviously low (B-R4 §57).

(4) Mutual criticality:
(a) Criticality of the business relationship to SupPF-A for Diagnosub: The criticality of the business relationship to SupPF-A was medium. They were important for Diagnosub to learn about the ways to make the photodetector with a lower price. In addition, they learned that software would probably solve the problem of the dynamic range of measurement. If SupPF-A had not terminated the business relationship with Diagnosub, they would have developed the photodetector together. When they ended the business relationship, the experts of the project team of CantisPF bought photodetectors from another project team at Diagnocom. Their project had been abandoned so the team of CantisPF could buy the photodetectors at a low cost. They developed the software about the dynamic range of measurement with another business partner later (B-R4 §58-61).
(b) Criticality of the business relationship to Diagnosub for SupPF-A: The business relationship to Diagnosub was completely substitutable for SupPF-A. SupPF-A decided to end the collaboration and did not work on similar projects later (B-R4 §62-63).

(5) Mutual commitment:
(a) Commitment of Diagnosub: Investments of Diagnosub in the business relationship to SupPF-A were low. Of course, some time and capacity of the experts were

spent to start the project. However, it was engineers who worked at Diagnosub and SupPF-A. They handled the project pragmatically and talked about the facts from the beginning (B-R4 §64-67).

(b) Commitment of SupPF-A: Due to the same reason investments of SupPF-A in the business relationship to Diagnosub were also low (B-R4 §68-69).

(6) Mutual trust:

(a) Diagnosub's trust in SupPF-A: Diagnosub's trust in SupPF-A was high during the collaboration and still is high. At the level of the engineers, no problems occurred during and after the collaboration (B-R4 §70-71). The head of technology development of CantisPF even wrote a letter to convince the program management to extend the contract to SupPF-A (B-R4 §51).

(b) SupPF-A's trust in Diagnosub: SupPF-A's trust in Diagnosub was assessed to be high, too (B-R4 §70-71).

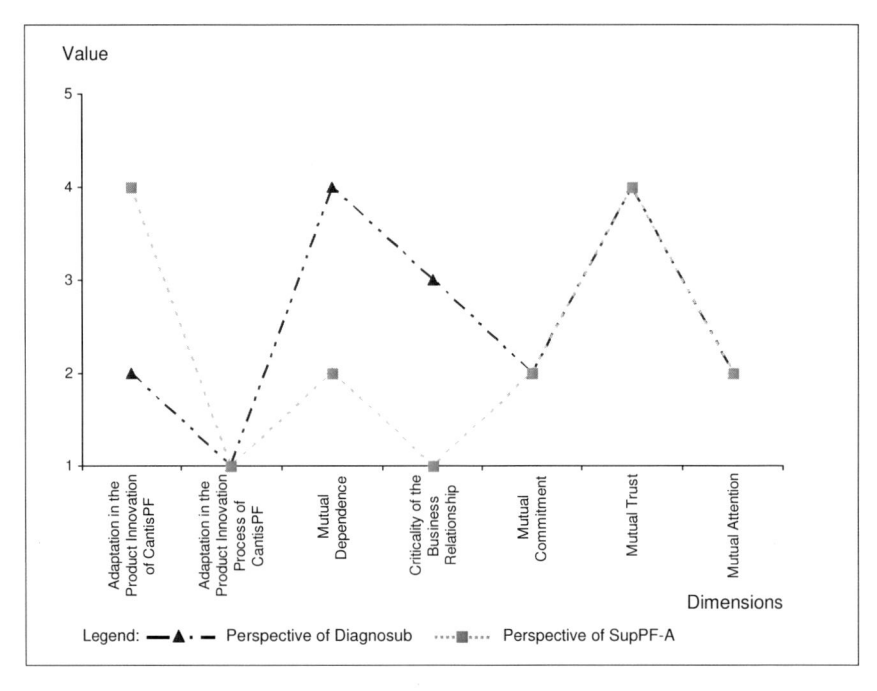

Figure 6-20: Embeddedness of the business relationship between Diagnosub and SupPF-A in the stages of basic and extended technology studies

(7) Mutual attention:

(a) Attention paid by Diagnosub to SupPF-A: The respondent described the attention that Diagnosub paid to SupPF-A as low. The stages of the collaboration are clear from the beginning (B-R4 §72-73).

(b) Attention paid by SupPF-A to Diagnosub: The attention paid by SupPF-A to Diagnosub was assessed to be low as well (B-R4 §72-73).

The criteria of the depth of the business relationship between Diagnosub and SupPF-A are depicted in figure 6-20.

6.3.2.2.2 Feasibility

At the time of conducting the interviews, CantisPF was entering the stage of feasibility. Diagnosub was in the selection process of an external business partner who would develop the final CantisPF. Two of four candidates were still in the process (B-R5 §30). However, as the collaboration to an external business partner at this stage was not yet established, the criteria of the depth and breadth of business relationships can not be discussed in detail. Thus, only a few remarks are made about the preparation of collaboration (for a more detailed description of the whole process see sub-section 6.2.2.2.2).

The selection process took about eight months. It began in November 2008 with the pre-selection of potential business partners, approaching them, presenting the product idea and the breadboard and asking for their development concept and estimation of costs (B-R5 §14-16, 18, 22, 30). A lot of knowledge was already transferred between Diagnosub and the candidates before the business relationship even started. Diagnosub needed to provide knowledge about CantisPF so that the candidates could develop their concept and estimation of costs (B-R5 §22). In return, candidates gave some suggestions on technical details that Diagnosub integrated in the product specifications (B-R5 §34). The early contacts not only served to exchange knowledge, they also served to build personal contacts between the R&D management at Diagnosub and experts at the business partners. Trust could be developed between Diagnosub and the potential business partners (B-R5 §49-50).

6.3.2.3 Summary of the Embeddedness of Business Relationships to External Business Partners during the Innovation Process of Cantis at Diagnosub

In the earlier sub-sections, the embeddedness of the business relationships of Diagnosub to external business partners in the product innovation processes of CantisCRC and CantisPF was analyzed. Thereby, a qualitative evaluation of the respondents was provided. The breadth of the relationships was specified and the depth was assessed by respondents on a five-point Likert scale. In this sub-section, the qualitative description of the business relationship is compared to the evaluation of the depth of the business relationships.[154] An overview over the embeddedness of business relationships is given in figure 6-21. It summarizes figures 6-17, 6-19 and 6-20. In figure 6-21, relationships to business partners during the product innovation process of CantisCRC are arranged in the first row. On the left hand side, the business relationship to CustCRC-A in idea description is depicted. On the right hand side, the business relationship to ClinCRC-A during basic and extended technology studies is shown. In the second row, the business relationship to SupPF-A during basic and extended technology studies of CantisPF is depicted. The criteria are arranged as follows from left to right: mutual adaptations concerning the product, mutual adaptations concerning the product innovation process, mutual dependence, mutual criticality of the business relationship, mutual commitment, mutual trust and mutual attention.[155]

(1) In the stage of **idea description of CantisCRC**, Diagnosub collaborated with CustCRC-A. CustCRC-A was a doctor at a British university hospital who gave Diagnosub feedback on their product idea of CantisCRC from a customer's point of view. She told experts from Diagnosub whether she would buy CantisCRC. She also advised Diagnosub on the specifications of the product. She told them what she would require in the product in order to buy it. In addition, she pointed Diagnosub to technologies that they had not considered yet. Hence, she was extraordinarily cooperative and took the perspective of Diagnosub. The business relationship between Diag-

---

[154] The breadth of the business relationship is not considered because all of the business partners collaborated in R&D only.
[155] In the first graph, the criterion of trust is split into emotional trust and openness of communication. Thus, eight instead of seven criteria are depicted in this graph.

nosub and CustCRC-A was described as very good. Long grown personal contact did not develop but professional contact was very good and trustful. The respondent was very thankful about the collaboration. Although the business relationship ended after this stage, experts from Diagnosub would still get in contact with her if necessary. Most criteria of the depth of business relationship were evaluated as similar for both business partners. Adaptation of CantisCRC to the suggestions of CustCRC-A was evaluated as very high. Processes both at Diagnosub and CustCRC-A were not adapted. Both partners paid much attention to each other. Pharmasub prepared meetings with CustCRC-A very carefully. CustCRC-A took Diagnosub's perspective and pointed them to competitors and technologies that they did not have in mind yet although she was not directly asked for it. Commitment of Diagnosub was a bit higher than that of CustCRC-A. For instance, as Diagnosub was interested in the input from CustCRC-A they flew to her and not vice versa. The criterion of trust was split in two dimensions by the respondent: emotional trust and openness in communication. While the first dimension was evaluated as high from both perspectives, the latter was assessed as very high. Mutual dependence and criticality of the business relationship were assessed as very low for both partners. Diagnosub could have chosen another business partner.

(2) At the stage of **basic and extended technology studies of CantisCRC**, Diagnosub collaborated with ClinCRC-A. ClinCRC-A was a university hospital that collected sample material from patients with CRC. Further, they delivered demographic information on the patients and on the type of CRC. Without this information, the sample material would have been of no value for Diagnosub. The business relationship between Diagnosub and ClinCRC-A was described as intense. They had frequent contact and discussed studies. ClinCRC-A was also very interested in the state of the product innovation process of CantisCRC after the collaboration on the studies was finished. Some of the professors of the university hospital also worked as consultants in later stages of the project or in other projects. Adaptations of CantisCRC to ClinCRC-A were assessed as medium. Diagnosub had a concept of CantisCRC and ClinCRC-A confirmed this concept which was an important signal for internal discussions at Diagnosub. Adaptations in the product innovation process at Diagnosub were assessed as very low while the adaptations of ClinCog-A were evaluated as very high. Of course, ClinCog-A collected the sample material and information

according to Diagnosub's demands. Dependence of Diagnosub was assessed as high while that of ClinCog-A was assessed as very low. Diagnosub depended on the quality of sample material and information and on ClinCRC-A's speed of collecting the material. In contrast ClinCRC-A's day-to-day work was hardly affected by the collaboration with Diagnosub. Criticality was evaluated as high for Diagnosub but very low for ClinCRC-A. For Diagnosub, terminating the collaboration with ClinCRC-A unsuccessfully and looking for another business partner would have caused delays, efforts and additional costs. ClinCRC-A would have had other contracts soon. Commitment from both partners was assessed as medium. Time was spent from both sides to explain and discuss issues. Mutual trust was perceived as very high for both partners. Trust encompassed three dimensions: quality of the sample material and information, up-to-date technologies and therapies of ClinCRC-A, and personal contact with the professor and study nurse at ClinCRC-A and the project team at Diagnosub. Attention was assessed as medium from Diagnosub and low from ClinCRC-A. More contact was initiated by Diagnosub than by ClinCRC-A because Diagnosub wanted to discuss results.

(3) In the product innovation process of **CantisPF**, Diagnosub collaborated with **SupPF-A at the stage of basic and extended technology studies**. SupPF-A developed a detector for the breadboard of CantisPF according to the specifications of Diagnosub. The business relationship between Diagnosub and SupPF-A was described as very good, pragmatic and uncomplicated. Engineers were working on the project both at Diagnosub and SupPF-A. As SupPF-A developed the detector according to the specifications of Diagnosub; adaptations of the product were high. In opposition, adaptations of CantisPF were only low. No adaptations in the development processes were reported at Diagnosub or SupPF-A. Dependence was assessed as high for Diagnosub and low for SupPF-A. Criticality was perceived as medium for Diagnosub while the business relationship was not critical for SupPF-A. In the end, SupPF-A decided to terminate the relationship. Commitment was low by both business partners. Mainly engineers worked together and handled the collaboration very pragmatically. Mutual trust was high on both sides and mutual attention was low.

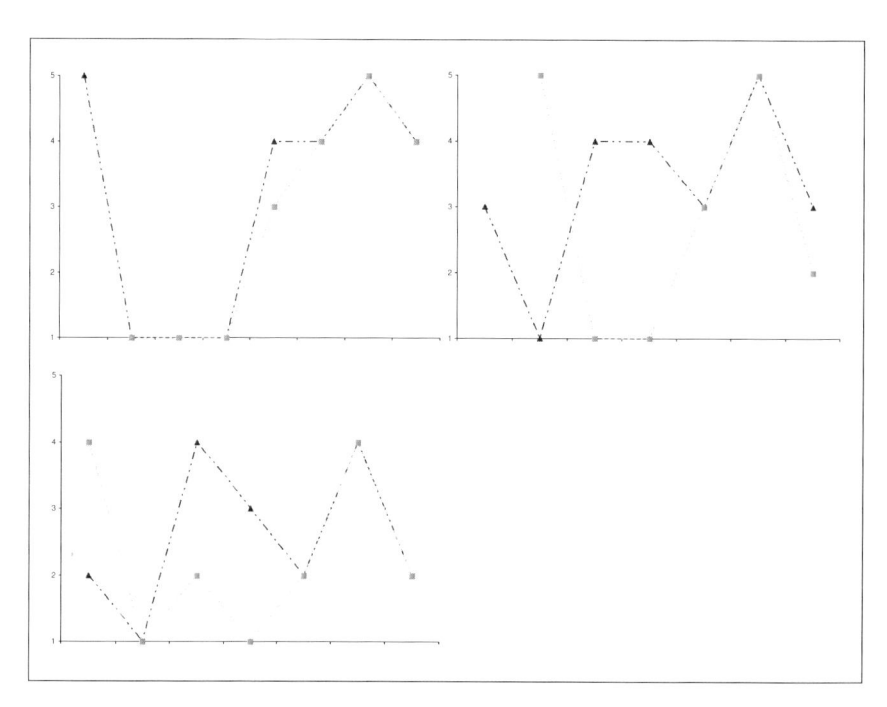

Figure 6-21: Overview over embeddedness of business relationships to the most influential business partners during the product innovation process of CantisCRC and CantisPF

Comparing the evaluations of business relationships in the case of CantisCRC and CantisPF, the business relationship to the most influential business partner, CustCRC-A, was described as the best business relationship. Seven of eight criteria were assessed similar for both business partners.[156] The business relationship to ClinCRC-A was evaluated as good professional business relationship. Most criteria were evaluated between medium and very high for Diagnosub. Dependence and criticality were higher than in the other business relationships. Two of six criteria were evaluated similarly for both business partners. The business relationship to SupPF-A was described as very pragmatic and uncomplicated. Four of seven criteria were assessed similarly for both business partners. The group of emotional factors of mutual

---

[156] The criterion of adaptations of the product was only assessed for Diagnosub in the collaborations with CustCRC-A and ClinCRC-A because they do not develop or produce a product for Diagnosub. Therefore, one of the seven criteria is left out when looking at similar evaluations. In the case of CustCRC-A, seven criteria are compared nevertheless. This is due to the fact that the criterion of trust was split up in two dimensions "emotional trust" and "openness of communication" which were evaluated for both partners.

commitment, mutual trust, and mutual attention were rated lower than in any other business relationship. While mutual trust was assessed as high, mutual commitment and mutual attention were only low. In the cases of CantisCRC and CantisPF, no adaptations of Diagnosub to business partners concerning the product innovation process were made. Trust was always high or very high.

6.3.3 Comparison and Conclusion of the Embeddedness of Business Relationships to External Business Partners during the Innovation Process of Cogis and Cantis

Studying the embeddedness of business relationships, a few points have been shown. They are summarized and explained in the following.

(1) First, in both cases, Cogis and Cantis, the **business relationships to the most influential business partners** in the product innovation process have been perceived as the best relationships. In the case of Cogis, the most influential business partner was ResCog-A at the stage of in vitro tests. The business relationship to him was assessed as excellent. Pharmasub invested a lot of effort to cultivate the business relationship. Adaptation of the product innovation process, dependence, criticality, commitment, trust and attention of Pharmasub were evaluated as very high.

The most influential business partner in the development of CantisCRC was CustCRC-A. She gave Diagnosub feedback whether the product idea was promising. In addition, she advised the experts which specifications the product should have. The business relationship to her was also evaluated as very good and better than the other two business relationships during the product innovation processes of CantisCRC and CantisPF. Adaptations concerning the product, commitment, trust and attention of Diagnosub were assessed as high or very high. Only dependence, criticality and adaptations regarding the product innovation process were very low.

In the qualitative description, the business relationship to ResCog-A was explained very enthusiastically. The business relationship to CustCRC-A was described warmly as a very good business relationship. In both cases, the business relationships were very good but no personal relationship between business partners existed. Hence, it is assumed that the criticality of the knowledge that both business partners transferred to the innovative subsidiaries affects the perception of the business relationship. If they deliver very critical knowledge and are reliable, respondents at the innovative subsidiaries are probably thankful and enthusiastic about the business relationship. This applies at least to the most important business relationships throughout the product innovation process. The assumed relationship is depicted in figure 6-22.

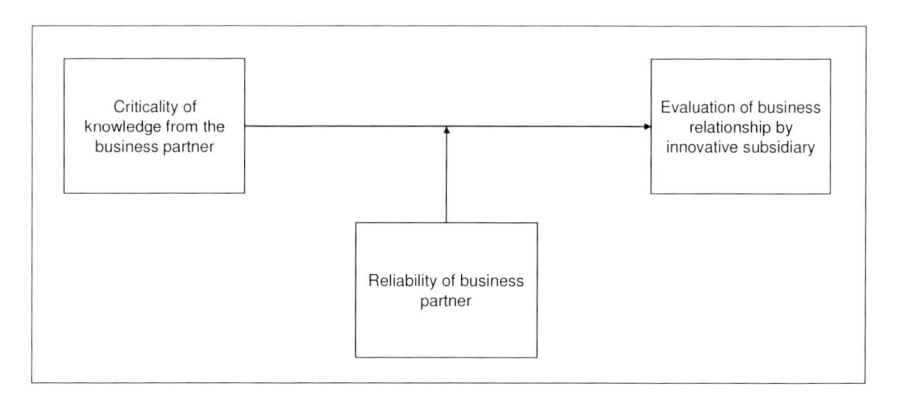

```
┌─────────────────────┐                              ┌─────────────────────┐
│   Criticality of    │                              │ Evaluation of business│
│ knowledge from the  │─────────────────────────────▶│   relationship by    │
│  business partner   │                              │ innovative subsidiary │
└─────────────────────┘              ▲               └─────────────────────┘
                                     │
                          ┌─────────────────────┐
                          │ Reliability of business│
                          │       partner        │
                          └─────────────────────┘
```

Figure 6-22: Assumed determining and moderating factor of the evaluation of very important business relationships

(2) Business relationships that were described as very good and harmonic got **similar evaluation of criteria** for both business partners by the respondents. Business relationships to CustCRC-A and ClinCog-C (in clinical trials II and III) differed only in one criterion. In the case of CustCRC-A, this was mutual commitment and with ClinCog-C it was mutual attention. In the business relationship between Pharmasub and ResCog-A, two variables differed: mutual criticality and mutual attention. In opposition, the relationships to business partners which were described with least enthusiasm, ClinCog-B and ClinCRC-A differed in four of seven criteria. Hence, it might be assumed that in more harmonic business relationships both partners are rated with the same values regarding the criteria.

(3) It becomes obvious in most evaluations of business relationships that **criteria were assessed very differently**. For instance, criteria of the business relationship to ClinCog-C in stages II and III of clinical trials ranged from very low to very high. Even

though the business relationship was described as very good and frame contracts were made with ClinCog-C, adaptations of the product innovation process were very low. However, dependence, criticality, trust and attention from Pharmasub were high or very high. In the business relationship with ClinCRC-A, adaptation of CRC due to the business relationship with ClinCRC-A were medium. However, dependence, criticality, trust and attention were assessed as high or very high. Hence, taking adaptation as the only measure of the embeddedness of business relationships, as was done in past studies, oversimplifies the relationship. The embeddedness of business relationships can not be fully grasped by this single measure.

(4) Only few respondents stated that the **business relationship developed** during the collaboration on Cogis, CantisCRC or CantisPF. Within the development of Cogis, the business relationship between Pharmanorth and ClinCog-A developed from a good but not too tight business relationship to a very good business relationship. The personal contact between experts of both firms got tighter and more informal during this time. Changes of the business relationship could be determined regarding the criteria "mutual adaptations in the product innovation process", "mutual commitment" and "mutual trust". While mutual trust increased from medium to very high, mutual adaptations and commitment increased from low to high. The other criteria did not evolve. Trust also evolved in the business relationship to CustCRC-A. Diagnosub had not worked with CustCRC-A before so that no trust before the collaboration on CantisCRC. During the collaboration, trust between the business partners got high and has stayed like this until now. Openness of communication got very high but decreased a bit when CustCRC-A did not continue the business relationship.

6.4   Characteristics of Knowledge and Knowledge Transfer

In this section, characteristics of exchanged knowledge and of knowledge transfer are analyzed. While in sub-section 6.4.1, knowledge transfer between Pharmasub and their business partners in the case of Cogis is examined, the same is done in sub-section 6.4.2 for Diagnosub and its business partners during the product innovation process of CantisCRC and in 6.4.3 for the case of CantisPF. In sub-section 6.4.4, the cases are compared and conclusions are drawn.

6.4.1 Characteristics of Knowledge Exchanged with and Knowledge Transfer to External Business Partners during the Innovation Process of Cogis at Pharmasub

6.4.1.1 Pre-clinic I: In vitro tests

6.4.1.1.1 Content of Knowledge Flows

Knowledge flows started in a kick-off meeting between the contact person at Pharmasub and ResCog-A. Cogis was explained and the problem of the olfactory toxicity was discussed. The meeting ended with the signing of contracts (A-R1 §102).

During the collaboration frequent contacts took place. They had two purposes. First, the collaboration was coordinated. For instance, Pharmasub and ResCog-A talked about delivery of material, toll, the time frame of particular activities and next steps. Second, results were gradually passed on from ResCog-A to Pharmasub. Both partners discussed about the interpretation of the results and possible implications for next steps of the study (A-R1 §98-100).

At the end of this stage, results were summarized in a report and transferred from ResCog-A to Pharmasub. The whole documentation of the studies was also provided to Pharmasub. After the study on olfactory toxicity had terminated ResCog-A kept working for Pharmasub for about two years as a consultant on further steps of the product innovation process (A-R1 §68, 104).

6.4.1.1.2 Characteristics of Knowledge

(1) Articulability: Exchanged knowledge was easily articulated orally by phone or by face-to-face discussions or in a written form in reports and documentation (A-R1 §98-104).

(2) Complexity of knowledge: Knowledge that Pharmasub received from ResCog-A was assessed as very complex. Pharmasub presented the problem to ResCog-A with very little knowledge on the solution of the problem of olfactory toxicity. Thus, ResCog-A started his studies from scratch. ResCog-A applied different scientific approaches to find out whether Cogis was toxic for humans. Some of these approaches are difficult to proceed on and interpret. One method was to exclude other possible explanations for the toxicity. This method was described as very complex (A-R1 §122).

(3) System dependence: The exchanged knowledge is system dependent because it is very specific pharmaceutical and medical knowledge (A-R1 §98).

(4) Detailedness: The knowledge that Pharmasub gave to ResCog-A was not more detailed than in other business relationships. Pharmasub always provides their business partners with detailed knowledge about the joint project. Apart from receiving good results, this serves to cultivate the business relationship (A-R1 §124-126). The degree of detailedness of knowledge that Pharmasub receives from their business partners differs, however. The documentation of ResCog-A about the study was very detailed. Although Pharmasub did not provide ResCog-A with strict guidelines on how to document the study and results, ResCog-A made a very detailed documentation. If something remained unclear, he added explanations (A-R1 §124-126).

(5) Holisticity of knowledge: The knowledge that Pharmasub received from ResCog-A was also very holistic. He had a lot of expertise about the problem of olfactory toxicity and provided all the knowledge in the reports and documentation that Pharmasub needed. If anything was unclear he did not hesitate to provide explanations. In other business relationships Pharmasub did not receive the knowledge that they needed. This may be the case because the business partner was not motivated to add lacking information. However, it mainly happened when the business partner did not have sufficient expertise about a subject (A-R1 §127-136).

6.4.1.1.3 Characteristics of Knowledge Flows

(1) Cross-border knowledge flows: ResCog-A worked at a private research institution in the USA so that knowledge flows were cross-border (A-R1 §122).

(2) Planned versus emerging knowledge flows: Knowledge flows between Pharmasub and ResCog-A were either planned or emerging. Of course, the first meeting was planned. The couple of times that experts from Pharmasub flew to the USA or ResCog-A or vice versa were also planned. Finally, the transfer of the summarized results and documentation was planned. Most of the operational issues were discussed in emerging contacts, though. This was also the case for part results because ResCog-A usually delivered them prior to the deadline (A-R1 §56, 106).

(3) Frequency of knowledge flows: Knowledge flows took place once or twice a month on average in the two years of the study (A-R1 §94-96).

(4) Coordinator of knowledge flows: Knowledge flows were coordinated by Pharmasub and ResCog-A. A third party was not involved (A-R1 §56, 107-108).

(5) Coordination of knowledge flows: Coordination between Pharmasub and ResCog-A took place rather informally. Of course, there were plans when ResCog-A should deliver part results (A-R1 §56, 106). Above that, a lot was discussed orally in personal contacts or on the telephone (A-R1 §110). Thus, coordination was mainly done by technocratic and personal coordination mechanisms.

(6) Criticality of knowledge flows: Knowledge flows from ResCog-A to Pharmasub were exceptionally crucial for Pharmasub. They strongly influenced the success of the product innovation process of Cogis. ResCog-A was one of two experts who could examine and prove the non-toxicity of Cogis to humans regarding the olfactory epithelium. Hence, if ResCog-A had not proven the non-toxicity and documented his studies thoroughly, Cogis probably could not even have been taken into the stages of clinical trials. Another expert on this field was by far not as experienced and well-equipped as ResCog-A. The documentation and interpretation of the results were essential for the success of the product innovation process (A-R1 §111-116). The

other way round, the knowledge that ResCog-A received from Pharmasub during the studies and afterwards was important but not crucial for him. Of course, he learned from Pharmasub as well, mainly about metabolism processes concerning Cogis (A-R1 §118).

(7) Problems of knowledge transfer: No problems in knowledge transfer between Pharmasub and ResCog-A were reported. Instead, it was emphasized that the business relationship and knowledge transfer were perceived as excellent (A-R1 §52-56, 141-142).

6.4.1.2   Pre-clinic II: In vivo tests

6.4.1.2.1   Content of Knowledge Flows

Kick-off meeting between Pharmasub and ClinCog-A took place at ClinCog-A. Pharmasub explained the substance of Cogis to experts at ClinCog-A, their existing data and the study that ClinCog-A was supposed to conduct. Apart from transferring knowledge, trust and commitment were supposed to be built (A-R1 §190, 220).

Knowledge flows happened frequently between Pharmasub and ClinCog-A. They served to transfers results bit by bit or to solve problems that arose. With the results, ClinCog-A also passed on their interpretation of results about which Pharmasub discussed with them. Part of the knowledge flows between Pharmasub and ClinCog-A happened at ClinCog-A's location. There, Pharmasub monitored the progress of studies and quality managers checked the studies and the whole firm. In addition, experts from Pharmasub and ClinCog-A discussed the study and part results. An important aim was to demonstrate to ClinCog-A the enthusiasm of Pharmasub about Cogis and to transfer this enthusiasm to ClinCog-A. Finally, face-to-face contacts helped to cultivate the business relationship between both partners (A-R1 §167-170, 221-224).

Knowledge flows ended with the termination of the study. Results were transferred to Pharmasub in a report. The whole documentation was added. ClinCog-A also sent Pharmasub a questionnaire to evaluate their performance (A-R1 §220).

6.4.1.2.2 Characteristics of Knowledge

(1) Articulability: Knowledge was articulated and taught. Important knowledge was articulated in a written way, for instance the report with final results and the documentation of the studies. This knowledge is passed on to external stakeholders like the administration that decides on the approval of drugs. The greatest part of knowledge was exchanged orally. These knowledge flows mainly encompassed operational issues on coordination of both business partners. Knowledge on how to take sample material for the studies from apes, for instance olfactory epithelium, was taught by Pharmasub (A-R1 §219-222, 232).

(2) Complexity: The knowledge that was exchanged between Pharmasub and ClinCog-A was described as very complex. It encompassed knowledge on all kinds of tissues, including olfactory tissue, hormones and spermiograms (A-R1 §235-238).

(3) System dependence: Knowledge on the studies was system dependent. Understanding medical and pharmaceutical language and processes was required to understand the knowledge (A-R1 §98).

(4) Detailedness: The knowledge that Pharmasub and ClinCog-A shared was evaluated as very detailed. For instance, Pharmasub explained to ClinCog-A in depth how to conduct the different studies. On the other hand, ClinCog-A discussed results of studies more intensively with Pharmasub than other business partners do (A-R1 §239-244).

(5) Holisticity: Knowledge exchange was also described to be more holistic in this business relationship than in average business relationships. This mainly applied for knowledge flows from Pharmasub to ClinCog-A. For instance, Pharmasub told ClinCog-A a lot about Cogis, the product innovation process and existing data on the

product. Additionally, they told ClinCog-A about data that they received from studies with human test persons and discussed comparisons between apes and humans (A-R1 §190, 242-248).

6.4.1.2.3 Characteristics of Knowledge Flows

(1) Cross-border knowledge flows: ClinCog-A is an international service contractor. For the in vivo studies of Cogis, Pharmasub collaborated with their German subsidiary so that knowledge flows were not cross-border (A-R1 §162).

(2) Planned versus emerging knowledge flows: Kick-off and final knowledge transfer were planned. Many of the contacts and knowledge flows on operational issues were emergent. Either Pharmasub or ClinCog-A called the business partner to discuss issues (A-R1 §225-226).

(3) Frequency of knowledge flows: During the in vivo studies on Cogis, Pharmasub and ClinCog-A had contact about once a week. They mainly served to talk about the progression of the studies, operational issues and part results (A-R1 §215-218, 222).

(4) Coordinator of knowledge flows: Coordinator of knowledge flows was a team of experts on Cogis and in vivo studies at Pharmasub and a team at ClinCog-A (A-R1 §227-228).

(5) Coordination of knowledge flows: Coordination between Pharmanorth and ClinCog-A took place mainly via two mechanisms: Experts from Pharmanorth went to ClinCog-A in order to explain the studies and to monitor them (A-R1 §165-170). Operational issues were discussed on the telephone (A-R1 §225-226). Both instruments are personal coordination mechanisms. Also, plans, budgets, and reports existed that determined which studies should be conducted in a particular timeframe (A-R1 §220, 258). Thus, technocratic coordination mechanisms were also used.

(6) Criticality of knowledge flows: Knowledge flows from ClinCog-A in the form of the results of the study were critical for Pharmasub. As the study was successful

Pharmasub did not need to conduct additional studies on the topics of toxicity and tolerance. This saved time and effort in the product innovation process of Cogis. Vice versa, ClinCog-A learnt new methods from Pharmasub. Pharmasub taught them how to do take tissues from the olfactory epithelium. Hormonal studies and spermiogram were new experiences for ClinCog-A as well. However, they could have learned that from literature. Hence, knowledge flows from ClinCog-A to Pharmasub were perceived to be more critical than those vice versa (A-R1 §180, 229-234).

(7) Problems of knowledge transfer: Problems with knowledge transfer were not reported by the respondent. Problems during the in vivo studies arose but were discussed very openly. Mistakes were made transparent as well (A-R1 §251-252). Thus, Pharmasub could identify and deal with defaults.

6.4.1.3 Clinical Trials Stage I

6.4.1.3.1 Content of Knowledge Flows

The basic structure of knowledge transfer between Pharmasub and ClinCog-B and ClinCog-C is quite similar during clinical trials I to III. It can be described in three instances. First, there was a kick off meeting in which Pharmasub provided ClinCog-B and ClinCog-C with knowledge on the specifications of the study. Specifications concerned the type of test persons that were needed for the study. For instance, female test persons of a particular age could be the target group of the medicine. Furthermore, instructions on the operational process of the study were given. ClinCog-B and ClinCog-C were told when to give the test persons the medicine and when and how to collect which data (A-R2&3 §374, 568-541).

During the study, ClinCog-B and ClinCog-C pass preliminary results on to Pharmasub. This was the biggest part of knowledge transfer which took place about once a week in the studies of stage I of the clinical trials. In the later studies, especially in stage III, these contacts happened less often. This is due to the fact that in stage I the medicine is tested with (healthy) human beings for the first time. Although it has been tested in vitro and in vivo with animals before, it can not be exactly foreseen how humans react to the medicine. In stage II, the basic tolerability is already confirmed and Cogis is given to patients with Chronic Obstructive Pulmonary Disease for the first time. At this stage, the effectiveness of the drug is verified. Thus, the uncertainty is not as big as in stage I (A-R2&3 §374). Stage III is called the confirmatory study because tolerability and efficacy have been proved (A-R2&3 §377). The results of the first two stages are only confirmed with a much bigger group of patients.

Pharmasub and ClinCog-B or ClinCog-C regularly talked about the progress of the study, for instance about the number of test persons that had been recruited (A-R2&3 §374). Monitoring of the study was another goal of the frequent telephone calls in order to guarantee the quality of the study (A-R2&3 §669). Pharmasub was furthermore interested whether test persons stayed with the study or if they quit the study (A-R2&3 §581). Of course, most important was how the test persons reacted to the medicine (A-R2&3 §377, 406, 581). It was made clear by the respondents that ClinCog-B and ClinCog-C did not deliver knowledge in the sense of combined information that was interpreted. Instead, they transferred single pieces of knowledge on physical reactions of test persons and patients to Pharmasub (A-R2&3 §403). The examiners at ClinCog-B and ClinCog-C did not know which disease was addressed by Cogis. Thus, they could hardly interpret the information they collect. They only passed the information on physical reactions of the test persons on to Pharmasub (A-R2&3 §369-373, 673). This is due to the fact that studies are double-blind. Because of legal regulations the system of drug development is hypersensitive. It is made sure that medical risks for test persons and patients during the studies and after the approval of the drug are as little as possible. Therefore, the people who collect the information are not the ones who interpret it (A-R2&3 §406).

In the end, ClinCog-B and ClinCog-C transferred final results to Pharmasub. Thus, the results were passed on in a condensed form. They were written down in the study book and transferred into databases at Pharmasub (A-R2&3 §377).

6.4.1.3.2 Characteristics of Knowledge

(1) Articulability: Pharmasub told ClinCog-B the specifications of the study. Specifications include the type of test persons needed and details on the frequency of giving medicine to the test persons and collecting physical data from them (A-R2&3 §374). During the study, ClinCog-B told Pharmasub how the study was progressing. This was done by telephone about once or twice a week (A-R2&3 §365, 374-377, 399). Moreover, ClinCog-B passed on preliminary data of the test persons to Pharmasub which was done both on the telephone and through email or templates (A-R2&3 §369, 377, 399). When the study was terminated, final data of the test persons were transferred to Pharmasub in the form of a study book or templates (A-R2&3 §377). Thus, the articulability of knowledge was assessed as very high.

(2) Complexity: Knowledge was assessed as complex. Test persons reported symptoms they perceived. In addition, data on reactions of the body to the drug were taken. Thus, different kinds of knowledge was transferred from ClinCog-B to Pharmasub (A-R2&3 §406).

(3) System dependence: Knowledge was perceived as system dependent because it contained mainly medical knowledge. Experts from other industries would have had difficulties understanding the exchanged knowledge (A-R2&3 §408).

(4) Detailedness: Knowledge was not assessed to be more detailed than in comparable business relationships. ClinCog-B conducted the studies and collected the expected data of the test persons. They transferred the expected knowledge but did not deliver more details (A-R2&3 §408).

(5) Holisticity of knowledge: Knowledge was not evaluated to be more holistic than in other business relationships. As in the case of detailedness, for this aspect also, ClinCog-B delivered the expected data but did not provide any knowledge beyond that (A-R2&3 §408).

6.4.1.3.3 Characteristics of Knowledge Flows

(1) Cross-border knowledge flows: As both Pharmasub and ClinCog-B were located in Germany, knowledge exchange was not cross-border (A-R2&3 §378-379).

(2) Planned versus emerging knowledge flows: Knowledge flows between Pharmasub and ClinCog-B were either planned or emergent. Of course, the first knowledge transfer about the specifications was planned. The final transfer of results was planned as well. Thus, contacts to the study manager were planned. However, knowledge transfers with the study doctor often were emerging spontaneously. With the study doctor, Pharmasub had frequent knowledge transfers about the progression of the study and preliminary results (A-R2&3 §380-393).

(3) Frequency of knowledge flows: Because of the high uncertainty of the study in stage I of the clinical trials, contact between Pharmasub and ClinCog-B was very frequent. They took place at least once a week while the study was proceeded (A-R2&3 §362-367).

(4) Coordinator of knowledge flows: Knowledge flows between Pharmasub and ClinCog-B were mainly coordinated by Pharmasub. At Pharmasub, one person was responsible for the coordination of communication with ClinCog-B (A-R2&3 §394-397).

(5) Coordination of knowledge flows: Pharmasub and ClinCog-B used plans, budgets, reports and templates to coordinate the strategic, long-term progress of the studies. Operational issues that arose during studies were mainly discussed on telephone calls (A-R2&3 §377, 399).

(6) Criticality of knowledge flows: Knowledge transfer from ClinCog-B was considered very critical by Pharmasub. Pharmasub could not proceed with clinical development or apply for approval without the data of tolerability of Cogis. Thus, if ClinCog-B had failed in delivering test person data this would have been a reason to terminate the business relationship (A-R2&3 §400-402). The product innovation process would have taken much longer.

(7) Problems of knowledge transfer: Problems of knowledge transfer did not occur. Rather misunderstandings concerning the interpretation of data happened. Data were collected by ClinCog-B. Physical data like blood pressure could be measured objectively. However, information on how the test persons felt was also collected. For instance, a test person had told the study doctor that he had headache. The study doctor wrote this information down in the study book and passed it on to Pharmasub. The study doctor interpreted this information as a neurological disease. The experts at Pharmasub disagreed; they thought that it was no symptom for any disease at all. However, no conflict arose out of the issue. This was mainly due to legal regulations. They determine that source data that are collected by the study center, i.e. by ClinCog-B in this case, stay in the study books. Thus, the information was in the documentation which was provided to the approval authorities like the Food and Drug Administration (FDA) in the USA. However, Pharmasub's interpretation was pivotal for its decision to continue with the studies and the development of the Cogis. They discussed it with experts at the department for pharmaceutical drug safety at Pharmasub before they took this decision (A-R2&3 §414-424). As the symptom did not show in later studies it would hardly be a problem in the approval process.

6.4.1.4 Clinical Trials Stage II

6.4.1.4.1 Characteristics of Knowledge

(1) Articulability: As the basic process of the study and the content of knowledge flows in stage II were the same as in stage I, the knowledge was easily and clearly articulated again (A-R2&3 §612-613).

(2) Complexity: For the same reason, the exchanged knowledge was complex like it was described in stage I of the clinical trials (A-R2&3 §612-613).

(3) System dependence: For the same reason, the exchanged knowledge was system dependent like it was described in stage I of the clinical trials (A-R2&3 §612-613).

(4) Detailedness: The knowledge that was exchanged between Pharmasub and ClinCog-C was not perceived as more detailed than in other business relationships (A-R2&3 §614-615).

(5) Holisticity of knowledge: The exchanged knowledge was not assessed to be more holistic either (A-R2&3 §614-615).

6.4.1.4.2 Characteristics of Knowledge Flows

(1) Cross-border knowledge flows: ClinCog-C has study centers in many countries. The study in stage II of the clinical trials took place on a worldwide basis. However, Pharmasub had contact with the German subsidiary of ClinCog-C. Thus, knowledge flows between Pharmasub and ClinCog-C were not cross-border. The contact subsidiary was chosen on the basis of the competence of subsidiaries in the disease, of available resources in the subsidiaries and because of its geographic location. Having too much time shift between Pharmasub and the subsidiary would have made communication on telephone more inconvenient (A-R2&3 §583-601).

(2) Planned versus emerging knowledge flows: In stage II of the clinical trials, physical reactions of patients are not as unforeseen as in stage I. Tolerability has been affirmed in stage I already. Thus, planned knowledge exchange with the study manager was basically the same as in stage I but emerging contacts to the study doctor on operational issues were less frequent (A-R2&3 §658-661).

(3) Frequency of knowledge flows: Knowledge flows between Pharmasub and ClinCog-C took place on a frequent basis. However, contacts to the study doctor were not as frequent as in stage I (A-R2&3 §571).

(4) Coordinator of knowledge flows: Knowledge flows between Pharmasub and ClinCog-C were mainly coordinated by Pharmasub. This was done by the same position in the subsidiary like in stage I (A-R2&3 §602-603).

(5) Coordination of knowledge flows: Like in stage I of the clinical trials, coordination instruments were both technocratic (plans, budgets, reports) and personal (telephone calls, meetings). However, personal coordination mechanisms were less spontaneous but more formalized and planned. Less telephone calls were conducted and more meetings and conferences are held (A-R2&3 §569-571).

(6) Criticality of knowledge flows: Knowledge transfer from ClinCog-C was considered very critical by Pharmasub. However, the criticality was a bit lower than in stage I because some data had already been collected in stage I. Nevertheless, if ClinCog-C had not delivered test person data Pharmasub would have ended the business relationship (A-R2&3 §610-611).

(7) Problems of knowledge transfer: No problems were reported with ClinCog-C. However, respondents pointed to other business partners who tried to conceal that they had made mistakes in the study or that they were not able to recruit as many patients as expected (A-R2&3 §619).

6.4.1.5 Clinical Trials Stage III

6.4.1.5.1 Characteristics of Knowledge

(1) Articulability: For the same reasons as in stage I, the exchanged knowledge was easily articulated (A-R2&3 §681).

(2) Complexity: The knowledge that was exchanged between Pharmasub and ClinCog-C in stage III of the clinical trials was evaluated as complex (A-R2&3 §681).

(3) System dependence: The exchanged knowledge was described as system dependent like in stages I and II of the clinical trials (A-R2&3 §681).

(4) Detailedness: The knowledge that was exchanged between Pharmasub and ClinCog-C in stage III was not perceived as more detailed than in other business relationships (A-R2&3 §683).

(5) Holisticity of knowledge: The exchanged knowledge was not assessed to be more holistic either (A-R2&3 §683).

6.4.1.5.2 Characteristics of Knowledge Flows

(1) Cross-border knowledge flows: In stage III, Pharmasub gave the mandate for the study to the same hospital like in stage II. Thus, the partner was ClinCog-C again. Like in stage II, Pharmasub's contact subsidiary was in Germany so that knowledge flows between the business partners were not cross-border (A-R2&3 §583-601).

(2) Planned versus emerging knowledge flows: In stage III, studies are confirmative. Thus, the uncertainty is much lower than in stage I and II. Hence, knowledge exchange with the study manager was basically the same as in stage I an II again, and contact to the study doctor was less frequent (A-R2&3 §658-661).

(3) Frequency of knowledge flows: Because of the confirmatory character of the study in stage III of the clinical trials, knowledge flows between Pharmasub and ClinCog-C were less frequent than in stage I and II (A-R2&3 §655).

(4) Coordinator of knowledge flows: Like in stage II, knowledge flows between Pharmasub and ClinCog-C were mainly coordinated by Pharmasub. This was done by the same position in the subsidiary like in stage I (A-R2&3 §602-603).

(5) Coordination of knowledge flows: Compared to stage II of the clinical trials, knowledge flows are more formalized. Of course, technocratic coordination instruments of plans and budgets are applied, again. However, as less operational contact takes place less personal contact is required (A-R2&3 §604-609).

(6) Criticality of knowledge flows: Although knowledge flows from ClinCog-C to Pharmasub are critical for the subsidiary, the criticality is not as high. Nevertheless, if ClinCog-C had not delivered test person data Pharmasub would have ended the business relationship (A-R2&3 §669, 679).

(7) Problems of knowledge transfer: No problems were reported with ClinCog-C (A-R2&3 §685).

6.4.1.6 Summary of the Characteristics of Knowledge and Knowledge Transfer of Cogis at Pharmasub

In the stage of pre-clinic I (in vitro tests), Pharmasub collaborated with ResCog-A. ResCog-A conducted studies for Pharmasub and proved the non-toxicity of Cogis to human beings. This business relationship was crucial for the product innovation process of Cogis. If ResCog-A had not proven the non-toxicity, Cogis probably would not even have entered clinical trials. Hence, knowledge flows from ResCog-A were extraordinarily critical for Pharmasub. Articulation of knowledge between Pharmasub and ResCog-A was assessed as easy. Knowledge that was transferred from ResCog-A to Pharmasub was very complex. ResCog-A applied different approaches during his studies that were all described in documents. As the exchanged knowledge was very special pharmaceutical and medical knowledge, it was very system dependent as well. The documented knowledge Pharmasub received from ResCog-A was very detailed. It was also very holistic. Knowledge flows were cross-border and took place about once or twice a month. While all of the strategic knowledge flows like the kick off meeting or transfer of final results were planned, many of the knowledge flows on operational issues emerged. Planned knowledge flows were co-ordinated mainly by technocratic coordination instruments while emergent knowledge flows were coordinated mainly by personal contact. Knowledge flows were coordinated by Pharmasub or ResCog-A. No problems in knowledge transfer between Pharmasub and ResCog-A were reported. Instead, it was emphasized that the business relationship and knowledge transfer were perceived as excellent.

In the stage of pre-clinical studies II (in vivo studies), Pharmasub collaborated with ClinCog-A. ClinCog-A conducted studies on apes with Cogis. Studies included several tissues and hormonal studies and were quite varied. The business relationship was not very critical for Pharmasub. They could have conducted in vivo studies with another service contractor. However, business relationship was evaluated as very good. Most of the knowledge that was transferred from Pharmasub to ClinCog-A was articulated. In the beginning of the studies, Pharmasub also taught knowledge when they showed ClinCog-A how to take sample material from apes. Since different kinds of tissues were the object of the studies, the knowledge was assessed as very complex. It was also evaluated as system dependent. Knowledge from ClinCog-A was perceived as more detailed than in average business relationships as ClinCog-A discussed results more intensively with Pharmasub. It was not perceived as particularly holistic. Knowledge flows were not cross-border. First and last knowledge flows were planned while many of the operational issues were discussed in emerging contacts. Operational contacts occurred about once a week. They were coordinated by personal contact mainly on the telephone. Planned knowledge flows took place both by technocratic (e.g. plans, budgets) and personal coordination instruments (mainly visitations at ClinCog-A). Knowledge flows were coordinated by both partners. Even if the business relationship was not perceived as critical for Pharmanorth, knowledge flows were critical. Well documented and successful studies saved further in vivo studies on Cogis. Problems of knowledge flows were not reported. In contrast, ClinCog-A was very open with problems during the studies.

In stage I of the clinical trials, Pharmasub collaborated with ClinCog-B. ClinCog-B conducted studies on healthy test persons with Cogis. Business relationship was described as good but with a few problems. This is mainly due to the fact that ClinCog-B did not recruit test persons as quickly as expected. Knowledge was articulated mainly on the telephone. Results were documented, of course. Knowledge was complex and system dependent but not more detailed or holistic than in comparable business relationships. Planned knowledge flows were coordinated mainly by technocratic coordination instruments, while emergent knowledge flows were coordinated mainly by personal contact. Knowledge flows took place once or twice a week. The high frequency was due to the high uncertainty of the studies. Knowledge flows were not cross-border. Again, kick off and final meetings were planned while the many contacts on operational issues and preliminary results emerged spontaneously. Knowledge flows were coordinated by Pharmasub and ClinCog-B. Knowledge flows from ClinCog-B were regarded as critical. Pharmasub needed the results of the study to continue with stages II and III of clinical trials and for approval process. If ClinCog-B had not documented studies and results properly, Pharmasub would have had to conduct the study again. Problems of knowledge transfer were not reported. However, Pharmasub and ClinCog-B sometimes had differing opinions regarding the evaluation of symptoms that test persons described.

Dimension	Stage / Business Partner	Degree
	Characteristics of knowledge	
Articulatedness	ResCog-A / Pre-clinic I	Easy
	ClinCog-A / Pre-clinic II	Easy
	ClinCog-B / Clinical Trials I	Easy
	ClinCog-C / Clinical Trials II	Easy
	ClinCog-C / Clinical Trials III	Easy
Teachability	ResCog-A / Pre-clinic I	-
	ClinCog-A / Pre-clinic II	Easy, how to conduct study
	ClinCog-B / Clinical Trials I	-
	ClinCog-C / Clinical Trials II	-
	ClinCog-C / Clinical Trials III	-
Dimension	**Stage / Business Partner**	**Degree**
	Characteristics of knowledge	
Complexity	ResCog-A / Pre-clinic I	Very complex
	ClinCog-A / Pre-clinic II	Very complex
	ClinCog-B / Clinical Trials I	Complex
	ClinCog-C / Clinical Trials II	Complex
	ClinCog-C / Clinical Trials III	Complex
System dependence	ResCog-A / Pre-clinic I	Very system dependent
	ClinCog-A / Pre-clinic II	System dependent
	ClinCog-B / Clinical Trials I	System dependent
	ClinCog-C / Clinical Trials II	System dependent
	ClinCog-C / Clinical Trials III	System dependent
Detailedness	ResCog-A / Pre-clinic I	Very detailed
	ClinCog-A / Pre-clinic II	Very detailed
	ClinCog-B / Clinical Trials I	Not particularly detailed
	ClinCog-C / Clinical Trials II	Not particularly detailed
	ClinCog-C / Clinical Trials III	Not particularly detailed
Holisticity	ResCog-A / Pre-clinic I	Very holistic
	ClinCog-A / Pre-clinic II	Not particularly holistic
	ClinCog-B / Clinical Trials I	Not particularly holistic
	ClinCog-C / Clinical Trials II	Not particularly holistic
	ClinCog-C / Clinical Trials III	Not particularly holistic

Characteristics of knowledge flows		
Cross-border flows	ResCog-A / Pre-clinic I	Yes
	ClinCog-A / Pre-clinic II	No
	ClinCog-B / Clinical Trials I	No
	ClinCog-C / Clinical Trials II	No
	ClinCog-C / Clinical Trials III	No
Planned versus emergent knowledge flows	ResCog-A / Pre-clinic I	Both
	ClinCog-A / Pre-clinic II	Both
	ClinCog-B / Clinical Trials I	Both
	ClinCog-C / Clinical Trials II	Both
	ClinCog-C / Clinical Trials III	Both
Frequency	ResCog-A / Pre-clinic I	Once or twice a month
	ClinCog-A / Pre-clinic II	Once a week
	ClinCog-B / Clinical Trials I	More than once a week
	ClinCog-C / Clinical Trials II	Frequently, but less than at stage I of clinical trials
	ClinCog-C / Clinical Trials III	Frequently, but less than at stages I and II of clinical trials
Dimension	**Stage / Business Partner**	**Degree**
Characteristics of knowledge flows		
Coordinator	ResCog-A / Pre-clinic I	ResCog-A and Pharmasub
	ClinCog-A / Pre-clinic II	ClinCog-A and Pharmanorth
	ClinCog-B / Clinical Trials I	ClinCog-B and Pharmasub
	ClinCog-C / Clinical Trials II	ClinCog-C and Pharmasub
	ClinCog-C / Clinical Trials III	ClinCog-C and Pharmasub
Coordination	ResCog-A / Pre-clinic I	Technocratic and personal mechanisms
	ClinCog-A / Pre-clinic II	Technocratic and personal mechanisms
	ClinCog-B / Clinical Trials I	Technocratic and personal mechanisms
	ClinCog-C / Clinical Trials II	Technocratic and personal mechanisms
	ClinCog-C / Clinical Trials III	Technocratic and personal mechanisms
Criticality	ResCog-A / Pre-clinic I	Very critical
	ClinCog-A / Pre-clinic II	Critical
	ClinCog-B / Clinical Trials I	Very critical
	ClinCog-C / Clinical Trials II	Very critical
	ClinCog-C / Clinical Trials III	Critical

Problems	ResCog-A / Pre-clinic I	No
	ClinCog-A / Pre-clinic II	No
	ClinCog-B / Clinical Trials I	No
	ClinCog-C / Clinical Trials II	No
	ClinCog-C / Clinical Trials III	No

Table 6-2: Characteristics of knowledge and knowledge transfer in the case of Cogis

In stages II and III of the clinical trials, Pharmasub collaborated with ClinCog-C. ClinCog-C was a university hospital that conducted exploratory and confirmatory studies with patients for Pharmasub. The business relationship was described as very good. ClinCog-C was described as more reliable and professional than ClinCog-B. Knowledge from ClinCog-C was articulated in documents and templates or orally on the telephone. Knowledge was perceived as complex and system dependent but not as more detailed or holistic than in other business relationships. Knowledge flows were not cross-border. Both kick off meeting and transfer of final results were planned but operational issues were discussed in emerging knowledge flows. Knowledge flows were less frequent in stages II and III than in stage I because reactions of patients to Cogis were not as unforeseen as in stage I. Like in stage II, knowledge flows between Pharmasub and ClinCog-C were mainly coordinated by Pharmasub. Planned knowledge flows were coordinated mainly by technocratic coordination instruments while emergent knowledge flows were coordinated mainly by personal contact. Coordination increasingly became more formal from stage I to stage III. Knowledge flows from ClinCog-C to Pharmasub were assessed as critical for the subsidiary but not as critical as in stage I. No problems were reported with ClinCog-C. The results of the characteristics of knowledge and knowledge transfer in the case of Cogis are summarized in table 6-2.

6.4.2 Characteristics of Knowledge Exchanged with and Knowledge Transfer to External Business Partners during the Innovation Process of CantisCRC at Diagnosub

6.4.2.1 Idea Description

6.4.2.1.1 Content of Knowledge Flows in Idea Description

About three contacts took place between Diagnosub and CustCRC-A during the stage of idea description. First, Diagnosub contacted CustCRC-A in order to find out if she was interested in discussing the product idea of CantisCRC. A broad idea of CantisCRC was given but no details were provided to CustCRC-A. This contact also served to get to know her and build trust between the business partners. The second time experts from Diagnosub presented the product idea of CantisCRC to CustCRC-A in detail. Both partners discussed the idea and CustCRC-A gave input on the specifications of the product. Furthermore, she gave her opinion on the degree of specificity and sensitivity that the test needed. Based on this input, Diagnosub decided to continue working on the project. Markers were searched for, which indicate the existence of CRC in serum. Trials with about 30 to 50 patients gave first impressions on the specificity and sensitivity of the test (B-R2 §117-119). With the data from these trials, experts of Diagnosub contacted CustCRC-A again. However, before the trails were conducted the project had faced a lag at Diagnosub. During this time Diagnosub did not have contact with CustCRC-A. So, when Diagnosub approached CustCRC-A on resumption of the project, she told them that she could not collaborate with them anymore. She already had made contracts with other firms. Her research now involved imaging diagnostic procedures. Thus, in the third contact Diagnosub and CustCRC-A did not discuss the data from the trials as normal. Instead, each partner explained his situation (B-R2 §47, 91-99).

6.4.2.1.2 Characteristics of Knowledge Exchanged during Idea Description

(1) Articulability: The knowledge that was exchanged between Diagnosub and CustCRC-A was articulable. Diagnosub depicted its product idea in PowerPoint

slides. This way, they visualized the workflow of the doctor and indicated at which point CantisCRC was supposed to be involved. In addition to this, Diagnosub's ideas on the attributes of CantisCRC were presented. The visualization made it easy for CustCRC-A to understand the idea of CantisCRC. In the discussion with Diagnosub, CustCRC-A gave her feedback and suggestions orally. No documents were used by her. Nevertheless, understanding the perspective of CustCRC-A was not difficult for Diagnosub. CustCRC-A's opinion whether the test was helpful and whether she would buy it was easy to discuss. Suggestions on attributes of CantisCRC were not difficult to articulate either (B-R2 §154-159).

(2) Complexity: Complexity of exchanged knowledge was perceived as low for Diagnosub and CustCRC-A. Knowledge on the basic idea and specifications that CantisCRC should have is rather elementary (B-R2 §159).

(3) System dependence: Knowledge was highly system dependent. This was indicated by the fact that experts understood the knowledge easily while other people would have had great difficulties (B-R2 §161-163).

(4) Detailedness: The knowledge that Diagnosub received from CustCRC-A was not described as more detailed than in other business relationships. However, the respondent stated that in other embedded business relationships knowledge exchange might be more detailed (B-R2 §164-165, 171).

(5) Degree of holistic knowledge: The knowledge that CustCRC-A provided Diagnosub with was more holistic than that from other business partners. CustCRC-A anticipated the need for knowledge of the experts from Diagnosub and told them about upcoming technologies by competitors. This was knowledge that Diagnosub had not explicitly asked for. Nevertheless, it was very helpful for Diagnosub. Taking the perspective of Diagnosub made CustCRC-A a very valuable partner that Diagnosub had a lot of trust in (B-R2 §168-171).

6.4.2.1.3 Characteristics of Knowledge Flows during Idea Description

(1) Cross-border knowledge flows: CustCRC-A is a doctor at a university hospital in the UK. Therefore, the knowledge flow was cross-border (B-R2 §43).

(2) Planned versus emerging knowledge flows: Knowledge flows between CustCRC-A and Diagnosub were always planned. Diagnosub approached CustCRC-A and flew to her to present and discuss the project idea. They also flew to her to discuss data of the first study with 30 to 50 patients (B-R2 §117-119). However, they did not give her the data because in the meanwhile she had committed to contracts from other pharmaceutical firms regarding imaging procedures to diagnose CRC (B-R2 §47). For the three contacts, experts of Diagnosub flew to CustCRC-A. Thus, the knowledge exchange was thoroughly planned. No emergent knowledge flows occurred. However, the respondent indicated that emergent knowledge flows might take place between long time business partners who have a very tight personal contact (B-R2 §122-123).

(3) Frequency of knowledge flows: Knowledge flows did not take place on a frequent basis. Experts from Diagnosub and CustCRC-A had contacts with each other on three occasions in the stage of idea description (B-R2 §117).

(4) Coordinator of knowledge flows: Knowledge exchange between Diagnosub and CustCRC-A was coordinated by experts of Diagnosub. They initiated the business relationship. As they needed knowledge from CustCRC-A, they prepared the meetings with her thoroughly and hence, managed the flow of knowledge between them and CustCRC-A. With the data from the first trials, they were also prepared to control the knowledge flow of the third meeting (B-R2 §117-119). However, CustCRC-A was not available anymore (B-R2 §47, 126-127).

(5) Coordination of knowledge flows: Coordination of knowledge flows between Diagnosub and CustCRC-A took place by personal coordination mechanisms only. This is mainly due to the fact that there were only three instances of knowledge flows. For every knowledge exchange, experts from Diagnosub flew to CustCRC-A (B-R2 §89, 117-119).

(6) Criticality of knowledge flows: In the stage of idea description, knowledge flows between Diagnosub and CustCRC-A were rather critical. Of course, Diagnosub needed the feedback and suggestions of external experts from hospitals. This feedback was valuable to promote the product idea internally at Diagnocom. Also, the suggestions of a potential customer were helpful to refine the product idea regarding its specifications. If CustCRC-A had not admitted to give it to Diagnosub, another business partner maybe would not have been that helpful. She was clearly an expert in the field of CRC. However, at this point in time CustCRC-A was exchangeable. She was actually exchanged at the end of the stage when she had made contracts with other pharmaceutical firms (B-R2 §148-151). For CustCRC-A, knowledge flows with Diagnosub were obviously exchangeable because she collaborated with other firms when the project stagnated at Diagnosub (B-R2 §47, 152-153).

(7) Problems of knowledge transfer: Within the three events of knowledge transfer, no problems were reported by the respondent. She found the knowledge transfer to be very open and holistic (B-R2 §177). CustCRC-A did not only answer to the explicit questions of Diagnosub's experts but also pointed to technologies of competitors that they had not yet taken into account (B-R2 §171). The only problem that arose was the termination of the collaboration due to the lag of the project at Diagnosub (B-R2 §173).

6.4.2.2 Basic and Extended Studies

6.4.2.2.1 Content of Knowledge Flows in Basic and Extended Technology Studies

In the beginning of the business relationship between Diagnosub and ClinCRC-A, Diagnosub transferred a lot of knowledge and know-how to ClinCRC-A. Knowledge was mainly transferred via written material that explained the study and which sample material and data should be collected. In addition to that, experts of Diagnosub went to ClinCRC-A and passed their know-how on to experts of ClinCRC-A. This was done by training the study nurse on how to proceed with the study. It included know-how on taking and processing the sample material, labeling the sample material and filling out the questionnaire on the patient (B-R3 §131). At the same time, experts of

Diagnosub and ClinCRC-A discussed details of the study proceeding. While the ancillary test for a particular marker was developed at Diagnosub, ClinCRC-A gave input on clinical issues of the test. Clinical issues encompassed questions on the grouping of patients in the study or the number of patients with particular forms of tumors in Germany, for example (B-R3 §111).

During the study, ClinCRC-A transferred sample material and the accompanying knowledge on patients to Diagnosub. Sometimes questions about the accompanying knowledge arose at Diagnosub that they posed to ClinCRC-A. ClinCRC-A also had questions or issues while collecting sample material and data. Hence, during the study steady knowledge flows went in both directions (B-R3 §131).

6.4.2.2.2 Characteristics of Knowledge Exchanged during Basic and Extended Technology Studies

(1) Articulability: Most of the knowledge was articulated in a written form. In the beginning of the study Diagnosub transferred the material on collecting sample material and data to ClinCRC-A (B-R3 §131). This was also done with the knowledge on patients and their disease that accompanied the sample material by ClinCRC-A. The study nurse at ClinCRC-A filled out the questionnaire and sent it to Diagnosub (B-R3 §45). Further, after each meeting, protocols were written (B-R3 §136-137). Part of the knowledge exchange consisted of teaching staff at ClinCRC-A on how to collect sample material and how to fill out the questionnaire (B-R3 §131).

(2) Complexity: The knowledge transferred between Diagnosub and ClinCRC-A was perceived as very complex. Even though experts at Diagnosub knew the diagnostic field and had conceptualized the ancillary test they sometimes did not understand the information of the medical staff at ClinCRC-A (B-R3 §139).

(3) System dependence: Knowledge was also system dependent because medical language was used in knowledge exchange, for instance in the questionnaires that were filled out by ClinCRC-A (B-R3 §139).

(4) Detailedness: Knowledge flows from Diagnosub to ClinCRC-A were described as more detailed than in other business relationships. This was mainly due to the fact that ClinCRC-A was interested in the knowledge that Diagnosub built on CRC. Other partners were not always interested in results from Diagnosub (B-R3 §141-143). Thus, extraordinarily detailed knowledge was passed from Diagnosub to ClinCRC-A but knowledge from ClinCRC-A was not more detailed than in average business relationships.

(5) Degree of holistic knowledge: The knowledge that was transferred from Diagnosub to ClinCRC-A was also described as more holistic. Results on markers that responded to CRC were told in half-year meetings. This was done as far as the situation of intellectual property allows. If a marker was patent relevant but not yet applied for patenting the name of the marker was not given (B-R3 §144-145). Knowledge from ClinCRC-A to Diagnosub was not more holistic than in average business relationships.

6.4.2.2.3 Characteristics of Knowledge Flows during Basic and Extended Technology Studies

(1) Cross-border knowledge flows: As ClinCRC-A was a German university hospital knowledge and know-how flows were not cross-boarder (B-R3 §53).

(2) Planned versus emerging knowledge flows: Part of the knowledge and know-how flows were planned. This was the fact for the start of the business relationship, half-year meetings and transfer of knowledge on patients and their disease (B-R3 §119-123). However, during the study questions arose both at Diagnosub and ClinCRC-A. Experts at Diagnosub asked for the meaning of medical language or missing data, for instance. Medical staff at ClinCRC-A asked for unclear steps in the collection of data (B-R3 §119).

(3) Frequency of knowledge flows: During the study, meetings took place every half a year. Between these meetings, staff of Diagnosub and ClinCRC-A regularly talked about ambiguities that arose for both (B-R3 §119).

(4) Coordinator of knowledge flows: Knowledge flows were coordinated by Diagnosub or ClinCRC-A without the participation of HQs or other units of Diagnocom. At Diagnosub a team was responsible for knowledge and know-how flows between Diagnosub and ClinCRC-A (B-R3 §127).

(5) Coordination of knowledge flows: Coordination between Diagnosub and ClinCRC-A took place by structural, technocratic and personal coordination instruments. At Diagnosub, experts in the team of the respondent were solely responsible for the coordination with university hospitals that delivered sample material and patient information (B-R3 §127). At ClinCRC-A, a study nurse was staffed to collect the material and information and transfer it to Diagnosub (B-R3 §55; structural coordination instrument). Technocratic instruments were plans and budget that built a frame for the studies (B-R3 §95). Personal coordination included telephone contact and meetings between both business partners (B-R3 §119).

(6) Criticality of knowledge flows: Knowledge flows from ClinCRC-A to Diagnosub were perceived as very critical for Diagnosub. If knowledge about patients and their tumors and treatment of CRC did not accompany the sample material, the sample material could hardly be used for the ancillary test of the marker (B-R3 §133). Knowledge flows from Diagnosub to ClinCRC-A were not evaluated as critical. They did not concern the every day work at the hospital and were case sensitive to the particular test. It might be, though, that the experts at ClinCRC-A learned a procedure of taking sample material that they could apply in another study as well (B-R3 §135).

(7) Problems of knowledge transfer: With ClinCRC-A no problems existed (B-R3 §84-85). However, with other hospitals some problems of knowledge transfer arose (B-R3 §133). Sometimes, knowledge was not transferred with the sample material because the hospital could not send them. For instance, Diagnosub asked for knowledge that was not included in the original version of the questionnaire. This might be due to changes in the expected specifications of CantisCRC. Sometimes this knowledge could not be transferred because the hospital could not ascertain it. Sometimes the reason was that the effort of ascertaining the data was quite high. Then motivational factors played a role. Some hospitals tried to ascertain the knowledge while others do not (B-R3 §149).

6.4.3 Characteristics of Knowledge Exchanged with and Knowledge Transfer to External Business Partners during the Innovation Process of CantisPF at Diagnosub

6.4.3.1 Basic and Extended Studies

6.4.3.1.1 Content of Knowledge Flows in Basic and Extended Technology Studies

Several instances of knowledge transfer took place. First, Diagnosub told SupPF-A about the specifications that they needed for the photodetector. The photodetector was supposed to have series maturity. They made it clear what the photodetector was supposed to do and what were the critical issues about it. They also told them the price ceiling for the photodetector. SupPF-A then set up a breadboard construction and started developing the photodetector (B-R4 §79). The whole collaboration lasted about a year. During this time, experts from Diagnosub and SupPF-A met every four to eight weeks (B-R4 §74-77). In these meetings, experts from Diagnosub and SupPF-A talked about additional specifications of the photodetector (B-R4 §79). SupPF-A presented them several stages of the breadboard construction. Diagnosub tested them and discussed with SupPF-A which specifications should be adjusted (B-R4 §73). Before series maturity was reached the contract was supposed to be extended. SupPF-A needed to have clarity on whether they would be allowed to produce CantisPF. At that time, Diagnosub was not able to assure this, so the contract was not extended. Hence, the final series maturity was not reached and the common project of the photodetector was not brought to the normal end (B-R4 §79).

6.4.3.1.2 Characteristics of Knowledge Exchanged during Basic and Extended Technology Studies

(1) Articulability: The knowledge that was exchanged between Diagnosub and SupPF-A during their collaboration on the photodetector obviously was articulable. Desired specifications and issues of the photodetector were provided in a written form to SupPF-A. Also, the model that was developed for the proof of principle was shown to SupPF-A. During the development of the photodetector at SupPF-A several

stages of breadboards were demonstrated to Diagnosub. Discussions took place orally or feedback was given by email (B-R4 §73, 79).

(2) Complexity: Knowledge that was exchanged between Diagnosub and SupPF-A was assessed as very complex by the respondent. Deep and specific physical knowledge on optical systems is required to understand the knowledge and calculations exchanged. The respondent emphasized that he was no physician who could understand the knowledge easily (B-R4 §86-87).

(3) System dependence: At Diagnosub and SupPF-A, engineers were in contact on the detector. Of course, experts at SupPF-A were more specialized in optical instruments. Even engineers at Diagnosub sometimes had problems understanding knowledge from SupPF-A (B-R4 §86-87).

(4) Detailedness: The knowledge that Diagnosub and SupPF-A exchanged was not less detailed than in other good business relationships. However, it was not described as particularly detailed (B-R4 §88-89).

(5) Degree of holistic knowledge: The knowledge exchange between Diagnosub and SupPF-A was not particularly holistic either (B-R4 §88-89).

6.4.3.1.3 Characteristics of Knowledge Flows during Basic and Extended Technology Studies

(1) Cross-border knowledge flows: As SupPF-A is a German firm, knowledge flows were not cross-border (B-R4 §24-25).

(2) Planned versus emerging knowledge flows: Knowledge was mainly exchanged in meetings at SupPF-A or Diagnosub. Of course, these meetings were planned. Emerging knowledge exchange was not reported but may have occurred. The respondent did not remember the form and frequency of knowledge exchange properly (B-R4 §75-77).

(3) Frequency of knowledge flows: Knowledge flows took place about every four to eight weeks when experts from Diagnosub and SupPF-A met. The whole stage of basic and extended technology studies took about one year (B-R4 §75-77).

(4) Coordinator of knowledge flows: Knowledge exchange between Diagnosub and SupPF-A was mainly coordinated by Diagnosub (B-R4 §81).

(5) Coordination of knowledge flows: Knowledge flows were mainly coordinated via documentation. Reports were written at several milestones of the development of the photodetector. After meetings of Diagnosub and SupPF-A, protocols were written (B-R4 §80-83). Thus, technocratic coordination prevailed but personal coordination instruments like meetings were also applied.

(6) Criticality of knowledge flows: Knowledge flows from SupPF-A to Diagnosub were evaluated as critical. It was important for Diagnosub to know that a low cost photodetector could be developed. Furthermore, Diagnosub needed to know how the problem of the dynamic range of measurement could be solved. However, if SupPF-A had not been able to find solutions and tell them Diagnosub, another firm would have been chosen (B-R4 §84-85).

(7) Problems of knowledge transfer: No problems of knowledge transfer between Diagnosub and SupPF-A were reported. However, in other business relationships cooperation partners were not willing to pass relevant parts of their knowledge on to Diagnosub. This was mainly due to unsettled intellectual property rights. In these cases the collaboration dealt with core competencies of the business partner. Especially small start-up firms were not willing to reveal too much knowledge or know-how. For instance, the business partner who developed a solution for mixing for CantisPF was very restrictive with know-how and knowledge. For instance, they sent an expert to Diagnosub to program the instrument so that they did not have to tell Diagnosub how to do it (B-R4 §89-91). Hence, the business relationship between Diagnosub and SupPF-A was not characterized by a particularly detailed or holistic transfer of knowledge but by the absence of problems of knowledge transfer.

6.4.3.2 Feasibility

6.4.3.2.1 Content of Knowledge Flows in Feasibility

Even before the actual business relationship began, a lot of knowledge was exchanged between Diagnosub and the potential business partners. Diagnosub presented the idea of CantisPF to them. It provided them with technical details so that the candidates could develop their concept of the final CantisPF and their estimation of costs. Further, knowledge on the timeline of the project and conditions of the selection of the business partner were given. Conditions included pre-financing of the development and the price of the product. The breadboard of CantisPF was demonstrated to the candidates (B-R5 §14-18, 22).

After having submitted the concept and the estimation of costs, two candidates were excluded from the selection process. They were given feedback on their submission. The two remaining candidates were provided with new technical specifications of the product. Some of these new technical details were integrated from the concepts of the candidates. They had a few ideas on how to design a part process of the workflow of the platform better. Hence, knowledge already flew from potential business partners to Diagnosub as well (B-R5 §30-36).

The two remaining candidates updated their concepts according to the new knowledge. Now, Diagnosub enters negotiation with both candidates to talk about intellectual property rights, for instance. Thus, in this stage of the selection process, more knowledge on business details flows between the potential business partners (B-R5 §36).

6.4.3.2.2 Characteristics of Knowledge Exchanged during Feasibility

As the business relationship between Diagnosub and a particular business partner is not yet established, knowledge flows between Diagnosub and its potential business partners can only be discussed regarding the selection process of the potential business partners.

(1) Articulability: During the selection process, knowledge was articulated both orally and written with PowerPoint presentations about Diagnocom and CantisPF (B-R5 §60). Technical issues were partly discussed orally and with the written concepts of final CantisPF by the candidates (B-R5 §22, 28-30).

(2) Complexity: Complexity of knowledge probably was medium. Of course, physical and engineerial knowledge was exchanged between Diagnosub and the candidates. This was especially done in the presentation of technical specifications of CantisPF and the concepts of the candidates. However, the knowledge that was exchanged was not too difficult because most technical details have already been discussed and decided at Diagnosub when developing the breadboard. Hence, few details had to be discussed with the candidates in depth because they were new. This was only the case when candidates made suggestions for improvement (B-R5 §14, 22, 32-34).

(3) System dependence: Knowledge that was exchanged between Diagnosub and the candidates was rather system dependent. Engineers discussed technical issues that would not be understood easily by experts from other fields (B-R5 §14, 22).

(4) Detailedness: Detailedness of knowledge from Diagnosub increased throughout the selection process. When experts from Diagnosub visited the four candidates at their locations, they told them about the product idea and about conditions of entering the selection process (e.g. pre-financing of development; B-R5 §14). When all candidates agreed to enter the competition for the project, they were provided with the necessary technical details to develop a concept and an estimation of costs (B-R5 §22). In an update of the concepts of the two remaining candidates, more technical details were added (B-R5 §30-34). Finally, Diagnosub now starts to negotiate with them about business details like intellectual property rights (B-R5 §36).

(5) Degree of holistic knowledge: Knowledge was not very holistic although it got more holistic throughout the selection process as well. First, only the idea was presented by Diagnosub, then technical details were provided and finally business issues concerning the contract are discussed (B-R5 §14, 22, 36).

6.4.3.2.3 Characteristics of Knowledge Flows during Feasibility

(2) Planned versus emerging knowledge flows: Knowledge flows between Diagnosub and the potential business partner throughout the selection process were usually planned. Meetings were made and deadlines for next steps were appointed (B-R5 §14, 22, 36).

(4) Coordinator of knowledge flows: Knowledge flows from Diagnosub to the potential business partners were coordinated jointly by the R&D project manager of CantisPF and the Program Manager at the Headquarters in Switzerland. The final decision requires the Program Management at HQs' approval (B-R5 §56).

(5) Coordination of knowledge flows: Coordination took place both between R&D project management and program management and between Diagnosub and potential business partners. Knowledge exchange between project and program management were coordinated in frequent meetings and telephone calls. Between Diagnosub and potential business partners, meetings were the main coordination instrument. Thus, personal coordination mechanisms prevailed.

6.4.3.3 Summary of the Characteristics of Knowledge and Knowledge Transfer of Cantis at Diagnosub

At the stage of idea description, Diagnosub collaborated with CustCRC-A. CustCRC-A was a university doctor in the UK who advised Diagnosub on the product idea of CantisCRC. The business relationship was described as very good and trustful but still not as personal as long grown business relationships. Knowledge from CustCRC-A was easily articulable. She told Diagnosub whether she would buy the product and made suggestions on attributes of CantisCRC. As exchanged knowledge was quite basic it was not perceived as very complex. However, it was highly system dependent. People of other professions would have great difficulties in understanding the exchanged knowledge. Knowledge from CustCRC-A was not assessed as more detailed than in other business relationships. However, it was described as more holistic than that from other business partners. When giving feedback on CantisCRC, CustCRC-A took the position of both a customer and Diagnosub. She told them more than Diagnosub had explicitly asked for. Knowledge flows were cross-border. Diagnosub had explicitly looked for a business partner in the UK because this is an important and special market. Knowledge flows between CustCRC-A and Diagnosub were always planned. They took place only three times. For kick off and discussions with CustCRC-A, experts from Diagnosub flew to her. They were also the ones who coordinated the knowledge exchange. As only meetings were held, coordination took place by personal coordination mechanisms only. Knowledge flows between Diagnosub and CustCRC-A were critical for CantisCRC. CustCRC-A gave very valuable input on the idea of CantisCRC. No problems were reported by the respondent.

At the stage of basic and extended technology studies of CantisCRC, Diagnosub collaborated with ClinCRC-A, a German university hospital that collected sample material and patient information for Diagnosub. Diagnosub needed sample material and information to test marker performance on CRC. The business relationship was described as a good professional relationship. Most of the knowledge was articulated, for instance the information on patients and their type of CRC. Part of the knowledge was taught by Diagnosub. They showed ClinCRC-A how to collect sample material and how to fill out the questionnaire. The knowledge transferred between Diagnosub and ClinCRC-A was perceived as very complex. Even though experts at Diagnosub knew the diagnostic field and have conceptualized the ancillary test they sometimes did not understand the information of the medical staff at ClinCRC-A. Knowledge was also system dependent because medical language was used in knowledge exchange. Knowledge flows from Diagnosub to ClinCRC-A was described as more detailed than in other business relationships because ClinCRC-A was interested in the knowledge that Diagnosub built on CRC. However, knowledge from ClinCRC-A was not perceived as more detailed than in other business relationships. It was not assessed as more holistic either. While kick off meeting, the transfer of final results and half-year meetings were planned, many knowledge flows on operational issues and ambiguities were discussed in emergent contacts. Knowledge flows were coordinated by Diagnosub or ClinCRC-A. They were coordinated applying structural, technocratic, and personal coordination instruments. Knowledge exchange was perceived as very critical for Diagnosub. If knowledge about patients and their tumors and treatment of CRC did not accompany the sample material, the sample material could hardly be used for the ancillary test of the marker. With ClinCRC-A no problems were reported.

In the stage of basic and extended technology studies, Diagnosub collaborated with SupPF-A. SupPF-A developed the detector for the breadboard of CantisPF. The business relationship was described as very pragmatic and uncomplicated as long as engineers acted on both sides. Knowledge between Diagnosub and SupPF-A was articulated. Desired specifications and issues of the photodetector were given in a written form to SupPF-A. In addition, Diagnosub showed SupPF-A the model that was developed for the proof of principle. During the development of the photodetector at SupPF-A several versions were demonstrated to Diagnosub. Knowledge that was exchanged between Diagnosub and SupPF-A was assessed as very complex because very specific physical knowledge on optical systems is required to understand it. It was also very system dependent. Even engineers at Diagnosub sometimes had problems understanding knowledge from SupPF-A. Knowledge from SupPF-A was not described as particularly detailed. It was not particularly holistic either. As SupPF-A is a German firm; knowledge flows were not cross-border. As knowledge was mainly exchanged in meetings every four to eight weeks, knowledge flows were planned. They were mainly coordinated by Diagnosub using mainly technocratic but also personal coordination instruments. Knowledge flows from SupPF-A to Diagnosub were perceived as critical. They needed to know that a technical solution for the detector could be found. No problems of knowledge transfer between Diagnosub and SupPF-A were reported.

Dimension	Stage / Business Partner	Degree
	Characteristics of knowledge	
Articulatedness	CustCRC-A / Idea description	Easy
	ClinCRC-A / Basic and extended technology studies	Easy
	SupPF-A / Basic and extended technology studies	Easy

Dimension	Stage / Business Partner	Degree
	Characteristics of knowledge	
Teachability	CustCRC-A / Idea description	-
	ClinCRC-A / Basic and extended technology studies	ClinCRC-A was taught how to collect sample material and how to fill out the questionnaire
	SupPF-A / Basic and extended technology studies	SupPF-A showed several stages of breadboards to Diagnosub
Complexity	CustCRC-A / Idea description	Not complex
	ClinCRC-A / Basic and extended technology studies	Very complex
	SupPF-A / Basic and extended technology studies	Very complex
System dependence	CustCRC-A / Idea description	Very system dependent
	ClinCRC-A / Basic and extended technology studies	System dependent
	SupPF-A / Basic and extended technology studies	Very system dependent
Detailedness	CustCRC-A / Idea description	Not particularly detailed
	ClinCRC-A / Basic and extended technology studies	Not particularly detailed from ClinCRC-A
	SupPF-A / Basic and extended technology studies	Not particularly detailed
Holisticity	CustCRC-A / Idea description	Very holistic
	ClinCRC-A / Basic and extended technology studies	Not particularly holistic from ClinCRC-A
	SupPF-A / Basic and extended technology studies	Not particularly holistic from ClinCRC-A

Characteristics of knowledge flows		
Cross-border flows	CustCRC-A / Idea description	Yes
	ClinCRC-A / Basic and extended technology studies	No
	SupPF-A / Basic and extended technology studies	No
Planned versus emergent knowledge flows	CustCRC-A / Idea description	Planned
	ClinCRC-A / Basic and extended technology studies	Both
	SupPF-A / Basic and extended technology studies	Planned
Frequency	CustCRC-A / Idea description	Not frequent, about three times
	ClinCRC-A / Basic and extended technology studies	Planned meetings every six months, emerging telephone calls more frequent
	SupPF-A / Basic and extended technology studies	Every four to eight weeks
Dimension	**Stage / Business Partner**	**Degree**
Characteristics of knowledge flows		
Coordinator	CustCRC-A / Idea description	Diagnosub
	ClinCRC-A / Basic and extended technology studies	Diagnosub and ClinCRC-A
	SupPF-A / Basic and extended technology studies	Diagnosub
Coordination	CustCRC-A / Idea description	Personal mechanisms
	ClinCRC-A / Basic and extended technology studies	Structural, technocratic and personal instruments
	SupPF-A / Basic and extended technology studies	Technocratic mechanisms prevails but also personal instruments
Criticality	CustCRC-A / Idea description	Very critical
	ClinCRC-A / Basic and extended technology studies	Very critical
	SupPF-A / Basic and extended technology studies	Critical
Problems	CustCRC-A / Idea description	Not during collaboration at this stage
	ClinCRC-A / Basic and extended technology studies	No
	SupPF-A / Basic and extended technology studies	No

Table 6-3: Characteristics of knowledge and knowledge transfer in the case of CantisCRC and CantisPF

At the moment of writing the thesis, the product innovation process of CantisPF was at the stage of feasibility. Diagnosub was selecting a business partner for developing the prototype of CantisPF which could then be produced in large scale. Thus, knowledge flows between Diagnosub and its potential business partners were only analyzed regarding the selection process of the potential business partners. During the selection process, knowledge was mainly sent by Diagnosub and was articulated both orally and written. Potential business partners offered their concept of CantisPF and their estimation of costs in a written form. Because of the early stage of the business relationship, knowledge that was provided was articulated very clearly from both sides. Complexity of knowledge was medium. Physical and engineerial knowledge was exchanged between Diagnosub and the candidates. Knowledge was not too difficult because most technical details have already been discussed and decided at Diagnosub when developing the breadboard. However, it was system dependent. Engineers discussed technical issues that would not be easily understood by experts from other fields. So far, knowledge was not very detailed because contracts and CDAs were not made yet. It was not very holistic either. Because of the early stage, knowledge flows were usually planned. They were coordinated jointly by the R&D project manager of CantisPF at Diagnosub and the Program Manager at the Headquarters in Switzerland. Coordination took place mainly applying personal coordination mechanisms. Final decision on the selection of the business partner would be made by program management. The results of the characteristics of knowledge and knowledge transfer in the case of CantisCRC and CantisPF are summarized in table 6-3. The stage of feasibility in the product innovation process of CantisPF is not integrated in the table because the final business partner was not selected yet. Thus, the characteristics of knowledge and knowledge transfer during the collaboration can not be described.

6.4.4 Comparison and Conclusion of the Characteristics of Knowledge and Knowledge Transfer during the Product Innovation Process of Cogis and Cantis

Looking at knowledge transfer in business relationships to external business partners during the innovation processes of Cogis and Cantis, some points are obvious.

(1) In all business relationships, some similarities are observed. (1a) First, in all business relationships **few incidents of knowledge transfer were planned**. At these incidents, knowledge on the object of the collaborations was exchanged. The kick off meeting and the final transfer of results were always planned. Sometimes, meetings to discuss the project were set up every few month. This was the case with ClinCRC-A. Most of the incidents of knowledge transfer emerged spontaneously, though. In emerging knowledge flows, business partners discussed operational issues like the delivery of material or problems in studies that were conducted. Preliminary results of studies are also transferred and discussed. Only in the business relationships to CustCRC-A and SuppF-A all knowledge flows were planned. In both business relationships knowledge flows were much rarer than in the others. Diagnosub met only three times with CustCRC-A and about every four to eight weeks with SupPF-A.

(1b) Second, **knowledge flows were always coordinated by the innovative subsidiary and its business partner**. Only in the stage of feasibility in the innovation process of CantisPF, HQs of Diagnosub are involved. However, this is probably due to the fact that knowledge flows in the selection process of a business partner are analyzed here. The business partner in this stage is very important because it will develop the final prototype of CantisPF and manufacture CantisPF in serial production. Coordination mechanisms were mainly technocratic for the planned knowledge exchanges and personal when operational issues were discussed.

(1c) Third, exchanged **knowledge was always described as very system dependent**. This was true both for medical knowledge and for engineerial knowledge. Sometimes even the experts at the innovative subsidiaries had problems understanding the knowledge that they received from their business partners.

(1d) Fourth, **in none of the business relationships problems of knowledge transfer were reported**. Problems in some business relationships arose. For instance, in the studies ClinCog-A conducted for Pharmasub some mistakes were made. This is usual for in vivo studies. However, ClinCog-A was very open and transparent about mistakes and problems during the studies. With ClinCog-B problems of recruitment of test persons were described. In the case of Pharmasub and ClinCog-B, they were of different opinion about the interpretation of a symptom that one test person reported. However, this is not a problem of knowledge transfer either. In other business relationships, some problems of knowledge transfer were described. For instance, in the stage of basic and extended technology studies of tests sample material and accompanying information is delivered by university hospitals. Sometimes, questionnaires are filled out fragmentarily. However, this was not the case in the business relationships that were described here. This is probably due to the fact that business relationships with problems in knowledge transfer were not regarded as the most influential business relationships.[157]

(2) In some business relationships, knowledge was completely **articulated**. In other business relationships, most of the knowledge was articulated while some of it was taught by the innovative subsidiaries. However, this did not depend on the embeddedness of the business relationship but on the type of business partner. In several stages of the innovation processes of Cogis and CantisCRC, Pharmasub, Pharmanorth, or Diagnosub collaborated with clinical service contractors or university hospitals that conducted studies for them. In the beginning of the business relationships the innovative subsidiaries taught their business partners how to take sample material, give the medicine or fill out questionnaires. The knowledge that the innovative subsidiaries received from their business partners was always articulated, irrespective of the type of business partner.

(3) The **criticality of knowledge** flows was assessed differently in business relationships. Knowledge flows from external business partners were evaluated as very critical in the cases of ResCog-A and CustCRC-A. Those are the business relationships that were evaluated as very good and important. Both collaborations took place in

---

[157] Another explanation is that respondents did not remember problems of knowledge transfer. However, as they remembered characteristics of business relationship and knowledge transfer this is doubted.

early stages of the product innovation processes of Cogis. At the stage of basic and extended technology studies, knowledge from ClinCRC-A was evaluated as very critical as well. Comparing ClinCog-B and ClinCog-C, knowledge transfer from ClinCog-B was evaluated as more critical than that from ClinCog-C. Respondent explained that stages II and III are not as uncertain as stage I of clinical trials. Hence, knowledge flows are more critical in the earlier stage. The business relationship to ClinCog-C was evaluated as much better than that to ClinCog-B, however. Hence, criticality probably depends on the stage of the product innovation process rather than on the embeddedness of business relationships.

The same applies to **complexity** of the transferred knowledge. It was described as very complex in almost all business relationships. This was because the objects of collaborations were very difficult or comprehensive. The only exception is the business relationship between Diagnosub and CustCRC-A. Knowledge from her was not described as complex. She told experts from Diagnosub about her opinion on the product idea and basic specifications that CantisCRC should have. Hence, in very early stages of product innovation processes knowledge is probably not as complex as in later stages.

(4) It was also evaluated differently by respondents how **holistic** the knowledge was that they received. Knowledge was assessed as much more holistic in the business relationship between Pharmasub and ResCog-A and between Diagnosub and CustCRC-A than in average business relationships. CustCRC-A looked at the issue from both the perspective of a customer and of Diagnosub. Thus, she gave more input on the product idea and potential technologies of competitors than Diagnosub had asked for. ResCog-A gave more holistic knowledge than other business partners because he made an extensive documentation of the studies. Pharmasub hardly asked for any supplementations. In contrast, it was not perceived as more holistic than usual in the business relationships to ClinCog-A, ClinCog-B and ClinCog-C and to ClinCRC-A and SupPF-A.

(5) Concerning the **detailedness** of exchanged knowledge, no correlations with the embeddedness of business relationships could be observed. While in the most important and most embedded business relationship in the product innovation process

of CantisCRC (to CustCRC-A), the subsidiary received extraordinarily detailed knowledge, this was not reported for the business relationship to ResCog-A. In other embedded relationships like the one between Pharmasub and ClinCog-A or ClinCog-C, the knowledge was not more detailed than in average business relationships either.

6.5 Transfer of Knowledge between Sub-units of the MNC

In this section, intra-organizational business relationships and knowledge flows are examined. It is found that knowledge flows are embedded in a very sophisticated organizational structure in both firms. The case of Pharmacom is described in sub-section 6.5.1 and the case of Diagnocom is depicted in sub-section 6.5.2. In sub-section 6.5.3, both cases are compared.

6.5.1 Organizational Structures and Processes to Facilitate the Intra-organizational Transfer of Knowledge in the Product Innovation Process of Cogis

The product innovation process of Cogis was mainly done at Pharmasub. Only the stage of pre-clinic II (in vivo studies) was coordinated at Pharmanorth. From Pharmasub, the product innovation is transferred to many countries in which products are sold by foreign subsidiaries of Pharmacom. In order to facilitate product innovation transfer, Pharmacom introduced organizational structures and processes which integrate the foreign subsidiaries from all countries into the product innovation process. The reasons for implementing the organizational structure are introduced in the first sub-section (6.5.5.1). Then, the organizational structures and processes are explained (6.5.5.2).

6.5.1.1 Reasons for Integrating Foreign Subsidiaries in the Product Innovation Process

Foreign subsidiaries are integrated into the product innovation process for several reasons: the experts at the subsidiaries are supposed to give their opinion on the clinical development plan after the first stage of clinical trials. They are asked to provide their feedback on the potential market success of the product in development, whether their market would be interested in the indication of the drug, and how many patients they expect for the medicine. Furthermore, they give advice on potential improvements of the product concept. The description of specifications of the product is called target product profile. With the target product profile they specify how the product should be designed in order to be successful in their market (A-R4 §29-31). Thus, experts of both medical affairs and marketing are involved at the foreign subsidiaries (A-R4 §13).

Apart from market assessments and specifications of the product, foreign subsidiaries are also involved for process reasons. Local professionals know which documents local approval authorities and health systems require in the approval and reimbursement process. They also know which studies and documents they need to convince customers to buy the medicine. Thus, before clinical trials begin, they can ask for additional studies or particular examinations that should be conducted during the clinical trials, for instance in order to obtain quality of life data. These studies may be demanded by health systems for cost benefit calculations (A-R4 §29-31). Knowing about the need for additional data, examinations in stage III of the clinical studies can be added, for instance. Thus, the market potential of the medicine in foreign markets can be enhanced (A-R4 §33).

With the assessment of market potential, improvement of product specifications and planning of documentation in early stages of the product innovation process, both the product innovation process and the market launch are organized more efficiently (A-R4 §11, 15). Indeed, no problems of knowledge transfer between the foreign subsidiaries and HQs were reported. Rather, subsidiaries like to give more input in the product innovation process now than they did some years ago (A-R4 §47). HQs discuss suggestions of the foreign subsidiaries carefully (A-R4 §17).

6.5.1.2 Organizational Structures and Processes for Incorporating Foreign Subsidiaries in the Product Innovation Process

At Pharmacom, product development and inlicensing of products are organized in project teams. They work quite autonomously and only approach the development board at predefined decision points when they apply for a budget for further work on the project. The core project team consists of the project leader and different functions. The functions depend on the stage that the project is at; they may for instance be at medical affairs, pharmacology, production, regulatory issues or marketing. Thus, the core project team manages the whole project from the idea to the approval of the product and the market launch. In order to support the medical affairs function, a clinical subteam is installed. In this clinical subteam, one or two medical directors or medical advisors represent all foreign subsidiaries. They are involved when the input of the foreign subsidiaries becomes important (A-R4 §37). The organization of the core project team and the clinical subteam is depicted in figure 6-23.

Organizational Structure	Corporate						Subsidiaries in Country Markets
	Core Project Team						
	Medical Affairs	Pharmacology	Production	Marketing	Regulatory	Etc.	
	Clinical Subteam	Two medical directors					

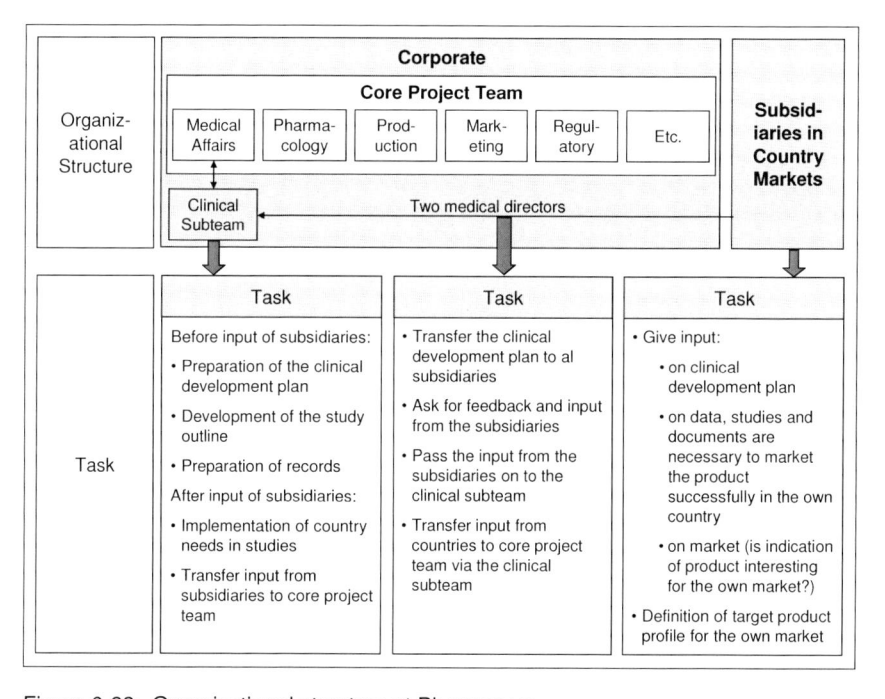

	Task	Task	Task
Task	Before input of subsidiaries: • Preparation of the clinical development plan • Development of the study outline • Preparation of records After input of subsidiaries: • Implementation of country needs in studies • Transfer input from subsidiaries to core project team	• Transfer the clinical development plan to al subsidiaries • Ask for feedback and input from the subsidiaries • Pass the input from the subsidiaries on to the clinical subteam • Transfer input from countries to core project team via the clinical subteam	• Give input: • on clinical development plan • on data, studies and documents are necessary to market the product successfully in the own country • on market (is indication of product interesting for the own market?) • Definition of target product profile for the own market

Figure 6-23: Organizational structure at Pharmacom

After stage I of clinical development, the clinical subteam prepares the clinical development plan. It includes the planning of clinical trials and outlines of clinical studies, among others. The clinical development plan also serves to plan the documentation for approval authorities and reimbursement. At this point, the input of foreign subsidiaries is needed. The representative medical directors are provided with the clinical development plan, background material and a particular deadline for the input from the foreign subsidiaries by the head of the clinical subteam and the Senior Director LOC Medical Relation. They approach their colleagues at all foreign subsidiaries, send them the clinical development plan and ask for their feedback (A-R4 §17).[158] At the foreign subsidiaries, medical directors and marketing experts discuss the clinical development plan and, if necessary, ask for adjustments of specifications of the product to fit their local market. Further, they can demand particular studies and documents that help them to market the product successfully in their region. They may request additional studies to demonstrate the improvement of quality of life, for instance. These documents may help local subsidiaries to get reimbursement from the national health system and to convince local opinion leaders (A-R4 §29-31). Pharmasub has about 40 subsidiaries in the world of which 34 have medical directors. Of course, not all of them respond to the request of the clinical subteam. Some products are not interesting for some countries because the indication does not exist there or is treated in another way (A-R4 §29, 43).

Medical directors collect the information from the countries and pass it on to the clinical subteam. At the clinical subteam meeting, it decides which suggestions are considered and how they affect the innovation process in the following. Together with the core project team, it implements the requests of the countries and passes the knowledge on to the core project team (A-R4 §17). After the clinical subteam meeting, the medical directors transfer the report of the meeting to the medical directors at the foreign subsidiaries (A-R4 §45). The tasks of the clinical subteam, the medical directors at the clinical subteam and the foreign subsidiaries are depicted in figure 6-23. The process of collecting information from the foreign subsidiaries is presented in figure 6-24.

---

[158] It is not regulated which representative medical director approaches which of the foreign subsidiaries (A-R4 §43).

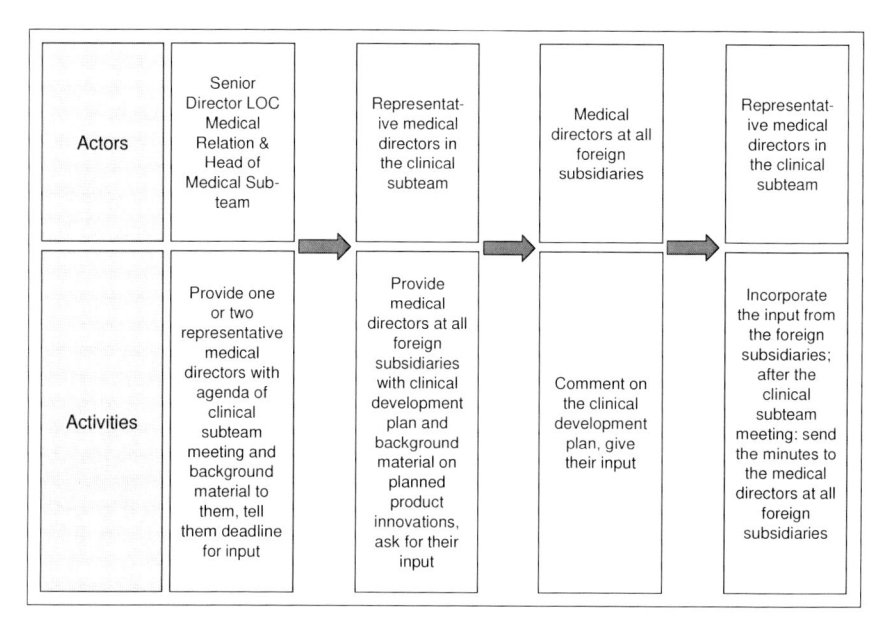

Actors	Senior Director LOC Medical Relation & Head of Medical Sub-team	Representative medical directors in the clinical subteam	Medical directors at all foreign subsidiaries	Representative medical directors in the clinical subteam
Activities	Provide one or two representative medical directors with agenda of clinical subteam meeting and background material to them, tell them deadline for input	Provide medical directors at all foreign subsidiaries with clinical development plan and background material on planned product innovations, ask for their input	Comment on the clinical development plan, give their input	Incorporate the input from the foreign subsidiaries; after the clinical subteam meeting: send the minutes to the medical directors at all foreign subsidiaries

Figure 6-24: Process of collecting information from the subsidiaries

Representative medical directors that are part of the medical subteam are selected by the head of the clinical subteam and the Senior Director LOC Medical Relation. The head of the clinical subteam defines the profile that the medical director or medical advisors should have in order to be helpful for the clinical subteam. Of course, the therapeutic area of the product is an important selection criterion. Not every foreign subsidiary has experts in each therapeutic area. They should also be experienced managers and be competent in collecting information from the foreign subsidiaries and prepare the information for the clinical subteam meeting. The Senior Director LOC Medical Relation sends the preferred profile to all medical directors and medical advisors at the foreign subsidiaries. The medical directors and advisors who are interested in the task get back to him. The senior director and the head of the clinical subteam decide for one or two representative medical directors together (A-R4 §39). The process is depicted in figure 6-25.

Actors	Head of Medical Sub-team	Senior Director LOC Medical Relation	Medical Directors	Senior Director LOC Medical Relation & Head of Medical Sub-team
Activities	Definition of preferred profile of country medical directors as representatives of subsidiaries	Sends preferred profile to all medical directors and medical advisors with a scientific background	Show their interest to Senior Director LOC Medical Relation and Head of Medical Sub-team	Decide for one or two medical directors

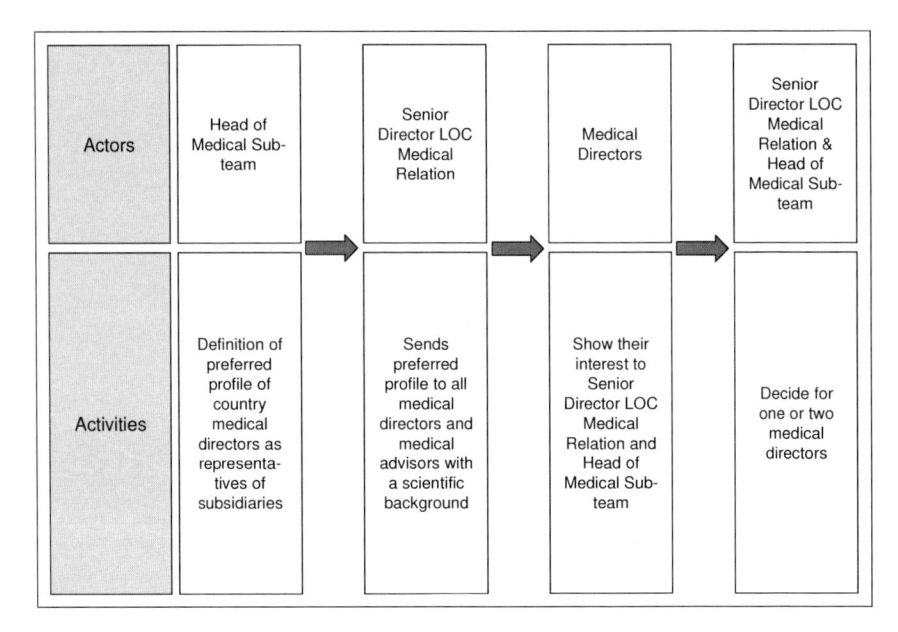

Figure 6-25: Process of selecting medical directors for the clinical subteam

6.5.2 Organizational Structures and Processes to Facilitate the Intra-organizational Transfer of Knowledge in the Product Innovation Process of Cantis

The whole product innovation process of Cantis is carried out at Diagnosub. Once the product innovation process is finished, the product is launched in many markets in the whole world. Marketing is coordinated by the global marketing organization at HQs. Hence, the product innovation must be transferred from the German subsidiary to HQs in Switzerland as a first step. Second, it has to be passed on from the Swiss HQs to many foreign subsidiaries because products are sold worldwide (B-R2 §139-141).

When analyzing product innovation transfer at Diagnocom it became clear that units are not the critical issue. It is not the business relationships between Diagnosub and HQs or between HQs and other foreign subsidiaries. Instead, communication between different functional areas was crucial. Particularly, the coordination between

R&D (at Pharmasub) and global marketing (at HQs) was problematic in the past and was therefore organized in elaborate organizational structures and processes (B-R6 §9). The reasons for establishing the organizational structures and processes are explained in sub-section 6.5.2.1.

In sub-section 6.5.2.2, it is depicted how the integration of functions in the product innovation process is organized. It is described that global and local marketing experts are already involved in early stages of the product innovation process. Their integration increases the more the product innovation process progresses (B-R6 §15). Hence, product innovation process and transfer do not happen one after the other but they are intertwined.

6.5.2.1 Reasons of Establishing Organizational Structures and Processes in the Product Innovation Process

Until about three years before the interviews, i.e. until about 2006, Diagnosub was very R&D driven. Their perspective on development of diagnostic products was a primarily scientific one. Business perspective was hardly taken into account during the product innovation process. Products were often developed because scientists were interested in the project and were successful in development. If the products could actually be sold was only considered after completion of product development. Until then, only two organizational levels were established: project and program management (B-R6 §77-81). At project level, the actual work of research and development was done. Program management was supposed to control project work and select the most promising projects for continuation (B-R6 §63). However, project management had more power than program management. Above that, the program level did not include experts from Marketing. Instead, R&D experts decided on the program level as well. Hence, it was only R&D experts at both levels who decided about the budget of a project (B-R6 §81-85).

The strong focus on R&D and little attention to the market perspective caused problems for Diagnocom. Some products were not as successful as expected. As Marketing entered the product innovation process only at the stage of the market launch, it could not influence which products it got and had to sell. Thus, serious conflicts arose between R&D and marketing (B-R6 §90-93). With products that were interesting for customers, other problems came up. With expensive tests, for instance, customers demanded studies that proved the effectiveness of the test. Only when they got reliable data on the effectiveness the test was reimbursed by the national health insurance. This system is particularly strict in the USA. Of course, studies on the test effectiveness had to be conducted before the market launch. However, they were not planned as part of the activities before the market launch (B-R6 §33-39). When a new CEO was appointed he identified the problems and started to reorganize the structure of Diagnocom. He also initiated the integration of the portfolio level and Product Portfolio Board in early stages of the product innovation process (B-R6 §93).

Another reason for integrating both functions of R&D and marketing is that corporate knowledge exchange is perceived much more difficult than knowledge flows to external business partners. This is due to the fact that knowledge on product innovations is always highly system dependent (see sub-section 6.4.4). System dependence of knowledge makes it difficult for experts from other functional areas to understand product innovations and product innovation processes (B-R2 §205). Additionally, marketing experts have a rather short-term perspective and tend to oppose new product ideas and innovations (B-R2 §143, 205). This fact impedes communication between R&D and marketing functions. As a lack of communication between both functions may endanger the success of a product innovation, comprehensive organizational structures and processes were built to assure coordination and communication between R&D and marketing. Bringing experts from both functional areas together in teams and frequent meetings enhances the understanding at both R&D and marketing experts (B-R2 §129, 137, B-R6 §33-39, 42-43, 77-86).

6.5.2.2 Organizational Structures and Processes for Incorporating Global Marketing and Foreign Subsidiaries in the Product Innovation Process

The product innovation process at Diagnocom is managed and controlled by several organizational levels. The actual work of research and development is done in teams.

Usually, several teams work at the stages of research and development of a particular product innovation process. These teams have project managers. They report to program management. Program managers control several interrelated projects. For instance, they are responsible for system solutions like Cantis (CantisPF and its applications) or reagent families (B-R6 §63). Program Management for one system solution consists of experts from both R&D and marketing (B-R6 §15). Program management is one of several departments of a Business Segment. This department encompasses all program managers. Business Segments are managed and controlled by the Core Management Team. Core Management Team is responsible for company-wide functions (B-R6 §51).

Program management is organized in two boards: Technology and Marker Board and Product Portfolio Board. In these boards, Program Managers of the whole Business Segment discuss product innovation projects.[159] Both boards decide about the budget for R&D and hence, they decide which projects should be continued (B-R4 §31, B-R6 §75). Projects compete in the boards. While the Technology and Marker Board accompanies the research stages of the product innovations project, the Product Portfolio Board acts at the development stages of the process. During research, mainly technological issues are discussed. However, Marketing experts are already involved in the Board. During development, more and more marketing and business development topics are discussed. Boards meet about every six to eight weeks. Thus, there is frequent exchange between R&D and marketing in these boards (B-R6 §75). The Program Managers have to report to the Product Portfolio Board which plan the marketing activities for a product (B-R6 §43-59). The structure of decision making on product innovation processes at Diagnocom is depicted in figure 6-26.

In the Product Portfolio Board, experts from the global marketing organization are included. Thus, during the R&D process, Marketing and Product Management are involved in the process. Global Marketing experts are responsible to inform regional and local marketing subsidiaries about planned products and get their feedback. In this way, foreign subsidiaries are integrated in the development process (B-R6 §11).

---

[159] Apart from these two basic boards, smaller teams are built in which experts from different functions meet to discuss a product idea. For instance, DAST (Disease Area Strategic Team) was set up. This team already meets at the stage of idea description (B-R2 §21, 131-133).

Frequent meetings are held by global and local marketing experts. In these meetings, global marketing experts introduce product plans to local marketing. Local marketing experts give their feedback on the product (B-R2 §139). For instance, they evaluate whether their customers would be interested in the product. Therefore, they either validate the market potential by asking customers themselves or they make the contact between HQs' global marketing experts and their customers (B-R6 §11).

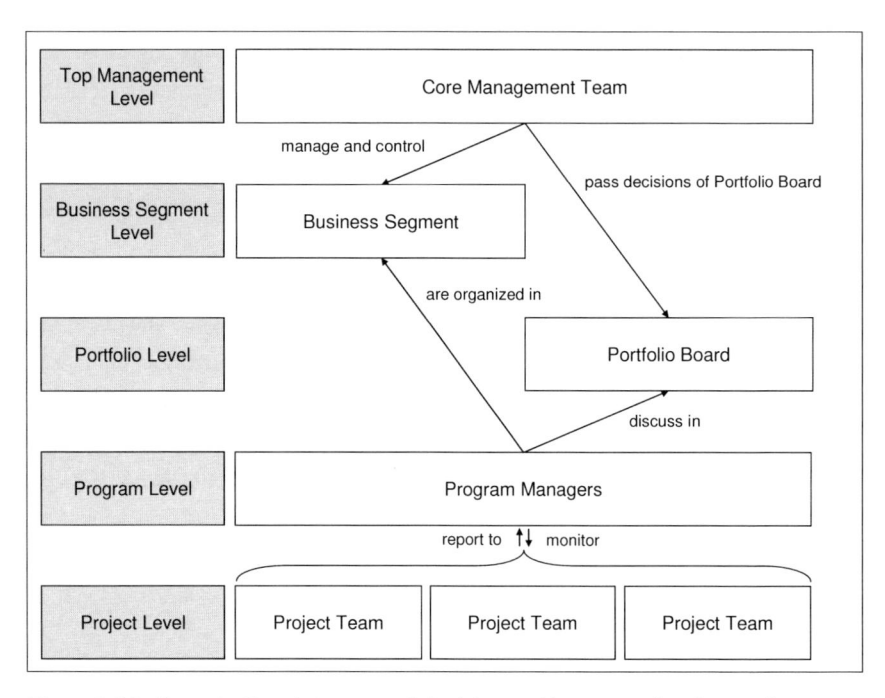

Figure 6-26: Organizational structure of decision making on product innovation at Diagnocom

At the beginning of development, at the stage of analysis, Global Marketing at HQs has already informed the foreign subsidiaries about the product that is being developed. As they will sell the product in their countries their feedback on the product is required. This feedback is given in the stage of feasibility. Further, either the subsidiaries suggest customers in their countries who test and evaluate the upcoming product or they validate the intended specifications of the product in their market (B-R6 §11). In the late stage of implementation, foreign subsidiaries are trained on the new product. Knowledge on the product and data are summarized in a launch binder. For instance, knowledge on the target group of the product, on pricing, profitability calculations and the Multi Customer Evaluation (MCE) are included (B-R6 §15).

Through the integration of R&D and Marketing functions in Program Management and the Technology and Marker Board and Product Portfolio Board, conflicts between the functions and sub-units are reduced. The situation that marketing professionals complain about product innovations made by R&D because they do not fit the market should not occur due to the early integration of Marketing in the product innovation process (B-R6 §43). However, problems can arise in the Technology and Marker Board and the Product Portfolio Board. First, sometimes experts from Marketing and Business Development take part who are not well-prepared or do not have the authority to make decisions. If they agree with the research or development plans at a particular stage, and if this affirmation is neglected by the authority, time and money is wasted as a result (B-R6 §77). Second, experts from R&D and from Marketing have a completely different view on the firm and the market. While R&D experts think a few years ahead, marketing experts are very focused on the present. They rather worry about sales in the present month or year. However, there are much less problems than some years ago.

6.5.3 Comparison and Conclusion of the Organizational Structures and Processes to Facilitate Intra-organizational Transfer of Product Innovations at Pharmacom and Diagnocom

The organizational structures and processes to facilitate the transfer of product innovations from the innovative subsidiaries to other units of the MNC were presented in the past sub-sections. Some common structures were identified in both firms and some differences in structures. They are discussed here.

(1) Similarities: In both innovative subsidiaries, the development of product innovations is organized in project teams. They do the actual work in the product innovation process. Usually, several project teams work on different R&D activities during the product innovation process. Each team has a project manager (A-R4 §37, B-R6 §15, 63).

In both firms, the budget for R&D activities is allocated by another level than the project team level. After each stage of the product innovation process, decision points are established. At these decision points, the results of the former stage are reviewed. A superior level decides whether the product innovation project is continued and assigns a budget to the project team (A-R1 §16, A-R4 §17, 37, B-R6 §63, 73-75).

(2) Differences: In product innovation transfers at both Pharmacom and Diagnocom, foreign subsidiaries that sell the product innovations in their local markets are occupied in the product innovation process. However, in the case of Pharmacom, they are involved at earlier stages of the product innovation process. In this case, their input on the product and product innovation process is required in stage I of the clinical trials in the beginning of development (A-R4 §51). It is done in order to be able to conduct additional studies in clinical trials that the foreign subsidiaries asked for (A-R4 §13, 29). In the case of Diagnocom, foreign marketing units are involved mainly in the late stages of development, about six to 18 months before the product innovation is launched (B-R6 §9, 25). Also, the process of involving foreign subsidiaries is organized in a more sophisticated way in the case of Pharmacom. While at Diagnocom meetings between global and local marketing experts are held (B-R2 §139), at Pharmacom two medical directors for each product innovation project are selected (A-R4 §39). They pass information about the planned product innovation on to foreign subsidiaries and collect their input (A-R4 §39-45).

At Pharmacom, positions in the teams that discuss product innovation projects are selected in a more thorough manner. The two medical directors that are involved in the clinical subteam are selected with a sophisticated process (A-R4 §39). The marketing experts in the Technology and Marker Board or Product Portfolio Board on the other hand are determined by their position. They are not selected just for the Boards (A-R4 §144-145, B-R6 §46-47).

7 Discussion

The results of the thesis are discussed in the present chapter. First, the major contributions are summarized in section 7.1 according to the research questions that were posed in section 1.2. Some of the results extend the concept of the Embedded MNC on which this contribution is based. They are reflected in detail in section 7.2. In section 7.3, implications for management praxis are drawn. Finally, limitations of this study are presented in section 7.4 and avenues for further research are presented in section 7.5.

7.1 Contributions

The first research question that the present study intended to address was the following: **How does the external business network of subsidiaries influence their product innovation process (research question 1)?** Within this research question, it was asked:

Which external business partners affect different stages of the product innovation process (research question 1.1)?

(1) In the present thesis, the **most influential stakeholder groups in the single stages of the product innovation process** in the pharmaceutical industry were studied. In order to do this, product innovation processes on both medicines (at Pharmasub and Pharmanorth) and diagnostic products (at Diagnosub) have been examined. In drug development, the stages of in vitro tests, in vivo tests and stages I to III of clinical trials were analyzed. At the stage of in vitro tests, the most influential business partner was a scientist at a private research institution (ResCog-A). At the stages of in vivo tests and clinical trials I, private study centers were most relevant for the innovative subsidiaries (ClinCog-A and ClinCog-B, respectively). At stages II and III of the clinical trials, a university hospital played the greatest role (ClinCog-C). While it is the core business to conduct studies for pharmaceutical companies for the business partners of in vivo studies and clinical studies I and to cure people in clinical trials II and III, the main interest of the business partner at in vitro tests is in research.

It was the most influential business partner for the whole product innovation process of Cogis. It proved the non-toxicity of Cogis for humans. The most important business partners in the product innovation process of Cogis are depicted in figure 6-8 in sub-section 6.2.1.3.

In the product innovation process of the diagnostic test, CantisCRC, a (potential) customer was involved in the first stage of idea description (CustCRC-A). The university doctor was also the most influential business partner in the whole product innovation process. During the stages of basic and extended technology studies, a university hospital was the most important business partner. In the product innovation process of the platform for diagnostic tests, CantisPF, suppliers were most crucial in basic and extended technology studies and in feasibility. The most important business partners in the product innovation process of CantisCRC and CantisPF are depicted in figure 6-9 in sub-section 6.2.2.3.

Thus, in opposition to past studies that focused only on customers and suppliers, here these stakeholder groups played a minor role in the product innovation process in the three cases. The issue of stakeholder groups is discussed in more detail in sub-section 7.2.1.

How does the relationship between the focal subsidiary and its most influential external business partners look like (research question 1.2)?
(How) Does the embeddedness of the relationship between the focal subsidiary and its external business partners develop during the product innovation process (research question 1.2.1)?

(2) Studying the embeddedness of business relationships revealed some new insights as well. The analysis showed that the innovative subsidiaries **had not collaborated with the most influential business partners** ResCog-A and CustCRC-A before. In spite of this, business relationships to the most influential business partners were also evaluated as the most embedded business relationships. The importance of the business partners was defined by their task and contribution in the product innovation process. This applies for both ResCog-A and CustCRC-A. The embeddedness of both business relationships was affected by the importance of the

business relationship for the product innovation process. This applies at least for the most important business relationships in the product innovation process. Respondents were particularly thankful for reliable business partners at these critical stages and perceived the business relationships as particularly embedded. The relationship between the criticality of the received knowledge and the evaluation of the business relationship is presented in figure 6-22 in sub-section 6.3.3.

(3) During the collaborations on Cogis, CantisCRC or CantisPF only few business relationships were perceived to have advanced. Respondents did not remember **developments in the embeddedness of business relationships** although they were explicitly asked about them. Only in three business relationships, changes were reported: in the business relationships to ClinCog-A (see 6.3.1.1.2), ClinCog-B (see 6.3.1.2.1), and CustCRC-A (see 6.3.2.1.1). They were described according to the criteria "mutual adaptations in the product innovation process", "mutual commitment" and "mutual trust".

Which knowledge is exchanged between the focal subsidiary and its external business partners during the product innovation process (research question 1.2.2)?

(4) Characteristics of knowledge that had been analyzed in studies before showed **different results** in the present research project. It had been stated by other authors that exchanged knowledge is more tacit, detailed and holistic, the more embedded the business relationship is (Uzzi 1996, pp. 677-678, 1997, pp. 45-47). However, the present research project showed that knowledge was always easily articulable. Only part of the knowledge was taught.[160] This was reported irrespective of the embeddedness of the business relationship. Hence, the relationship between the embeddedness of the business relationship and the articulability of knowledge could not be demonstrated here. However, knowledge was more holistic in more embedded business relationships. Regarding the detailedness of knowledge no trend could be observed.

---

[160] This was the case in collaborations with service contractors and university hospitals that conducted studies for the innovative subsidiaries. They were taught how to conduct respective studies, e.g., how to take particular tissue.

(5) Compared to past publications, **two characteristics of knowledge were added** to this study: complexity and system dependence. Knowledge was described as complex in all business relationships. The only exception was the business relationship between Diagnosub and CustCRC-A. At this early stage of idea description, the knowledge that was passed on between the business partners was quite elementary. CustCRC-A gave her opinion on the usefulness of CantisCRC and the specifications the diagnostic test would need. Exchanged knowledge was always described as very system dependent as well. This was the case for both medical knowledge and for engineerial knowledge. The characteristics of knowledge and knowledge transfer have been summarized in the table in the sub-section for the case of Cogis and in the table in the sub-section for the cases of CantisCRC and CantisPF.

How does the relationship of the subsidiary to other units of the MNC affect the transfer of the subsidiary's product innovation in the MNC (research question 2)?

(6) During the study an interesting observation was made regarding the product innovation transfer. As was suggested in the introduction of this dissertation, product innovations at Pharmacom and Diagnocom were always transferred from the innovative subsidiary to HQs and foreign subsidiaries of the MNC. In this transfer however, from an R&D perspective **HQs and other subsidiaries as units are not the most critical issue in product innovation transfer**. Instead, coordination with other functions, mainly marketing and business development, was crucial for product innovation transfer and selling product innovations in worldwide markets, especially in the case of Diagnocom. The involvement of foreign subsidiaries in the product innovation process was a focus in both cases.

It became clear that MNCs in the pharmaceutical industry had sophisticated organizational structures and processes to facilitate product innovation transfer from the innovative subsidiary to the global marketing organization which was located at HQs and foreign subsidiaries. The structures and processes are supposed to avoid conflicts between R&D and marketing by integrating marketing in the product innovation process. Some years ago, conflicts between R&D and marketing arose because product innovations were driven very much by science. The marketability of products was hardly analyzed during the product innovation process. Now, global marketing experts are integrated in R&D teams to give their input on product innovation projects. They are even involved when deciding about the budget for further research on a project. At stages of development, local marketing experts from foreign subsidiaries are involved in the product innovation process as well. However, they are not integrated directly but are approached by global marketing. Organizational structures to integrate Marketing professionals and experts from foreign subsidiaries are depicted in figure 6-23 in sub-section 6.5.1.2 for the case of Pharmacom and figure 6-26 in sub-section 6.5.2.2 for the case of Diagnocom.

Other contributions

(7) For the first time, the **single stages of the product innovation process** were analyzed in a study on the influence of subsidiaries' external business partners on product innovations. Past publications used product innovations as an outcome of collaborations but they did not examine the process that led to the result of product innovations. Investigating the product innovation process in detail made it possible to reveal all the most influential business partners along the process that contributed to the product innovation. Studying the product innovation process also enabled the author not only to analyze the business relationships and knowledge transfer but also to compare the results of the stages. This fostered the insight that most crucial business relationships for the entire process were evaluated most harmonically by subsidiaries.

(8) Apart from the results regarding the research questions, a methodological contribution has been made to the **measurement of embeddedness of business relationships**. Seven criteria for measuring embeddedness of business relationships were taken into account. So far, adaptations between business partners were the main (and sometimes the only) criterion used by authors of previous studies (see table 4-2 in section 4.4). In most assessments of the embeddedness of business relationships in the present research project, the seven criteria got different values between "very low" and "very high" by respondents. Thus, it seems too simple to employ only one criterion to measure the embeddedness of business relationship. Instead, it seems helpful to apply the seven characteristics used in the present study.

The measures of the embeddedness of business relationships are presented in table 5-2 in sub-section 5.1.3.3. The evaluation of the embeddedness of business relationships are depicted in figure 6-16 in sub-section 6.3.1.3 for the case of Cogis and in figure 6-21 in sub-section 6.3.2.3 for the cases of CantisCRC and CantisPF.

(9) In the empirical study it was found that some respondents split the **attribute of trust into two to three sub-criteria**. In the case of ClinCog-B, respondents talked about the trust in competence of the business partner and quality of the results on the one hand and trust in delivery on time on the other hand. While the first remained constant during the collaboration on Cogis, trust in delivery decreased. In the business relationship between Diagnosub and CustCRC-A, the emotional dimension of trust and the openness of communication (CustCRC-A) was mentioned. The emotional dimension was high from the beginning and stayed high even after the breakdown of the collaboration. The openness in communication however, declined. The expert who was interviewed about the business relationship between Diagnosub and ClinCRC-A distinguished between three dimensions of trust: trust in the quality of the delivered material and information and their delivery, trust in modern technologies of the business partner, and personal trust in the contact persons.

(10) A **new criterion to measure the intensity of product innovations** was added during the study. In line with sophisticated studies of Hauschildt and Schlaak (2001) and Lettl, seven criteria were planned to be applied to assess the intensity of the product innovations Cogis and Cantis. However, when discussing the intensity of CantisCRC and CantisPF the Head of Innovation Management talked about the (anticipated) uncertainty of the market. This variable involves the acceptance of the new test and platform with new technology in the market. Both doctors and health insurance providers have to be convinced that the new test has benefits as compared to other diagnostic methods for colorectal cancer. The (anticipated) uncertainty of the market was not included in the study from the beginning and it is not part of the technological dimension of product innovations. Looking at the other dimensions which were identified in the study of Hauschildt and Schlaak (sales market, purchasing, production process, formal and informal organization, Hauschildt/Schlaak 2001, p. 175), the new criterion fits the market dimension. However, none of the questions asked by the authors in this dimension suit the issue described here. It is not a crite-

rion in the study of Lettl and his co-authors either (Lettl/Hienerth/Gemuenden 2008, p. 229). The measures of the intensity of product innovations (as originally applied) are listed in table 5-1 in sub-section 5.1.3.1.1. The intensity of CantisCRC is depicted in figure 6-4 in sub-section 6.1.2.3.1 while the intensity of CantisPF is shown in figure 6-5 in sub-section 6.1.2.3.2.

7.2 Reflection of Results on the Concept of the Embedded MNC

7.2.1 Stakeholder Groups

As was stated in section 7.1, several stakeholder groups were identified as most influential in the product innovation process in the pharmaceutical industry in this thesis. Private research institutions, private study centers and university hospitals played a role in the development of new medicines while customers, suppliers, and university hospitals were most important for the development of a diagnostic test and platform.

In theoretical discussions of the concept of the Embedded MNC, authors include all kinds of stakeholder groups. They do not limit their considerations to particular groups (e.g., Blankenburg Holm/Eriksson/Johanson 1999, Andersson/Björkman/ Forsgren 2005, Forsgren/Holm/Johanson 2005). However, it was revealed in section 4.4 that in their empirical studies mainly customers and suppliers were analyzed (see also table 4-2). If other external stakeholders were taken into account, they were subsumed as "others". It was assumed in this dissertation that past studies focused on customers and suppliers because they specifically analyzed Business-to-Business industries that mainly involve engineerial expertise such as industrial equipment, paper or plant building. In plant building for instance, product innovations are specifically adapted to the customer. However, there are many other industries that are obviously not covered by the research of the Embedded MNC stream. Hence, the concept of the Embedded MNC should be expanded and refined.

In the product innovation process of CantisPF, mainly engineerial knowledge was required as well. In this product innovation process, two business partners were engaged at three stages. Both of them were suppliers. In opposition, chemical knowledge was mainly involved in the product innovation processes of Cogis and CantisCRC. In total six business partners were inhered in both cases. Only one of them was a customer, the others were research institutions and clinical study centers. Hence, it may be concluded that suppliers are the most influential business partners when engineerial knowledge is required whereas in the case of chemical knowledge other business partners are more important. In the case of pharmaceutical products, business partners who conduct studies to test and prove the effectiveness of medicine and diagnostic tests are crucial.

In the case of CantisCRC, the customer was involved in the first stage of the product innovation process, the idea description. This was the only business relationship of all analyzed relationships in which the exchanged knowledge was described as not complex. The (potential) customer was a doctor at a university hospital who gave her opinion on the first ideas of Diagnosub on the specifications and use of CantisCRC. Hence, it can be assumed that the complexity of the knowledge that is required from the business partner by the innovative subsidiary influences which type of stakeholder the business partner is. Since the subsidiary needs different degrees of the complexity of knowledge at each of the stages of the product innovation process, the stage has an indirect influence on the stakeholder group. Also, the content of the knowledge that is needed by the innovative subsidiary determines which stakeholder is most crucial at each stage of the product innovation process. If R&D experts need input on the market potential of their product idea at an early stage of the product innovation process, (potential) customers are likely to be most influential at this stage.

7.2.2 Embeddedness of Business Relationships

Several contributions were made in the present thesis on the embeddedness of business relationships: (1) more criteria than in the past have been employed to measure the embeddedness, (2) the relationship between the embeddedness of business relationships and the characteristics of knowledge that were proposed in the past have hardly been supported by the present empirical study, and (3) very important and tight business relationships were embedded right from the start without the business partners having known each other earlier and business relationships hardly developed throughout the collaboration in the product innovation process.

(1) First, on the methodological level more criteria to measure embeddedness of business relationships were employed in the empirical study. As was discussed in section 4.4, authors of the research stream of the Embedded MNC describe embeddedness of business relationships as a very complex phenomenon. However, they apply only few criteria to measure the phenomenon in their empirical studies. As listed in table 4-2, mostly the measure of adaptations (one way or mutual) is used. In several studies, this was the only measure that was employed. In other articles, this measure is combined with one or several of the following measures: dependence, commitment, importance of the business partner (as indicators of the depth of business relationship) and number of functional areas involved with the business partner (indicating the breadth of business relationship). Some characteristics that were used as key criteria in explaining the embeddedness of business relationships were not employed in empirical studies at all: criticality, trust and attention.

In the present contribution, the depth of business relationships was measured by the criteria: mutual adaptations, mutual dependence, mutual criticality, mutual commitment, mutual trust and mutual attention. In addition, the breadth of business relationships was measured by the number of functional areas of the innovative subsidiary that were involved with the business partner. Respondents often rated the single measures quite differently. For instance, criteria of the business relationship to Clin-Cog-C in stages II and III ranged from very low to very high. Even though the business relationship was described as very good and frame contracts were made with ClinCog-C, adaptations of the product innovation process were reported to be very low. However, dependence, criticality, trust and attention from Pharmasub were assessed as high or very high. In the business relationship with ClinCRC-A, adaptation of CantisCRC due to the business relationship with ClinCRC-A were evaluated as medium. However, dependence, criticality, trust and attention were assessed as high or very high. Hence, taking adaptation as the only measure of the embeddedness of business relationships oversimplifies the relationship: the embeddedness of business relationships can not be fully grasped by this single measure.

The evaluation of the embeddedness of a business relationship from both the perspective of the innovative subsidiary and its business partner by the same respondent revealed another interesting phenomenon. Originally, it was planned to have the business relationship assessed by both the innovative subsidiaries and their business partners. However, as business partners could not be interviewed, respondents at the innovative subsidiaries were asked to judge it from both perspectives. It became obvious that more embedded business relationships were assessed with similar values for both perspectives while the values of less embedded ones were rather different. Thus, the harmony of business relationships is seen in the harmony of the evaluation of their embeddedness.

(2) The concept of the Embedded MNC and embeddedness literature was extended with two characteristics of knowledge: complexity and system dependence. Knowledge was described as complex in all business relationships. The only exception was the business relationship between Diagnosub and CustCRC-A. In this early stage of idea description, exchanged knowledge was quite basic. Exchanged knowledge was always described as very system dependent as well. This was the case for both for medical knowledge and for engineerial knowledge.

Characteristics of knowledge that had been analyzed in existing publications had different results in the present research project. It had been stated by other authors that exchanged knowledge is more tacit, detailed and holistic, the more embedded the business relationship is (Uzzi 1996, pp. 677-678, 1997, pp. 45-47). However, the present research project showed that knowledge was always easily articulable. Only part of the knowledge was taught.[161] This was reported irrespective of the embeddedness of the business relationship. Hence, the correlation of the embeddedness of the business relationship and the articulability of knowledge could not be demonstrated here. However, knowledge was more holistic in more embedded business relationships. Regarding the detailedness of knowledge no trend could be observed.

---

[161] This was the case in collaborations with service contractors and university hospitals that conducted studies for the innovative subsidiaries. They were taught how to conduct their respective studies. However, in all business relationships knowledge from the external business partners was easily articulable or teachable.

(3) Authors of the concept of the Embedded MNC and the similar concept of embeddedness have stated that some long term relationships evolve into embedded ones. As more tacit, detailed and holistic knowledge is passed on in embedded business relationships, these business partners are particularly important for the product innovation process (e.g. Uzzi 1996, pp. 677-678, 1997, pp. 45-47).

However, in the present contribution the innovative subsidiaries had not collaborated with the most influential business partners of the whole product innovation processes of Cogis and CantisCRC, ResCog-A and CustCRC-A, before. Nevertheless, business relationships with these two most influential business partners were evaluated as the most embedded business relationships of all the business relationships that were analyzed. The importance of the business partners was therefore not affected by the history of the business relationship. Instead, it was defined by the criticality of the knowledge they transferred to the innovative subsidiaries. For both the innovation processes of Cogis and CantisCRC the knowledge from ResCog-A and Cust-CRC-A respectively, was the most critical. The contribution of these business partners was the greatest. Thus, in opposition to the assumptions and findings of earlier publications, the embeddedness of both business relationships was affected by the criticality of the knowledge received for the product innovation process and not vice versa. This applies at least for the most important business relationships in the product innovation process. However, the influence of the criticality of knowledge is most likely moderated by the reliability of the business partner. Respondents were particularly thankful for reliable business partners in these critical stages and perceived the business relationships as particularly embedded.

Apart from the fact that very embedded business relationships did not have a long history, most business relationships were not perceived to have evolved during the collaboration in the product innovation process either. It was found that only two business relationships advanced during the collaboration on Cogis, CantisCRC or CantisPF. The business relationship between Pharmasub and ClinCog-A developed as a result of the adaptation of ClinCog-A to Pharmasub, the commitment of Pharmasub and the mutual trust between the business partners. The business relationship between Diagnosub and CustCRC-A evolved due to mutual trust. The respondent split trust into an emotional dimension of trust and openness in communication. From the first contact to the discussion of the ideas of CantisCRC, the value of the emotional dimension of trust went up from one to four. Emotional trust was still as high after the end of the business relationship. In opposition, the openness of communication increased to very high (value five) during the discussion of the product ideas but decreased to low (value two) after the end of the business relationship. Other dimensions were not reported to have increased by the respondents. Thus, measuring the embeddedness of business relationships with the seven criteria is also helpful when assessing the development of business relationships.

7.3 Implications for Management Praxis

What implications do the contributions of the present thesis have for management praxis? (1) It was stated in sub-section 4.3.1.4, that the role of subsidiaries is influenced by both its external and corporate business partners. All of them have expectations regarding the behavior of the subsidiary. This may lead to a role conflict between the expectations of external business partners and those of corporate business partners, especially HQs. HQs try to coordinate and control the subsidiaries so that they serve the goals of the MNC as accurately as possible (Andersson/Forsgren 1996, p. 489, Andersson/Forsgren/Pedersen 2001, p. 6, Schmid/Daniel 2009, Daniel 2010). In order to do so, HQs must know what and who affects the actions of each subsidiary. Hence, HQs should identify about the most important (external and corporate) business partners of each subsidiary (Renz 1998, pp. 80-81). Of course, this is even more crucial for subsidiaries that play a big role for long-term operations of the MNC (Holm/Johanson/Thilenius 1995, pp. 115-116). Subsidiaries that develop new products are very important for the whole MNC especially if the product innovations are passed on to other units of the MNC and marketed by them. Thus, in order to increase the success of the MNC, HQs must understand how to support the development of the capabilities of the innovative subsidiaries. It became clear in this study that innovative subsidiaries learn a lot from their external business partners at each of the stages of the product innovation processes. Hence, HQs must know about these external business partners and how to support the business relationships to them in order to enhance the development of subsidiary's capabilities (Holm/Johanson/Thilenius 1995, pp. 109-110).

This publication reveals that top management of HQs (and of the focal subsidiary, of course) should not take only customers and suppliers into account when thinking about the most important external stakeholders of their subsidiaries. At least in the case of the pharmaceutical industry, HQs must also consider private research institutions and service contractors (both private study centers and university hospitals) when coordinating and controlling the innovative subsidiaries. Since the product innovation process at subsidiaries is crucial for the business activity of the whole MNC, the external business partners that are influential during the innovation process must not be overlooked. Instead, HQs should take them into consideration when taking decisions that concern the innovative subsidiary. For example, HQs might want to frame contracts with important business partners that collaborate with sub-units regularly. In this case, HQs should not only consider customers and suppliers but also private study centers or university hospitals.

(2) The present publication also supports managers regarding the organization of product innovation transfer within the MNC. It was assumed that the business relationship between the sending subsidiary and the receiving HQs have an impact on the transfer of the finalized product innovation. Instead, it was found that it is not the relationship between units but those between the functional areas of R&D and Marketing that are crucial for the transfer. A couple of years ago, experts from Marketing were only involved in the process when the product innovation was already made. At this point, they took over and planned the Marketing activities to sell the new product. However, Marketing experts often complained that products were developed without assessing their market potential first. Hence, problems arose between Marketing and R&D experts. In order to reduce the problems, organizational structures were established that include Marketing experts at different milestones of the product innovation process. They are not only part of the project team that is in charge of product development but are also involved in organizational structures that decide on the budget of project teams.

In the past couple of years, foreign subsidiaries were integrated in the product innovation process. Their opinion on the potential of the product idea in their local markets is esteemed. They also have the opportunity to ask for particular studies in the product innovation process for local approval and which reimbursement authorities demand.

Both changes in organizational structures were done in the past years by the MNCs that were analyzed in this contribution. Hence, probably other MNCs in the pharmaceutical industry are in the same process of changing their organizational structure and processes. They can take an example in the organizational structures and processes that are presented in this publication on the two MNCs that were investigated.

7.4 Limitations

As was previously shown, the present thesis has made several contributions to fill research gaps concerning both the product innovation process at subsidiaries and the product innovation transfer within MNCs. However, it has limitations, which are explained as follows:

(1) As a case study design was used in the empirical study, results of the study are not statistically generalizable. Generalizability is limited due to several reasons: First, only two cases were analyzed and both cases were not selected randomly. This procedure is common in qualitative case study research because it does not aim at statistical generalizability. Rather, analytical generalization is applied in case studies (Yin 2009, p. 15). Second, generalizability of results of the present study is limited because in both cases German subsidiaries of Swiss MNCs were studied. This was done because sociological issues like the embeddedness of relationships are evaluated differently across national cultures (Sandström 1992, p. 51, Kutschker/Bäurle/ Schmid 1997, p. 8). However, it may limit the generalizability of results to subsidiaries and MNCs from other countries.

(2) An important limitation is that the embeddedness of business relationships and characteristics of knowledge and knowledge transfer between business partners were only assessed by respondents of the innovative subsidiaries. They evaluated the research questions not only from their own perspective but also from the perspective of their business partners. Of course, their perception of the perspective of

the business partner may be incorrect. However, it was not possible to conduct interviews with experts from the external business because the innovative subsidiaries and their business partners made CDAs. CDAs prohibited the names of business partners from being mentioned. Thus, contacts could not be made. However, as described above, this limitation might also have brought a new insight. Business relationships that were described as very good tended to be assessed with similar values for both business partners by the respondents.

(3) In both cases not all stages of the product innovation processes could be analyzed. In the case of Cogis, five stages of the product innovation process were studied: pre-clinic I (in vitro studies), pre-clinic II (in vivo studies) and clinical trials I, II, and III. Earlier stages of target definition and pre-clinic 0 could not be analyzed because they were carried out too long ago and the experts had left the firm. With CantisCRC, all the three stages of research were analyzed: idea description, basic and extended technology studies. Stages of development could not be studied because CantisCRC is only about to enter the development part of the process. However, with the test CantisCRC not much development work needs to be done. The main task is the upscaling of marker production. Regarding CantisPF, the stage of idea description was not analyzed. This stage took place too long ago in this case. Stages of basic and extended technology studies are examined and the selection process of a business partner at the feasibility stage is looked at. Further stages have not yet been passed.

7.5 Avenues for Further Research

There are innumerable possibilities to extend this study. In this section, some opportunities regarding methodology and content are presented.

Methodology

(1) Results of this research project could be tested on a large sample in a quantitative study. This way, statistical generalizability could be achieved. The seven measures for the embeddedness of business relationships could be employed. They

should be evaluated by both business partners if possible. In addition, subsidiaries and MNCs from countries other than Germany and Switzerland should be included in the research. It might be interesting to analyze whether there are differences in product innovation processes and product innovation transfer due to a larger geographical or cultural distance.

(2) Also, other industries other than the pharmaceutical industry should be analyzed. Although the broad categories of basic research, applied research and development apply for most industries, it is industry specific what happens in these stages and how they are further detailed. It should also be kept in mind that that the pharmaceutical industry is more regulated by laws than most other industries. Many external business partners are collaborated with each other in order to fulfill the demands of approval authorities.

(3) Future studies should intend to look at all stages from the very beginning of the product development process to market launch. Taking all stages into account might help to gain further insights into which stakeholder groups at which stages of the process are the most important business partners.

Content

(4) Another interesting issue is the change in the role of a business partner during the product innovation process. For instance, in the case of CantisCRC the most influential business partner at the stage of idea description was CustCRC-A. She was a doctor at a hospital and gave her opinion on the product idea of CantisCRC as a potential customer. Due to stagnation of the product innovation process at Diagnosub, the business relationship to CustCRC-A ended after the first stage. Usually, CustCRC-A would also have conducted clinical studies at the stages of basic and extended technology studies. In this case, her role as a business partner would no longer have been that of a (potential) customer but of a provider of clinical studies. She would have belonged to the stakeholder group of university hospitals and would have been called ClinCRC-A in the present empirical study. It would be interesting to find out how the business relationship between the innovative subsidiary and the

business partner and the exchanged knowledge changes when another role is taken on.

(5) Researchers should also try to explain different findings regarding the characteristics of knowledge. While past studies revealed that knowledge is more detailed in embedded business relationships (Uzzi 1996, 1997, Uzzi/Lancaster 2003), in the present dissertation no effect of the embeddedness on the detailedness of exchanged knowledge was observed. This could have several reasons, e.g. the fact that studies took place in different industries. Moderating and modifying variables that influence the relationship between the embeddedness and detailedness of knowledge should be addressed.

(6) Regarding the intra-organizational transfer of product innovations it would be interesting to study whether such sophisticated organizational structures are able to integrate different functional areas and foreign subsidiaries in the product innovation process in industries other than the pharmaceutical industry. As product innovation processes in the pharmaceutical industry take a lot of time and require high investments it is possible that MNCs in this industry attach a higher importance to involving different perspectives. However, it may also be that different functional areas and units are included in the product innovation process in other industries in order to increase the success of the product innovation.

Appendix

Appendix A: Interview Guideline

Background Information:
- Provide the respondent with my definition of a subsidiary.
- Which position do you have in the MNC?
- Which role do you play in the product innovation process?

Product innovation:
1. Please describe the product innovation.
   Aim: To understand the product innovation.
   - What is the aim of the product innovation? For instance, which disease shall be cured with the drug, which disease will be diagnosed by the diagnostic method?
   - What is the innovative part, e.g. which is the active ingredient of the drug?
   - Please explain what exactly is innovative about it.

2. Is the product innovation radical?
   - Do you develop a completely new product or do you improve an existing product?
   - How novel is the mode of action/technology of the product innovation on a five-point scale between "not at all novel" and "very novel"?
   - How much new knowledge was obtained in your subsidiary while working on the product innovation? Please evaluate the degree of new knowledge on a five-point scale between "no new knowledge" and "a high amount of new knowledge".
   - How much experience did your subsidiary have with the mode of action/technology before this product innovation process started? Please evaluate the degree of experience on a five-point scale between "no experience" and "a lot of experience".
   - How complex is the mode of action/technology of the product innovation on a five-point scale between "not at all complex" and "very complex"?

- Please evaluate the risk that the product innovation process is not successful on a five-point scale between "no risk" and "very high risk".
- Please evaluate the uncertainty regarding the length of the product innovation process on a five-point scale between "no uncertainty" and "very high uncertainty".
- Please evaluate the uncertainty regarding the cost of the product innovation process on a five-point scale between "no uncertainty" and "very high uncertainty".

Product innovation process:

1. The product innovation process in general:
- How long does the product innovation process take so far?
- When did it start and at which point of the product innovation process are you now?
- Which stage of the product innovation process are you working on?
- What exactly happened at this stage of the product innovation process?
- How long did this stage take?
- Which sub-units of the MNC were involved in the other stages of the product innovation process?

2. Which type of product innovation process according to Bartlett and Ghoshal is this process?
    - Which stages of the product innovation process are conducted at your subsidiary?
    - Which is result of your stage of the innovation process?
    - Which sub-units receive the result of your stage of the innovation process?
    - Which stages of the innovation process are carried out in the sub-unit which receives your result?

Business relationships:

1. Actor:
- With which business partners did you collaborate at your stage of the product innovation process? They might be firms (customers, competitors, private research institutions) or universities, for instance.

- Do you collaborate with these business partners in other functional areas? Are they customers or suppliers, for example?
- Which of these business partners affected the product innovation process the most?

(From now on questions refer to the most important actor):

- In which country is the HQ of the business partner situated? If it is a multinational firm, which sub-unit in which country do you work with?
- Do you work with this actor on other stages of the innovation process?
- Why did you select this business partner for collaboration at this stage of the process?
- Who selected this business partner? Was it your subsidiary, the management of R&D or the HQ?

2. Business relationship:

- Starting point:
    - Have you collaborated with this actor before?
    - If so when have you worked with him for the first time? How often, how tight and for which occasions did you work together?
    - How would you describe the relationship to this business partner in the beginning of this innovation process in your subsidiary? (open question)
- Breadth of the business relationship:
    - In how many functional areas did you work with the business partner at the beginning of the innovation process?
    - In how many functional areas is your subsidiary involved? (if more than R&D is mentioned)
    - Did this number increase or decrease during the collaboration?
- Depth of the business relationship:
    - Adaptations:
        - How much have you adapted the product innovation specifically to this business partner?
        - How much have you adapted the product innovation process specifically to this business partner?
        - How much has your business partner adapted the product innovation (component) specifically to you?

- How much has your business partner adapted the product innovation process specifically to you?
    - Dependence:
        - How strong is the dependence of your subsidiary on the business partner on a technological, social, economical, legal and knowledge level?
        - How strong is the dependence of the business partner on the business partner on a technological, social, economical, legal and knowledge level?
    - Criticality:
        - How severe would the consequences be for your subsidiary if the business relationship to the partner terminated?
        - How severe would the consequences be for your business partner if the business relationship to your subsidiary terminated?
    - Commitment:
        - How high are the investments of your subsidiary in the business relationship?
        - How high are the investments of your partner in the business relationship?
    - Trust:
        - How trustful do you perceive the business relationship to the business partner?
        - How trustful does your business partner perceive the business relationship to you?
    - Attention:
        - Do you pay a lot of attention to the needs of your business partner during the collaboration?
        - Does you business partner pay a lot of attention to your needs during the collaboration?

Exchange of knowledge:

1. Flows of knowledge:
- Content of knowledge flows:
    - What were the contacts about?
    - Which knowledge was exchanged during the collaboration?
- Frequency of knowledge exchange:
    - How often did you have contact to the business partner?

- What was the reason for these contacts?
1. Generation of knowledge flows:
    - Did you plan the knowledge flows?
    - Which of the knowledge flows were planned?
    - Were there any emergent knowledge flows?
    - Why did they occur?
- Coordination of knowledge flows:
    - Who coordinates the knowledge flows? Is this your subsidiary?
    - How do you coordinate the knowledge flows?
- Criticality of knowledge flows:
    - How critical are knowledge flows for your subsidiary? How severe would be the consequences concerning the knowledge flows if the business relationship ended?
    - How critical are knowledge flows for your business partner? How severe would be the consequences concerning the knowledge flows if the business relationship ended?

2. Knowledge:
- Tacitness von knowledge:
    - Which knowledge did you exchange with the business partner?
    - To which degree are results articulated, for instance through written or oral reports, software etc.
    - If knowledge was not articulated was it taught by employees?
- Was the exchanged knowledge more complex than in similar business relationships?
- Was the exchanged knowledge more system dependent than in similar business relationships?
- Was the exchanged knowledge more detailed than in similar business relationships?
- Was the exchanged knowledge more holistic than in similar business relationships?
- Were there any problems with single "events" of knowledge transfer?

Would knowledge exchange be preceded the same way if business relationship to the partner was different?

Are there any remarks you would like to make about the study?

Appendix B: Final Code List as Used in this Study

Categories	Codes	Definition
Characteristics of Product Innovations		
Intensity/Radicality of product innovation (RAD)		
Completely new product	RAD New	The innovation is intended to become a completely new product.
Newness of technology	RAD Tech	Respondent assesses the newness of technology of the product innovation.
New knowledge	RAD Know	Respondent assesses the amount of new knowledge that was learnt during the product innovation process.
Past experience with technology	RAD Exp	Respondent assesses the experience that the innovative subsidiary had with the technology of the product innovation.
Complexity of technology	RAD Com	Respondent assesses the complexity of technology of the product innovation.
Uncertainty of technology	RAD UncTech	Respondent assesses the uncertainty of the feasibility of technology at the beginning of the product innovation process.
Uncertainty of development time	RAD UncTime	Respondent assesses the uncertainty of the duration of the product innovation process at its beginning.
Uncertainty of development costs	RAD UncCost	Respondent assesses the uncertainty of the costs of the product innovation process at its beginning.
(Anticipated) Uncertainty of Market	RAD UncMarket	Respondent assesses the uncertainty of the acceptance of the product innovation by the market, i.e. by customers, doctors and health insurances.
Geographical scope of product innovation (GEO)		
Geographical scope of product innovation (locally-leveraged vs. globally-linked)	GEO LL	Respondent talks about the sub-units that were involved in the product innovation process.
Characteristics of the Product Innovation and Product Innovation Process		
Description of Product Innovation	PI	Respondent describes the product innovation.
Description of product innovation process	PIP	Respondent describes the product innovation process.
Aim of Product Innovation	AIM	Respondent explains the aim of the product innovation.
Innovative Technology	INNTECH	Respondent talks about the innovative technology of the product innovation.

Categories	Codes	Definition
Characteristics of the Product Innovation and Product Innovation Process		
Time frame of Innovation Process	TIME	Respondent assesses the timeline of the product innovation process.
Current stage	CURSTAGE	Respondent talks about the current stage of the product innovation process.
Stakeholders[162]		
External actors/business partners (EBR)		
Stakeholder groups	EBR SG	Respondent talks about the stakeholders that have affected a particular stage of the product innovation process in general.
Customers	EBR Cus	The most influential business partner in a particular stage of the product innovation process was a customer.
Suppliers	EBR Sup	The most influential business partner in a particular stage of the product innovation process was a supplier.
Universities	EBR Uni	The most influential business partner in a particular stage of the product innovation process was a university.
Private research institutions	EBR Res	The most influential business partner in a particular stage of the product innovation process was a private research institution.
Collaboration in more stages of the product innovation process	EBR Stage	Respondent explains whether the innovative subsidiary collaborates with the most influential business partner in other stages of the product innovation process as well.
Selection of business partners (SEL)		
Reason	SEL Reason	Respondent explains why the most influential business partner in a particular stage was chosen as a business partner.
Unit/position	SEL Pos	Respondent describes who chose the most influential business partner in a particular stage. This refers to the sub-unit and/or the position that chose the business partner.

---

[162] Only external stakeholder groups are listed in the code table because on the corporate level, HQ and subsidiaries were not coded. Instead, organizational structures and processes were coded rather broadly.

Categories	Codes	Definition
Characteristics of Business Relationships		
Past experience with business partner	EXP BR	Respondent states whether (and how often) the subsidiary collaborated in past product innovation processes with the most influential business partner.
Characteristics of business relationship	CHAR BR	Respondent describes the business relationship to the most influential business partner in his own words.
Role of business relationship	ROLE BR	Respondent explains which consequences a more or less embedded business relationship has on the collaboration.
Reflection on business relationships	BR Reflection	Respondent describes differences between more and less embedded business relationships in general.
Development of business relationship	DEV BR	Respondent talks about the development of the business relationship.
Functional areas (FUNC)[163]		
R&D	FUNC RD	The subsidiary and the most influential business partner collaborate in R&D.
Marketing & sales	FUNC Mark	The subsidiary and the most influential business partner collaborate in marketing and sales.
Supply	FUNC Sup	The subsidiary and the most influential business partner collaborate in supply.
Mutual adaptation (ADAP)		
Adaptations of subsidiary to business partner regarding product innovation	ADAP Sub PI	Respondent assesses and describes the adaptations made by the subsidiary to the business partner regarding the product innovation.
Adaptations of business partner to subsidiary regarding product innovation	ADAP BP PI	Respondent assesses and describes the adaptations made by the business partner to the subsidiary regarding the product innovation.
Adaptations of subsidiary to business partner regarding product innovation process	ADAP Sub PIP	Respondent assesses and describes the adaptations made by the subsidiary to the business partner regarding the product innovation process.
Adaptations of business partner to subsidiary regarding product innovation process	ADAP BR PIP	Respondent assesses and describes the adaptations made by the business partner to the subsidiary regarding the product innovation process.

---

[163] From the six functional areas that were suggested in sub-section 4.3.1.1.2 (R&D, production, marketing & sales, logistics & distribution, purchasing and human resource management) only two were identified in the case studies.

Categories	Codes	Definition
Characteristics of Business Relationships		
Mutual dependence (DEP)		
Dependence of subsidiary on business partner	DEP Sub	Respondent assesses and describes the operational dependence of the subsidiary on the business partner in the product innovation process.
Dependence of business on subsidiary	DEP BR	Respondent assesses and describes the operational dependence of the business partner on the subsidiary in the product innovation process.
Mutual criticality (CRIT)		
Degree of severity of consequences for subsidiary	CRIT Sub	Respondent assesses and describes the strategic criticality of the business partner for the subsidiary.
Degree of severity of consequences for business partner	CRIT BR	Respondent assesses and describes the strategic criticality of the subsidiary for the business partner.
Mutual commitment (COMM)		
Investments made by subsidiary in business relationship	COMM Sub	Respondent assesses and describes the investments that the subsidiary made in the business relationship, e.g. time spent.
Investments made by business partner in business relationship	COMM BR	Respondent assesses and describes the investments that the business partner made in the business relationship, e.g. time spent.
Mutual trust		
Trust of the subsidiary in the business relationship	TRUST Sub	Respondent assesses and describes the trust of the subsidiary in the business relationship.
Trust of the business partner in the business relationship	TRUST BR	Respondent assesses and describes the trust of the business partner in the business relationship.
Mutual attention (ATT)		
Degree of attention paid by the subsidiary	ATT Sub	Respondent assesses and describes the attention that the subsidiary paid to the business partner during the collaboration.
Degree of attention paid by the business partner	ATT BR	Respondent assesses and describes the attention that the business partner paid to the subsidiary during the collaboration.

Categories	Codes	Definition
Characteristics of Knowledge		
Articulatedness	K Art	Respondent talks about how knowledge was articulated during the exchanges.
Complexity	K Comp	Respondent talks about the complexity of knowledge that was exchanged.
System dependence	K SysDep	Respondent talks about the system dependence of knowledge that was exchanged.
Detailedness	K Detail	Respondent talks about the detailedness of knowledge that was exchanged.
Degree of holistic knowledge	K Holist	Respondent talks about the system dependence of knowledge that was exchanged.
Characteristics of Flows of Knowledge		
Content of knowledge flow	KF Cont	Respondent explains the content of knowledge flows between business partners.
Cross-border knowledge flow	KF Cross	Respondent stated whether the business partner was located in the same country like the innovative subsidiary (i.e. Germany) or was located in another country.
Planning of knowledge flows	KF Plan	Respondent states whether knowledge flows between the innovative subsidiary and its business partners were planned or emerging.
Criticality of knowledge flows from the business partner for the subsidiary	KF Crit SUB	Respondent evaluated how critical knowledge flows from the business partner were for the product innovation process at the subsidiary.
Criticality of knowledge flows from the subsidiary for the business partner	KF Crit BR	Respondent evaluated how critical knowledge flows from the subsidiary were for business partner.
Frequency of knowledge flows	KF Freq	Respondent describes how often and how regularly knowledge flows between the business partners took place.
Coordinator of knowledge flows	KF Coordinator	Respondent states whether knowledge flows were coordinated by the innovative subsidiary, the business partner or a third person.
Coordination of knowledge flows	KF Coordination	Respondent explains whether structural, technocratic or personal coordination mechanisms were applied in order to coordinate knowledge flows.
Problems of knowledge transfer	KF Prob	Respondent describes problems of knowledge flows between the innovative subsidiary and its business partner.

Categories	Codes	Definition
Organization of Product Innovation Transfer within MNCs (ORG)		
Aim of the organizational structure	ORG Aim	Respondent explains the aims of establishing a particular organizational structure (future perspective).
Reasons to establish organizational structure	ORG Reason	Respondent explains the reasons for establishing a particular organizational structure (past perspective).
Description of organizational structure	ORG Structure	Respondent describes details of the organizational structure to facilitate product innovation transfer within the MNC.
Processes concerning the organizational structure	ORG Process	Respondent describes processes concerning facilitate product innovation transfer within the organizational structure.
Organizational problems	ORG Prob	Respondent describes organizational problems of the firm.
Others		
Diagnosub: Test	TEST	Respondent talks about the test CantisCRC.
Diagnosub: Platform	PLATFORM	Respondent talks about the platform CantisPF.
Pharmasub: Clinical Trials Stage one	CR Stage 1	Respondent talks about stage I of the clinical trials.
Pharmasub: Clinical Trials Stage two	CR Stage 2	Respondent talks about stage II of the clinical trials.
Pharmasub: Clinical Trials Stage three	CR Stage 3	Respondent talks about stage III of the clinical trials.
Pharmasub: In vitro studies	In Vitro	Respondent talks about in vitro studies (pre-clinic I).
Pharmasub: In vivo studies	In Vivo	Respondent talks about in vivo studies (pre-clinic II).

References

Abecassis-Moedas, Celine/Mahmoud-Jouini, Sihem B. (2008): Absorptive Capacity and Source-Recipient Complementarity in Designing New Products: An Empirically Derived Framework. In: Journal of Product Innovation Management, Vol. 25, No. 5, 2008, pp. 473-490.

Aboulnasr, Khaled/Narasimhan, Om/Blair, Edward/Chandy, Rajesh (2008): Competitive Response to Radical Product Innovations. In: Journal of Marketing, Vol. 72, No. 3, 2008, pp. 94-110.

Abramovici, Marianne/Bancel-Charensol, Laurence (2004): How to Take Customers into Consideration in Service Innovation Projects. In: Service Industries Journal, Vol. 24, No. 1, 2004, pp. 56-78.

Ali, Abdul (1994): Pioneering Versus Incremental Innovation: Review and Research Propositions. In: Journal of Product Innovation Management, Vol. 11, No. 1, 1994, pp. 46-61.

Almeida, Paul (1996): Knowledge Sourcing by Foreign Multinationals: Patent Citation Analysis in the U.S. Semiconductor Industry. In: Strategic Management Journal, Vol. 17, Winter Special Issue, 1996, pp. 155-165.

Almeida, Paul/Phene, Anupama (2004): Subsidiaries and Knowledge Creation: The Influence of the MNC and Host Country on Innovation. In: Strategic Management Journal, Vol. 25, No. 8/9, 2004, pp. 847-864.

Ambos, Björn (2005): Foreign Direct Investment in Industrial Research and Development: A Study of German MNCs. In: Research Policy, Vol. 34, No. 4, 2005, pp. 395-410.

Anderson, Erin/Weitz, Barton (1992): The Use of Pledges to Build and Sustain Commitment in Distribution Channels. In: Journal of Marketing Research, Vol. 29, No. 1, 1992, pp. 18-34.

Anderson, James C./Håkansson, Håkan/Johanson, Jan (1994): Dyadic Business Relationships within a Business Network Context. In: Journal of Marketing, Vol. 58, No. 4, 1994, pp. 1-15.

Andersson, Ulf (2003): Managing the Transfer of Capabilities within Multinational Corporations: The Dual Role of the Subsidiary. In: Scandinavian Journal of Management, Vol. 19, No. 4, 2003, pp. 425-442.

Andersson, Ulf/Björkman, Ingmar/Forsgren, Mats (2005): Managing Subsidiary Knowledge Creation: The Effect of Control Mechanisms on Subsidiary Local Embeddedness. In: International Business Review, Vol. 14, No. 5, 2005, pp. 521-538.

Andersson, Ulf/Forsgren, Mats (1995): Using Networks to Determine Multinational Parental Control of Subsidiaries. In: Paliwoda, Stanley J./Ryans Jr., John K. (Eds., 1995): International Marketing Reader. Routledge, London et al., 1995, pp. 72-87.

Andersson, Ulf/Forsgren, Mats (1996): Subsidiary Embeddedness and Control in the Multinational Corporation. In: International Business Review, Vol. 5, No. 5, 1996, pp. 487-508.

Andersson, Ulf/Forsgren, Mats (2000): In Search of Centre of Excellence: Network Embeddedness and Subsidiary Roles in Multinational Corporations. In: Management International Review, Vol. 40, No. 4, 2000, pp. 329-350.

Andersson, Ulf/Forsgren, Mats/Holm, Ulf (2001): Subsidiary Embeddedness and Competence Development in MNCs: A Multi-Level Analysis. In: Organization Studies, Vol. 22, No. 6, 2001, pp. 1013-1034.

Andersson, Ulf/Forsgren, Mats/Holm, Ulf (2002): The Strategic Impact of External Networks: Subsidiary Performance and Competence Development in the Multinational Corporation. In: Strategic Management Journal, Vol. 23, No. 11, 2002, pp. 979-996.

Andersson, Ulf/Forsgren, Mats/Holm, Ulf (2007): Balancing Subsidiary Influence in the Federative MNC: A Business Network View. In: Journal of International Business Studies, Vol. 38, No. 5, 2007, pp. 802-818.

Andersson, Ulf/Forsgren, Mats/Pedersen, Torben (2001): Subsidiary Performance in Multinational Corporations: The Importance of Technology Embeddedness. In: International Business Review, Vol. 10, No. 1, 2001, pp. 3-23.

Araujo, Luis/Easton, Geoffrey (1996): Networks in Socio-economic Systems: A Critical Review. In: Iacobucci, Dawn (Ed., 1996): Networks in Marketing. Sage, Thousand Oaks et al., 1996, pp. 63-107.

Axelsson, Björn (1992): Network Research: Future Issues. In: Axelsson, Björn/Easton, Geoffrey (Eds., 1992): Industrial Networks: A New View of Reality. Routledge, London, New York, 1992, pp. 237-251.

Baden, Axel (2001): Shareholder Value- oder Stakeholder-Ansatz? Zur Vorteilhaftigkeit der beiden Konzepte. In: Wirtschaftswissenschaftliches Studium, Vol. 30, No. 8, 2001, pp. 398-403.

Barden, Jeffrey Q./Mitchell, Will (2007): Disentangling the Influences of Leaders' Relational Embeddedness on Interorganizational Exchange. In: Academy of Management Journal, Vol. 50, No. 6, 2007, pp. 1440-1461.

Barney, Jay B. (1991): Firm Resources and Sustained Competitive Advantage. In: Journal of Management, Vol. 17, No. 1, 1991, pp. 99-120.

Bartlett, Christopher A. (1984): Organization and Control of Global Enterprises: Influences, Characteristics and Guidelines. Harvard Business School, Boston, 1984.

Bartlett, Christopher A./Ghoshal, Sumantra (1986): Tap Your Subsidiaries for Global Reach. In: Harvard Business Review, Vol. 64, No. 6, 1986, pp. 87-94.

Bartlett, Christopher A./Ghoshal, Sumantra (1987): Managing Across Borders: New Organizational Responses. In: Sloan Management Review, Vol. 29, No. 1, 1987, pp. 43-53.

Bartlett, Christopher A./Ghoshal, Sumantra (1989): Managing Across Borders: The Transnational Solution. Harvard Business School Press, Boston, 1989.

Bartlett, Christopher A./Ghoshal, Sumantra (1990a): Internationale Unternehmensführung: Innovation, globale Effizienz, differenziertes Marketing. Campus, Frankfurt, New York, 1990a.

Bartlett, Christopher A./Ghoshal, Sumantra (1990b): Managing Innovation in the Transnational Corporation. In: Bartlett, Christopher A./Doz, Yves/Hedlund, Gunnar (Eds., 1990b): Managing the Global Firm. Routledge, London, New York, 1990b, pp. 215-255.

Bartlett, Christopher A./Ghoshal, Sumantra (1998): Managing Across Borders: The Transnational Solution. 2nd edition, Harvard Business School Press, Boston, 1998.

Becker, Selwyn W./Whisler, Thomas L. (1967): The Innovative Organization: A Selective View of Current Theory and Research. In: Journal of Business, Vol. 40, No. 4, 1967, pp. 462-469.

Beckert, Jens (2007): The Great Transformations of Embeddedness: Karl Polanyi and the New Economic Sociology. MPIfG Discussion Paper No. 07/1, Max-Planck-Institut für Gesellschaftsforschung, Köln, 2007.

Belliveau, Maura A./O'Reilly III, Charles A./Wade, James B. (1996): Social Capital at the Top: Effects of Social Similarity and Status on CEO Compensation. In: Academy of Management Journal, Vol. 39, No. 6, 1996, pp. 1568-1593.

Belsey, Mark J./Pavlou, Alex K. (2005): Trends Underlying Early-stage Drug Discovery and Development Collaborations from October 2002 to September 2004. In: Journal of Commercial Biotechnology, Vol. 11, No. 4, 2005, pp. 369-373.

Bendt, Antje (2000): Wissenstransfer in multinationalen Unternehmen. Gabler, Wiesbaden, 2000.

Benito, Gabriel R. G./Grøgaard, Brigitte/Narula, Rajneesh (2003): Environmental Influences on MNE Subsidiary Roles: Economic Integration and the Nordic Countries. In: Journal of International Business Studies, Vol. 34, No. 5, 2003, pp. 443–456.

Berger, Peter L./Luckmann, Thomas (1966): The Social Construction of Reality: A Treatise in the Sociology of Knowledge. Doubleday & Comp., Garden City, 1966.

Bick, Markus (2004): Knowledge Management Support System: Nachhaltige Einführung organisationsspezifischen Wissensmanagements. Zugl. Diss., Essen, 2004.

Birkinshaw, Julian (1997): Entrepreneurship in Multinational Corporations: The Characteristics of Subsidiary Initiatives. In: Strategic Management Journal, Vol. 18, No. 3, 1997, pp. 207-229.

Birkinshaw, Julian/Fry, Nick (1998): Subsidiary Initiatives to Develop New Markets. In: MIT Sloan Management Review, Vol. 39, No. 3, 1998, pp. 51-61.

Birkinshaw, Julian/Holm, Ulf/Thilenius, Peter/Arvidsson, Niklas (2000): Consequences of Perception Gaps in the Headquarters-Subsidiary Relationship. In: International Business Review, Vol. 9, No. 3, 2000, pp. 321-344.

Birkinshaw, Julian/Hood, Neil (1998): Multinational Subsidiary Evolution: Capability and Charter Change in Foreign-owned Subsidiary Companies. In: Academy of Management Review, Vol. 23, No. 4, 1998, pp. 773-795.

Birkinshaw, Julian M./Morrison, Allen J. (1995): Configurations of Strategy and Structure in Subsidiaries of Multinational Subsidiaries. In: Journal of International Business Studies, Vol. 26, No. 4, 1995, pp. 729-753.

Birkinshaw, Julian/Ridderstråle, Jonas (1999): Fighting the Corporate Immune System: A Process Study of Subsidiary Initiatives in Multinational Corporations. In: International Business Review, Vol. 8, No. 2, 1999, pp. 149-180.

Björkman, Ingmar/Stahl, Günter K./Vaara, Eero (2007): Cultural Differences and Capability Transfer in Cross-border Acquisitions: The Mediating Roles of Capability Complementarity, Absorptive Capacity, and Social Integration. In: Journal of International Business Studies, Vol. 38, No. 4, 2007, pp. 658-672.

Blankenburg Holm, Desirée/Eriksson, Kent/Johanson, Jan (1999): Creating Value through Mutual Commitment to Business Network Relationships. In: Strategic Management Journal, Vol. 20, No. 5, 1999, pp. 467-486.

Boehe, Dirk Michael (2007): Product Development in MNC Subsidiaries: Local Linkages and Global Interdependencies. In: Journal of International Management, Vol. 13, No. 4, 2007, pp. 488-512.

Bogdan, Robert C./Biklen, Sari Knopp (1992): Qualitative Research for Education: An Introduction to Theory and Methods. 2nd edition, Allyn and Bacon, Boston et al., 1992.

Bonoma, Thomas V. (1985): Case Research in Marketing: Opportunities, Problems, and a Process. In: Journal of Marketing Research, Vol. 22, No. 2, 1985, pp. 199-208.

Borgatti, Stephen P./Foster, Pacey C. (2003): The Network Paradigm in Organizational Research: A Review and Typology. In: Journal of Management, Vol. 29, No. 6, 2003, pp. 991-1013.

Bortz, Jürgen/Döring, Nicola (2002): Forschungsmethoden und Evaluation für Human- und Sozialwissenschaftler. 3rd Edition edition, Springer, Berlin, Heidelberg, New York, 2002.

Braganza, Ashly (2004): Rethinking the Data-Information-Knowledge Hierarchy: Towards a Case-based Model. In: International Journal of Information Management, Vol. 4, 2004, pp. 347-356.

Branstetter, Lee G./Fisman, Raymond/Foley, C. Fritz (2006): Do Stronger Intellectual Property Rights Increase International Technology Transfer? Empirical Evidence from U.S. Firm-level Panel Data. In: Quarterly Journal of Economics, Vol. 121, No. 1, 2006, pp. 321-349.

Brass, Daniel J. (1984): Being in the Right Place: A Structural Analysis of Individual Influence in an Organization. In: Administrative Science Quarterly, Vol. 29, No. 4, 1984, pp. 518-539.

Braun, Dietmar/Benninghoff, Martin (2003): Policy Learning in Swiss Research Policy: The Case of the National Centres of Competence in Research. In: Research Policy, Vol. 32, No. 10, 2003, pp. 1849-1863.

Brink, Alexander (2000): Holistisches Shareholder-Value-Management: Eine regulative Idee für globales Management in ethischer Verantwortung. Hampp, München, 2000.

Britton, John N. H. (2004): High Technology Localization and Extra-regional Networks. In: Entrepreneurship & Regional Development, Vol. 16, No. 5, 2004, pp. 369-390.

Brockhoff, Klaus K. (1992): Forschung und Entwicklung: Planung und Kontrolle. 3rd edition, Oldenbourg, München, Wien, 1992.

Brühl, Rolf/Buch, Sabrina (2006): Einheitliche Gütekriterien in der empirischen Forschung? – Objektivität, Reliabilität und Validität in der Diskussion. Working Paper No. 20, ESCP-EAP European School of Management Berlin, 2006.

Bryman, Alan (1989): Research Methods and Organization Studies. Unwin Hyman, London, 1989.

Burt, Ronald S. (1992): Structural Holes: The Social Structure of Competition. Harvard University Press, Cambridge, 1992.

Cantwell, John A./Dunning, John H./Janne, Odile E. M. (2004): Towards a Technology-seeking Explanation of U.S. Direct Investment in the United Kingdom. In: Journal of International Management, Vol. 10, No. 1, 2004, pp. 5-20.

Cantwell, John/Iammarino, Simona (1998): MNCs, Technological Innovation and Regional Systems in the EU: Some Evidence in the Italian Case. In: International Journal of the Economics of Business, Vol. 5, No. 3, 1998, pp. 383-408.

Cantwell, John/Mudambi, Ram (2005): MNE Competence-Creating Subsidiary Mandates. In: Strategic Management Journal, Vol. 26, No. 12, 2005, pp. 1109-1128.

Capon, Noel/Christodoulou, Chris/Farley, John U./Hulbert, James M. (1987): A Comparative Analysis of the Strategy and Structure of United States and Australian Corporations. In: Journal of International Business Studies, Vol. 18, No. 1, 1987, pp. 51-74.

Carrero, Virginia/Peiro, Jose M./Salanova, Marisa (2000): Studying Radical Organizational Innovation through Grounded Theory. In: European Journal of Work & Organizational Psychology, Vol. 9, No. 4, 2000, pp. 489-514.

Casson, Mark (2007): Multinational Enterprises: Their Private and Social Benefits and Costs. In: World Economy, Vol. 30, No. 2, 2007, pp. 308-328.

Cepeda, Gabriel/Martin, David (2005): A Review of Case Studies Publishing in Management Decision 2003-2004: Guides and Criteria for Achieving Quality in Qualitative Research. In: Management Decision, Vol. 43, No. 6, 2005, pp. 851-876.

Chandy, Rajesh K./Tellis, Gerard J. (1998): Organizing for Radical Product Innovation: The Overlooked Role of Willingness to Cannibalize. In: Journal of Marketing Research, Vol. 35, No. 4, 1998, pp. 474-487.

Chen, Yen-Chung (2007): The Upgrading of Multinational Regional Innovation Networks in China. In: Asia Pacific Business Review, Vol. 13, No. 3, 2007, pp. 373-403.

Ciabuschi, Francesco (2004): On the Innovative MNC: Leveraging Innovations and the Role of IT Systems. Uppsala Universitet, Doctoral Thesis, No. 111, Uppsala, 2004.

Ciabuschi, Francesco/Kang, Olivia H./Ståhl, Benjamin (2004): Leveraging Innovations in MNCs: The Effect of Transfer Mechanisms and Organizational Structure on Innovation Transfer Performance. In: Ciabuschi, Francesco (Ed., 2004): On the Innovative MNC: Leveraging Innovations and the Role of IT Systems. Företagsekonomiska instituionen, Uppsala Universitet, Doctoral Thesis, No. 111, Uppsala, Paper III, 2004.

Cohen, Wesley M./Levinthal, Daniel A. (1990): Absorptive Capacity: A New Perspective on Learning and Innovation. In: Administrative Science Quarterly, Vol. 35, No. 1, 1990, pp. 128-152.

Cook, Karen S./Emerson, Richard M. (1978): Power, Equity, Commitment in Exchange Networks. In: American Sociological Review, Vol. 43, No. 5, 1978, pp. 721-738.

Cooper, Robert G. (1979): The Dimensions of Industrial New Product Success and Failure. In: Journal of Marketing, Vol. 43, No. 3, 1979, pp. 93-103.

Cooper, Robert G. (2005): Product Leadership: Pathways to Profitable Innovation. 2nd edition, Basic Books, New York, 2005.

Creswell, John W. (2003): Research Design: Qualitative, Quantitative, and Mixed Methods Approaches. 2nd edition, Sage, Thousand Oaks, 2003.

Criscuolo, Paola (2004): R&D Internationalisation and Knowledge Transfer: Impact on MNEs and their Home Countries. Zugl. Diss. Universiteit Maastricht, 2004.

Criscuolo, Paola/Narula, Rajneesh/Verspagen, Bart (2005): Role of Home and Host Country Innovation Systems in R&D Internationalisation: A Patent Citation Analysis. In: Economics of Innovation & New Technology, Vol. 14, No. 5, 2005, pp. 417-433.

Cummings, Larry L./O'Connell, Michael J. (1978): Organizational Innovation: A Model and Needed Research. In: Journal of Business Research, Vol. 6, No. 1, 1978, pp. 33-50.

D'Cruz, Joseph (1986): Strategic Management of Subsidiaries. In: Etemad, Hamid G./Séguin, Dulude (Eds., 1986): Managing the Multinational Subsidiary: Response to Environmental Changes and to Host Nation R&D Policies. Croom Helm, London, 1986, pp. 75-89.

Dacin, M. Tina/Ventresca, Marc J./Beal, Brent D. (1999): The Embeddedness of Organizations: Dialogue & Directions. In: Journal of Management, Vol. 25, No. 3, 1999, pp. 317-356.

Damanpour, Fariborz (1991): Organizational Innovation: A Meta-analysis of Effects of Determinants and Moderators. In: Academy of Management Journal, Vol. 34, No. 3, 1991, pp. 555-590.

Daniel, Andrea (2010): Perception Gaps between Headquarters and Subsidiary Managers: Differing Perspectives on Subsidiary Roles and their Implications. Gabler, Wiesbaden, 2010.

Daniels, John D./Cannice, Mark V. (2004): Interview Studies in International Business Research. In: Marschan-Piekkari, Rebecca/Welch, Catherine (Eds., 2004): Handbook of Qualitative Research Methods for International Business. Edward Elgar, Cheltenham, Northampton, 2004, pp. 185–206.

Davenport, Thomas H./Harris, Jeanne G./De Long, David W./Jacobson, Alvin L. (2001): Data to Knowledge to Results: Building an Analytic Capability. In: California Management Review, Vol. 43, No. 2, 2001, pp. 117-138.

Davis, Lee N./Meyer, Klaus E. (2004): Subsidiary Research and Development, and the Local Environment. In: International Business Review, Vol. 13, No. 3, 2004, pp. 359-382.

De Luca, Luigi M./Atuahene-Gima, Kwaku (2007): Market Knowledge Dimensions and Cross-Functional Collaboration: Examining the Different Routes to Product Innovation Performance. In: Journal of Marketing, Vol. 71, No. 1, 2007, pp. 95-112.

Descotes, Raluca Mogos/Walliser, Björn/Xiaoling, Guo (2007): Capturing the Relevant Institutional Profile for Exporting SMEs: Empirical Evidence from France and Romania. In: International Management Review, Vol. 3, No. 3, 2007, pp. 16-26.

Dewar, Robert D./Dutton, Jane E. (1986): The Adoption of Radical and Incremental Innovations: An Empirical Analysis. In: Management Science, Vol. 32, No. 11, 1986, pp. 1422-1433.

Dhanaraj, Charles/Lyles, Marjorie A./Steensma, H. Kevin/Tihanyi, Laszlo (2004): Managing Tacit and Explicit Knowledge Transfer in IJVs: The Role of Relational Embeddedness and the Impact on Performance. In: Journal of International Business Studies, Vol. 35, No. 5, 2004, pp. 428-442.

Doz, Yves L./Prahalad, Coimbatore K. (2005): Managing DMNCs: A Search for a New Paradigm. In: Ghoshal, Sumantra/Westney, D. Eleanor (Eds., 2005): Organization Theory and the Multinational Corporation. 2nd edition. Palgrave Macmillan, Basingstoke et al., 2005, pp. 24-50.

Doz, Yves. L./Prahalad, Coimbatore K. (1991): Managing DMNCs: A Search for a New Paradigm. In: Strategic Management Journal, Vol. 12, No. 4, 1991, pp. 145-164.

Dunning, John H. (1988): The Eclectic Paradigm of International Production: A Restatement and Some Possible Extensions. In: Journal of International Business Studies, Vol. 19, No. 1, 1988, pp. 1-31.

Dunning, John H. (1994): Re-evaluating the Benefits of Foreign Direct Investment. In: Transnational Corporations, Vol. 3, No. 1, 1994, pp. 23-51.

Easton, Geoffrey (1992): Industrial Networks: A Review. In: Axelsson, Björn/Easton, Geoffrey (Eds., 1992): Industrial Networks: A New View of Reality. Routledge, London, New York, 1992, pp. 3-27.

Easton, Geoffrey/Araujo, Luis (1989): The Network Approach: An Articulation. In: Cavusgil, S. Tamer/Hallén, Lars/Johanson, Jan (Eds., 1989): Advances in International Marketing. A Research Annual. Volume 3. JAI, Greenwich, London, 1989, pp. 97-119.

Eisenhardt, Kathleen M. (1989): Building Theories from Case Study Research. In: Academy of Management Review, Vol. 14, No. 4, 1989, pp. 532–550.

Eisenhardt, Kathleen M./Graebner, Melissa (2007): Theory Building from Cases. Opportunities and Challenges. In: Academy of Management Journal, Vol. 50, No. 1, 2007, pp. 25-32.

Elias, Arun A./Cavana, Robert Y./Jackson, Laurie S. (2002): Stakeholder Analysis for R&D Project Management. In: R&D Management, Vol. 32, No. 4, 2002, pp. 301-310.

Emsley, David/Nevicky, Barbara/Harrison, Graeme (2006): Effect of Cognitive Style and Professional Development on the Initiation of Radical and Non-radical Management Accounting Innovations. In: Accounting & Finance, Vol. 46, No. 2, 2006, pp. 243-264.

Ensign, Prescott C. (1999): Innovation in the Multinational Firm with Globally Dispersed R&D: Technological Knowledge Utilization and Accumulation. In: Journal of High Technology Management Research, Vol. 10, No. 2, 1999, pp. 203-221.

Erramilli, M. Krishna/Rao, C. P. (1990): Choice of Foreign Market Entry Modes by Service Firms: Role of Market Knowledge. In: Management International Review, Vol. 30, No. 2, 1990, pp. 135-150.

Feinberg, Susan E./Majumdar, Sumit K. (2001): Technology Spillovers from Foreign Direct Investment in the Indian Pharmaceutical Industry. In: Journal of International Business Studies, Vol. 32, No. 3, 2001, pp. 421-437.

Felker, Greg B. (2003): Southeast Asian Industrialisation and the Changing Global Production System. In: Third World Quarterly, Vol. 24, No. 2, 2003, pp. 255-282.

Ferdows, Kasra (1997): Making the Most of Foreign Factories. In: Harvard Business Review, Vol. 75, No. 2, 1997, pp. 73-86.

Fisch, Jan Hendrik (2003): Optimal Dispersion of R&D Activities in Multinational Corporations with a Genetic Algorithm. In: Research Policy, Vol. 32, No. 8, 2003, pp. 1381-1396.

Fischer, Dagmar/Breitenbach, Jörg (Eds., 2007): Die Pharmaindustrie: Einblick - Durchblick - Perspektiven. 2nd edition, Elsevier, Spektrum Akademischer Verlag, München, Heidelberg, 2007.

Fischer, Harald M./Pollock, Timothy G. (2004): Effects of Social Capital and Power on Surviving Transformational Change: The Case of Initial Public Offerings. In: Academy of Management Journal, Vol. 47, No. 4, 2004, pp. 463-481.

Ford, David/Håkansson, Håkan/Johanson, Jan (1994): How Do Companies Interact? In: Johanson, Jan/Associates (Eds., 1994): Internationalization, Relationships and Networks. Uppsala, 1994, pp. 123-135.

Forsgren, Mats/Hägg, Ingemund/Håkansson, Håkon/Johanson, Jan/Mattson, Lars-Gunnar (1995): Firms in Networks: A New Perspective on Competitive Power. Acta Universitatis Upsaliensis, Studia Oeconomiae Negotiorum No. 38, 1995.

Forsgren, Mats/Holm, Ulf/Johanson, Jan (1992): Internationalization of the Second Degree: The Emergence of European-based Centres in Swedish Firms. In: Young, Stephen/Hamill, Jim (Eds., 1992): Europe and the Multinationals: Issues and Responses for the 1990s. Edward Elgar, Hants, Vermont, 1992, pp. 235-253, 291-309 (References).

Forsgren, Mats/Holm, Ulf/Johanson, Jan (1995): Division Headquarters Go Abroad: A Step in the Internationalization of the Multinational Corporation. In: Journal of Management Studies, Vol. 32, No. 4, 1995, pp. 475-491.

Forsgren, Mats/Holm, Ulf/Johanson, Jan (2005): Managing the Embedded Multinational: A Business Network View. Edgar Elgar, Cheltenham, Northampton, 2005.

Forsgren, Mats/Johanson, Jan (1992a): Managing in International Muti-centre Firms. In: Forsgren, Mats/Johanson, Jan (Eds., 1992a): Managing Networks in International Business. Gordon and Breach, Philadelphia et al., 1992a, pp. 19-30.

Forsgren, Mats/Johanson, Jan (1992b): Managing Internationalization in Business Networks. In: Forsgren, Mats/Johanson, Jan (Eds., 1992b): Managing Networks in International Business. Gordon and Breach, Philadelphia et al., 1992b, pp. 1-16.

Forsgren, Mats/Olsson, Ulf (1992): Power Balancing in an International Business Network. In: Forsgren, Mats/Johanson, Jan (Eds., 1992): Managing Networks in International Business. Gordon and Breach, Philadelphia et al., 1992, pp. 178-193.

Forsgren, Mats/Pahlberg, Cecilia (1992): Subsidiary Influence and Autonomy in International Firms. In: Scandinavian International Business Review, Vol. 1, No. 3, 1992, pp. 41-51.

Forsgren, Mats/Pedersen, Torben (1996): Are There Any Centres of Excellence among Foreign-Owned Firms in Denmark? 22nd Annual Conference of the European International Business Academy (EIBA), Stockholm.

Forsgren, Mats/Pedersen, Torben (1997): Centres of Excellence in Multinational Companies: The Case of Denmark. In: Birkinshaw, Julian/Hood, Neil (Eds., 1997): Multinational Corporate Evolution and Subsidiary Developement. 1997.

Freeman, Christopher/Soete, Luc (2004): The Economics of Industrial Innovation. 3rd edition, Routledge, London et al., 2004.

Freeman, R. Edward (1984): Strategic Management: A Stakeholder Approach. Pitman, Boston et al., 1984.

Frost, Tony S. (2001): The Geographic Sources of Foreign Subsidiaries' Innovations. In: Strategic Management Journal, Vol. 22, No. 2, 2001, pp. 101-123.

Frost, Tony S./Birkinshaw, Julian M./Ensign, Prescott C. (2002): Centers of Excellence in Multinational Corporations. In: Strategic Management Journal, Vol. 23, No. 11, 2002, pp. 997-1018.

Frost, Tony/Zhou, Changhui (2000): The Geography of Foreign R&D Within a Host Country. In: International Studies of Management & Organization, Vol. 30, No. 2, 2000, pp. 10-43.

Galbraith, Craig S. (1990): Transferring Core Manufacturing Technologies in High-Technology Firms. In: California Management Review, Vol. 32, No. 4, 1990, pp. 56-70.

Garcia, Rosanna/Calantone, Roger (2002): A Critical Look at Technological Innovation Typology and Innovativeness Terminology: A Literature Review. In: Journal of Product Innovation Management, Vol. 19, No. 2, 2002, pp. 110-132.

Gatignon, Hubert/Tushman, Michael L./Smith, Wendy/Anderson, Philip (2002): A Structural Approach to Assessing Innovation: Construct Development of Innovation Locus, Type, and Characteristics. In: Management Science, Vol. 48, No. 9, 2002, pp. 1103-1122.

Gatignon, Hubert/Xuereb, Jean-Marc (1997): Strategic Orientation of the Firm and New Product Performance. In: Journal of Marketing Research, Vol. 34, No. 1, 1997, pp. 77-90.

Gerstlauer, Michael (2005): Eignung neuer Informations- und Kommunikationstechnik zur Erhöhung der Internationalität von Forschung und Entwicklung: Möglichkeiten und Grenzen. Zugl. Diss. Universität Bamberg, 2005.

Ghauri, Pervez/Grønhaug, Kjell (2005): Research Methods in Business Studies. 3rd edition, Prentice Hall, London, 2005.

Ghoshal, Sumantra/Bartlett, Christopher A. (1988a): Creation, Adoption, and Diffusion of Innovations by Subsidiaries of Multinational Corporations. In: Journal of International Business Studies, Vol. 19, No. 3, 1988a, pp. 365-388.

Ghoshal, Sumantra/Bartlett, Christopher A. (1988b): Innovation Processes in Multinational Corporations. In: Tushman, Michael L. /Moore, William L. (Eds., 1988b): Readings in the Management of Innovation. Ballinger Publishing Company, Cambridge, 1988b, pp. 499-518.

Ghoshal, Sumantra/Nohria, Nitin (1993): Horses for Courses: Organizational Forms for Multinational Corporations. In: Sloan Management Review, Vol. 34, No. 2, 1993, pp. 23-35.

Gittell, Jody Hoffer/Weiss, Leigh (2004): Coordination Networks Within and Across Organizations: A Multi-level Framework. In: Journal of Management Studies, Vol. 41, No. 1, 2004, pp. 127-153.

Glaser, Barney G./Strauss, Anselm L. (1979): Die Entdeckung gegenstandsbezogener Theorie: Eine Grundstrategie qualitativer Sozialforschung. In: Hopf, Christel/Weingarten, Elmar (Eds., 1979): Qualitative Sozialforschung. Klett-Cotta, Stuttgart, 1979, pp. 91-111.

Gnyawali, Devi R./Madhavan, Ravindranath (2001): Cooperative Networks and Competitive Dynamics: A Structural Embeddedness Perspective. In: Academy of Management Review, Vol. 26, No. 3, 2001, pp. 431-445.

Golder, Peter N./Tellis, Gerard J. (1993): Pioneer Advantage: Marketing Logic or Marketing Legend? In: Journal of Marketing Research, Vol. 30, No. 2, 1993, pp. 158-170.

Grabher, Gernot (1993): The Weakness of Strong Ties: The Lock-in of Regional Development in the Ruhr Area. In: Grabher, Gernot (Ed., 1993): The Embedded Firm: On the Socioeconomics of Industrial Networks. Routledge, London et al., 1993, pp. 255-277.

Grandori, Anna/Soda, Giuseppe (1995): Inter-firm Networks: Antecedents, Mechanisms and Forms. In: Organization Studies, Vol. 16, No. 2, 1995, p. 183.

Granovetter, Mark (1985): Economic Action and Social Structure: The Problem of Embeddedness. In: American Journal of Sociology, Vol. 91, No. 3, 1985, pp. 481-510.

Granovetter, Mark (1992): Problems of Explanation in Economic Sociology. In: Nohria, Nitin/Eccles, Robert G. (Eds., 1992): Networks and Organizations: Structure, Form, and Action. Harvard Business School Press, Boston, 1992, pp. 25-56.

Gulati, Ranjay (1995): Social Structure and Alliance Formation Patterns: A Longitudinal Analysis. In: Administrative Science Quarterly, Vol. 40, No. 4, 1995, pp. 619-652.

Gulati, Ranjay (1999): Network Location and Learning: The Influence of Network Resources and Firm Capabilities on Alliance Formation. In: Strategic Management Journal, Vol. 20, No. 5, 1999, pp. 397-420.

Gulati, Ranjay/Gargiulo, Martin (1999): Where Do Interorganizational Networks Come From? In: American Journal of Sociology, Vol. 104, No. 5, 1999, pp. 1439-1493.

Gulati, Ranjay/Nohria, Nitin/Zaheer, Akbar (2000): Strategic Networks. In: Strategic Management Journal, Vol. 21, No. 3, 2000, pp. 203-215.

Gummesson, Evert (1991): Qualitative Methods in Management Research. Sage, Newbury Park et al., 1991.

Gupta, Anil K./Becerra, Manuel (2003): Impact of Strategic Context and Inter-unit Trust on Knowledge Flows within the Multinational Corporation. In: McKern, Bruce (Ed., 2003): Managing the Global Network Corporation. Routledge, London et al., 2003, pp. 23-39.

Gupta, Anil K./Govindarajan, Vijay (1991): Knowledge Flows and the Structure of Control within Multinational Corporations. In: Academy of Management Review, Vol. 16, No. 4, 1991, pp. 768-792.

Hadjikhani, Amjad/Thilenius, Peter (2005): Non-business Actors in a Business Network: A Comparative Case on Firms' Actions in Developing and Developed Countries. Elsevier, Amsterdam et al., 2005.

Håkanson, Lars/Nobel, Robert (2001): Organizational Characteristics and Reverse Technology Transfer. In: Management International Review, Vol. 41, No. 4, 2001, pp. 395-420.

Håkansson, Håkan (Ed., 1982): International Marketing and Purchasing of Industrial Goods: An Interaction Approach. John Wiley & Sons, Chichester et al., 1982.

Håkansson, Håkan/Ford, David (2002): How Should Companies Interact in Business Networks? In: Journal of Business Research, Vol. 55, 2002, pp. 133-139.

Håkansson, Håkan/Henders, Barbara (1992): International Co-operative Relationships in Technological Development. In: Forsgren, Mats/Johanson, Jan (Eds., 1992): Managing Networks in International Business. Gordon and Breach, Philadelphia et al., 1992, pp. 32-46.

Håkansson, Håkan/Johanson, Jan (1992): A Model of Industrial Networks. In: Axelsson, Björn/Easton, Geoffrey (Eds., 1992): Industrial Networks: A New View of Reality. Routledge, London, 1992, pp. 28-34.

Håkansson, Håkan/Johanson, Jan (1993): Industrial Functions of Business Relationships. In: Cacusgil, S. Tamer/Sharma, D. Deo (Eds., 1993): Advances in International Marketing: Industrial Networks. Vol. 5. JAI, Greenwich, London, 1993, pp. 13-29.

Håkansson, Håkan/Snehota, Ivan (1989): No Business is an Island: The Network Concept of Business Strategy. In: Scandinavian Journal of Management, Vol. 5, No. 3, 1989, pp. 187-200.

Håkansson, Håkan/Snehota, Ivan (1995): Developing Relationships in Business Networks. Routledge, London, 1995.

Håkansson, Lars/Nobel, Robert (2001): Organizational Characteristics and Reverse Technology Transfer. In: Management International Review, Vol. 41, No. 4, 2001, pp. 395-420.

Halinen, Aino/Törnroos, Jan-Åke (1998): The Role of Embeddedness in the Evolution of Business Networks. In: Scandinavian Journal of Management, Vol. 14, No. 3, 1998, pp. 187-205.

Hall, Jeremy K./Martin, Michael J. (2005): Disruptive Technologies, Stakeholders and the Innovation Value-added Chain: A Framework for Evaluating Radical Technology Development. In: R&D Management, Vol. 35, No. 3, 2005, pp. 273-284.

Hallén, Lars/Johanson, Jan/Seyed-Mohamed, Nazeem (1991): Interfirm Adaptation in Business Relationships. In: Journal of Marketing, Vol. 55, No. 2, 1991, pp. 29-37.

Hallin, Christina (2008a): Subsidiaries as Sources and Recipients of Innovations in the Multinational Corporation. Uppsala Universitet, Doctoral Thesis, No. 136, Uppsala, 2008a.

Hallin, Christina (2008b): The Usefulness of Innovation Transfer in the Multinational Corporation. In: Hallin, Christina (Ed., 2008b): Subsidiaries as Sources and Recipients of Innovations in the Multinational Corporation. Uppsala Universitet, Doctoral Thesis, No. 136, Uppsala, Paper II, 2008b.

Hallin, Christina/Holm, Ulf/Sharma, D. Deo (2008): Embeddedness and Innovation Exploitation in MNC Subsidiaries: Effects on Business Performance. In: Hallin, Christina (Ed., 2008): Subsidiaries as Sources and Recipients of Innovations in the Multinational Corporation. Uppsala Universitet, Doctoral Thesis, No. 136, Uppsala, Paper III, 2008.

Hallin, Christina/Kang, Olivia H. (2008): Family or Friends? The Impact of Internal and External Collaboration on MNC Subsidiary Innovation. In: Hallin, Christina (Ed., 2008): Subsidiaries as Sources and Recipients of Innovations in the Multinational Corporation. Uppsala Universitet, Doctoral Thesis, No. 136, Uppsala, Paper I, 2008.

Hansen, Morten T. (1999): The Search-Transfer Problem: The Role of Weak Ties in Sharing Knowledge across Organization Subunits. In: Administrative Science Quarterly, Vol. 44, No. 1, 1999, pp. 82-111.

Hansen, Morten T./Nohria, Nitin (2004): How To Build Collaborative Advantage. In: MIT Sloan Management Review, Vol. 46, No. 1, 2004, pp. 22-30.

Hardy, Cynthia/Phillips, Nelson/Lawrence, Thomas B. (2003): Resources, Knowledge and Influence: The Organizational Effects of Interorganizational Collaboration. In: Journal of Management Studies, Vol. 40, No. 2, 2003, pp. 321-347.

Harzing, Anne-Wil/Noorderhaven, Niels (2006): Geographical Distance and the Role and Management of Subsidiaries: The Case of Subsidiaries Down-under. In: Asia Pacific Journal of Management, Vol. 23, No. 2, 2006, pp. 167-185.

Hauschildt, Jürgen/Schlaak, Thomas M. (2001): Zur Messung des Innovationsgrades neuartiger Produkte. In: Zeitschrift für Betriebswirtschaft, Vol. 71, No. 2, 2001, pp. 161-182.

Healey, Michael J./Rawlinson, Michael B. (1993): Interviewing Business Owners and Managers: A Review of Methods and Techniques. In: Geoforum, Vol. 24, No. 3, 1993, pp. 339-355.

Hedlund, Gunnar (1986): The Hypermodern MNC - a Heterarchy? In: Human Resource Management, Vol. 25, No. 1, 1986, pp. 9-35.

Hedlund, Gunnar/Kogut, Bruce (1993): Managing the MNC: The End of the Missionary Era. In: Hedlund, Gunnar (Ed., 1993): Organization of Transnational Corporations. Routlegde, London, 1993, pp. 343-358.

Helble, Yvonne/Chong, Li Choy (2004): The Importance of Internal and External R&D Network Linkages for R&D Organisations: Evidence from Singapore. In: R&D Management, Vol. 34, No. 5, 2004, pp. 605-612.

Heppner, Karsten (1997): Organisation des Wissenstransfers: Grundlagen, Barrieren und Instrumente. Deutscher Universitätsverlag, Wiesbaden, 1997.

Hill, Wilhelm (1997): Der Shareholder Value und die Stakeholder. In: Die Unternehmung, Vol. 50, No. 6, 1997, pp. 411-420.

Hillebrand, Bas/Biemans, Wim G. (2004): Links between Internal and External Cooperation in Product Development: An Exploratory Study. In: Journal of Product Innovation Management, Vol. 21, No. 2, 2004, pp. 110-122.

Holm, Ulf/Johanson, Jan/Thilenius, Peter (1995): Headquarters' Knowledge of Subsidiary Network Contexts in the Multinational Corporation. In: International Studies of Management & Organization, Vol. 25, No. 1/2, 1995, pp. 97-119.

Hongwu, Ouyang (2008): Resources, Absorptive Capacity, and Technology Sourcing. In: International Journal of Technology Management, Vol. 41, No. 1/2, 2008, pp. 183-202.

Hurmelinna-Laukkanen, Pia/Sainio, Liisa-Maija/Jauhiainen, Tiina (2008): Appropriability Regime for Radical and Incremental Innovations. In: R&D Management, Vol. 38, No. 3, 2008, pp. 278-289.

IMP-Group (1990): An Interaction Approach. In: Ford, David (Ed., 1990): Understanding Business Markets: Interaction, Relationships and Networks. Academic Press, London et al., 1990, pp. 7-26.

Ivarsson, Inge/Jonsson, Thommy (2003): Local Technological Competence and Asset-seeking FDI: An Empirical Study of Manufacturing and Wholesale Affiliates in Sweden. In: International Business Review, Vol. 12, No. 3, 2003, pp. 369-386.

Janne, Odile E. M. (2002): The Emergence of Corporate Integrated Innovation Systems across Regions: The Case of the Chemical and Pharmaceutical Industry in Germany, the UK and Belgium. In: Journal of International Management, Vol. 8, No. 1, 2002, pp. 97-119.

Jarillo, J. Carlos (1988): On Strategic Networks. In: Strategic Management Journal, Vol. 9, No. 1, 1988, pp. 31-41.

Jarillo, J. Carlos/Martinez, Jon I. (1990): Different Roles for Subsidiaries: The Case of Multinational Corporations in Spain. In: Strategic Management Journal, Vol. 11, No. 7, 1990, pp. 501-512.

Jeong, Insik (2003): A Cross-national Study of the Relationship between International Diversification and New Product Performance. In: International Marketing Review, Vol. 20, No. 4, 2003, pp. 353-376.

Johanson, Jan/Pahlberg, Cecilia/Thilenius, Peter (1996): Who Controls MNC Introduction of New Products? In: Pahlberg, Cecilia (Ed., 1996): Subsidiary-Headquarters Relationships in International Business Networks. Uppsala Universitet, Doctoral Thesis, No. 61, Uppsala, Paper 7, 1996.

Johanson, Jan/Vahlne, Jan-Erik (1977): The Internationalization Process of the Firm: A Model of Knowledge Development and Increasing Foreign Market Commitments. In: Journal of International Business Studies, Vol. 8, No. 1, 1977, pp. 25-34.

Johanson, Jan/Vahlne, Jan-Erik (1978): The Internationalization Process of the Firm. In: International Executive, Vol. 20, No. 1, 1978, pp. 19-21.

Johanson, Jan/Vahlne, Jan-Erik (2003): Business Relationship Learning and Commitment in the Internationalization Process. In: Journal of International Entrepreneurship, Vol. 1, No. 1, 2003, pp. 83-101.

Johnson, Joshua H./Dilts, David M. (2006): Acquire and Forget: The Conflict of Information Acquisition and Organizational Memory in the Development of Radical Innovations. AMA Winter Educators' Conference Proceedings, American Marketing Association, 2006, pp. 254-255.

Johnston, Stewart/Paladino, Angela (2007): Knowledge Management and Involvement in Innovations in MNC Subsidiaries. In: Management International Review, Vol. 47, No. 2, 2007, pp. 281-302.

Jones, Gary K./Teegen, Hildy J. (2000): The Role of National Culture in Locating Global R&D: An Emerging Markets Perspective. Global Management Research Working Paper Series, School of Business and Public Management, George Washington University, 2000.

Jones, Mark/Samalionis, Fran (2008): From Small Ideas to Radical Service Innovation. In: Design Management Review, Vol. 19, No. 1, 2008, pp. 20-27.

Kasper, Helmut (1980): Innovation in Organisationen: Konzeptionelle Arbeit mit empirischen Befunden. Facultas, Wien, 1980.

Katz, Ralph/Allen, Thomas J. (1982): Investigating the Not Invented Here (NIH) Syndrome: A Look at the Performance, Tenure, and Communication Patterns of 50 R&D Project Groups. In: R&D Management, Vol. 12, 1982, pp. 7-20.

Keating, Patrick J. (1995): A Framework for Classifying and Evaluating the Theoretical Contributions of Case Research in Management Accounting. In: Journal of Management Accounting Research, Vol. 7, No. 3, 1995, pp. 66–86.

Khilji, Shaista E./Mroczkowski, Tomasz/Bernstein, Boaz (2006): From Invention to Innovation: Toward Developing an Integrated Innovation Model for Biotech Firms. In: Journal of Product Innovation Management, Vol. 23, No. 6, 2006, pp. 528-540.

King, Nigel (1994): The Qualitative Research Interview. In: Cassell, Catherine/Symon, Gillian (Eds., 1994): Qualitative Methods in Organizational Research: A Practical Guide. Sage London et al., 1994, pp. 14–36.

Klein, Katherine J./Sorra, Joann S. (1996): The Challenge of Innovation Implementation. In: Academy of Management Review, Vol. 21, No. 4, 1996, pp. 1055-1080.

Knight, Kenneth E. (1967): A Descriptive Model of the Intra-firm Innovation Process. In: Journal of Business, Vol. 40, No. 4, 1967, pp. 478-196.

Kogut, Bruce/Zander, Udo (1993): Knowledge of the Firm and the Evolutionary Theory of the Multinational Corporation. In: Journal of International Business Studies, Vol. 24, No. 4, 1993, pp. 625-645.

Kormann, Hermut (1970): Die Steuerpolitik der internationalen Unternehmung. 2nd edition, Verlagsbuchhandlung des Instituts der Wirtschaftsprüfer, Düsseldorf, 1970.

Körnert, Jan (2003): Balanced Scorecard: Theoretische Grundlagen und Perspektivenwahl für Kreditinstitute. Berliner Wissenschaftsverlag, Berlin, 2003.

Kotabe, Masaaki/Swan, K. Scott (1994): Offshore Sourcing: Reaction, Maturation, and Consolidation of U.S. Multinationals. In: Journal of International Business Studies, Vol. 25, No. 1, 1994, pp. 115-140.

Kretschmer, Katharina (2008): Performance Evaluation of Foreign Subsidiaries. Gabler, Wiesbaden, 2008.

Kuemmerle, Walter (1999): Foreign Direct Investment in Industrial Research in the Pharmaceutical and Electronics Industries. In: Research Policy, Vol. 28, No. 2/3, 1999, pp. 179-194.

Kutschker, Michael (1990): The Multi-organizational Interaction Approach to Industrial Marketing. In: Ford, David (Ed., 1990): Understanding Business Markets: Interaction, Relationships and Networks. Academic Press, London et al., 1990, pp. 421-439.

Kutschker, Michael/Bäurle, Iris/Schmid, Stefan (1997): Quantitative und qualitative Forschung im Internationalen Management: Ein kritisch-fragender Dialog. Diskussionsbeiträge der Wirtschaftswissenschaftlichen Fakultät Ingolstadt No. 82, Katholische Universität Eichstätt, 1997.

Kutschker, Michael/Schmid, Stefan (2008): Internationales Management. 6th edition, Oldenbourg, München, 2008.

Kutschker, Michael/Schurig, Andreas/Schmid, Stefan (2002): Centers of Excellence in MNCs - An Empirical Analysis from Seven European Countries. In: Larimo, J./Julkaisuja, Vaasan Yliopiston (Eds., 2002): Current European Research in International Business. Vol. 86. 2002, pp. 224-245.

Lamnek, Siegfried (1995): Qualitative Sozialforschung: Band 2. Methoden und Techniken. 3rd edition, Beltz, Psychologie Verlags Union, Weinheim, 1995.

Lamnek, Siegfried (2005): Qualitative Sozialforschung. 4th edition, Beltz, Weinheim, Basel, 2005.

Lane, Peter J./Lubatkin, Michael (1998): Relative Absorptive Capacity and Interorganizational Learning. In: Strategic Management Journal, Vol. 19, No. 5, 1998, pp. 461-477.

Lane, Peter J./Salk, Jane E./Lyles, Marjorie A. (2001): Absorptive Capacity, Learning, and Performance in International Joint Ventures. In: Strategic Management Journal, Vol. 22, No. 12, 2001, pp. 1139-1161.

Lettl, Christopher/Hienerth, Christoph/Gemuenden, Hans Georg (2008): Exploring How Lead Users Develop Radical Innovation: Opportunity Recognition and Exploitation in the Field of Medical Equipment Technology. In: IEEE Transactions on Engineering Management, Vol. 55, No. 2, 2008, pp. 219-233.

Macharzina, Klaus/Oesterle, Michael-Jörg (2002): Das Konzept der Internationalisierung im Spannungsfeld zwischen praktischer Relevanz und theoretischer Unschärfe. In: Macharzina, Klaus/Oesterle, Michael-Jörg (Eds., 2002): Handbuch Internationales Management. Grundlagen - Instrumente - Perspektiven. 2nd Edition edition. Gabler, Wiesbaden, 2002, pp. 3-21.

Machlup, Fritz (1983): Semantic Quirks in Studies of Information. In: Machlup, Fritz/Mansfield, Una (Eds., 1983): The Study of Information: Interdisciplinary Messages. John Wiley, New York, 1983, pp. 641-671.

Marschan-Piekkari, Rebecca/Welch, Catherine (2004): Qualitative Research Methods in International Business: The State of the Art. In: Marschan-Piekkari, Rebecca/Welch, Catherine (Eds., 2004): Handbook of Qualitative Research Methods for International Business. Edward Elgar, Cheltenham, Northampton, 2004, pp. 5-24.

Martin, Graeme/Beaumont, Phil (2001): Transforming Multinational Enterprises: Towards a Process Model of Strategic Human Resource Management Change. In: International Journal of Human Resource Management, Vol. 12, No. 8, 2001, pp. 1234-1250.

Mattson, Lars-Gunnar (1989): Development of Firms in Networks: Positions and Investments. In: Cavusgil, S. Tamer/Hallén, Lars/Johanson, Jan (Eds., 1989): Advances in International Marketing. A Research Annual, Volume 3. Vol. 3. JAI, Greenwich, London, 1989, pp. 121-139.

Meißner, Wolfgang (1989): Innovation und Organisation: Die Initiierung von Innovationsprozessen in Organisationen. Verlag für Angewandte Psychologie, Stuttgart, 1989.

Merkens, Hans (2007): Auswahlverfahren, Sampling, Fallkonstruktion. In: Flick, Uwe/von Kardoff, Ernst/Steinke, Ines (Eds., 2007): Qualitative Forschung: Ein Handbuch. 5th edition. Rowohlt Taschenbuch, Reinbek bei Hamburg, 2007, pp. 286-299.

Miles, Matthew B./Huberman, A. Michael (1994): Qualitative Data Analysis: An Expanded Sourcebook. 2nd edition, Sage, Thousand Oaks, 1994.

Miles, Raymond E./Snow, Charles C. (1986a): Network Organizations: New Concepts for New Forms. In: McKinsey Quarterly, No. 4, 1986a, pp. 53-66.

Miles, Raymond E./Snow, Charles C. (1986b): Organizations: New Concepts for New Forms. In: California Management Review, Vol. 28, No. 3, 1986b, pp. 62-73.

Minbaeva, D./Pedersen, Torben/Björkman, Ingmar/Fey, C. F./Park, H. J. (2003): MNC Knowledge Transfer, Subsidiary Absorptive Capacity, and HRM. In: Journal of International Business Studies, Vol. 34, No. 6, 2003, pp. 586-599.

Mitchell, Ronald K./Agle, Bradley R./Wood, Donna J. (1997): Toward a Theory of Stakeholder Identification and Salience: Defining the Principle of Who and What really Counts. In: Academy of Management Review, Vol. 22, No. 4, 1997, pp. 853-886.

Mitra, Debanjan/Golder, Peter N. (2002): Whose Culture Matters? Near-Market Knowledge and Its Impact on Foreign Market Entry Timing. In: Journal of Marketing Research (JMR), Vol. 39, No. 3, 2002, pp. 350-365.

Moore, Karl J. (2000): The Competence of Formally Appointed Centres of Excellence in the UK. In: Holm, Ulf/Pedersen, Torben (Eds., 2000): The Emergence and Impact of MNC Centres of Excellence: A Subsidiary Perspective. Macmillan, London, 2000, pp. 154–166.

Moore, Karl J. (2001): A Strategy for Subsidiaries: Centres of Excellences to Build Subsidiary Specific Advantages. In: Management International Review, Vol. 41, No. 3, 2001, pp. 275-290.

Moran, Peter (2005): Structural vs. Relational Embeddedness: Social Capital and Managerial Performance. In: Strategic Management Journal, Vol. 26, No. 12, 2005, pp. 1129-1151.

Mote, Jonathon/Jordan, Gretchen/Hage, Jerald (2007): Measuring Radical Innovation in Real Time. In: International Journal of Technology, Policy & Management, Vol. 7, No. 4, 2007, pp. 355-377.

Mu, Shaohua Carolyn/Gnyawali, Devi R./Hatfield, Donald E. (2007): Foreign Subsidiaries' Learning from Local Environments: An Empirical Test. In: Management International Review, Vol. 47, No. 1, 2007, pp. 79-102.

Müller, Kristian/Rajala, Risto/Westerlund, Mika (2008): Service Innovation Myopia? A New Recipe for Client-Provider Value Creation. In: California Management Review, Vol. 50, No. 3, 2008, pp. 31-48.

Muralidharan, Raman/Phatak, Arvind (1999): International Activity of US MNCs: An Empirical Study with Implications for Host Government Policy. In: Multinational Business Review, Vol. 7, No. 2, 1999, pp. 97-105.

Newburry, William (2001): MNC Interdependence and Local Embeddedness Influences on Perceptions of Career Benefits from Global Integration. In: Journal of International Business Studies, Vol. 32, No. 3, 2001, pp. 497-507.

Nohria, Nitin (1992): Is a Network Perspective a Useful Way of Studying Organizations? In: Nohria, Nitin/Eccles, Robert G. (Eds., 1992): Networks and Organizations: Structure, Form, and Action. Harvard Business School Press, Boston, 1992, pp. 1-22.

Nonaka, Ikujiro (1994): A Dynamic Theory of Organizational Knowledge Creation. In: Organization Science, Vol. 5, No. 1, 1994, pp. 14-37.

Nonaka, Ikujiro/Takeuchi, Hiro (1995): The Knowledge-creating Company: How Japanese Companies Create the Dynamics of Innovation. Oxford University Press, New York, Oxford, 1995.

O'Dowd, Paul/McQuade, Eamonn/Murphy, Eamonn (2005): A Model for Innovation in Manufacturing Subsidiaries Based in Ireland. In: Irish Journal of Management, Vol. 26, No. 1, 2005, pp. 136-148.

OECD (1994): The Measurement of Scientific and Technological Activities: Using Patent Data as Science and Technology Indicators. Patent Manual 1994, No. OCDE/GD(94)114, Organisation for Economic Co-operation and Development (OECD), 1994.

OECD (2002): Frascati Manual: Proposed Standard Practice for Surveys on Research and Experimental Development. Organisation for Economic Co-operation and Development (OECD), Paris, 2002.

Ogawa, Susumu (1998): Does Sticky Information Affect the Locus of Innovation? In: Research Policy, Vol. 26, No. 7/8, 1998, pp. 777-790.

Orsenigo, Luigi/Pammolli, Fabio/Riccaboni, Massimo/Bonaccorsi, Andrea/Turchetti, Giuseppe (1998): The Evolution of Knowledge and the Dynamics of an Industry Network. In: Journal of Management & Governance, Vol. 1, No. 2, 1998, pp. 147-175.

Papanastassiou, Marina (1999): Technology and Production Strategies of Multinational Enterprise (MNE) Subsidiaries in Europe. In: International Business Review, Vol. 8, No. 2, 1999, pp. 213-232.

Pearce, Robert D. (1999): Decentralised R&D and Strategic Competitiveness: Globalised Approaches to Generation and Use of Technology in Multinational Enterprises (MNEs). In: Research Policy, Vol. 28, No. 2/3, 1999, pp. 157-178.

Pearce, Robert/Papanastassiou, Marina (1999): Overseas R&D and the Strategic Evolution of MNEs: Evidence from Laboratories in the UK. In: Research Policy, Vol. 28, No. 1, 1999, pp. 23-41.

Penrose, Edith T. (1959): The Theory of the Growth of the Firm. Oxford University Press, New York, Oxford, 1959.

Perlmutter, Howard V. (1969a): Some Management Problems in Spaceship Earth: The Megafirm and the Global Industrial Estate. In: Academy of Management Proceedings, 1969a, pp. 59-87.

Perlmutter, Howard V. (1969b): The Tortuous Evolution of the Multinational Corporation. In: Columbia Journal of World Business, Vol. 4, No. 1, 1969b, pp. 9-18.

Perlmutter, Howard V. (1971): Toward Research on and Development of Nations, Unions, and Firms as Worldwide Institutions. In: International Studies of Management & Organization, Vol. 1, No. 4, 1971, pp. 419-449.

Persson, Magnus (2006): Unpacking the Flow: Knowledge Transfer in MNCs. Uppsala Universitet, Doctoral Thesis, No. 118, Uppsala, 2006.

Peterson, Richard B. (2004): Empirical Research in International Management: A Critique and Future Agenda. In: Marschan-Piekkari, Rebecca/Welch, Catherine (Eds., 2004): Handbook of Qualitative Research Methods for International Business. Edward Elgar, Cheltenham, Northampton, 2004, pp. 25-55.

Pfeffer, Jeffrey/Salancik, Gerald R. (1978): The External Control of Organizations: A Resource Dependence Perspective. Harper & Row, New York et al., 1978.

Pfister, Etienne/Deffains, Bruno (2005): Patent Protection, Strategic FDI and Location Choices: Empirical Evidence from French Subsidiaries' Location Choices in Emerging Economies. In: International Journal of the Economics of Business, Vol. 12, No. 3, 2005, pp. 329-346.

Phene, Anupama/Almeida, Paul (2008): Innovation in Multinational Subsidiaries: The Role of Knowledge Assimilation and Subsidiary Capabilities. In: Journal of International Business Studies, Vol. 39, No. 5, 2008, pp. 901-919.

Podolny, Joel M./Page, Karen L. (1998): Network Forms of Organization. In: Annual Review of Sociology, Vol. 24, No. 1, 1998, pp. 57-76.

Polanyi, Karl (1957): The Great Transformation. Beacon, Boston, 1957.

Polanyi, Michael (1966): The Tacit Dimension. Doubleday, Garden City, 1966.

Porter, Michael E. (1999): Wettbewerbsvorteile: Spitzenleistungen erreichen und behaupten. 5th edition, Campus, Frankfurt/Main, New York, 1999.

Powell, Walter W. (1990): Neither Market Nor Hierarchie: Network Forms of Organization. In: Staw, Barry M./Cummings, Larry L. (Eds., 1990): Research in Organizational Behaviour. An Annual Series of Analytical Essays and Critical Reviews, Volume 12. JAI, Greenwich, London, 1990, pp. 295-336.

Powell, Walter W./Koput, Kenneth W./Smith-Doerr, Laurel (1996): Interorganizational Collaboration and the Locus of Innovation: Networks of Learning in Biotechnology. In: Administrative Science Quarterly, Vol. 41, No. 1, 1996, pp. 116-145.

Putnam, Robert D. (1995): Bowling Alone: America's Declining Social Capital. In: Journal of Democracy, Vol. 6, 1995, pp. 65-78.

Ramstetter, Eric D. (1999): Comparisons of Foreign Multinationals and Local Firms in Asian Manufacturing over Time. In: Asian Economic Journal, Vol. 13, No. 2, 1999, pp. 163-203.

Ranft, Annette L./Marsh, Sarah J. (2008): Accessing Knowledge through Acquisitions and Alliances: An Empirical Examination of New Market Entry. In: Journal of Managerial Issues, Vol. 20, No. 1, 2008, pp. 51-67.

Reichart, Sybille von (2002): Kundenorientierung im Innovationsprozess: Die erfolgreiche Integration von Kunden in den frühen Phasen der Produktentwicklung. Deutscher Universitäts-Verlag, Wiesbaden, 2002.

Reiss, Thomas/Hinze, Sybille (2000): Innovation Process and Techno-scientific Dynamics. In: Jungmittag, Andre/Reger, Guido/Reiss, Thomas (Eds., 2000): Changing Innovation in the Pharmaceutical Industry. Springer, Berlin et al., 2000, pp. 53-69.

Renz, Timo (1998): Management in internationalen Unternehmensnetzwerken. Gabler, Wiesbaden, 1998.

Richardson, George B. (1972): The Organisation of Industry. In: Economic Journal, Vol. 82, No. 327, 1972, pp. 883-896.

Ritter, Thomas/Gemünden, Hans Georg (2003): Interorganizational Relationships and Networks: An Overview. In: Journal of Business Research, Vol. 56, No. 9, 2003, pp. 691-697.

Robinson, Sandra L. (1996): Trust and Breach of the Psychological Contract. In: Administrative Science Quarterly, Vol. 41, No. 4, 1996, pp. 574-599.

Rothwell, R. (1994): Towards the Fifth-generation Innovation Process. In: International Marketing Review, Vol. 11, No. 1, 1994, pp. 7-31.

Rowley, Tim/Behrens, Dean/Krackhardt, David (2000): Redundant Governance Structures: An Analysis of Structural and Relational Embeddedness in the Steel and Semiconductor Industries. In: Strategic Management Journal, Vol. 21, No. 3, 2000, pp. 369-386.

Rygl, David (2008): Länderübergreifende Innovations- und Wissensnetzwerke: Eine empirische Studie in der pharmazeutischen Industrie. Rainer Hampp, München, Mering, 2008.

Sadowski, Bert M./Sadowski-Rasters, Gaby (2006): On the Innovativeness of Foreign Affiliates: Evidence from Companies in The Netherlands. In: Research Policy, Vol. 35, No. 3, 2006, pp. 447-462.

Sandström, Madelene (1992): The Culture Influence on International Business Relationships. In: Forsgren, Mats/Johanson, Jan (Eds., 1992): Managing Networks in International Business. Gordon and Breach, Philadelphia et al., 1992, pp. 47-60.

Sanna-Randaccio, Francesca/Veugelers, Reinhilde (2007): Multinational Knowledge Spillovers with Decentralised R&D: A Game-theoretic Approach. In: Journal of International Business Studies, Vol. 38, No. 1, 2007, pp. 47-63.

Sarangee, Kumar R. (2007): The Impact of Strategic New Product Alliances on Radical Product Innovation. In: AMA Winter Educators' Conference Proceedings, Vol. 18, 2007, pp. 148-149.

Scapens, Robert W. (1990): Researching Management Accounting Practice: The Role of Case Study Methods. In: British Accounting Review, Vol. 22, No. 3, 1990, pp. 259-281.

Schmid, Stefan (1996a): Multikulturalität in der internationalen Unternehmung: Konzepte, Reflexionen, Implikationen. Gabler, Wiesbaden, 1996a.

Schmid, Stefan (1996b): Nicht Shareholder-Orientierung, sondern Stakeholder-Orientierung! Diskussionsbeiträge der Wirtschaftswissenschaftlichen Fakultät Ingolstadt No. 76, Katholische Universität Eichstätt, 1996b.

Schmid, Stefan (1998): Shareholder-Value-Orientierung als oberste Maxime der Unternehmensführung? Kritische Überlegungen aus der Perspektive des Strategischen Managaments. In: Zeitschrift für Planung, Vol. 9, No. 3, 1998, pp. 219-238.

Schmid, Stefan (2000): Foreign Subsidiaries as Centres of Competence − Empirical Evidence from Japanese Multinationals. In: Larimo, Jorma/Kock, Sören (Eds., 2000): Recent Studies in Interorganizational and International Business Research. Vol. 58. Vaasan Yliopiston Julkaisuja, Vaasa, 2000, pp. 182-204.

Schmid, Stefan (2003): How Multinational Corporations Can Upgrade Foreign Subsidiaries: A Case Study from Central and Eastern Europe. In: Stüting, Heinz-Jürgen/Dorow, Wolfgang/Claassen, Frank/Blazejewski, Susanne (Eds., 2003): Change Management in Transition Economies: Intergrating Corporate Strategy, Structure and Culture. Palgrave Macmillan, Basingstoke, Hampshire et al., 2003, pp. 273-290.

Schmid, Stefan (2004): The Roles of Foreign Subsidiaries in Network MNCs – A Critical Review of the Literature and Some Directions for Future Research. In: Larimo, Jorma/Rumpunen, Sami (Eds., 2004): European Research on Foreign Direct Investment and International Human Resource Management. Vol. 112. Vaasan Yliopiston Julkaisuja, Vaasa, 2004, pp. 237-255.

Schmid, Stefan (2005): Kooperation: Erklärungsperspektiven interaktionstheoretischer Ansätze. In: Zentes, Joachim/Swoboda, Bernhard/Morschett, Dirk (Eds., 2005): Kooperationen, Allianzen und Netzwerke: Grundlagen - Ansätze - Perspektiven. 2nd edition. Gabler, Wiesbaden, 2005, pp. 237-256.

Schmid, Stefan/Bäurle, Iris/Kutschker, Michael (1998): Tochtergesellschaften in international tätigen Unternehmungen: ein "State-of-the-Art" unterschiedlicher Rollentypologien. Diskussionsbeiträge der Wirtschaftswissenschaftlichen Fakultät No. 104, Katholische Universität Eichstätt, 1998.

Schmid, Stefan/Daniel, Andrea (2007): Are Subsidiary Roles a Matter of Perception? A Review of the Literature and Avenues for Future Research. Working Paper No. 30, ESCP-EAP European School of Management, 2007.

Schmid, Stefan/Daniel, Andrea (2009): Subsidiary Roles, Perception Gaps and Conflict: A Social Psychological Approach. In: Schmid, Stefan (Ed., 2009): Management der Internationalisierung. Festschrift zum 65. Geburtstag von Michael Kutschker. Gabler, Wiesbaden, 2009, pp. 183-202.

Schmid, Stefan/Daub, Matthias (2007): Embeddedness in International Business Research - The Concept and its Operationalization. Working Paper No. 23, ESCP-EAP European School of Management, 2007.

Schmid, Stefan/Machulik, Mario (2006): What has Perlmutter Really Written? A Comprehensive Analysis of the EPRG Concept. ESCP-EAP Working Paper No. 16, ESCP-EAP European School of Management, 2006.

Schmid, Stefan/Maurer, Julia (2008): Relationships Between MNC Subsidiaries: Towards a Classification Scheme. Working Paper No. 35, ESCP-EAP European School of Management, 2008.

Schmid, Stefan/Schurig, Andreas (2003): The Development of Critical Capabilities in Foreign Subsidiaries: Disentangling the Role of the Subsidiary's Business Network. In: International Business Review, Vol. 12, No. 6, 2003, pp. 755-782.

Schmid, Stefan/Schurig, Andreas/Kutschker, Michael (2002): The MNC as a Network: A Closer Look at Intra-Organizational Flows. In: Lundan, Sarianna M. (Ed., 2002): Network Knowledge in International Business. Edward Elgar, Cheltenham, Northampton, 2002, pp. 45-72.

Schmid, Uwe (1997): Das Anspruchsgruppen-Konzept. In: WISU – Das Wirtschaftsstudium, Vol. 26, No. 7, 1997, pp. 633-635.

Schnell, Rainer/Hill, Paul Bernhard/Esser, Elke (2005): Methoden der empirischen Sozialforschung. 7th edition, Oldenbourg, Munich, Wien, 2005.

Schumpeter, Joseph A. (1934): The Theory of Economic Development: An Inquiry into Profits, Capital, Interest and the Business Cycle. Harvard University Press, Cambridge, 1934.

Schumpeter, Joseph A. (1939): Business Cycles: A Theoretical, Historical, and Statistical Analysis of the Capitalist Process. McGraw-Hill, New York et al., 1939.

Seyed-Mohamed, Nazeem/Bolte, Maria (1992): Taking a Position in a Structured Business Network. In: Forsgren, Mats/Johanson, Jan (Eds., 1992): Managing Networks in International Business. Gordon and Breach, Philadelphia et al., 1992, pp. 215-231.

Shannon, Claude E./Weaver, Warren (1949): The Mathematical Theory of Communication. University of Illinois Press, Urbana, 1949.

Sharma, D. Deo (1993): Introduction: Industrial Networks in Marketing. In: Cavusgil, S. Tamer/Sharma, D. Deo (Eds., 1993): Advances in International Marketing: Industrial Networks. Vol. 5. Greenwich/London, 1993, pp. 1-9.

Shatz, Howard J. (2003): Gravity, Education, and Economic Development in a Multinational Affiliate Location. In: Journal of International Trade & Economic Development, Vol. 12, No. 2, 2003, pp. 117-150.

Shimizutani, Satoshi/Todo, Yasuyuki (2008): What Determines Overseas R&D Activities? The Case of Japanese Multinational Firms. In: Research Policy, Vol. 37, No. 3, 2008, pp. 530-544.

Shuy, Roger W. (2001): In-Person versus Telephone Interviewing. In: Gubrium, Jaber F./Holstein, James A. (Eds., 2001): Handbook of Interview Research. Sage, Thousand Oaks et al., 2001, pp. 537–555.

Sieber, Eugen H. (1970): Die multinationale Unternehmung, der Unternehmenstyp der Zukunft? In: Zeitschrift für betriebswirtschaftliche Forschung, Vol. 22, No. 7, 1970, pp. 414-438.

Siggelkow, Nicolaj (2007): Persuasion with Case Studies. In: Academy of Management Journal, Vol. 50, No. 1, 2007, pp. 20-24.

Siler, Pamela/Chengqi, Wang/Xiaming, Liu (2003): Technology Transfer within Multinational Firms and its Impact on the Productivity of Scottish Subsidiaries. In: Regional Studies, Vol. 37, No. 1, 2003, pp. 15-25.

Silverman, David (2000): Doing Qualitative Research: A Practical Handbook. Sage, London, 2000.

Simon, Ethan S./McKeough, David T./Ayers, Alan D./Rinehart, Ed/Alexia, Barry (2003): How Do You Best Organize for Radical Innovation? In: Research & Technology Management, Vol. 46, No. 5, 2003, pp. 17-20.

Smith, Bruce L./Barfield, Claude E. (Eds., 1996): Technology, R&D, and the Economy. The Brokings Institution, Washington, 1996.

Solomon, Robert F./Ingham, Keith P. (1977): Discriminating between MNC Subsidiaries and Indigenous Companies: A Comparative Analysis of the British Mechanical Engineering Industry. In: Oxford Bulletin of Economics & Statistics, Vol. 39, No. 2, 1977, pp. 127-138.

Sölvell, Örjan/Zander, Ivo (1995): Organization of the Dynamic Multinational Enterprise: The Home-based and the Heterarchical MNE. In: International Studies of Management & Organization, Vol. 25, No. 1/2, 1995, pp. 17-38.

Sorescu, Alina B./Chandy, Rajesh K./Prabhu, Jaideep C. (2003): Sources and Financial Consequences of Radical Innovation: Insights from Pharmaceuticals. In: Journal of Marketing, Vol. 67, No. 4, 2003, pp. 82-102.

Specht, Günter/Beckmann, Christoph (1996): F&E-Management. Schäffer-Poeschel, Stuttgart, 1996.

Ståhl, Benjamin (2004): Innovation and Evolution in the Multinational Enterprise. Uppsala Universitet, Doctoral Thesis, No. 112, Uppsala, 2004.

Steinke, Ines (2004): Quality Criteria in Qualitative Research. In: Flick, Uwe/von Kardorff, Ernst/Steinke, Ines (Eds., 2004): A Companion to Qualitative Research. Sage, London et al., 2004, pp. 184–190.

Story, Vicky/O'Malley, Lisa/Hart, Susan/Saker, Jim (2008): The Development of Relationships and Networks for Successful Radical Innovation. In: Journal of Customer Behaviour, Vol. 7, No. 3, 2008, pp. 187-200.

Sun, Yifei/Von Zedtwitz, Maximilian/Simon, Denis Fred (2007): Globalization of R&D and China: An Introduction. In: Asia Pacific Business Review, Vol. 13, No. 3, 2007, pp. 311-319.

Sundaram, Anant K./Black, J. Stewart (1992): The Environment and Internal Organization of Multinational Enterprises. In: Academy of Management Review, Vol. 17, No. 4, 1992, pp. 729-757.

Surlemont, Bernard (1996): Types of Centers within Multinational Corporations: An Empirical Investigation. In: Institute of International Business (Ed., 1996): Innovation and International Business. Proceedings of the 22nd EIBA Annual Conference. Vol. 2. EIBA, Stockholm, 1996, pp. 745-765.

Swamy, M. R. Kumara (2003): Financial Management Relating to Transfer of Technology to Developing Countries: Focus on Arbitrage and Capital Gear Ratio Analysis. In: Journal of Financial Management & Analysis, Vol. 16, No. 1, 2003, pp. 84-96.

Sydow, Jörg (1992): Strategische Netzwerke: Evolution und Organisation. Gabler, Wiesbaden, 1992.

Szulanski, Gabriel (1995): Unpacking Stickiness: An Empiricial Investigation of the Barriers to Transfer Best Practice Inside the Firm. Academy of Management Proceedings, 1995/08//, Academy of Management, 1995, pp. 437-441.

Szulanski, Gabriel (1996): Exploring Internal Stickiness: Impediments to the Transfer of Best Practice within the Firm. In: Strategic Management Journal, Vol. 17, Winter Special Issue, 1996, pp. 27-43.

Szulanski, Gabriel (2000): The Process of Knowledge Transfer: A Diachronic Analysis of Stickiness. In: Organizational Behavior & Human Decision Processes, Vol. 82, No. 1, 2000, pp. 9-27.

Szulanski, Gabriel/Cappetta, Rossella (2003): Stickiness: Conceptualizing, Measuring, and Predicting Difficulties in the Transfer of Knowledge within Organizations. In: Easterby-Smith, Mark/Lyles, Marjorie A. (Eds., 2003): The Blackwell Handbook of Organizational Learning & Knowledge Management. Blackwell, Malden et al., 2003, pp. 513-534.

Taggart, James H. (1997a): Autonomy and Procedural Justice: A Framework for Evaluating Subsidiary Strategy. In: Journal of International Business Studies, Vol. 28, No. 1, 1997a, pp. 51-76.

Taggart, James H. (1997b): An Evaluation of the Integration-Responsiveness Framework: MNC Manufacturing Subsidiaries in the UK. In: Management International Review, Vol. 37, No. 4, 1997b, pp. 295-318.

Thibaut, John W./Kelley, Harold H. (1959): The Social Psychology of Groups. John Wiley, New York et al., 1959.

Thompson, Jeffery A. (2005): Proactive Personality and Job Performance: A Social Capital Perspective. In: Journal of Applied Psychology, Vol. 90, No. 5, 2005, pp. 1011-1017.

Thorelli, Hans B. (1986): Networks: Between Markets and Hierarchies. In: Strategic Management Journal, Vol. 7, No. 1, 1986, pp. 37-51.

Tregaskis, Olga (2003): Learning Networks, Power and Legitimacy in Multinational Subsidiaries. In: International Journal of Human Resource Management, Vol. 14, No. 3, 2003, pp. 431-447.

Tsai, Wenpin (2001): Knowledge Transfer in Intraorganizational Networks: Effects of Network Position and Absorptive Capacity on Business Unit Innovation and Performance. In: Academy of Management Journal, Vol. 44, No. 5, 2001, pp. 996-1004.

Tsai, Wenpin/Ghoshal, Sumantra (1998): Social Capital and Value Creation: The Role of Intrafirm Networks. In: Academy of Management Journal, Vol. 41, No. 4, 1998, pp. 464-476.

Twiss, Brian C. (1980): Managing Technological Innovation. 2nd edition, Longman, London et al., 1980.

Uzzi, Brian (1996): The Sources and Consequences of Embeddedness for the Economic Performance of Organizations: The Network Effect. In: American Sociological Review, Vol. 61, No. 4, 1996, pp. 674-698.

Uzzi, Brian (1997): Social Structure and Competition in Interfirm Networks: The Paradox of Embeddedness. In: Administrative Science Quarterly, Vol. 42, No. 1, 1997, pp. 37-69.

Uzzi, Brian/Gillespie, James J. (2002): Knowledge Spillover in Corporate Financing Networks: Embeddedness and the Firm's Debt Performance. In: Strategic Management Journal, Vol. 23, No. 7, 2002, pp. 595-618.

Uzzi, Brian/Lancaster, Ryon (2003): Relational Embeddedness and Learning: The Case of Bank Loan Managers and Their Clients. In: Management Science, Vol. 49, No. 4, 2003, pp. 383-399.

Vahs, Dietmar/Burmester, Ralf (1999): Innovationsmanagement: Von der Produktidee zur erfolgreichen Vermarktung. Schäffer-Poeschel, Stuttgart, 1999.

Van de Ven, Andrew H. (1988): Central Problems in the Management of Innovation. In: Tushman, Michael L./Moore, William L. (Eds., 1988): Readings in the Management of Innovation. 2nd edition. Ballinger, Cambridge, 1988, pp. 103-122.

Van den Bosch, Frans A. J./Van Wijk, Raymond/Volberda, Henk W. (2003): Absorptive Capacity: Antecedents, Models, and Outcomes. In: Easterby-Smith, Mark/Lyles, Marjorie A. (Eds., 2003): Blackwell Handbook of Organizational Learning & Knowledge Management. Blackwell, Malden et al., 2003, pp. 278-301.

Venkatraman, N./Lee, Chi-Hyon (2004): Preferential Linkage and Network Evolution: A Conceptual Model and Empirical Test in the U.S. Video Game Sector. In: Academy of Management Journal, Vol. 47, No. 6, 2004, pp. 876-892.

Verganti, Roberto (2008): Design, Meanings, and Radical Innovation: A Metamodel and a Research Agenda. In: Journal of Product Innovation Management, Vol. 25, No. 5, 2008, pp. 436-456.

Voelker, Rainer/Stead, Richard (1999): New Technologies and International Locational Choice for Research and Development Units: Evidence from Europe. In: Technology Analysis & Strategic Management, Vol. 11, No. 2, 1999, pp. 199-209.

Von Hippel, Eric (1994): "Sticky Information" and the Locus of Problem Solving: Implications for Innovation. In: Management Science, Vol. 40, No. 4, 1994, pp. 429-439.

Walliser, Björn (2003a): An International Review of Sponsorship Research: Extension and Update. In: International Journal of Advertising, Vol. 22, No. 1, 2003a, pp. 5-40.

Walliser, Björn (2003b): L'Évolution et l'État de l'Art de la Recherche Internationale sur le Parrainage. In: Recherche et Applications en Marketing, Vol. 18, No. 1, 2003b, pp. 65-94.

Welch, Catherine/Marschan-Piekkari, Rebecca/Penttinen, Heli/Tahvanainen, Marja (2002): Corporate Elites as Informants in Qualitative International Business Research. In: International Business Review, Vol. 11, No. 5, 2002, pp. 611-628.

West, Michael A./Farr, James L. (1990): Innovation at Work. In: West, Michael A./Farr, James L. (Eds., 1990): Innovation and Creativity at Work: Psychological and Organizational Strategies. John Wiley & Sons, Chichester et al., 1990, pp. 3-13.

White, Roderick E. /Poynter, Thomas A. (1989): Achieving Worldwide Advantage with the Horizontal Organization. In: Business Quarterly, Vol. 54, No. 2, 1989, pp. 55-60.

White, Roderick E./Poynter, Thomas A. (1984): Strategies for Foreign-Owned Subsidiaries in Canada. In: Business Quarterly, Vol. 49, No. 2, 1984, pp. 59-69.

Williamson, Peter J. (2005): Strategies for Asia's New Competitive Game. In: Journal of Business Strategy, Vol. 26, No. 2, 2005, pp. 37-43.

Winter, Sidney (1987): Knowledge and Competence as Strategic Assets. In: Teece, David J. (Ed., 1987): The Competitive Challenge: Strategies for Industrial Innovations and Renewal. Ballinger, Cambridge, 1987, pp. 159-184.

Witt, Jürgen (1996): 1. Teil: Grundlagen für die Entwicklung und die Vermarktung neuer Produkte. In: Witt, Jürgen (Ed., 1996): Produktinnovation: Entwicklung und Vermarktung neuer Produkte. Vahlen, München, 1996, pp. 1-110.

Wright, Lorna L. (2004): The Need for International Qualitative Research. In: Punnett, Betty Jane/Shenkar, Oded (Eds., 2004): Handbook for International Management Research. 2nd Edition edition. The University of Michigan Press, Ann Arbor, 2004, pp. 49-67.

Wrona, Thomas (2005): Die Fallstudienanalyse als wissenschaftliche Forschungsmethode. Working Paper No. 10, ESCP-EAP Europäische Wirtschaftshochschule Berlin, 2005.

Yamawaki, Hideki (2004): The Determinants of Geographic Configuration of Value Chain Activities: Foreign Multinational Enterprises in Japanese Manufacturing. In: International Economics & Economic Policy, Vol. 1, No. 2/3, 2004, pp. 195-213.

Yin, Robert K. (1981): The Case Study Crisis: Some Answers. In: Administrative Science Quarterly, Vol. 26, No. 1, 1981, pp. 58–65.

Yin, Robert K. (2009): Case Study Research: Design and Methods. 4th edition, Sage, Los Angeles et al., 2009.

Young, Stephen/Tavares, Ana Teresa (2004): Centralization and Autonomy: Back to the Future. In: International Business Review, Vol. 13, No. 2, 2004, pp. 215-237.

Zaltman, Gerald/Duncan, Robert/Holbek, Jonny (1973): Innovations and Organizations. John Wiley & Sons, New York et al., 1973.

Zander, Ivo (1994): The Tortoise Evolution of the Multinational Corporation: Foreign Technological Activity in Swedish Multinational Firms, 1890-1990. Institute of International Business (IIB) & Ivo Zander, Stockholm, 1994.

Zander, Ivo (1998): The Evolution of Technological Capabilities in the Multinational. In: Research Policy, Vol. 27, No. 1, 1998, pp. 17-35.

Zander, Ivo (2002): The Formation of International Innovation Networks in the Multinational Corporation: An Evolutionary Perspective. In: Industrial & Corporate Change, Vol. 11, No. 2, 2002, pp. 327-353.

Zander, Udo/Kogut, Bruce (1995): Knowledge and the Speed of the Transfer and Imitation of Organizational Capabilities: An Empirical Test. In: Organization Science, Vol. 6, No. 1, 1995, pp. 76-92.

Ziggers, Gerrit W. (2005): Radical Product Innovation in the Dutch Food Industry: An Empirical Exploration. In: Journal of Food Products Marketing, Vol. 11, No. 3, 2005, pp. 43-65.

PLANUNG, ORGANISATION UND UNTERNEHMUNGSFÜHRUNG

Herausgegeben von Prof. Dr. Dr. h. c. Norbert Szyperski, Köln, Prof. Dr. Winfried Matthes †, Wuppertal, Prof. Dr. Udo Winand, Kassel, Prof. (em.) Dr. Joachim Griese, Bern, Prof. Dr. Harald F. O. von Kortzfleisch, Koblenz, Prof. Dr. Ludwig Theuvsen, Göttingen, und Prof. Dr. Andreas Al-Laham, Mannheim

Band 124
Nicole Sodeik
Projektmanagement wertorientierter Mergers & Acquisitions
Lohmar – Köln 2009 ♦ 440 S. ♦ € 68,- (D) ♦ ISBN 978-3-89936-805-5

Band 125
Christoffer-Martin F. Seubert
Build, Ally or Acquire – Die strategische Entscheidung über den Entwicklungsweg
Lohmar – Köln 2010 ♦ 420 S. ♦ € 67,- (D) ♦ ISBN 978-3-89936-886-4

Band 126
Maren S. D. Breuer
Socio-Cognitive Dynamics in Strategic Processes
Lohmar – Köln 2010 ♦ 360 S. ♦ € 64,- (D) ♦ ISBN 978-3-89936-954-0

Band 127
Shakib Manouchehri Far
Social Software in Unternehmen – Nutzenpotentiale und Adoption in der innerbetrieblichen Zusammenarbeit
Lohmar – Köln 2010 ♦ 268 S. ♦ € 57,- (D) ♦ ISBN 978-3-89936-970-0

Band 128
Michaela Schaschke
Kultivierung von Kundenwissen – Ein Systematisierungsrahmen für das Customer Knowledge Management
Lohmar – Köln 2010 ♦ 372 S. ♦ € 65,- (D) ♦ ISBN 978-3-89936-975-5

Band 129
Swantje Hartmann
External Embeddedness of Subsidiaries – Influences on Product Innovation in MNCs
Lohmar – Köln 2011 ♦ 392 S. ♦ € 66,- (D) ♦ ISBN 978-3-8441-0037-2

JOSEF EUL VERLAG